THE FUTURE OF ENGLISH TEACHING WORLDWIDE

The seminal Dartmouth Conference (1966) remains a remarkably influential moment in the history of English teaching. Bringing together leading voices in contemporary English education, this book celebrates the Conference and its legacy, drawing attention to what it has achieved, and the questions it has raised.

Encompassing a multitude of reflections on the Dartmouth Conference, *The Future of English Teaching Worldwide* provides fresh and revisionist readings of the meeting and its leading figures. Chapters showcase innovative and exciting new insights for English scholars, and address both theoretical and practical elements of teaching English in a variety of settings and countries. Covering topics including the place of new media in English curricula, the role of the canon, poetry and grammar, the text is divided into three accessible parts:

- Historical perspectives
- Dartmouth today: why it still matters
- Reflections: but for the future.

This powerful collection will be of value to researchers, postgraduate students, literature scholars, practitioners, teacher educators, trainee and in-service teachers, as well as other parties involved in the teaching and study of English.

Professor Andrew Goodwyn is President of IFTE, Head of Education at The University of Bedfordshire, and Emeritus Professor at the University of Reading, UK.

Associate Professor Cal Durrant is Associate Professor (Adjunct) in the School of Education at Murdoch University, Australia.

Professor Wayne Sawyer is Director of Research in the School of Education, Western Sydney University, Australia.

Dr Lisa Scherff is a Faculty member at South Fort Myers High School, USA.

Professor Don Zancanella is Professor Emeritus at the University of New Mexico, where he has taught since 1988.

NATE

The National Association for the Teaching of English (NATE), founded in 1963, is the professional body for all teachers of English from primary to post-16. Through its regions, committees and conferences, the association draws on the work of classroom practitioners, advisers, consultants, teacher trainers, academics and researchers to promote dynamic and progressive approaches to the subject by means of debate, training and publications. NATE is a charity reliant on membership subscriptions. If you teach English in any capacity, please visit **www.nate.org.uk** and consider joining NATE, so the association can continue its work and give teachers of English and the subject a strong voice nationally.

This series of books co-published with NATE reflects the organisation's dedication to promoting standards of excellence in the teaching of English, from early years through to university level. Titles in this series promote innovative and original ideas that have practical classroom outcomes and support teachers' own professional development.

Books in the NATE series include both pupil and classroom resources and academic research aimed at English teachers, students on PGCE/ITT courses and NQTs.

Titles in this series include:

The Future of English Teaching Worldwide
Celebrating 50 years from the Dartmouth Conference
Andrew Goodwyn, Cal Durrant, Wayne Sawyer, Lisa Scherff, and Don Zancanella

Teaching English Language 16–19, 2nd edition
A comprehensive guide for teachers of AS and A Level English language
Martin Illingworth and Nick Hall

For more information about this series, please visit: www.routledge.com/National-Association-for-the-Teaching-of-English-NATE/book-series/NATE

THE FUTURE OF ENGLISH TEACHING WORLDWIDE

Celebrating 50 Years From the Dartmouth Conference

Edited by Andrew Goodwyn, Cal Durrant, Wayne Sawyer, Lisa Scherff, and Don Zancanella

LONDON AND NEW YORK

First published 2019
by Routledge
2 Park Square, Milton Park, Abingdon, Oxon OX14 4RN

and by Routledge
711 Third Avenue, New York, NY 10017

Routledge is an imprint of the Taylor & Francis Group, an informa business

British Library Cataloguing in Publication Data
A catalogue record for this book is available from the British Library

Library of Congress Cataloging in Publication Data
A catalog record has been requested for this book

ISBN: 978-1-138-49521-0 (hbk)
ISBN: 978-1-138-49522-7 (pbk)
ISBN: 978-1-351-02446-4 (ebk)

Typeset in Bembo
by Swales & Willis Ltd, Exeter, Devon, UK

DEDICATION

This volume is dedicated to all the participants at the 1966 Dartmouth conference whose ideas and influences are alive and well today, and especially to John Dixon whose report on the conference *Growth through English*, has had such an important and sustained value to English teachers around the world.

CONTENTS

Foreword   *x*

Contributors and editors   *xiii*

Introduction: the enduring significance of the Dartmouth
Seminar of 1966   1
Andrew Goodwyn

PART I

Historical perspectives   **13**

1 London English, the Dartmouth Seminar and *Growth
   through English*   15
   Simon Gibbons

2 *Growth through English* and *The Uses of English*: literature,
   knowledge and experience   27
   Wayne Sawyer

3 Re-reading Dartmouth: an American perspective on the
   pasts and presents of English teaching   42
   Jory Brass

4 The impact of the Blue Books prior to Dartmouth   52
   Lorna Smith

5 Dartmouth and Personal Growth in Australia: the New
   South Wales and Western Australian curricula of the 1970s   65
   Wayne Sawyer and Cal Durrant

6 The manifold ways in which language works: the generation
   after Dartmouth   81
   John Willinsky

7 The many voices of Dartmouth   93
   John Hodgson and Ann Harris

PART II
Dartmouth today: why it still matters   **107**

8 From Personal Growth (1966) to Personal Growth and
   Social Agency (2016) – proposing an invigorated
   model for the 21st century   109
   Andrew Goodwyn

9 Dartmouth's Growth Model reconceived from a
   social perspective   123
   Peter Smagorinsky

10 The status and relevance of the Growth model for a new
   generation of English teachers in New South
   Wales, Australia   133
   Jacqueline Manuel and Don Carter

11 Growing the nation: the influence of Dartmouth on the
   teaching of literature in subject English in Australia   146
   Larissa McLean Davies, Lucy Buzacott and Susan K. Martin

12 Language and experience: re-reading *Growth through
   English*   159
   Brenton Doecke and John Yandell

PART III
Reflections: but for the future   **173**

13 W(h)ither media in English?   175
   Steve Connolly

14 Back to the future: the restoration of canon and the
backlash against multiculturalism in secondary
English curricula   191
Lesley Nelson-Addy, Nicole Dingwall, Victoria Elliott and
Ian Thompson

15 Finding and keeping poetry   203
Sue Dymoke

16 Reading for pleasure in English class: developing reading
dispositions and identities in a digital society   215
Joanne O'Mara and Catherine Beavis

17 Culturally sustaining pedagogy and the problem of
poverty: from cultural identity to political subjectivity   227
Todd DeStigter

18 The Dartmouth Conference revisited: changing views of
grammar – or not?   241
Annabel Watson and Debra Myhill

19 "What is English?": new directions for the discipline in a
transnational world   254
Allison Skerrett and Saba Vlach

Index   *267*

FOREWORD

John Dixon

When 20 or more scholars and teachers from each side of the Atlantic met for a month to thrash out a new approach to English, they obviously hoped for some degree of consensus, and with luck, glimpses of a new vision. At Dartmouth College in 1966, I believe some of those hopes were fulfilled.

First, the central activities of English lessons were redefined: in part, talk (classroom discussion and conversations), drama and role play; in part, writing and 'reading' – with a new extension. And a crucial interplay was sketched in between those oral and written forms, for the sake of language and learning. This is perhaps a prime success of the seminar: still a solid foundation for English Studies.

Along with it went a longer-term vision. Most of the delegates had been brought up in a print culture, but they proposed alongside printed texts, the study of film and television. It would be 10 to 15 years before videos and later DVDs began to make the audio-visual easily accessible in the average classroom, but they were looking ahead. And quite rightly. (They couldn't foresee, of course, the way audio-visual interaction would become a staple feature of everyday life on the street and in the workplace, as it is today.) But their sense of future possibilities has to be credited.

Then came a firm negative. A band of distinguished professors of English language from both sides of the Atlantic, declared the study of grammar – for so long favoured for 11–16-year-olds – to be irrelevant, and instead opted, after pilot studies, for a more general option: post-16 studies of language and its uses.

Finally, for the moment, the seminar accepted – against early expectations – that a model of language development was the best hope for giving a sense of 'continuity' to English studies. Thus, with an agreed focus on learning, it was the cumulative corpus of an individual's achievements in oral, written and (progressively) audio-visual communication that would offer evidence for progress in English.

These proposals themselves count as a major group achievement. In the UK, they formed an effective riposte to the standard English language course culminating in the GCE O Level exam at 16+ – an exam that had as recently as 1964 come near to being totally rejected by a national panel. In the USA, they seriously unsettled a similar tradition, the Tripod of Grammar, Composition and Literature. So they opened the way – against entrenched traditions in textbooks, exams, and 'mind-forged manacles' – for a decade or two of struggles to elaborate on and extend those key positions.

End of story? I think not. There were hints of deeper implications that were not spelled out in the conference papers – but became more pressing across the English-speaking world, as Scotland, Canada, Australia, New Zealand, Northern Ireland and others took up the challenge. Here are three.

Cultural exchange and learning. Students come to school with a culture derived from the home, extended family, neighbourhood, region, and prevailing media. Increasingly, too, within the global village one classroom may need to embrace several different kinds of cultural roots. Personally, my friends and I had learned in an inner-city London school to start with our 11-year-olds by celebrating stories of events – funny, rueful, dismaying, enjoyable – drawn from their slum streets. These became the 'literature of the classroom' (hinted at by Dartmouth). Then, we did our best to read stories and poems back that we hoped would resonate, however obliquely, with their own experiences, yet suggest or even open up new, different worlds. There's no knowing of course, what will resonate: going down to the Hall for an early drama session, I was a bit taken aback when Terry said eagerly, "Sir, Sir, can we do Beowulf?" It does stretch your teacherly imagination. . .

That interplay between the cultures that students bring to school (if we let them) and the cultural products we offer back (some in response, some just fishing perhaps): that interplay was not analysed in the seminar – despite the rising wave of black freedom protests in the US of the early Sixties. Of course, we also hadn't today's easy access to film and television, either – the world of the media some of our students were steeped in. And unfortunately (ironically?) to right the balance, Stuart Hall and Richard Hoggart were too preoccupied setting up their new Centre for Cultural Studies to accept their invitations.

Critical perspectives on a mediated world. Similarly, despite the growing hold of television by 1966, and those other long-term forces behind the Press and magazines, this was not an explicit focus at Dartmouth. A mediated world unexamined: it's obvious whose interests were served at the time! However, I already knew several departments, like my own, that offered a critical study of these major influences on our students' lives, starting with advertising and moving on to (comparative) press cuttings and (more schematically) popular TV series. Nowadays, of course, the pervasive impact of social media has intensified the questions we raised. It's not just what we intend to buy, but our emotional drives, attitudes, opinions, beliefs, propensities to act – deeper elements in our psyche – that are being insidiously got at by powerful corporations and their allies. Quite apart from the blatant selling of fake news. A new generation in English teaching and beyond has had to take up the challenge.

Finally, classroom discussion in a democratic society. Again, this topic was not foregrounded, though many of us from the UK were engaged in the question. In fact, portable tape recorders were beginning to make this a potentially central focus for studies of teaching and learning. A wake-up call – for all of us in London's ATE – came from the earliest tapes of small groups discussing without the teacher. When invited to talk over a poem, they were just too good. We were manifestly missing in our teaching a powerful contribution by students to their own learning. (But when Les Stratta, Doug Barnes and I put forward a joint research proposal to the SSR Council, they weren't exactly excited.)

Equally, taping a full class in discussion, with a teacher in the chair, was not really technologically feasible in the Sixties. Yet both these poles needed to be explored and investigated in depth: they weren't, and they still lack international backing, to the best of my knowledge. The results – with international surveys showing most teachers relentlessly in control – are uncontestable.

Well, one seminar, however high-powered, cannot achieve everything. There were plenty of forces in the UK and US that were resolutely against the changes it proposed, in any case. Besides, a generation after 1966, Thatcher and Reagan, with backing from much more powerful lobbies, were sweeping away those aspirations of teachers and students – working together to explore new curricular horizons. Instead, from the 1990s the central ministries would declare the goals and use their testing agencies to enforce them. Are the first signs of an alternative thrust just beginning to show?

Coda. This, I believe, is my swansong for English studies as such – and all my generation owes to them. But for me, the idea of curricular territories has always been suspect. In the Sixties, the likes of Richard Hoggart and Stuart Hall led me off into cultural studies, while Jimmy Britton, Les Stratta and my colleague Irene Farmer swept me up into language (and writing) development and social interaction. In retirement I've been drawn into histories – local, curricular and more broadly intellectual. Before the end of this century, who knows, might these all be seen as components within a comprehensive view of Human Studies – a reconstruction of the Humanities? Aren't the current boundaries just a challenge to new creative spirits – my current readers among them, I hope?

CONTRIBUTORS AND EDITORS

Catherine Beavis is Professor of Education at Deakin University, Australia. She teaches and researches in the areas of English, literature and literacy pedagogy and curriculum, and around digital culture, young people and new media. Her work has a focus on the changing nature of text and literacy, and the implications of young people's experience of the online world for contemporary constructions of English and literacy curricula. Her research particularly explores young people's engagement with computer games, the nature of games as text, and the experience and expectations students bring to English regarding texts, community and communication in contemporary times.

Jory Brass is an independent scholar with a PhD in Curriculum, Teaching, and Educational Policy from Michigan State University. His research has traced the changing contexts of English education and often draws from the work of Foucault and related scholars to historicise ideas and practices that often get taken for granted in education. With Allen Webb, he edited a recent Routledge book on English teacher education, *Reclaiming English Language Arts Methods Courses: Critical Issues and Challenges for Teacher Educators in Top-down Times*. He has also published widely in leading national and international journals of English education, curriculum studies, education policy, and the history and philosophy of education.

Lucy Buzacott is a Research Fellow and Project Coordinator at the Melbourne Graduate School of Education at the University of Melbourne. She currently manages the Australian Research Council-funded project *Investigating Literary Knowledge in the Making of English Teachers* as well as contributing to projects related to national literatures, literary knowledge, and English curriculum. She has a PhD in Literary Studies from the University of Queensland. Her current research interests include Australian and American literature, critical race and whiteness studies, and secondary and tertiary English education.

Don Carter is a Senior Lecturer in Education at the University of Technology, Sydney. He has a PhD, Master of Education (Honours), Master of Education (Curriculum), Bachelor of Arts and a Diploma of Education. Don is a former Inspector of English at the New South Wales curriculum authority and led a range of projects, including the *English K-10 Syllabus*. His research interests include the effects of standardised testing, literacy pedagogies and curriculum theory, and history. Don has published extensively on a range of issues including curriculum reform, English education and mass literacy testing.

Steve Connolly is a Senior Lecturer in Teacher Education at the University of Bedfordshire, who has worked in schools and colleges for more than 20 years teaching Media, English and Film. His PhD research focused on how students learn to make video projects, and learning processes in all their forms (social, cognitive, cultural etc.) continue to be an area of research interest for him. His current research projects include: evaluating and developing resources for the Structural Learning tool (www.structural-learning.com), compiling a history of the study of media texts within the UK English curriculum, and looking at the relationship between academic and vocational media studies in the UK. He is a Visiting Fellow at the Centre for Excellence in Media Practice at the University of Bournemouth and a member of the DARE Collaborative, based at the London Knowledge Lab.

Todd DeStigter, a former high school English, Spanish, and social studies teacher (and tennis coach), is Associate Professor of English at the University of Illinois, Chicago. His primary research interests are English teacher education and the intersection of literacy, culture, and political theory. He is the author of *Reflections of a Citizen Teacher: Literacy, Democracy, and the Forgotten Students of Addison High*, which was selected for the Richard A. Meade Award by the NCTE. Todd's current book project, *Teaching in the Shadows of Pragmatism: Urban Literacies on the Spectrum of Politics*, is based on ethnographic research in a Chicago public high school and explores the range of political subjectivities represented in the American pragmatist tradition. Todd is currently serving his second term on the Executive Committee of the Conference on English Education.

Nicole Dingwall is a Curriculum Tutor on the PGCE English course and a supervisor on the MSc in Learning and Teaching at the University of Oxford. Previously, Nicole taught English in secondary schools in Australia and the UK. She is currently conducting research at doctoral level on the cultures of secondary school English departments.

Brenton Doecke is Emeritus Professor in the Faculty of Arts and Education, Deakin University, Australia. He has published widely in the fields of English curriculum and pedagogy and teacher education. The focus of his current research is on the relationship between English teaching and the maintenance of a social democracy. He is engaged (with Larissa McLean Davies, Philip Mead, Wayne Sawyer and Lyn Yates) in a major Australian Research Council Project on the role that literary knowledge might play in the professional learning and practice of early career English teachers.

Cal Durrant retired as Associate Professor in English Curriculum and Director of the Literacy Research Hub at the Australian Catholic University in Sydney in 2013, but continued to work part-time as Research Officer of the innovative Pilbara Cities Internship Program in the School of Education at Murdoch University in Perth, Western Australia, until 2017. He is currently the Secretary of IFTE (International Federation for the Teaching of English). He also spent 16 years on the AATE (Australian Association for the Teaching of English) Council as Research and Initiatives Officer and then Commissioning Editor of the highly acclaimed *Interface* series. Cal's research covers the areas of English literacy and technology and media education, and over the past two decades he has been involved in projects that have applied ICTs to a range of teaching and learning contexts.

Sue Dymoke is a poet, Reader in Education and National Teaching Fellow in the School of Education at the University of Leicester, UK. She was the Editor of English in Education from 2010–2015 and in June 2017 received The Terry Furlong Research Award from NATE. Sue's research focuses primarily on aspects of poetry pedagogy and curriculum. Publications include *Making Poetry Matter: International research on poetry pedagogy* and *Making Poetry Happen: Transforming the poetry classroom* (both from Bloomsbury) and *Drafting and Assessing Poetry* (Sage/ Paul Chapman). Her third full poetry collection *What They Left Behind* is due from Shoestring Press in October 2018). She also blogs at suedymokepoetry.com.

Victoria Elliott is Associate Professor of English and Literacy Education at the University of Oxford. Her main research interests are in policy, curriculum and assessment in English teaching at secondary level. She is currently working on a book on classroom discourse research methods.

Simon Gibbons began his career as a teacher of English, Media and Drama in an East London comprehensive school. After 10 years working in London schools, he moved, via a role as a Local Authority Consultant, into the university sector. He has led both university- and employment-based initial teacher training programmes and is currently the Director of Teacher Education at King's College London and a Senior Lecturer in English and Education. His main area of research is the historical development of English as a school subject, an interest reflected in his 2017 book *English and its Teachers: a History of Policy, Pedagogy and Practice*, published by Routledge. He was Chair of the National Association for the Teaching of English from 2011–13.

Andrew Goodwyn is currently President of The International Federation for the Teaching of English and a Fellow of the Royal Society of Arts. He is a Professor and Head of The School of Education and English Language, and also Director of The Institute for Research in Education, at The University of Bedfordshire; he is also Emeritus Professor at The University of Reading where he was Head of Education (2007–15). He is convenor of the English in Education, Special Interest Group as part of The British Educational Research Association. After 12 years teaching English in comprehensive schools in Coventry and London, he moved to work in teacher education and research. He has been a member of NATE for 35 years and is a former Chair. His research focuses on first-language education and on the concept of teacher expertise. He has published extensively, including single-authored and edited books, contributed to many scholarly journals and given lectures and presentations around the world. He is on the editorial board of numerous journals.

Ann Harris is Professor of Education and Culture at the University of Huddersfield. Before joining the university, she taught English in the UK and Australia and was Head of English and Media at a sixth form college for 7 years. She is a Fellow of the Higher Education Academy and a Fellow of the Royal Society of Arts. Her doctoral research explored innovation in curriculum and assessment in English departments. Ann has co-authored, with John Hodgson, journal articles on student writing across the transition from school/college into higher education. She has also written on education and popular culture, and on cultural pedagogies. She is Associate Editor of *English in Education* and is on the Sholokhov Moscow State University Humanities Bulletin Editorial Board. Ann is currently writing on *Doctor Who*, cultural identities and professionalism.

John Hodgson has taught English, Media and Cultural Studies in secondary and higher education in the UK and USA. His experience as Head of English in a large rural secondary school inspired his doctoral study of the literacy practices of a group of adolescents from the south-west of England. After joining the University of the West of England, he conducted studies for the UK Higher Education Academy on the student experience of university English and has published, with Ann Harris, a number of studies of student writing across the transition from later secondary schooling to higher education. He is currently editor of *English in Education* and believes that key research from 50 years of English education can help contemporary teachers sustain their identity and develop a fruitful approach to global educational changes. John writes a professional blog, *research.english*, and a personal blog, *Living in the Future Present*.

Jacqueline Manuel is an Associate Professor of English Education in the Sydney School of Education and Social Work at the University of Sydney. She holds a BA (Hons 1) in English, a Dip Ed and a PhD in English Literature from the University of New England. She is Program Director of the Master of Teaching (Secondary) and Secondary English Curriculum Co-ordinator in the School. Jackie's teaching and research interests include: teenagers' reading; creative pedagogies in secondary

English; pre-service English teacher motivation; early-career teacher experience, and English curriculum history.

Susan K. Martin is Professor in English and Associate PVC (Research) in the College of Arts, Social Sciences and Commerce, La Trobe University, Australia. She taught Australian and Victorian literature and Australian Studies for many years. She publishes on 19th–21st century Anglophone literature and culture, including cultures of reading, garden history, literature and the environment, in journals including *English Studies*; *Studies in The History of Gardens and Designed Landscapes*; *ALS* and *Postcolonial Studies*. Her books include *Reading the Garden: the Settlement of Australia* with Katie Holmes and Kylie Mirmohamadi, (MUP, 2008), *Women and Empire (Australia)* (Routledge, 2009), and *Sensational Melbourne* (2011) and *Colonial Dickens* (ASP, 2012) with Kylie Mirmohamadi.

Larissa McLean Davies is an Associate Professor in Language and Literacy, and Associate Dean, Learning and Teaching, in the Melbourne Graduate School of Education at the University of Melbourne. Larissa's research is broadly concerned with the way in which English teachers conceptualise and account for literature and its role in subject English, and she is specifically interested in the teaching of Australian literatures. She is lead Chief Investigator, with fellow CIs Wayne Sawyer, Philip Mead, Lyn Yates and Brenton Doecke, on the Australian Research Council-funded project *Investigating Literary Knowledge in the Making of English Teachers*.

Debra Myhill is Professor of Education at the University of Exeter, UK. Her research has focused particularly on young people's composing processes and their metacognitive awareness of them; the inter-relationship between metalinguistic understanding and writing; the talk-writing interface; and the teaching of writing. She is Director of the Centre for Research in Writing, which promotes inter-disciplinary research, drawing on psychological, socio-cultural and linguistic perspectives on writing. Over the past 15 years, she has led a series of research projects in these areas, in both primary and secondary schools, and has conducted several commissioned research studies. Debra runs numerous professional education courses for teachers, examining the practical classroom implications of her research on the teaching of writing, and in 2014, her research team was awarded the Economic and Social Research Council award for Outstanding Impact in Society.

Lesley Nelson-Addy is a teacher of English at Didcot Girls' School, currently in her fourth year of teaching, having completed her PGCE in the Department of Education at the University of Oxford. In her previous school, as the Lead Teacher of Higher Prior Attaining students, she collaboratively created an extracurricular programme for disadvantaged, higher-ability students called *Symposium*, which has been running now for 3 years. She explored the impact of this extracurricular academic programme on students' engagement in English during the final year of her

MSc in Learning and Teaching. Within her current school, she has taken an active role in developing the Year 9 and 10 Curriculum in preparation for GCSEs. In addition to her Key Stage 3, 4 and 5 Language and Literature teaching, Lesley continues to develop her interest in education research with lecturers at the University of Oxford Department of Education.

Joanne O'Mara is an Associate Professor in Language and Literature Education in the Faculty of Arts and Education, Deakin University, Australia. An experienced secondary English and Drama teacher, she has continued to work with young people and schools through her university research. She is also an avid reader, and reading fiction is one of the great pleasures of her life. Her research and scholarship focuses on: emergent literacies and new textual practices; digital games; drama pedagogy, and the spatial, social and temporal dimensions of teachers' work. A hallmark of Joanne's research programme has been the focus on the establishment of ongoing strategic partnerships with inbuilt benefits to all parties, working in collaboration with students, teachers, schools, professional associations and key education authorities.

Wayne Sawyer is a Professor of Education at Western Sydney University and a member of the Centre for Educational Research. He researches in the fields of secondary English curriculum, curriculum history in English, and engaging pedagogy in low-SES school communities. He is currently working on an Australian Research Council project on literary knowledge in the making of English teachers (with Larissa McLean Davies, Brenton Doecke, Philip Mead and Lyn Yates). He is an Honorary Life Member of the NSW English Teachers Association and the Australian Association for the Teaching of English, and a former Chair of the English Curriculum Committee for the New South Wales curriculum authority. He has authored or edited over 30 books for audiences of teachers and academics.

Lisa Scherff teaches Advanced Placement Research and English at South Fort Myers High School, Florida. She previously taught English education at the University of Tennessee, the University of Alabama and Florida State University. Her research interests include opportunity to learn, teacher preparation and development, and student–teacher discussions of young adult literature. Her work has appeared in journals such as the *Journal of Teacher Education, Journal of Adolescent & Adult Literacy, Journal of Literacy Research, Research in the Teaching of English* and *Teaching and Teacher Education*. Lisa is Past-Chair of the Amelia Elizabeth Walden Award.

Allison Skerrett is Associate Professor of Language and Literacy Studies in the Department of Curriculum and Instruction at The University of Texas, Austin. Dr. Skerrett's teaching and research focus on adolescents' literacy practices, both in and outside school, and secondary English education in contexts of racial, cultural, and linguistic diversity. Dr. Skerrett's recent book, *Teaching Transnational Youth: Literacy and Education in a Changing World* (2015), is published by Teachers College Press. It is the first book to examine the educational opportunities and challenges arising from increasing numbers of students who live and attend school across different countries. Dr. Skerrett was selected for the Literacy Research Association's Early Career Achievement Award in 2013 and serves on the organisation's Board of Directors. She was appointed in June 2016 to Scotland's International Council of Education Advisers.

Peter Smagorinsky is Distinguished Research Professor at The University of Georgia, USA, where he has taught since 1998, and Distinguished Visiting Scholar at the Universidad de Guadalajara, Mexico, through his work with their literacy education faculty since 2016. Since 2012 he has served as faculty advisor to the student-edited *Journal of Language and Literacy Education* at The University of Georgia. Recent awards include the 2017 UGA College of Education Aderhold Distinguished Professor Award and 2017 National Council of Teachers of English Distinguished Service Award. Recent books include: *Creativity and Community among Autism-Spectrum Youth: Creating Positive Social Updrafts through Play and Performance*; the second edition of *Teaching English by Design: How to Create and Carry Out Instructional Units*, and the forthcoming *The Disabling Environments of Education: Creating New Cultures and Environments for Accommodating Difference* and *Teacher Education in National Context: Developing A Literacy Education Program in Guadalajara for the New Mexico*.

Lorna Smith leads the PGCE English programme at the University of Bristol. Her main current research interest, and the field for her doctoral studies, is the impact of the latest national curriculum (2014) on creativity in the English classroom. Further select publications explore the impact of technology-enhanced learning (particularly the contribution that ICT can make to an English classroom) and developing oracy through storytelling. She launched a successful local Teachers as Writers group in 2013 as part of the National Writing Project, which seeks to explore the impact of teachers' writing on their work with children in the classroom. Lorna has been working in Initial Teacher Education since 2002, having previously spent 10 years teaching English in a comprehensive school in the South West of England, including a spell as acting Head of Faculty.

Ian Thompson is an Associate Professor of English Education and PGCE Course Director at the University of Oxford. He previously taught English for 16 years in state secondary schools in England. Ian's research focuses on English pedagogy, teacher education, and social justice in education. His most recent book is *Tackling Social Disadvantage through Teacher Education* (Critical Publishing).

Saba Vlach is a PhD Candidate in the Language and Literacy Studies programme at The University of Texas, Austin. Saba taught elementary school for 17 years before pursuing her PhD, and it was those years in the classroom that shaped her research interests. Her research focuses on the enactment of critical pedagogy, and literacy teaching and learning in elementary contexts, and her research interests include multicultural children's literature, critical sociocultural knowledge, discourse analysis, and teacher education. Saba has had the opportunity to work on multiple research projects at UT in the areas of literacy instruction and pre-service teacher education, literacy and transnationalism, and a critical discourse study on current 'word gap' narratives.

Annabel Watson is a Senior Lecturer at the University of Exeter, where she leads the secondary English PGCE and School Direct programme. As a member of the Exeter Centre for Research in Writing, her research interests lie in the interrelationship of metalinguistic understanding and writing development, teacher beliefs about writing and composition on digital platforms.

John Willinsky is Khosla Family Professor of Education and Director of the Program in Science, Technology, and Society at Stanford University, as well as Professor (part-time) of Publishing Studies at Simon Fraser University. He directs the Public Knowledge Project, which conducts research and develops open-source scholarly publishing software in support of greater access to knowledge. His books include the *Empire of Words: the Reign of the OED* (Princeton, 1994); *Learning to Divide the World: Education at Empire's End* (Minnesota, 1998); *Technologies of Knowing* (Beacon 2000); and *The Access Principle: the Case for Open Access to Research and Scholarship* (MIT Press, 2006) and *The Intellectual Properties of Learning: a Prehistory from Saint Jerome to John Locke* (Chicago, 2017).

John Yandell taught in inner-London secondary schools for 20 years before moving to the Institute of Education, University College London, where he has worked since 2003. He is the editor of the journal, *Changing English: Studies in Culture and Education* and the author of *The Social Construction of Meaning: Reading Literature in Urban English Classrooms* (Routledge, 2013). Other recent publications include *Rethinking Education: Whose Knowledge is it Anyway?* (with Adam Unwin, New Internationalist, 2016), and *Critical Practice in Teacher Education: a Study of Professional Learning*, which he co-edited with Ruth Heilbronn.

Don Zancanella is Professor Emeritus at the University of New Mexico, where he has taught since 1988. His research focuses on the politics and policy of literacy education, the teaching and learning of literature, and the history of English language arts. His work has appeared in journals such as *Research in the Teaching of English, English Journal, Education Evaluation and Policy Analysis*, and *English*

Education. He is a former chair of the Conference on English Education. He is also an award-winning fiction writer who has received an O. Henry Award and whose collection of stories, *Western Electric,* won the Iowa Short Fiction Award. Recent stories are in *The Beloit Fiction Journal, The Hopkins Review,* and elsewhere.

INTRODUCTION

The enduring significance of the Dartmouth Seminar of 1966

Andrew Goodwyn

This book is about the fundamental importance of English and its teachers. English remains the subject where young people can consider and reflect upon their emergent identities in the many cross cultural and ideological currents in which they try to swim and survive. In 1966 an extraordinary and unique event took place when a group of educators, all from an 'English' background, met for a month in Dartmouth College, USA, to consider what was meant by 'English' and what was its purpose and place in the curriculum; where 'English' is defined as a subject taught in schools by a professional group called English teachers; this is not to diminish the importance of terms such as 'The Language Arts', but Dartmouth was about something called 'English' at the time.

The 1960s remains an iconic decade. On the one hand the Cold War was at its height and the Dartmouth seminar was funded because the US was terrified of falling behind the Soviet Union, whether in regards to the technologies of the space race or the basic quality of education for all its citizens. On the other hand, this was the decade of love and peace and radical challenges to the establishment.

The 50th anniversary of Dartmouth (2016) produced a range of activities, from specialist conferences to a range of publications. This publication was conceived as a focal point to reflect on the event itself and its lasting significance, and to draw on the attention that the anniversary had created. This collection is organised into three parts, the first loosely labelled 'historical', the second 'Dartmouth today' and the final part 'the future'. However, the spirit of the collection is that all chapters are infused by the ideas of Dartmouth and they all raise the same questions as did the seminar: what actually is English? – or perhaps what should it be? – and what is its place and purpose in the curriculum now and in the coming decades? We look back – to look forward – with more knowledge and understanding and more conviction that we have learned from the journey. On the journey we have also learned that the idealism of the 1960s was an inspiring spring of hope but that the establishment was also learning;

it had no plans to relinquish its control. Around the world English teachers have never been more constrained and under surveillance than they are now, students have never been more tested and strait-jacketed, curricular are so narrow they leave almost no room for the notion of a quicksilver subject – as Dixon put it in *Growth through English* – a subject impossible to contain. English is everywhere contained, constrained and its teachers – all too often – drained.

Through this volume we celebrate Dartmouth, not nostalgically, but dynamically. The collection offers much critique of the ideas that emerged at the time but also traces the extraordinary influence that those ideas have had across the Anglophone World – and continue to have. This enduring legacy did come from a particular age but its debates are very much for all time. We should never allow the endless attempts to contain the subject of English and to confine its teachers, to contain or confine our passionate engagement with making English the most interesting educational domain for every student to experience and to enjoy.

Part I: historical perspectives

Simon Gibbons opens the collection with a close examination of 'London English' and the Dartmouth Seminar, focusing on John Dixon's book *Growth through English* (1967). Ostensibly an account of an apparent consensus reached at Dartmouth on the pre-eminence of a personal growth view of English, many of the ideas in the text reflect the views that were taken to the seminar by NATE delegates, particularly those, such as John Dixon, who had worked in the post-war decades in London schools and in association with colleagues involved in the London Association for the Teaching of English (LATE) and the London Institute for Education. Such colleagues included such highly influential figures as James Britton, Nancy Martin and Harold Rosen, who – under the umbrella of LATE – forged a new, progressive model of English in the context of the capital's radically changing school systems and population. Drawing on documentary and oral history, this chapter offers an important overview of the development of the 'new' English in London schools in the decades prior to the Dartmouth seminar, evaluating the importance of this work, and the major figures associated with it, for events at Dartmouth and the lasting legacies of the seminar for English pedagogy and curriculum.

This chapter is followed by Wayne Sawyer's comparative examination of the two central books that came out of the Dartmouth conference: John Dixon's *Growth through English* and Herbert Muller's *The Uses of English*. He argues that they are very different texts with different roles and different audiences. Muller aimed for 'objective' reporting, Dixon argued for a normative curriculum position. Literature became at the time a particular focus for critique of the Growth model, of Dixon, and of Dartmouth, in particular as Dixon critiques the deployment of a cultural heritage model in the teaching of literature. Literature is almost the defining element in what Muller in particular argues are the differences between the then American and British views of English. Sawyer considers the actual or implied 'British' and 'American' differences and their origins, and the role knowledge plays in literature. He argues that Dixon in *Growth through English* was conceptualising a number of networked relations in defining the place of literature in English – and that these shifted over time as different versions of *Growth through English* were published during the 1960s and 1970s.

The next chapter, by Jory Brass, provides an American re-reading of Dartmouth, arguing that advocates of the Personal Growth model have identified Dartmouth as a key break in English's curriculum history, including John Dixon's (1967) germinal book. In contrast, his chapter re-reads a series of 1960s and 1970s publications from the US that suggest that the simple view of Dartmouth as a progressive break in the history of English teaching glosses over important struggles and multiple temporalities in English's curriculum history. To build this line of argument, his historical analysis reads with and against a range of English journal articles published in the wake of the Dartmouth conference that complicate any singular history, consensus reading, or simple narrative of progress/decline in the teaching of English. The chapter illustrates how familiar narratives of Dartmouth overlook important ways in which the Growth model overlaps historically with earlier progressive traditions in English teaching, including the Anglo-Australian New Education of the 1900s and American progressivism of the 1930s. Next, it further denaturalises received views of the British vs. American contributions to Dartmouth by exploring how the surprising conservatism among American educators of the 1960s can be explained in part by the unusual political coalitions and Cold War panics that made Dartmouth possible.

Lorna Smith offers a very illuminating account of work that occurred before the seminar, examining the impact of what were known as the Blue Books. From 1905 to 1955, a series of advisory pamphlets – which gradually turned into books – was published by the Board of Education in England. Initially entitled, 'Suggestions for the Consideration of Teachers and Others Concerned in the Work of Public Elementary Schools', they became 'Handbook of Suggestions for Teachers;' their blue covers led to them becoming known as The Blue Books. Each has a chapter on the teaching of English and there was one (1924) devoted entirely to English teaching. In terms of English teaching, the series recognises and recommends child-centred, creative practice (such as promoting the importance of speaking and listening, encouraging wide reading, creative approaches to the teaching of writing, involving drama and, gradually, embracing media (the wireless and nascent television). The fact that the series spans 50 years suggests that it was valued by stakeholders. The chapter explores the main themes of the Blue Books and compares them to the literature proceeding from Dartmouth. It asks what might have prevented the Blue Books' child-centred 'suggestions' being taken up, and what might have caused English educationists to be receptive to similar ideas when they were re-disseminated in the late 1960s.

Cal Durrant and Wayne Sawyer add to our historical understandings through a close examination of the decade immediately following Dartmouth. They trace how the ideas expressed in *Growth through English* were taken up enthusiastically in Australia. They examine curricula and curriculum debate from the 1970s from two

Australian states, New South Wales [NSW] and Western Australia [WA], along
with writings on English that appeared in the national journal *English in Australia* in
one selected year – to demonstrate the nature of vernacular inflections in Australia
of the 'Personal Growth' model. The two curricula discussions are different and
are more comprehensive because of that difference. One focus is specifically on
the detail of the relevant NSW Years 7–10 Syllabus in the 1970s in that state, and
the other ranges more broadly over curriculum debates in WA in roughly the same
period. The chapter provides a clear sense of both breadth and depth in relation
to Australia's institutionalised versions of Personal Growth in the years following
Dartmouth, as well as its representation in curricular debates.

Dartmouth was fundamentally a gathering of UK and US scholars of English.
Canada had one representative, Merron Chorny (only an 'observer') but the
influence of Dartmouth on Canada was significant. Therefore, John Willinsky's
retrospective account 'as a Canadian school teacher and teacher educator who
came of age during the 1960s and began teaching school in 1972' and who was
tutored personally by Chorny, is extremely valuable for this collection. He explains
that it took another decade before he learned about the Anglo-American Seminar
on the Teaching of English held at Dartmouth College in the summer of 1966.
By that point, he suggests, Dartmouth already looked like the English teacher's
San Francisco Summer of Love, which began the following year with the legendary Monterey Pop Festival. He described how 'you didn't have to be there', was
the general feeling, with 'flowers in your hair', because 'all across the nation . . .
there's a whole generation / with a new explanation', as Scott Mackenzie sang
at Monterey in the song 'San Francisco'. In the years that followed Dartmouth,
Monterey Pop, and the Summer of Love, Willinsky recounts how all that came
to be associated, beyond anything that could have been imagined at the time,
with a self-conscious calling out of the moment for the generation involved in
and touched by those events. For Willinsky, it took the form of a professional
self-awareness of the calling, as English teachers took stock of their trade and its
place in the culture. He recounts very personally how the conference provided its
own Monterey Pop headliners for his generation of teachers, led by James Britton
and including Douglas Barnes, Basil Bernstein, Wayne Booth, John Dixon, Joshua
Fishman, James Moffett, Walter Ong, Alan Purves, Connie Rosen, James Squires,
and Denys Thompson. He describes how English teaching in Canada operated
at the intersection of the Anglo-American exchange of educational ideas but was
especially influence by one the 'pop stars' of Dartmouth, namely James Britton.

This collection is appropriately a mixture of the critical and the celebratory, and
John Dixon's extraordinarily influential book receives a great deal of forensic attention. It is, therefore, a tremendously valuable contribution that we have in the final
chapter in this part, because it draws on a recent interview with John Dixon himself,
on his contribution to this volume in our preface, and on unpublished papers from
Dartmouth. John Hodgson and Annie Harris reveal his response to the interpersonal
dynamics of the conference, as well as his personal history as a teacher of English,
and how it shaped the report. They locate Dixon's account in the context of his

early experiences of teaching and his published books for the classroom, and they give voice to participants whose contribution, they believe, may not have been adequately recognised in *Growth through English*. They conclude by suggesting that a fuller appreciation of the complexity of the influences on the conference and the diverse contributions of the work of the participants actually heightens the significance of the Dartmouth conference.

Part II: Dartmouth today – why it still matters

Andrew Goodwyn's chapter opens this part by arguing for the enduring place of Personal Growth in English teaching worldwide, and especially in the UK. His research in England over the last 25 years demonstrated consistently that English teachers value the Personal Growth [PG] model of English as summarised in the Cox Report (1989). Despite all the changes to curriculum and assessment over that time, PG remains their basic philosophy of English teaching. He demonstrates how English teachers have found each manifestation of the National Curriculum to be moving away from their child-centred approach towards an inflexible Cultural Heritage model, beloved of right-wing politicians, increasingly a model obsessed with only a singular version of Heritage, and that is not even a British heritage but *The* English Literary Heritage. The chapter explores this contradiction and proposes that, as the school system in England has become increasingly fragmented and the National Curriculum disapplied to more than half of all schools, so an updated and invigorated model of PG can challenge this imposed version of heritage and be effective where it matters most, in the diverse classrooms of schools in England.

By contrast, Peter Smagorinsky takes a strong critical stance towards what he sees as the limitations of the Growth model, arguing it lacked a truly social perspective. He considers that the conference of 1966 took place during a time when Romanticism had a strong hold on educational thought, generating individualistic conceptions of the student, grounded in both Piagetian psychology and Rousseauian notions of society's corrupting influence, celebrating such notions as 'do your own thing' and other anti-establishment sentiments that suggested that individuals could simply defy their circumstances and be who and what they wanted to be. He critiques *Growth through English* as celebrating the idea that each individual child's personal growth trajectory could be cultivated through such means as classroom drama through which students explored their identities. This leads him to suggest that the field's later 'social turn' made this valuing of the individual seem questionable. He argues for a more social view of human development, through which any individual's personal development is inherently subject to cultural mediation, with schools having deep structures that help to shape the conduct of teaching in ways that in turn shape how students learn in school. The consequences for English teachers in taking this social, cultural, and historical approach lead to a very modified notion of the 'Personal'. Whilst he sees Dartmouth's values demonstrated in schools as sites for developmental processes, he challenges Dartmouth's optimistic, Rousseauian, culture-defying assumptions. He insists we need to view learning as a socially-situated, culturally-mediated development; this is the necessary condition of humanity that educators cannot ignore in spite of the appeal of the notion of unbridled possibilities that Dartmouth suggested.

As Dartmouth was very much about the 'idea of English' so, inevitably, much of this collection is concerned with big ideas and concepts. However, some of the chapters, as with this one, are strongly grounded in empirical research, as with Goodwyn's above. Here Jacqueline Manuel and Don Carter present the findings of a recent study conducted with New South Wales' English teachers. The chapter draws attention to the remarkable professional, curricular, pedagogical and disciplinary sway of the Dartmouth Conference in shaping subject English and English teachers' beliefs and values in NSW since the 1970s. It argues that teachers have remained 'faithful' to the ideas of Personal Growth because of its far-reaching impact and continuing legacy. Once it was the 'new English' – becoming instantiated in the 1971 NSW junior secondary English syllabus – but it still retains an enduring salience with the same principles, philosophy and values more than four decades later. However, the research shows how difficult it is becoming for English teachers in NSW to stay 'faithful' because of the diminishing role of teacher agency, the challenges to the nature of teacher professionalism and the narrowing scope of student learning opportunities. The research reveals questions about the problematic future direction of subject English in an increasingly systematised and standardised educational landscape.

Rather than treating *Growth through English* as some kind of founding statement or declaration of truths that we hold to be self-evident, Brenton Doecke and John Yandell, situate it in a continuing dialogue about subject English, thereby relocating it within the tradition of practitioner inquiry into the complexities of language and education out of which the original book emerged. They state that their aim is to reaffirm the salience of that tradition to a fully knowing practice today and to revisit the question of language and experience. They argue that, for Dixon, a consciousness of that relationship is at the heart of English curriculum and pedagogy, involving sensitivity on the part of teachers to efforts by their students to give meaning to experience through the language available to them. They argue that to be sensitive to that struggle for students is to acknowledge the struggle that we all have – teachers and pupils alike – when it comes to creating representations of our experience in order to achieve a sense of our identities and an understanding of our place within society. This is the starting point for conceptualising classrooms as sites for enacting a social democracy. They conclude that Dixon's concept of 'experience' is not something that pre-exists language, as some kind of personal realm to be cherished; it is predicated on a Vygostkian understanding of language as mediating between the private realm of 'self' and the public realm that people negotiate each day, between the 'personal' and the 'social'.

The chapter by Larissa McLean Davies, Lucy Buzacott and Susan K. Martin argues that it is again time to consider what we 'do' in English in response to the needs of diverse students. At a time when social media has paradoxically made it possible to establish and market textual individuality, for one's face to virtually become a 'book', their chapter considers a twenty-first-century, relational notion of 'growth'. They present case studies from two Australian, specifically Victorian, secondary schools, which are each differently attempting to leverage subject English to support both personal and community growth in culturally and linguistically diverse contexts. A theme throughout the chapter is the consideration of what place should Australian literature specifically play in contemporary schooling. This is a subject of much heated national debate. They explore some of the tensions that exist for teachers and curriculum and policy writers as they negotiate contemporary possibilities of 'growth through English' in the context of the teaching of literature in Australia. They examine how the ideological complexity of applying personal growth approaches in post-colonial contexts is refracted through the unquestioned 'dominance' of British and American canonical literature in late twentieth- and early twenty-first-century articulations of subject English in Australia. They analyse the distinctions made in curriculum and practice between student growth and national cultural knowledge and understanding. In exploring the implications of these tensions for the future teaching of literature in subject English, they conclude by outlining considerations for a model of growth that is sustainable and generative in the twenty-first century in a post-colonial, pluralistic national context.

Part III: reflections – but for the future

This part opens with an important consideration and one that was unsurprisingly almost absent from the dialogues of Dartmouth – that is, the place of media study within English. Although the famous critic F.R. Leavis trumpeted the call to English teachers back in the 1930s to 'discriminate and resist' the encroachments of what was then termed the Mass Media, there was none of that sentiment expressed at Dartmouth. Generally speaking, most English teachers in the anglophone countries have steadily absorbed teaching about the media and, more recently, multimodal texts, into their everyday practice. As Steve Connolly demonstrates, this trend has also been present in many curricular documents and policies around the world. How extraordinary then, in the second decade of the twenty-first century, to find such work effectively 'disappeared' in England, put neatly in his punning title, 'W(h)ither Media in English?' The chapter provides a historical perspective on the study of media texts within English curricula. A number of countries have, across the last few decades, chosen to include the study of media texts within their national and regional school curricula. In some instances (Australia and New Zealand, for example) this has occurred in the subject area of English, while for others (USA, Latvia, Greece) it has been found in other locations in the school curriculum. Connolly uses the UK as an example of the way that the study of media texts has been characterised in the English subject curriculum and its relationship to that subject, from the inception of the National Curriculum in 1988 to its most recent manifestation in 2014.

He demonstrates that the place of the study of media texts of all types (print, moving image and digital) within 'Subject English' has shifted considerably, from being seen as an integral part of modern curricular versions of the subject, externally assessed and fundamentally connected to traditional conceptions of reading and writing, to something much less significant. Using a range of documentary and discourse analysis research methodologies, this chapter looks at the way that the National Curriculum and its related policy and practice documents have sought to treat media texts, and more generally, the notions of representation and audience within curricular English. Within this account, there is the desire to achieve three key aims; first, to examine how the study of media texts has been and is conceived by those writing and interpreting the National Curriculum for English; second, to analyse how this changing conception manifested itself in classroom practice; and finally, to explore the ways that teachers who want to make a study of media texts within English lessons might do so – when faced with a current National Curriculum in which there is very little acknowledgement of the idea that such study might be an important part of English.

Another aspect of English that barely featured at Dartmouth was what became known later as 'multiculturalism', now a much contested term. However, in their chapter, Lesley Nelson-Addy, Nicole Dingwall, Victoria Elliott and Ian Thompson examine what they consider to be the restoration of the canon and the backlash against multiculturalism in secondary English curricula. They consider that the Personal Growth model of English that came to significance after Dartmouth drew heavily on the concept of relevance to young people's lives and led to a wealth of multicultural texts entering the classroom (Gibbons, 2017). They consider that the framing of texts as being 'from other cultures' can been seen as problematic (Rogers, 2015) in terms of both the ways students understand them and some teachers frame issues of diversity for the English classroom. However, they argue, in both the UK and the US, curriculum 'reform' in favour of cultural literacy and core knowledge has led to a reduction in the place of multicultural texts in English, and more generally has led to a backlash against multiculturalism in the whole curriculum (see for example the status of Mexican-American studies in Arizona) and in society. In England, in particular, this is seen through the renaissance of the (largely) 'dead white male' canon for statutory study at 14–16.

They review how canonical literature is now promoted as a means of acquiring cultural capital linked to social mobility (and therefore to not teach it is an immoral decision, which makes teachers 'enemies of promise'). Yet the amount of cultural literacy required even to access and to analyse the new set texts in England exposes and produces further problems of equity. The removal of representation of non-white, non-middle-class voices from the curriculum produces another ethical dilemma for teachers who believe in the need for such representation. The authors argue that wider representation not only benefits those who then see themselves in the texts before them, but also society as a whole, providing for a more empathetic and balanced understanding of the people who make up the population of, for example, the UK or the US. The moral balance needs to be struck between personal life opportunities as represented by exam success and the potential for social agency (as framed in Goodwyn's (2016) revisiting of the Personal Growth model of English teaching). They explore the ethical dilemmas surrounding the teaching of the canon and of multicultural texts 50 years after Dartmouth and look towards the future for teaching literature in diverse societies.

In *Growth through English*, Dixon used many examples of student's work to illustrate what was meant by 'Personal Growth'. Naturally a number of these texts were either poems or poetic in nature. In Sue Dymoke's very personal chapter, we learn about her relationship to poetry as a person, as a teacher and as a poet herself. She draws initially on a personal milestone, the moment she gave the Harold Rosen Memorial Lecture at NATE's 2016 research symposium to celebrate '50 Years After Dartmouth' where she revisited certain aspects of her own English education (between the ages of 5–18 years) in the Sixties and Seventies. In focusing on this formative period, she explores the nature of language and personal growth (Dixon 1967, p.1) which were central elements of the original month-long seminar in 1966. She reflects on how poetry came to be such a key influence on her learning, teaching and writing and what lessons might be drawn from these experiences to inform future pedagogical practice or research in the field. In doing so, the chapter references previously published research on drafting, reading and performing poetry, poetic identity, poetry pedagogy and spoken word to consider how young people can find and keep poetry for themselves in ways that will continue to enrich them throughout their adult lives.

Catherine Beavis and Joanne O'Mara consider a variety of approaches to encourage reading for pleasure in secondary school English classes. They provide a historical trajectory, beginning with post-Dartmouth responses in Australia to Dixon's growth model (1967), mapping some of the rise and fall of reading for pleasure programmes, and examining the current resurgence of reading for pleasure in English classes. They analyse the range of approaches that we have seen, draw from data generated across several research projects and consider what might the place of reading for pleasure be in the digital society? They show emphatically that enjoyment is linked not just to success, but to purpose and identity, arguing that as we are in a post-typographic era, as Merchant (2015) suggests, then what does this mean for books and reading in English classes, and what might the pleasures be? They argue that if we want the reading of print texts to be an enjoyable, and hence valued, activity for all students, we need to change and broaden both the types of text that might be brought into the English/literacy classroom, and the ways we approach text in the English curriculum.

The Dartmouth Conference profoundly questioned the purpose of English and initiated a historical shift in the teaching of English from a focus on subject matter to an attention to process and student-centred learning. Todd DeStigter argues that among the recent manifestations of this emphasis on the student-learner has been the rise of Culturally Sustaining Pedagogy (CSP), which prioritises actively sustaining the cultures of racial, ethnic, and linguistic minority students. Using research based on three semesters of ethnographic research in an urban high school that serves almost exclusively Mexican-American and poor students, DeStigter examines the stories/experiences of these students and their ELA teachers to offer a friendly critique of CSP. More specifically, he argues that CSP is insufficiently attentive to poverty and wealth inequality, and concludes by suggesting ways in which CSP may more fully achieve its aspirations for social justice. He suggests that 50 years after Dartmouth, poverty and wealth inequality are defining characteristics of our time, and his chapter is motivated by the belief that among the best ways to sustain a culture is to ensure that those who identify with it are economically secure.

Grammar and its teaching were much discussed at Dartmouth and Annabel Watson and Debra Myhill, 'revisit' the debate, but with a view to the future of English teaching. They present an analysis of the significant and lasting effect that the Dartmouth Conference had on professional and classroom views of the role of grammar in the school curriculum in many Anglophone countries. They argue that it marked the abandonment of formal grammar teaching across many English-speaking jurisdictions in favour of more naturalistic methods of learning grammar, and to an extent shifted the focus from knowing about language to being a language user. To contextualise the impact of this on the language curriculum and professional practice, they present the reflections of leading educational researchers on the influence of the Dartmouth thinking about grammar in their own national jurisdictions. The chapter concludes with an analysis of recent developments in theoretical thinking about grammar and current curriculum and professional practice in the teaching of grammar with implications for future practice.

This volume has demonstrated just how much Dartmouth has remained an internationally significant event. Were such an event to take place again it would be most unlikely that it would only really involve the US, the UK, and a 'token' Canadian. It must be noted that the US government's funding for the event came from an essentially nationalistic motivation inspired by Cold War angst about the Soviet Union. However, an unintended consequence of the event was the creation, some years later, of the International Federation for the Teaching of English, a genuinely globally inclusive organisation. It is fitting to complete this volume with the contribution of Allison Skerrett and Saba Vlach, who once more ask, 'What is English?' and propose some new directions for the discipline, but adding that it exists now in a 'Transnational World'. They first consider the conversations at Dartmouth about new approaches to English education in response to sweeping changes in social life within and across world nations and relate them to the expanding social phenomenon with which they are concerned, that is transnationalism. 'Transnationalism' refers to the circumstance wherein people, through a mix of necessity and choice, live their lives across two or more countries. This lifestyle, they argue, generates familial, social, cultural, economic, socio-political and other networks and commitments, and feelings of belongingness, spanning two or more nations (Levitt, 2001). All of this is manifest in schools today worldwide, they are now populated by more transnational youths than ever before (Coe, Reynolds, Boehm, Hess, & Rae-Espinoza 2011; Zúñiga & Hamman, 2009). Given this situation, they argue that it is critical that English education today, in the spirit of the responsiveness, intellectual curiosity, creativity, and social justice stances of Dartmouth, reconsider how the discipline's practices can promote learning for this demographic and all students who sit alongside them in classrooms. They describe a conceptual approach with related instructional practices for English education called a transnationally-inclusive approach to literacy education (Skerrett, 2015). They demonstrate this approach, drawing on research with a diverse group of secondary-aged students in the highly transnational and post-colonial Caribbean nation of Dutch St. Maarten. They position their research as a kind of microcosm of the dichotomy at Dartmouth and the problems and possibilities we continue to grapple with 50 years later.

This Introduction comes to an end, but without a neat concluding paragraph. This volume explores the history and significance of the Dartmouth seminar, but without demanding a singular interpretation. The seminar itself was a debate and a dialogue, full of healthy and stimulating challenge and disagreement, but with all participants listening and engaged in developing forms of 'English' relevant to the emerging future. We have seen extraordinary changes in societies across the planet since 1966 but this need for debate, currently stifled in many Anglophone countries, is more important than ever. We hope that this volume will play its own part in that healthy debate and may offer some inspiration and hope for the future of English and its teachers worldwide.

PART I

Historical perspectives

1

LONDON ENGLISH, THE DARTMOUTH SEMINAR AND *GROWTH THROUGH ENGLISH*

Simon Gibbons

Introduction

For many, the most important tangible outcome of the 1966 Dartmouth Seminar was the publication of *Growth through English* (Dixon, 1967). Though there were other published outcomes from the seminar – an American summary of events appeared as *The Uses of English* (Muller, 1967) whilst other texts looked at drama and creativity in English (Barnes, 1968; Summerfield, 1968) – it is *Growth through English* that is considered to be the representative tome on proceedings. It is from the title to this text – ironically not Dixon's preferred choice, as he favoured something like 'Language in Operation' as more fitting – that many people's understanding of the growth model of English comes[1].

Within *Growth through English* is the claim – both explicit and implicit – that the text reflects the consensus reached by the seminar, that it is the acceptance of a new articulation of growth English, to supersede the heritage and skills models of the subject that had previously been seen to be dominant. There is debate surrounding to what extent any consensus was in fact reached at the Seminar. The relative contexts from which delegates from opposite sides of the Atlantic came meant that the starting points for discussions about the subject were very different. In the States, where things such as Russia's apparent superiority is the space race were causing anxiety amongst policymakers, resulting in more prescriptive ideas about curriculum content, there was already a federally funded Project English underway. Its aim was 'to define a sequenced curriculum for the study of language and literature from kindergarten to college' (Harris, 1991, p.635). At Dartmouth, the Americans were apparently drawing on this in proposing a structured curriculum which would specify 'certain literary works and genres to be studied based on the tripod of language, literature and composition' (Shafer, 1986, p.22). The English delegates, on the other hand, were advocating 'a shift in attention from the subject matter of English to the learners in English classes' (Smagorinsky, 2002, p.24).

Following the Seminar, eleven points of agreement were published (see Simmons et al, 1990, p.109) but some evidence contradicts such a harmonious outcome. Whilst NCTE's executive director regarded the event as 'stimulating, often stunning' (Squires, 1966) and claimed the group did reach 'much general agreement', one British delegate later recalled that there had been 'very little meeting of minds' and that there had been a 'bemused intellectual climate' (Whitehead, 1976, p.13). Apparently, 'arguments rose to fever pitch every day and in virtually every gathering' (Simmons, J., Shafer, R. and Shadiow, L., 1990, p.108). When talking of Dartmouth, Douglas Barnes,[2] another of the British delegation said 'all sorts of other things went on there besides what John reported' but that, significantly 'many of them not so much to our taste'. NCTE, according to Barnes 'weren't unwilling to accept that [*Growth through English*] as a version of what happened' however he confessed that 'You still meet American teachers who know the truth is very different'. Ultimately, even Dixon himself has recently acknowledged that the synthesis reached at Dartmouth, although powerful, was not 'all-inclusive' (Dixon, 2015, p.432).

It is, then, highly contestable to claim that *Growth through English* is a reflection of any consensus reached at the Dartmouth Seminar. If not the product of the Seminar's forty days of debate one might ask from where this version of English sprang. One clear answer to this question can be found in the work that Dixon and other British delegates James Britton, Harold Rosen and Douglas Barnes undertook in London in the decade and more prior to 1966. In this work in London schools and within the network of the London Association for the Teaching of English (LATE), a vision for English had been evolving since the post-war years. To a large extent it is this vision that appears in *Growth through English*, so much so that when one examines the development of this work it is not too fanciful to believe *Growth through English* might have contained more or less the same vision whether Dartmouth had happened or not. In this chapter I will briefly consider the development of a new English in London in the post-war years showing how, through the voices of Dixon, Barnes, Rosen and Britton, this view of the subject emerged as the perceived consensus of the seminar.

The development of London English: the formation and work of the London Association for the Teaching of English

That a new model for the teaching of English emerged from London schools in the immediate post-war years is no coincidence. A radical overhaul in secondary education in England had begun with the Education Act of 1944, which for the first time ensured all children to the age of fifteen, and ultimately sixteen, would attend school. Whilst the education act envisaged a tri-partite school system, with grammar, technical and secondary modern schools tailored to the perceived differing needs of different groups of young people, provision was made within the act for local education authorities to determine their own school landscape, with the scope offered for the introduction of comprehensive secondary schooling. The London County Council in its post-war educational London Plan seized this opportunity to boldly plan for a fully comprehensive system. It has been claimed that, uniquely, the London Plan powerfully promoted the development of the comprehensive as part of a project for social unity (Rubinstein and Simon, 1973). London's plans for comprehensivisation were seemingly inspired by a hope for the enthusiasm and optimism that would be generated for those who would have been previously hopeless in establishments other than grammar schools (Limond, 2007). This was apparently not an educational decision – at least not one informed by any evidence that the comprehensive system would result in raised academic outcomes. It was a bold attempt to rebuild a city ravaged by war with schools seen as the building blocks of a fairer, more just society.

These noble aims resulted in some stark difficulties for English teachers in the capital, many of whom were either newly – and rapidly – trained to meet a teacher shortage, or used to teaching a literature-based Leavisite-version of English in the grammar schools. This version of English, Cambridge English as it is often termed, was not fit for the new purpose of educating the whole cohort of secondary-aged children in classes catering for the full ability range. The necessity for a new kind of English led colleagues working at the London Institute of Education, specifically Perceval Gurrey, James Britton and Nancy Martin, to launch the London Association for the Teaching of English in the summer of 1947. This new voluntary subject association was formed to provide a network for English teachers in the capital, and indeed beyond, to share and disseminate practice, research their own classroom teaching and campaign on key issues.

A full account of the birth, growth and development of the London Association for the Teaching of English (Gibbons, 2013) clearly illustrates how this new network functioned to fashion a new model for the teaching of English. Fundamental to the approach was that the emergence of this model was genuinely 'bottom-up'; English teachers would identify challenges in their own classrooms, and – through working in LATE study groups – seek to find solutions to these problems. The findings would be disseminated through publications and conferences. Even in the earliest LATE projects, around aspects of the subject such as the marking of composition or the teaching of comprehension, a new English could be seen to be emerging. Those who have written about the emergence of this model (see for example Ball, 1985) have variously labelled it London English, English as Language or growth English, sometimes casting it as a directly opposing paradigm to the Cambridge, English as Literature, model that dominated in grammar schools in the pre-war years. As I have suggested (Gibbons, 2017) it may be unhelpful to seek an easy title for the model of English that was emerging. In reality there were many different strands, with key figures in LATE pursuing different strands of interest as years passed: James Britton, for example, became increasingly concerned with child language and thought development; Harold Rosen in the role and function of the language of the working classes; Douglas Barnes in talk in the classroom; Michael Halliday and Peter Doughty in grammar and knowledge about language. According to Tony Burgess,[3] the task before LATE was 'to try and build a sort of framework, or ongoing knowledge and theory. . . . the commitment to an underlying rationale for the teaching of English that could go on developing as a body of ideas'. A unifying philosophy or single overarching rationale did not emerge from the work of LATE and the teachers in London schools, but there were elements that brought the different strands together, notably the fundamental belief that the child, her language and her experience, should be the starting point and foundation for work in English. The subject was not about content – be that expressed as a canon of literature or the rules of the language – it was the means by which children would develop and express their growing understanding of their own worlds and the worlds of others.

This refocusing of the subject, the development of what might be termed child centredness in its most positive sense, was clearly evident in LATE's campaign to transform the assessment of English of school leavers through the GCE 'O' level language examination in the early 1950s. This lengthy and hard-fought campaign (see Gibbons, 2009) saw LATE devise, pilot and ultimately introduce an alternative examination that sought to resolve what Britton saw for teachers as 'the conflict of loyalties – to the subject they teach or the child who is taught' (Britton, 1955, p.178). It was a campaign that began with what can only be described as Harold Rosen's distain for then current 'O' level papers, given their apparent image of pupils taking the exam. Considering the types of choice offered for composition in the papers Rosen remarked at the time, 'the sort of children the examiners had in mind were children who visited pen friends abroad, who were chairmen of school dramatic clubs, and who arranged private dances. Was this symptomatic of the examiners' 'sympathy' with children?' (LATE, 1952, p.1). The new English was not simply about putting children's language and experience at the heart of the subject, it was about ensuring that the mass of 'ordinary' children now in the school system were represented in the curriculum and in assessment mechanisms.

LATE's *The Aims of English Teaching*

By the mid-1950s, the work of LATE had already led to a relatively well-formed theory of English being articulated. This is evident in a document that was prepared by the Association and sent to members in 1956. This document (LATE, 1956), entitled *The Aims of English Teaching* was written by LATE for British Council Study Boxes to be used in schools in India. That LATE was approached to write this document is in itself striking; one must assume that the British Council considered that the Association would be able to offer something of an authoritative overview of subject English. Given LATE had been in existence less than a decade at this point, this would appear to indicate the impact the Association was having within the field of English education; there doesn't seem to be any evidence to suggest that the LATE pamphlet was one of several springing from different sources (the English Association, for example), rather it appears to be the single publication used to offer a 'definitive' view on the subject for those studying overseas.

In its introduction *The Aims of English Teaching* acknowledged that in itself it could not be representative of the full range of work of the English teacher, and most notably in this respect it stressed that oral work 'seems to us to be of utmost importance' (p.1). Following the introduction, there were sections that outlined the scope of work in English. Significantly, the section placed at the beginning was 'Language and Experience', within which there were remarkably clear and confident statements that demonstrate the thinking of the Association.

'Experience comes first' (LATE, 1956, p.2) was the bold assertion and the English teacher's aim was to 'assist the development of language adequate to the child's experience' (p.2). No individual authors were named on the document but it is not unreasonable to suggest at least one member of the team responsible for its writing. The remarks on the relationship between language and experience indicated the emerging thinking of James Britton, and the growth of an as yet not fully developed philosophy, and one which was not yet supported by the theories of Vygotsky, theories that would ultimately reinforce the claims. The effect of language on experience was, the document proclaimed, 'to deepen it, order it, and make it accessible' (p.2). The pamphlet went on:

> By language we require a measure of control over our own experience and thereby are able to learn from it. It is commonplace that language helps us to think: our formulation implies also that language similarly helps us to perceive and feel and act.
>
> *(LATE, 1956, p.2)*

The use of language to represent experience, to make sense of one's world, would appear to foreshadow the ideas Britton developed through the 1960s around the notion of 'language in the spectator role' which came to maturity in *Language and Learning* (Britton, 1970). The explicit links between language and thought, though not fully developed here, would similarly form a critical part of Britton's later work.

When talking specifically about language the message was clear; children have language when they come to school and this should be the foundation on which development is built 'there should be no break' (2). Perhaps here, in the emphasis on embracing the home language and dialect of the child, the influence of Harold Rosen can be detected in the document. There was a stress, too, placed on the social dimensions to both language and experience:

> Experience is not had in isolation, but it is something shared with a social group. Language is the prime medium of social communication.
>
> *(LATE, 1956, p.2)*

In describing appropriate methods to use in the classroom to foster the development of language and experience, the stress was laid on what is called 'expressiveness' or 'fidelity to experience' as oppose to 'acceptability'; that is,. children should be allowed to use their own language or dialect to relate experience either in spoken or written form, and that notions of acceptability – or grammatical correctness – should come later, as insistence on 'correctness' in use of language can be at the expense of expression. The section on 'Language and Experience' concluded with the idea that children should have a strong choice in what they choose to speak and write about, given that such language use ought to be rooted in their experience.

The opening section of the document, then, which it is logical to accept was a summary of a developing philosophy of English teaching, given the title of the pamphlet, its purpose and its intended audience, was certainly bold in the way in which it prioritised language and experience, with the child at the centre of learning and teaching. The remainder of the pamphlet included sections on reading, poetry, drama, language study and literature in the sixth form. Within the language study section, the ongoing argument about the place and teaching of grammar in English – reflecting the concerns James Britton came into the teaching profession with – took centre stage. The pamphlet came out very strongly against what might be called 'traditional' grammar teaching through a prescriptive approach. Grammar study should, it was asserted, 'be a consideration of the structure of the language in so far as that affects meaning' (LATE, 1956, p.8), in what alluded to a 'functional' approach to language study, though it is unlikely that such a term would have had any common currency in the mid-1950s. Similarly, rather than decontextualised exercises focused on word classes or parsing contrived sentences, the starting point for any grammatical study should be 'the study of actual utterances' (p.9).

LATE, Walworth School and *Reflections*

In its content and style, *The Aims of English Teaching* certainly foreshadows the later *Growth through English*. Although John Dixon's involvement with LATE was more peripheral that that of fellow Dartmouth attendees such as Britton, Barnes and Rosen, his inextricable link to the development of the new English emerging in London was ensured when he took up the post of head of English at Walworth school in South London. Walworth had been one of the first experimental comprehensive schools, established in the late 1940s. Guy Rogers, a key early figure in LATE, had been head of English and then headteacher. Harold Rosen took on the leadership of the English department in 1956, and in 1958 wrote an English syllabus that articulated the vision of English emerging through the work of LATE. In their fascinating case study of Walworth school included in *English Teachers in a Postwar Democracy* (Medway, Hardcastle, Brewis and Crook, 2014) the authors point to the 'strikingly unconventional declaration' that opens the syllabus, and reproduce its opening lines:

> The teaching of English at Walworth calls for a sympathetic understanding of the pupils' environment and temperament. Their language experience is acquired from their environment and from communication with the people who mean most to them. . . Whatever language the pupils possess, it is this which must be built on rather than driven underground. . . The starting point for English work must be the ability to handle effectively their own experience
> *(Harold Rosen's 1958 English syllabus, quoted in Medway et al, 2014, p.90)*

This was a clear articulation of LATE thinking, a restatement of the arguments in *The Aims of English Teaching* and foreshadowing what was to come in *Growth through English*. The syllabus went on to detail what was a practical realisation of growth English, or English as language, for the comprehensive classroom. It was into this environment that John Dixon walked when he took on the head of English role from Rosen in January 1959. And it was in this working context that Dixon collaborated with Walworth colleagues Simon Clements and Leslie Stratta to produce the course book *Reflections* along with its accompanying *Teachers' book* (Clements, Dixon and Stratta, 1963a, 1963b).

Ostensibly the English course for the fourth form at Walworth, it has been rightly acknowledged that *Reflections* was 'innovative in several ways: in the quality of its production (good paper, typography, and photographs) and the absence from the main text of the customary comprehension exercises and instruction about usage' (Medway et al, 2014, p.102). Most striking was the thematic arrangement of the course so that some critics, such as Shayer (1970), felt it was more like a sociology course than an English one. Chapters in *Reflections* include those on 'Family, Community and Work', 'The Mass Media' and 'Questions of Our Time', each packed with excerpts for pupils to read. The texts used in the book include what would be recognised as established literature – writing from D.H. Lawrence and William Faulkner is present – but also include examples from contemporary writers such as Alan Sillitoe and Richard Wright. Additionally, there are many non-fiction texts, some taken from newspapers but others from documents produced by expert groups – the United Nations and the Royal Institute of British Architects, for example. The texts and pictures provide stimuli for children to write and respond both in imaginative and in critical and reflective ways.

Though innovative, there is no doubt that *Reflections* is a form of, or perhaps more accurately an extension of, some of the thinking about English that had been developing through LATE. The Preface to the *Teachers' book* makes this explicit:

'Many of the principles in this book come from the traditions of Walworth School and from many long and exciting discussions with colleagues and friends in the London Association for the Teaching of English' (Clements, Dixon and Stratta, 1963b, p.4). According to Dixon himself,[4] '*Reflections* is one very good outcome of all the ferment that was going on in LATE and in our own school in addition'. Clements was equally clear about the close relationship between *Reflections* and the ongoing work of LATE. During a presentation on the text to a LATE conference in 1965, Clements declared that *Reflections* was 'more than a book; it represents a state of affairs. It represents a long period of working with LATE' (LATE, 1965, p.6) and that:

> *The Teachers' Book* is really a kind of discussion representing a relationship between the teacher and the material of the book and it therefore represents a view of culture, and this is a crystallisation of what LATE has been working on for 10 years.
>
> *(p.6)*

Going on to articulate what might be seen as a common school culture, Clements used the phrase 'ordinary living' (p.7) and suggested that 'LATE has been trying for years to get children to write about these ordinary values because writing makes them articulate' (p.7). Creating an analogy with the development in the teaching of art beyond line drawing and painting into a concern 'to create. . . .a tactile and visual sensibility which will be useful in ordinary living' (p.7), Clements suggested that this was precisely what was happening in English, using language to 'create a sensibility which will be useful in living' (p.7). The report then records Clements' view that:

> This is not mere child centred learning. When we get children to write, we are establishing the validity of their experience. This is the creative milieu in which anything at all can happen.
>
> *(p.7)*

London English and Dartmouth

By the time of Dartmouth, then, LATE had been in existence nearly twenty years, and delegates such as John Dixon, Harold Rosen, James Britton and Douglas Barnes took with them to the Seminar well-formed ideas about effective English curriculum and pedagogy that had been forged through classroom-based collaboration, research and action and which had been articulated in publications such as *The Aims of English Teaching* and *Reflections*. It may of course be that the articulation of this notion of the subject was accepted at Dartmouth, despite what apparently was an initial rejection of it by American delegates. Reporting to LATE following the Seminar, John Dixon suggested that,

> At the beginning the Americans were surprised to hear the English apparently
> defending an 'outmoded progressivism'. One of the by-products in the States
> of the Russian Sputnik had been a revulsion from what many considered was
> flabby in the progressive school system.
>
> *(LATE, 1966, p.1)*

Perhaps surprisingly, given his own assessment of the Dartmouth proceedings,
it was Frank Whitehead who, according to Dixon, 'brilliantly demolished the
Americans' case for a structured curriculum' (p.1) with Dixon later recalling[5] that
'what came through in Dartmouth – and Frank Whitehead was mostly responsible
for this – was when you looked at all of the models available in the States, and in
England at the time, only a developmental model would give you any basis for
describing an English curriculum'.

As we've seen, the evidence about a consensus at Dartmouth is, at best, mixed.
What I would suggest is not in dispute is that the product of the seminar – *Growth
through English* – is in fact an articulation of the version of English worked on and
refined by Dixon, Britton, Barnes, Rosen and others working in London schools
through the 1950s and 1960s.

The continuity is clear. The central organising concepts of English being
about language and experience, that the starting point for English work should
be the child's own language and that fidelity to this is critical are already
articulated very clearly in *The Aims of English Teaching* and in *Reflections*.
An examination of the extensive archive of LATE conference reports and
research publications covering the twenty years between its formation and the
Dartmouth Seminar reveals the evolution of the model and the extent to which
it grew to encompass the study of popular culture and media, drama, the language of the working classes and so much more. Some of the 'big ideas' in
Growth through English are refinements of thinking that was already publicly
part of LATE work. For example, in Chapter 2 of *Growth through English* the
key concepts of language in the spectator and language in the participant role
are referenced. These ideas were most closely associated with the work of
James Britton, who had used them first in a public lecture at the Institute of
Education in 1962. It is possible – though opinions differ here – that the ideas
about spectator and participant derived from work by D.W. Harding, originally
an English specialist who was on the editorial board of *Scrutiny* before turning
his attentions to psychology. Certainly, his piece for *Scrutiny* 'The Role of the
Onlooker' (Harding, 1937) would seem to be a direct antecedent of Britton's
later formulations of spectator and participant. This piece is referenced in
Growth through English, though according to Tony Burgess 'Jimmy didn't know
about it and he produced the role of the spectator quite independently at the
same sort of time'.[6] Where this idea originally came from is less important than
the fact that its promotion in *Growth through English* stems from the work of

those developing London English. Even down to the examples of children's work reproduced in *Growth through English*, LATE work is critical: the extract of children's dialogue used on page 24 of the text, for example, came from a LATE conference held in the early 1960s, and the poem 'Domestic Abuse' on page 53 was reproduced from a LATE anthology of children's writing, *And When You Are Young* (LATE, 1960).

Conclusion

Part of my argument is that whether or not there was a consensus that emerged from Dartmouth, an agreement on a new model for the teaching and learning of English, is in some ways not particularly important. We will never know to what extent there was agreement, given that even those present at the Seminar differ on their views as to how much accord there was. What we have from Dartmouth, in the shape of *Growth through English*, is the articulation of a model of English that is almost indistinguishable from that which Britton, Barnes, Rosen and Dixon packed in their suitcases as they made the trip across the Atlantic in 1966. Did they so powerfully sell this to the Americans that it was universally embraced as a new orthodoxy? This is highly unlikely. More believable is that Dixon, armed with his own experience of working in London comprehensives and given his close collaboration with Britton, Barnes and Rosen, could have written *Growth through English* without the Dartmouth Seminar having ever even taken place.

That may sound heretical when the Seminar itself is seen by many as a watershed moment in the history of English teaching, and so important in proposing a new model for the subject. It may seem even more odd in the context of a book inspired by the fiftieth anniversary of the event. Does it mean that in and of itself Dartmouth has little significance for the English teaching profession today? I don't think this is the case. If, as I contend, the content of *Growth through English* is not the result of the discussions at the Seminar this does not mean it was an unimportant event. In one sense, Dartmouth stands as a powerful reminder of a time when the development of pedagogy and curriculum was, to a very large extent, in the hands of teachers. It points to a model of professionalism, of teacher agency and autonomy that we would do well to champion today.

In another sense, one could argue that the importance of Dartmouth was that it brought London English, or English as Language, to a much wider audience than would have been possible without it. In the guise of Personal Growth English, this model of the subject proved acceptable and attractive to a huge number of English teachers, even if the model itself was far from fully formed, singular and coherent. Growth English – however we may want to define or characterise it – did not rely on Dartmouth for its existence, but must surely rely on Dartmouth, to no little degree, for its enduring legacy.

Notes

1 In an interview with the author, referring to the title of *Growth through English*, John Dixon said, 'I said I thought of calling it something like *Language in Operation*. You see not a very brilliant title. So somebody – in fact one of the most reactionary North Americans said, well it's about growth why don't we call it *Growth through English*?'.
2 Douglas Barnes' comments taken from an interview with the author.
3 Tony Burgess' comments taken from an interview with the author.
4 John Dixon's comments taken from an interview with the author.
5 John Dixon's comments taken from an interview with the author.
6 Tony Burgess' comments taken from an interview with the author.

References

Ball, S. (1985). 'English for the English Since 1906'. In Goodson, I. (ed.), *Social histories of the secondary curriculum*. Sussex: Falmer Press.

Britton, J. (1955). 'The Paper in English Language at Ordinary Level'. *The Use of English*, 6(3), 178–184.

Clements, S., Dixon, J. and Stratta, L. (1963a). *Reflections*. Oxford: Oxford University Press.

Clements, S., Dixon, J. and Stratta, L. (1963b). *Reflections – teacher's book*. Oxford: Oxford University Press.

Dixon, J. (1967). *Growth through English*. London: Penguin.

Dixon, J. (2015). 'Developing English'. *English Teaching Practice and Critique* 14(3), 427–434.

Gibbons, S. (2009). 'Back to the future? A Case Study in Changing Curriculum and Assessment: The Story of the London Association for the Teaching of English's Alternative 'O' level English Language Paper'. *English in Education* 43(1), 19–31.

Gibbons, S. (2013). *The London Association for the Teaching of English 1947–1967: a history*. London: Institute of Education/Trentham Press.

Gibbons, S. (2017). *English and its teachers: a history of policy, pedagogy and practice*. Oxford: Routledge.

Harris, J. (1991). 'After Dartmouth: Growth and Conflict in English'. *College English*, 53(6), 631–646.

LATE (1952). 'Report of meeting on GCE examinations in English March 11th 1952'. Unpublished LATE Archive material.

LATE (1956). *The Aims of English teaching* 'A pamphlet prepared for British Council Study Boxes to be used in India'. Unpublished LATE Archive material.

LATE (1960). *And when you are young: prose and verse by young writers, 5–18* London: The Joint Council for Education through Art.

LATE (1965). 'English in the education of the 14–16 Year Old'. Unpublished LATE Archive material.

Limond, D. (2007). 'Miss Joyce Lang, Kidbrooke and 'The Great Comprehensives Debate': 1965–2005'. *History of Education*, 36(3), 339–352.

Medway, P, Hardcastle. J, Brewis. G and Crook, D (2014). *English teachers in a postwar democracy: emerging choice in London schools, 1945–1965*. New York: Palgrave Macmillan.

Muller, H. (1967). *The Uses of English*. New York: Holt, Reinhart and Winston.

Rubinstein, D. and Simon, B. (1973). *The evolution of the comprehensive school 1926–1972*. London: Routledge and Keegan Paul.

Shayer, D. (1972). *The teaching of English in schools 1900–1970*. London: Routledge and Keegan Paul.

Shafer, R. (1986). 'Dartmouth and Beyond'. *The English Journal*, 75(3), 22–26.

Simmons, J., Shafer, R. and Shadiow, L. (1990). 'The swinging pendulum: teaching English in the USA, 1945–87'. In Britton, J., Shafer, R., and Watson, K. (eds.), *Teaching and learning English worldwide*. Philadelphia: Multilingual Matters Ltd.

Smagorinsky, P. (2002). '*Growth through English* Revisited'. *The English Journal*, 91(6), 23–29.

Squires, J. (1966). *Post Dartmouth memorandum* available at http://archives.library.illinois.edu/ncte/about/about_images/dartmouth/memorandum01.jpg.

Summerfield, G. (1968). *Creativity in English* Urbana, IL: NCTE.

Whitehead, F. (1976). 'The Present State of English Teaching: Stunting the Growth'. *The Use of English*, 28(1), 11–17.

Note on LATE Archive material

The unpublished LATE documents are held in an archive at University College London Institute of Education Library.

2

GROWTH THROUGH ENGLISH AND *THE USES OF ENGLISH*

Literature, knowledge and experience

Wayne Sawyer

In the British 'zone' of the English education world, which Australia largely inhabited throughout the twentieth century, the key book that came out of Dartmouth was John Dixon's *Growth through English*. Some in the British 'zone' may not even be aware of the equivalent American book, Herbert Muller's *The Uses of English*. 2017 was the 50th anniversary of the publication of these texts and seems a useful time to re-visit some of their key ideas. Here I want to examine these books from the perspective of what they had to say about literature in particular and, in turn, about 'knowledge' and 'experience'.

Muller distinguished the books as his being 'a report on the proceedings of the seminar designed for the general reader', and Dixon's as 'a report addressed to the professional community' (Muller, 1967: vi). Dixon's discussion centres far more on exploring a normative curriculum position (though, as I argue below, not by himself presenting a final position). He says in the Preface to his second edition that his aim had been to 'draw from the discussions and reports at Dartmouth such ideas as are directly relevant to my own work in class and to that of teachers that I know' (1969/1972: xi). Though American and British differences on particular issues are presented by Muller – with his own views sometimes clear, sometimes not – the extent to which either book represents any 'national position' via its author is problematic. Suffice to say at this point that it is Muller's book, rather than Dixon's, that engages in the more extended discussion of this sort.

Literature and the nation

The theme of Dartmouth was 'What is English?' and on the question of literature and its role in English curriculum, Dixon and Muller begin from positions which are occasionally different, but interestingly overlapped at particular points. Muller argues that literature is at 'the very heart of their subject' for teachers, though 'the ordinary citizen regards it as only a kind of elegant pastime, not really essential to an education . . . (compared to) the practical importance of writing and speaking well' (Muller, 1967, pp.4–5.) Where 'most Americans' see value in literature, it is as a means of building a national culture around 'the sanctity of the flag, home, religion and private property – the heart of the American Way of Life' (p.78). This view of literature's differential roles for the teacher and the 'ordinary citizen' exactly reflects in each of its points the views put forward by another American, Albert Kitzhaber, in his own essay entitled 'What is English?' that opened 'Working Paper No. 1' at Dartmouth:

> As for the teaching of literature . . . literary scholars and English teachers in the schools would defend it as the chief bulwark of the humanities in public education . . . The average citizen, on the other hand, is more likely to tolerate literature . . . than to support it wholeheartedly . . . He regards it as effete if not effeminate. But . . . often . . . sees it as a convenient way of inculcating . . . a belief in orthodox social philosophy and moral standards, or merely the stock responses to flag, home, and mother.
>
> *(Kitzhaber, 1966, pp.2–3)*

As for the British, Dixon's book was most widely criticised in the following years from a literature-centred school who saw his emphasis on pupil experience, and the idea that pupils' own writing was itself suitable literature for classroom consideration, as denigrating the curriculum (Allen, 1980; Hansen, 1979; Inglis, 1975; Whitehead, 1976). However, Dixon's argument was not a turning away from literature – of the British and Americans at Dartmouth, he says that 'the common ground we found lay in the teaching of imaginative literature' (Dixon, 1975, p.123). Rather, what Dixon wanted to turn away from is the way literature had been deployed as nation-building (not unlike Muller's and Kitzhaber's claims about the way 'the average citizen' or 'most Americans' saw literature's role) and as 'civilising':

> Great literature offers, in Arnold's phrase, a criticism of life: what better could the children be reading? Here was a content for English that all could respect. . . Through literature all that was best in national thought and feeling could be handed on to a generation that knew largely slums and economic depression.
>
> *(Dixon, 1975, pp.2–3)*

There are two fundamental problems with this 'cultural heritage' vision, according to Dixon. One is that in classrooms the '"precious lifeblood of a master-spirit" (became) a series of inky marginal annotations and essay notes'. The other – more fundamental – is that '(i)n the heritage model the stress was on culture as a *given*'. Dixon's was not a rejection of canonical literature as a category, but rather an emphasising of the place of pupils' cultures and their interaction with 'the world of the writer' – a point pursued further below in the section on experience (Dixon, 1975, p.3). Muller's reporting is curious on this issue. According to Muller, any notion that literature teaching should mean a '"great books" program', or require 'the teaching of certain writers' was questioned not by the British specifically, but by the whole Seminar (Muller, 1967, p.79). While Dixon's position on the cultural heritage was not to reject the canon as a category, Muller reports that '(t)he litera- ture study group[1] specifically questioned the assumption that our cultural heritage required the teaching of '"great books"' or 'certain writers' (Muller, 1967, p.79). While one can see how teaching classical mythology, European folk and fairy tales, foreign literature, film, radio and television and '"good" books' (the Seminar's list of appropriate texts for study – Muller, 1967, p.79) constitutes a nicely broad and highly appropriate programme, it is not altogether clear how a 'cultural heritage' curriculum could avoid 'the teaching of certain writers'. In fact, Muller – in one of his occasional, often cynical, interjections – effectively argues that American classrooms are already successfully bypassing the cultural heritage:

> An American might have remarked that a play or two of Shakespeare are about the only classics that many high school students read.
>
> *(Muller, 1967, p.80)*

Muller himself argues that in not supporting the canon, the needs of society and students were both 'slighted' (p.89). One can glean from scattered statements such as these a sense of what Muller considered to be – sometimes in practice, some- times as a set of ideals- the aims of literature teaching. These included:

- knowledge of cultural heritage and history (pp.5, 12, 34, 89)
- being a bulwark against 'standardized mass society' (pp.8, 18). The British were also seen by Muller as 'defending the all-important human values that are being neglected in the interests of economy and efficiency' (p.176)
- presenting values/presenting diverse visions of life/ learning how to live (pp.18, 77, 81, 176)
- developing sensitive judgements and taste and recognition of quality (pp.18, 84)
- developing critical, literate, discriminating citizens (p.19)
- developing the personality, character and identity of the child as an individual (pp.35, 176)
- developing pleasure in language and literature themselves (pp.79, 176)
- turning out good 'common readers' (p.180)
- improving writing (p.78)

Dixon, as I argued above, tagged the cultural heritage model as having nation- building and 'civilising' aims that were thwarted in practice, while at the same time neglecting the opportunity to use language to explore, order and organise one's experience in Britton's 'spectator' role – l where Britton himself also situates literature (Dixon, 1975, pp.4, 8, 9, 28–29). Literature is to add to the store of shared experience in the classroom by 'bringing new voices into the classroom' and 'helping to bring order and meaning to parts of (a student's) experience' (Dixon, 1975, pp.13, 30, 36, 44). The Seminar, according to Dixon, tentatively proposed English as a joint literary-linguistic discipline, 'the one investigating with more detachment the intuitions of the other' (p.11). In his chapter specifically dedicated to the 'question of knowledge', Dixon argues for two specific areas in which a body of knowledge *about* language becomes most useful. One is to provide for older students 'the tools of linguistic thought' in order to 'study problems' in language (pp.79–80); the other is to provide a way of analysing the language of literature (p.80). Finally, also highly controversial was the defining of students' own work as 'the literature of the classroom' (p.55).

Literature and knowledge

It is on the question of knowledge that Muller highlights, at many points, key differences between the American and British 'positions' at Dartmouth. Their stance on 'knowledge' for Muller constitutes the quintessential, defining British position at Dartmouth, and the key site on which the knowledge issue plays out is literature:

> In the teaching of literature [the British] shied away from any emphasis on 'knowledge' which to them implied a body of inert facts; they deplored the tendency to present a body of historical or critical knowledge *about* literature, instead wanting to concentrate on the understanding and appreciation of particular literary works.
>
> *(Muller, 1967, p.12; see also pp.51, 81, 85–87)*

> The British aversion to teaching knowledge about literature extended to knowledge of literary forms, genres and techniques. . .Whitehead . . .objected that this approach 'leads our attention away from the unique work of literature'. . .towards. . . his *bete noir*, knowledge *about* literature.
>
> *(p.84)*[2]

In fact, this debate between a focus on the individual text, its meanings and readers' experiences – as opposed to knowledge about literature which, as a manifestation of curriculum, might include knowledge about history, authors, techniques (and genres in particular) – had been playing itself out within England both before and since the establishment of English literature as a legitimate curriculum area at both school and university levels. This debate could be conceptualised as one between 'knowledge' and (textual) 'experience', with the latter also able to be viewed as 'response'. 'Knowledge' and 'experience/response' have often been positioned as binaries in developing British curricula for literary study. In relation to Victorian Britain, Atherton shows that literary 'criticism' struggled to find its role in universities against the opposition of, particularly, historical and philological scholarship.Resistance to literary study as an academic discipline in a number of universities 'focused. . .on the belief that it was concerned with judgements rather than knowledge' (Atherton, 2005, p.221).[3] Later, Cambridge under Leavis was seen as valuing close reading, while London and Oxford were valuing literary history over 'criticism' and over a culture of 'individual responses to texts' (Hilliard, 2012, p.9). Response to the individual work – the importance of the literary *experience* – had been standing up for some time as a curricular principle against bodies of knowledge which were considered by some as simply external to that central experience.

Any American position on the teaching of literature is complex. The British, Muller says, favoured experience and response to the particular literary work as against historical knowledge and critical knowledge (Muller, 1967, pp.12, 89). They rejected knowledge about forms, genres and techniques in place of 'experiencing effects' (pp.84–85). The Americans, it is implied in other places, were less averse to such knowledge ('they argued for the importance of basic subject matter' – p.12), particularly as the US delegates were said to have favoured more the claims of the discipline against the British claims of the child (p.50). The Americans were more inclined to favour 'some explicit teaching about literary forms and critical vocabulary' (p.87), but felt that in regard to literary history in particular, the schools have been teaching 'far too much inert knowledge, such as names and dates' (p.80). In fact, Muller also described American delegates as reflecting a 'modified influence' of the New Critics in favouring 'sensitive appreciation' of literature over 'historical knowledge' (in fact, both the British and Americans are said to have welcomed New Critical stress on 'aesthetic values and closer reading')[4] (p.87). The year after Muller's publication, James Moffett, who had been an American delegate to Dartmouth, also argued about the dangers of 'organizing the whole literature course in historical-survey fashion or . . . assigning books of literary history' (Moffett, 1968, pp.4). In the same year as Moffett, a national study of high school English programs in the US was published by James Squire and Roger Applebee. Their *High School Instruction Today* characterised literature teaching as emphasising 'ideas', and concern with literary history. Knowledge *about* literature was seen as far too often the substance of high school English programs – knowledge about 'the age. . . in which a work was written. . . the writer himself. . . the literary genre as an abstraction to be perceived in and for itself' (Squire and Applebee, 1968, p.106) – as opposed to 'the experience of literature itself' (p.97). Really 'exciting' literature teaching was concerned with 'the emotional, intellectual, and artistic demands of the text' (p.97) and with refining 'the processes of learning to read. . . with insight and discrimination. . . analytical reading. . . as a process' (pp.108–109). The NCTE published five monographs (the Dartmouth Seminar Papers) on the conference that reflected the work of the Study Groups.[5] One of these, edited by Squire, was *Response to Literature* (1968b). It repeatedly reflects the knowledge/experience binary:

> The direct study of literary criticism, literary history or critical theory do not seem necessary in the elementary and secondary school, nor do courses like 'The History of American Literature'.
>
> *(Working Party Number One, in Squire, 1968a, p.49)*

> We can probably all agree that conscious awareness of formal characteristics . . . should play some part in a student's literary education . . . From the British standpoint what may well be in dispute is the magnitude of the contribution that can be made by such awareness to the reader's ability to respond fully and appropriately to any specific literary work.
>
> *(Frank Whitehead, in Squire, 1968a, pp.50–51)*

> There are at present considerable differences about the *knowledge* of literature to be expected from students. On the one hand there are those who favour the study of genre, literary forms, chronological arrangement. Others believe that information about literature is not important enough for any time to be given to it. . . Our literature programs tend to place far too little attention to the *close* reading of literary texts, far too much on superficial coverage and talking about texts.
>
> *(Denys Thompson, in Squire, 1968a, pp.51–52)*

Importantly, this Literature Study group 'were concerned', according to Muller, with 'the expansion of the child's experience, not of his formal knowledge of literature' (Muller, 1967, p.81) and a joint Anglo-American statement suggested a curriculum based on 'experience, rather than knowledge' (p.81).

In fact, cognition generally is treated as problematic in both books, as both Muller and Dixon reported a strong concern at the Seminar with affect. The Study Group on literature were said by Muller to have chiefly discussed '"affective" responses, since they were wary of knowledge, explicit analysis, demands for "formulation" of response, etc.' (p.91).[6] In the project of English generally, Muller himself deplored the emphasis in a liberal education on '"knowledge", not powers of thought, broad comprehension, or philosophy, still less on enlargement of the imagination' (p.179). He agreed that teachers of English should do more than impart 'a body of knowledge or mere techniques' (p.54). However, on 'experience' in general, he sought to distance himself from the British position:

> The British preference for focusing on the personal and inner life, helping the child to order, extend, and enrich his experience instead of imparting a body of knowledge or mere techniques, still required attention to his knowing and knowing how as well as his feelings.
>
> *(Muller, 1967, p.40)*

It is to 'experience' in its curricular relation to 'literature', that I now turn.

Literature and experience

While this relationship between literature and knowledge plays out in quite similar terms in Dixon's account of the Seminar ('the search for. . . "structure" as a guiding principle leads to retrogressive emphasis on "knowledge" [knowledge. . .*about* literature]' – Dixon, 1975, p.84), far more interesting in *Growth through English* is the relationship between literature and experience.

I made the point earlier that Dixon's was not a rejection of canonical literature as a category, but rather a re-thinking of the way literature had been used in classrooms as representing the only cultural heritage there was. Nine years after Raymond Williams had declared that 'culture is ordinary' (Williams, 1958), Dixon wanted to foreground culture 'as the pupil knows it, a network of attitudes to experience and personal evaluations that he develops in living response to his family and neighbourhood' (Dixon, 1975, p 3). Moving the pupils' culture(s) to the centre of the curriculum and at the same time emphasising pupil response to literature – their interaction with 'the world of the writer' – were no doubt a set of radical moves. While Dixon stressed the 'interplay' between the world of the pupil and the world of the writer, he felt that the heritage model, 'by re-emphasizing the text', had moved too far in simply 'presenting experience' to students (Dixon, 1975, p.3), rather than having experience as 'the vital core of English work' (Dixon, 1975, p.48):

> The English specialist is often tempted to restrict himself to looking at life through fictions – quite forgetting that one can also look at people and situations direct.
>
> *(Dixon, 1975, p.54)*

Dixon's own teaching at Walworth (Medway et al, 2014) and his foregrounding the cultures of his students as presented in the Walworth English course *Reflections* (Clements et al, 1963) is, of course, itself 'reflected' here. *Growth through English* carries within it not just a foregrounding of pupil experience, but of working class experience, at the same time as it is almost definitively urban. The thematic titles of some of the *Reflections* chapters give a sense of the central concerns:

'Homes for the ageing'

'Paul brings Clara home'

'Living-rooms and kitchens'

'White-collar girl'

'Boys weeklies'

'The pay packet'

'The arrest'

'Causes of crime?'

'Borstal boy'

Dixon felt that there was a curriculum balance too far in the direction of 'fictions'. Ten to 15 years later, and often conflating the Dartmouth conference with *Growth through English* specifically and the Growth model generally, critics of an alleged neglect of literature, such as Inglis (1975), Whitehead (1976) and Allen (1980), were arguing also in binary terms that the curriculum balance had moved too far towards 'experience'. To them the focus on experience represented a downgrading of the curriculum and a lowering of standards. In Australia, the NSW English Teachers' Association in 1977 published a major text, *English in Secondary Schools: Today and Tomorrow*, which included a section on 'Current issues' with two chapters entitled, 'Towards a Literature-Centred English' (Smith, 1977) and 'Towards an Experience-Centred English' (Walshe, 1977). David Homer, in his important (1973) history of the subject since the 1920s, reported that by the late 60s, 'child-centredness' had become so strong that people were wondering whether there was a role for literature at all (p.142).

Some of this criticism was expressed in terms that specifically rejected the urban working class/poor origins of 'growth':

> relevance in English classrooms meant the presentation of local material to stimulate talk. 'What's it like in your house when the truant officer comes?'. . . The urban underprivileged were marked for salvation. . . English teachers began to. . .cut back on the freight of literature or jettison it altogether. If all pupils cannot cope with literature, then none need have it.
>
> *(Hansen, 1979, p.6)*[7]

An over-emphasis on talk and on language were also caught up in this critique. The irony of this criticism is that today, Dixon and Growth are criticised for being too linked to literature via Leavis and Romanticism (eg Jones, 2017) especially by advocates of genre-based writing pedagogy (see, for example, Christie, 1981, 1990, 1993, 1995 and Christie et al, 1991).[8]

Of course, the overarching area of English that sits above all of this is language. As discussed above, Dixon sees language in terms that echo notions of language as organising experience, but also in terms of Britton's (1970; Britton et al, 1975) spectator and participant roles (see, for example, pp.27–30 of *Growth through English*). One view of literature discussed at the Seminar was as a 'joint literary-linguistic discipline' where literary 'intuitions' are given 'detach(ed)' rigour (Dixon, 1975, pp.11, 80). Dixon's focus on language becomes more elaborated in curriculum terms as *Growth through English* evolves from edition to edition. The chapter on 'Processes in language learning' remains the core discussion, but the Preface to the second edition highlights such things as: the neglect at Dartmouth of the 'language resources a pupil brings to school'; the need for more investigation of classroom dialogue, and the need for a greater focus on argument, persuasion and 'the intellectual uses of language' (Dixon, 1969/1972: xii–xiv). By the third edition with its chapter 'In the perspective of the seventies', Dixon is discussing curriculum-programmatic issues such as: the place of the participant role and the work of the Writing Research Unit at London; sequencing levels of abstraction, especially as emanating from the work of James Moffett, and the uses of language as classroom investigations, as in the *Language in Use* materials. I now turn to a more schematic discussion of the relationship between language, literature and experience in Dixon's book.

Bill Green (1988, 2018) has represented the terrain of English in this way:

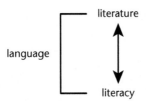

When Green used this model in 1988 to describe the history of the subject, but also to 'map the territory' of English, he conceptualised the subject in terms of the '*secondary* modelling systems' of literature and literacy *in relation to each other* and also *in relation to* the '*primary* modelling system' of language (Green 1988, p.48). Green views these elements primarily in terms of their 'network of relations'. I think this notion of the relations between primary and secondary modelling systems is particularly generative in thinking about the elements of English. One can see the ways in which Dixon's conceptualisations could find useful parallels here. There is a potentially useful network of relationships between literature, language (including relationships between spectator roles and participant roles), experience and experiences (lived experiences and textual experiences). Particularly apt might be this network of relationships:

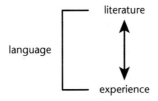

This sees Dixon as being rather more exploratory in his discussion than is usually presented in critiques of 'Growth' generally or of *Growth through English* specifically (eg Moon, 2012; Jones, 2017; Christie passim). Dixon is exploring not just the place of these elements in English, but also the relationships between them. Dixon's own hesitations around declaring the book a manifesto for subject English needs to be recognised and taken seriously, I believe. His preface to the 1969/1972 second edition, argues that 'in taking from the dialogue of the Seminar what would help me make sense of English as I know it, my aim has not been to make an end of discussion. . .but rather to propose a new starting point' (Dixon, 1969/1972: xi). This point is repeated here:

> I have never suggested that the seminar at Dartmouth represented a final view of English teaching. . . As an essay it is often skeletal. And I am glad that it is so, since this lays the book more open to the pressure of development and re-interpretation – and occasionally reinforcement – as work in teaching English progresses.
>
> *(Dixon, 1969/1972: xiv)*

This second edition of *Growth through English* ends indeed with a discussion that is worth quoting at length and considering in some detail:

> How an 'experience-based curriculum' relates to a curriculum that is subject-based is a further issue. Clearly English as defined in this report stands as a bridge between the two: our subject is experience, wherever language is needed to penetrate and bring it into a new and satisfying order. But equally our specialist knowledge of how language relates to experience and society is just beginning to take on a real cutting edge. English will be pulled it two directions, and in resolving the tension we may gain a new clarification of our work. Is a new model for education struggling to emerge, just as the point when we have spelt out for ourselves the fuller implications of a model based on personal growth? Very well. The limits of the present model *will* be reached that is certain, and thus a new model will be needed to transcend its descriptive power – and in doing so redirect our attention to life as it really is.
>
> *(Dixon, 1969/1972, p.114)*

Certainly, this contains a declaration of the centrality of experience and a recognition of 'personal growth' as constituting 'the present model'. However, the reference to ordering experience brings us back to the spectator role and the notion that ordering experience is as much the work of literature as is the students' exploring their own personal experience – a reading we should also take into the very final clause. Moreover, the present model is simply subject to history: its limits will be reached, indeed they may already have been. Most interesting is that the definition of subject 'English' is not *as* experience, nor *as* subject- (presumably at this point 'literature') -based, but rather as a 'bridge' between the two. It is here that I think reading Dixon's book as far more tentative, nuanced and exploratory than is usually presented, arrives at its key issue. In the final chapter of the book's third edition ('In the perspective of the Seventies'), Dixon conceptualises one school of thought as 'literature-centred', the other as 'experience-centred', with the latter usually dismissed by the former as 'sociology'. Though intended by its users to be dismissive, Dixon in fact takes up that disciplinary title and extends it: that school of thought which emphasises the *pupils'* construction of experience [original italics] is at the borderland with 'sociology, psychology, history etc.' Naming specific disciplines in this way is, I believe, telling. One distinction we can make in thinking about the history of English is the distinction between the school subject and the academic discipline(s) from which it derives and/or on which it draws. The ways in which, and the degree to which, school English can simply be 'read off' the academic discipline is one of the ongoing problematics of the subject. Ultimately, I believe, *Growth through English* is attempting to explore the ways in which the school subject English positions itself in terms of particular academic disciplines and how, in turn, those disciplines relate to each other in the discursive formation of the school subject English. 'Literature' and the 'sociology, psychology, history etc.' cluster do, however, need to be joined in this network by studies of language – language being always central to Dixon's formulations, but increasingly elaborated from edition to edition. As he says, 'English is the meeting point of experience, language and society' (Dixon, 1975, p.85).

Conclusion

While Muller mostly sought to play down or rationalise the differences between the Americans and the British at Dartmouth ('The British and Americans could. . . understand one another readily. . . because. . . they passed one another in mid-Atlantic. The Americans were upholding the traditional British ideal of intellectual discipline, the British were clamoring for the individual freedom that Americans have always prized in theory' [Muller, 1967, p.13]), Roger Applebee presents a very different view of the conference in terms that focus on specifically national differences:

> at Dartmouth. . . the fragile formality gave way; family differences erupted into quarrels: rhetoric became sharp; some participants became intractable. . . the essence of Dartmouth is in the differences in viewpoints towards the profession of English, differences that were best revealed in the heat of discussion and debate. In general, American participants pressed for structure, sequence and system, while British participants held out for self-discovery, spontaneity and growth. . . there was little consensus evident at the conclusion of the Seminar in August 1966.
>
> *(Applebee, 1973, p.53)*

Stephen Ball (1982, 1983, 1985) characterised the period in England before WWII as driven by a tripartite curriculum of *grammar, literature* and *pupil self-expression* (or *composition*). If Ball is correct and if there was some consensus on this structure at that time, it has certainly disappeared in England (and in Australia) since. In those contexts, models of English – personal growth, critical literacy, basic skills, cultural studies etc. – are usually presented (rightly or wrongly – see Doecke and Yandell, this volume) as engaged in Kuhnian struggles for a kind of paradigmatic dominance. This has been a clear difference from the American scene where there has been a remarkable degree of (academic) consensus around the foundational elements of the subject: *language, literature, composition* (e.g. CEEB, 1965, p.13; Muller, 1967, p.54: Kitzhaber, 1966, Abstract; Miller, 1969, pp.11–12;[9] Applebee, 1978, p.38; Parker, 1979, p.34; Kantor, 1979, p.29; Tchudi and Mitchell, 1989, p.13; Harris, 1991, p.634; Gerlach, 2000, p.314).

I do not think, however, that the two books can be said to be simply playing out national differences. They did issue out of different contexts and different histories and they eventually were to have different kinds of influence and different degrees of influence in particular contexts. They played out different aims – reporting in the one case or exploring a normative curriculum position in the other. Of course, a richer study of the two texts would consider far more the historical and geographical contexts which produced each of them (see, for example, Brass, 2016), but my focus on the three central areas of knowledge, experience and literature and their relationships meant a different kind of reading. I see *The Uses of English* as useful in clearly laying out the terms of particular debates of the time – the place of knowledge in literary study being a key one considered here. *Growth through English*, I think, is more nuanced than is often conceded and the more interesting because of that. Australia is experiencing at the moment the early days of our first national curriculum being played out and at any such moment in which fundamental issues of English curriculum are under consideration *Growth through English* always repays another reading.

Notes

1 The 6 Study Groups focused on: Drama, Language, Myth, Literature, Creativity, and Sequence and Continuity.
2 Whitehead's important *The Disappearing Dais* was published in the same year as the Dartmouth conference.
3 It was also philology specifically that literary criticism was struggling to assert itself 'against' in the US. Graff, for example, talks of the humanist critics defending 'appreciation over investigation and values over facts' (1987, p.55; see also McComiskey, 2006).
4 According to Muller, both sets of delegates did, nevertheless, see the New Critics as too schematic and analytical and potentially interfering with 'the enjoyment . . . the direct personal response of the student' (p.87).
5 Only the Sequence and Continuity study group did not produce a paper in the *Dartmouth Seminar Papers* series published by the NCTE.
6 Muller does note, however, that the Study Group 'nevertheless assumed, at least tacitly, that literature itself is a significant way of "knowing" about life' (p.91).
7 To be completely fair to Hansen, this passage occurs within an argument that recognises that focus on the 'deprived' was long overdue, that the notion of relevance was well-intentioned, and that neglecting literature was the position of 'the extreme' (p.6). Nevertheless, the implicitly class-based nature of his language here is telling.
8 Bill Green and Catherine Beavis are correct to argue that '(c)oncepts and historical-philosophical movements such as 'Progressivism' and 'Romanticism' are all too often deployed with neither theoretical rigour nor historical grounding and reference' (1996, p.1).
9 Miller said of Dartmouth: 'The trinity for the Americans was made up of the familiar trio – language, composition, literature. The first large question set for the conference had been: "What is English?". The Americans knew, if they knew anything, the answer to that question' (1969, pp.11–12).

References

Allen, D. (1980). *English teaching since 1965: How much growth?* London: Heinemann.

Applebee, R. K. (1973). 'The Transatlantic dialogue', in N. Bagnall (ed.) *New Movements in the study and teaching of English,* London: Temple Smith: 51–62.

Applebee, R. K. (1978). *Tradition and reform in the teaching of English: a history.* Urbana, Ill: NCTE.

Atherton, C. (2005). 'The Organisation of literary knowledge: the study of English in the late nineteenth century', in M. Daunton (ed.), *The Organisation of knowledge in Victorian Britain.* Oxford: Oxford University Press.

Ball, S. J. (1982) 'Competition and conflict in the teaching of English: a socio-historical analysis', *Journal of Curriculum Studies,* 14(1), 1–28.

Ball, S. J. (1983). 'A Subject of privilege: English and the school curriculum 1906–35', in M. Hammersley & A. Hargreaves (eds.) *Curriculum practice: some sociological case studies.* London and New York: The Falmer Press.

Ball, S. J. (1985). 'English for the English since 1906', in I. F. Goodson (ed.) *Social histories of the secondary curriculum: subjects for study.* London and Philadelphia: The Falmer Press.

Brass, J. (2016). 'Re-reading Dartmouth: an American perspective', *English in Australia,* 51(3), 52–57.

Britton, J. (1970). *Language and learning,* London: Penguin.

Britton, J., Burgess, T., Martin, N., McLeod, A. and Rosen, H. (1975). *The Development of writing abilities (11–18),* London and Basingstoke: Macmillan Education.

Christie, F. (1981). The 'Received Tradition' of English language study in schools: the decline of rhetoric and the corruption of grammar. Unpublished MA thesis, University of Sydney.

Christie, F. (1990). 'The Changing face of literacy', in F. Christie (ed.) *Literacy for a Changing World.* Hawthorn: ACER.

Christie, F. (1993). 'The "Received Tradition" of English teaching: the decline of rhetoric and the corruption of grammar', In B. Green (ed.), *The Insistence of the letter: literacy studies and curriculum theorizing.* Pittsburgh: University of Pittsburgh Press.

Christie, F. (1995). Defining directions for language and literacy education in contemporary Australia. Inaugural professorial lecture, University of Melbourne.

Christie, F., Devlin, B., Freebody, P., Luke, A., Martin, J.R., Threadgold, T. and Walton, C. (1991). *Teaching English literacy: a project of national significance on the preservice preparation of teachers for teaching English literacy – Volume 1.* Canberra: Department of Employment, Education and Training.

Clements, S., Dixon, J. and Stratta, L. (1963). *Reflections (Walworth English course): an English course for students aged 14–18.* London: Oxford University Press.

College Entrance Examination Board (CEEB) (1965). *Freedom and discipline in English: report of the commission in English.* New York: College Entrance Examination Board.

Dixon, J. (1969/1972, 2nd edn.). *Growth through English: a report based on the Dartmouth Seminar.* London: NATE.

Dixon, J. (1975, 3rd edn.). *Growth through English: set in the perspective of the Seventies.* London: Oxford University Press.

Gerlach, J. (2000). 'Teaching "English" in the United States', in R. Peel, A. Patterson and J. Gerlach (eds.), *Questions of English: ethics, aesthetics, rhetoric, and the formation of the subject in England, Australia and the United States.* London: Routledge Falmer: 303–322.

Graff, G. (1987). *Professing literature: an institutional history.* Chicago: University of Chicago.

Green, B. (1988). 'Literature as curriculum frame: a critical perspective', in K. Hart (ed.) *Shifting frames: English/literature/writing.* Deakin University: Centre for Studies in Literary Education: 46–71.

Green, B. (2018). *Engaging curriculum: bridging the curriculum theory and English education divide.* New York and London: Routledge.

Green, B. and Beavis, C. (1996). 'Introduction: English teaching and curriculum history', in B. Green and C. Beavis (eds.) *Teaching the English subjects: essays on curriculum history and Australian schooling.* Geelong: Deakin University Press.

Hansen, I. V. (1979). 'The case for literature study in secondary schools: some difficulties'. *The Teaching of English*, 36, May, 3–16.

Harris, J. (1991). 'After Dartmouth: growth and conflict in English', *College English*, 53(6), October: 631–646.

Hilliard, C. (2012). *English as a vocation: the* Scrutiny *movement.* Oxford: Oxford University Press.

Homer, D. B. (1973). Fifty years of purpose and precept in English teaching (1921–71): an overview with special reference to the teaching of poetry in the early secondary years. Unpublished MEd Thesis: Melbourne University.

Inglis, F. (1975). *Ideology and the imagination.* Cambridge: Cambridge University Press.

Jones, J. (2017). The ambivalent legacy of Dartmouth five decades on: What, now, should we teach the English teachers?', *English in Australia*, 52(2), 65–72.

Kantor, K. J. (1979). 'The revolution a decade later: confessions of an aging Romantic', *The English Journal*, 68(6), September, 28–31.

Kitzhaber, A. R. (1966). 'What is English?', in A. R. Kitzhaber et al, 'Working party paper No1; Response, report to the seminar, and supporting papers one through six', ERIC document number ED082201: 2–3. Available: http://files.eric.ed.gov/fulltext/ED082201.pdf. Accessed 31 January 2018.

McComiskey, B. (2006). 'Introduction', in B. McComiskey (ed.) *English studies: an introduction to the discipline(s).* Urbana, Ill: NCTE.

Medway, P., Hardcastle, J., Brewis, G. and Crook, D. (2014). *English teachers in a postwar democracy: emerging choice in London schools, 1945–1965.* New York: Palgrave Macmillan.

Miller, J. E. (1969).'What happened at Dartmouth? (A query by one who was there)'. ERIC document number 039249. Available: https://ia801300.us.archive.org/24/items/ERIC_ED039249/ERIC_ED039249.pdf. Accessed 31 January 2018.

Moffett, J. (1968). *Teaching the universe of discourse.* Boston: Houghton Mifflin.

Moon, B. (2012). 'Remembering rhetoric: recalling a tradition of explicit instruction in writing', *English in Australia*, 47(1), 37–52.

Muller, H. J. (1967). *The Uses of English: guidelines for the teaching of English from the Anglo-American conference at Dartmouth College.* New York: Holt, Rinehart, Winston.

Parker, R. P.(1979). 'From Sputnik to Dartmouth: trends in the teaching of composition' *The English Journal*, 68(6), September, 32–37.

Smith, B. (1977). 'Towards a literature-centred English', in K.D. Watson and R.D. Eagleson (eds.), *English in secondary schools: today and tomorrow.* Ashfield: English Teachers' Association of New South Wales.

Squire, J. R. (ed.) (1968a). 'Gleanings from the Dartmouth Discussions', in J. R. Squire (ed.) Response to literature: papers relating to the Anglo-American seminar on the teaching of English at Dartmouth College, New Hampshire, 1966. Champaign, IL: NCTE.

Squire, J. R. (ed.) (1968b). *Response to literature: papers relating to the Anglo-American seminar on the teaching of English at Dartmouth College, New Hampshire, 1966.* Champaign, Ill: NCTE.

Squire, J. R. and Applebee, R. K. (1968). *High school English instruction today: the National Study of High School English Programs.* New York: Appleton-Century-Crofts.

Tchudi, S. and Mitchell, D. (1989). *Explorations in the teaching of English*. New York: Harper and Row.

Walshe, R. D. (1977). 'Towards an experience-centred English', in K.D. Watson and R. D. Eagleson (eds.), *English in secondary schools: today and tomorrow*. Ashfield: English Teachers' Association of New South Wales.

Whitehead, F. (1966). *The Disappearing dais: a study of the principles and practice of English teaching*. London: Chatto and Windus.

Whitehead, F. (1976). 'The present state of English teaching: (1) Stunting the growth', *The Use of English*, 28(1), Autumn, 11–17.

Williams, R. (1958). 'Culture is ordinary', in N. McKenzie (ed.) *Conviction*, London: MacGibbon & Kee: 74–92.

3

RE-READING DARTMOUTH

An American perspective on the pasts and presents of English teaching

Jory Brass

The 1966 Anglo-American Seminar at Dartmouth stands as a landmark event in the history of English teaching. Among other things, Dartmouth popularized the 'growth model' of English (Dixon, 1967), which shaped my practice as a self-identified 'student-centered' English teacher who began his career in the 1990s. At the same time, the practice of locating Dartmouth as a progressive moment that spawned the 'New English' can overlook social and political struggles of the 1960s that not only shaped the past of English teaching, but also its present. This chapter offers an American perspective on Dartmouth based on early 1970s publications that offered contradictory accounts of the post-Dartmouth moment of English teaching. It reads with, across, and against these texts to complicate progressive readings of Dartmouth and sensitize us to historical shifts and struggles from the (post)Dartmouth-era that have influenced present struggles over the teaching of English across Anglophone countries.

Re-reading Dartmouth

Many advocates of the Personal Growth model have identified Dartmouth as a key shift in English's curriculum history, including John Dixon's (1967) germinal book, *Growth through English*. According to Dixon (1967), the British contingent at Dartmouth helped usher in the 'New English' centered on talk, drama, personal writing, and response to literature – with the Americans at Dartmouth focused on more traditional concerns about literature, disciplinary knowledge, and curriculum scope and sequence. Dixon (1967) centered the 'new' contributions of Dartmouth on the 'Anglo' side of the Anglo-American hyphen, and he cemented the British leadership of progressive English teaching with a memorable image of the American and British delegations 'passing each other in the mid-Atlantic.' As Harris (1991, p.639) later described it:

the irony of Dartmouth was that the British were reacting against almost precisely the view of English that the Americans were trying to achieve. In turn, many of the Americans at the seminar balked at the ideas of growth theory because they seemed so much like the very kind of progressive schooling that they had built their own sense of English against.

No doubt, Dixon popularized a 'progressive' narrative that represented important national differences at the Seminar, even if his admittedly partial view likely overstated both the consensus and binary oppositions that emerged in and after Dartmouth. Dixon's (1967) *Growth through English*, for instance, was clearly more progressive than the American report on Dartmouth, Herbert Muller's (1967) *The Uses of English*, a painfully boring book that I could not force myself to finish in graduate school. Still, I want to trouble the received Dartmouth narrative here – not to redeem my home country, but to complicate Dixon's assumptions of historical progress and to revisit political cross-currents that shaped Dartmouth in the 1960s and reverberate now in present struggles around the teaching of English.

Locating Dartmouth historically

One of my concerns is that locating Dartmouth as a progressive rupture in English teaching overlooks important ways that the Growth model overlaps historically with earlier progressive traditions in English teaching. For example, my historical work in the US has illustrated how many of the ideas and practices that came to typify the Growth model – the centrality of language in ordering thought and worlds, linking texts to lived experiences, and response-based literary pedagogies – were already established in English education in the early twentieth century and had important precursors in nineteenth-century Christian literary education (Brass, 2011). In another study that examined a century of research on secondary English teaching (Brass and Burns, 2011), my archival work also suggested that the post-Dartmouth progressivism that shaped my teaching was not as politically progressive as much of the field's pedagogical writing of the 1930s. My histories built upon curriculum histories from Australia, including Green and Cormack's (2008) archival work that documented important links between the 'new education' of the 1900s–1920s and the 'New English' of the 1960s and 1970s. Our studies are among several curriculum histories in English that challenge the extent to which post-Dartmouth English teaching did, in fact, constitute an important break with past practices. Importantly, then, the 'new English' of the 1960s was not particularly new, and post-Dartmouth English teaching may not be as politically progressive as its proponents often assume.

These historical continuities and differences with earlier progressive movements were not lost on some American educators of the late 1960s and early 1970s. In her review of *Growth through English* (Dixon, 1967), for example, Margaret Early (1968, p.260) argued that Dixon's writing would 'evoke a certain *nostalgia*' (my italics) among English teachers in the US who had been

reluctant 'to abandon principles of learning theories in the enthusiasm for [cur-
riculum] structure in English' and had not forgotten Progressive experiments
in democratic education, such as the 8-year Study, which had been 'lost in the
United States since the race with the Russians began.' In this nostalgic reading of Dartmouth, Americans would 'detect echoes of the thirties' in Dixon's
(1967) discussions of personal growth, affective response, language and experience that were 'good to hear, this time in a British accent' (Early, 1968,
pp.260–261). Likewise, Dixon (1967) not only 'freshened familiar ideas' from
American progressive education from the 1930s–1940s, but English teachers
would 'also recognize that these old ideas have been modified and strengthened by infusions of linguistic scholarship and modern literary criticism' (Early,
1968, p.261). From this standpoint, Dixon's (1967) Growth model was less of
a progressive step forward as an important step backwards in time – particularly
in a decade when the National Council of Teachers of English had distanced
itself from progressive education in its bids for federal grants to enlist English
teachers to 'compete with Russian rocket scientists' in a post-Sputnik world
(Early, 1968).

Early's (1968) less than subtle critiques of the NCTE draw attention to the unusual historical conditions that made Dartmouth possible. The Dartmouth seminar
was one of a series of summer seminars that the NCTE co-hosted with the Modern
Language Association (MLA) in the 1960s as part of their joint pursuit of federal
funding through the National Defense in Education Act (NDEA). Beginning in
1958, the NDEA mobilized education in the fight for national defense in response
to post-Sputnik panics about the rise of Soviet Union as a scientific, military, and
political power. The NDEA identified math, science, foreign languages, and gifted
education as central to national defense in the Cold War; however, the NCTE,
MLA, and other associations lobbied to include English and the humanities in subsequent versions of the NDEA. In a bid for NDEA funding, the NCTE marshaled
post-Sputnik crisis rhetoric in its publication of *The National interest and the teaching
of English* (NCTE, 1961). This publication challenged the rigor of subject English
and the rigor of research on English teaching to build a case for the federal government to fund a series of initiatives to provide a stronger scientific and disciplinary
basis for English teaching in primary and secondary schools. Years of lobbying
eventually led to federal funding, as well as philanthropic funding through the
Ford and Carnegie Foundations, to fund 'Project English' centers at select universities that would develop curriculum models and scientific curriculum sequences
in subject English. This funding also led to series of summer teacher institutes
and conferences where primary and secondary school teachers would learn from
university English faculty (Hook, 1979). Without these ideological and material
conditions, the NCTE, MLA, and Carnegie foundation would not have co-hosted
the Dartmouth Seminar in 1966.

Importantly, this Cold War political settlement was a significant departure
from the networks of relations that had shaped US English teaching for more than
50 years. At its emergence in 1911, for example, the NCTE comprised a coalition of

secondary teachers, education faculty, and university English faculty who opposed the nineteenth-century model of elite universities determining secondary school curricula through uniform reading lists and university entrance examinations (Applebee, 1974). In a near reversal, the American representatives at Dartmouth excluded all but a few 'educationists' – a derisive term for classroom teachers and teacher education faculty – and was instead dominated by university English professors whom were primarily culled from traditional, élite universities. In addition, the American 'consultants' at Dartmouth were primarily cognitive psychologists and Project English staff funded by the NDEA and the Carnegie foundation to develop scientific curriculum sequences and model curricula for secondary schools based on traditional 'academic' knowledge of English. For the Americans, then, the Dartmouth seminar constituted a professional hierarchy in which faculty from the humanities and sciences would regulate English education through externally defined curriculum sequences, cognitive science, and professional partnerships with the federal government and corporate philanthropy. Likewise, Dartmouth also followed from NCTE's rise as a policy entrepreneur – where the organization sought to increase its status and funding by distancing itself from 'progressive education' and leveraging crisis narratives that questioned the professional qualifications of classroom teachers and the university faculty who worked most closely with primary and secondary schools (Mason, 2011; Applebee, 1974).

In many ways then, Dartmouth's charge to answer the question 'What is English?' was not narrowly pedagogical – it was about the politics of knowledge and the governance of English education. The Dartmouth seminar replayed longstanding struggles over the American curriculum, including struggles to articulate the relationships between universities and secondary schools, debates regarding the affordances and limitations of educational psychology, and the competing aims of conservative, liberal/progressive, and critical/radical schooling (Kliebard, 1995). At the same time, Sputnik-era reforms also turned to scientists and to university faculty in traditional academic disciplines to restore rigor and credibility to the education professions had supposedly lost their way across progressive education reforms (Applebee, 1974).

These political and professional shifts often played out in the multiple and sometimes contradictory forms of 'professionalism' that came out of Dartmouth. Particularly on the American side, Dartmouth set up a series of hierarchical distinctions between the sciences and humanities, English faculty and education faculty, and university faculty and primary/secondary teachers. NCTE's federal and philanthropic grants had positioned cognitive psychologists and literary faculty outside of education as the field's professionals and disciplinary experts; in this professional hierarchy, Project English centers and cognitive psychologists developed the curriculum models that teachers should implement and the scientific sequences they should follow. In contrast, US educator James Moffett imagined professional English teachers as teacher-scholars who developed student-centered curricula with their students and developed as professionals through practitioner inquiry and reflecting on their experience. Dixon (1967) may have positioned the Growth model as a professional 'consensus,' but 'no English teachers [would] miss the dissent lurking in between the lines' (Early, 1968, p.261) – or miss the significance of their tokenistic representation among the American delegation at Dartmouth.

Not surprisingly then, the Dartmouth seminar lent itself to a spectrum of reactions that went beyond 'consensus' or competing 'American' and 'British' camps. Some NCTE leaders welcomed federal funding and the turn to university literature professors to restore academic rigor to a school subject that had been diluted and distorted by progressive education (e.g. Hook, 1979). At the same time, many teachers and teacher education faculty excluded from Dartmouth worried that the British educators and American English professors might not be aware of American experiments in democratic education, such as the 8-year study in the 1930s, and they suspected that cognitive psychologists were developing an English curriculum that might be scientific, 'but at the expense of feeling and common sense' (Early, 1968, p.260). Within 5 years, Dartmouth participants themselves took contrasting positions on Dartmouth as they alternately described the seminar as a positive site of international dialogue, a relic of a past era, a retreat from crucial issues, a mistake whose findings should be ignored, a waste of Carnegie money, a return to the 1930s and 1940s (that Americans either celebrated or disdained), and a missed opportunity to consider minority community voices and to wrestle with sociological, racial, and sociopolitical aspects of English teaching (Donlan, 1974).

The politics of post-Dartmouth progressivism

Among other things, then, Dartmouth clearly represented an important moment in the historical struggle over progressive English teaching in the US. On one hand, the British model popularized at Dartmouth encouraged some educators in the US to reassert progressive concerns from earlier in their careers (Applebee, 1974). By the early 1970s, for example, Americans gave the Dartmouth seminar at least some credit for the resurrection of Louise Rosenblatt's (1938) *Literature as Exploration*, alternative models of writing development and student-centered English teaching (e.g. Moffett, 1968a, 1968b; Emig, 1971; Britton et al, 1975), and the formation of the National Writing Project (Gray, 2000), which helped popularize notions of the teacher-writer, writing as process, workshop pedagogies, and teacher inquiry as professional development (e.g. Whitney & Friedrich, 2013).

On the other hand, NCTE's 1970s histories of English teaching positioned post-Dartmouth progressivism as an historical correction to the 'excesses' and 'distortions' of progressive reforms from the late 1920s–1940s (Applebee, 1974; Hook, 1979). For Applebee (1974), the progressivism of the 1970s offered a more 'authentic' synthesis of 'tradition' and 'reform' in the teaching of English than the previous progressive movement. In contrast to 1930s progressives and social reconstructionists, for example, the American academics and British educators who worked 'to re-establish. . . some of the better parts of the progressive vision' at Dartmouth were also 'the men who were deeply involved in developing the academic model' (p.232). Thus, Dartmouth afforded an 'academic' (and masculine) correction to progressive English teaching that offered secondary teachers in the U.S. 'a more moderate and subject-oriented position. . . that reestablished meaningful limits to the universe of English instruction' (p.131). In Applebee's (1974) history, this post-Dartmouth progressivism improved upon its historical predecessors because it avoided both the 'radical rhetoric. . . that helped to plunge progressives as well as the 'social reconstructionists' into disfavor' in the 1930s (p.116) and the 'excesses' of the 'life adjustment' movement of the 1940s that had lost track of traditional disciplines of language and literary study (p.177).

Similarly, Hook's (1979) accounts of Project English and the NCTE/MLA summer seminars of the late-1950s and 1960s (including Dartmouth) credited them with forging a 'middle road' between traditional 'academic Puritanism' and the 'abuses' of progressive reforms that followed from the previous generation's attempts to make English more 'relevant' to youth (p.247). In this view, the British Growth model offered a viable pedagogical alternative to rote learning and traditional teaching, yet it also reasserted English's traditional subject matter – the 'tri-pod' of literature, language, and composition that progressive education had unhinged as it aligned subject English with concerns about democratic citizenship, social and economic equality, personal autonomy, community, and communication across contexts (Hook, 1979).

Importantly then, the post-Dartmouth progressivism that the NCTE and National Writing Project re-assembled in the 1970s was not as politically progressive as the progressive education movement of the first half of the twentieth century. The American growth-oriented writing published in the decade after Dartmouth united the individualistic and social goals of English education (McKenzie, 2017); in the 1970s, however, these social goals had largely moved away from sociopolitical concerns that were more overt in 1930s progressivism, including progressives' explicit focus on democratic citizenship, along with frequent critiques of capitalism and the ways in which schools might help to reconstruct a more socially and economically just society (Applebee, 1974).

Along these lines, it is also important to note that Dixon's (1967) 'British Model' was just one of two progressive counter-movements discussed at Dartmouth (Applebee, 1974). Like the British Growth model, this second strand of progressive English teaching began with the progressive tenet that the starting point in English teaching was student interest and involvement; however, it also challenged inequities in the resources and curricular materials in suburban and urban schools, the racial dynamics of tracking or streaming, segregation, the preponderance of texts with white authors and characters in the English curriculum, and negative myths about the language and cultures of poor and 'disadvantaged' youth, including the damaging view that black children and poor children needed more direct and explicit teaching, behavior management, and skills-based instruction (Applebee, 1974). Walter Loban and Richard Corbin presented these ideas at Dartmouth on behalf of their federally funded research on disadvantaged schools (Loban) and NCTE's Task Force on Teaching English to the Disadvantaged (Corbin) (Applebee, 1974).

In the decade after Dartmouth, American writers offered alternative interpretations of Dartmouth beyond Applebee's (1974) and Hooks' (1979) embrace of
its more 'modest' progressivism. Already in 1971, some Dartmouth participants
acknowledged that the seminar was in some respects an insular event that was
distanced from minority community voices and insufficiently aware of growing sociopolitical pressures on schools (Donlan, 1974); thus, they argued that
subsequent professional dialogues needed to reflect a stronger 'socio-political
concern for the teacher and the student, including how literature, language,
and writing can be made relevant to racial and ethnic minorities' who rightfully
deserved more attention in the United States and United Kingdom (Donlan,
1974, p.174). A revised edition of *Growth through English* (Dixon, 1975) similarly conceded that Dartmouth critics had 'rightfully criticized the deliberations
for failing to relate the teaching of English to the sociopolitical contexts in
which young people live today' (Squire and Britton, 1975, p.xi.). In particular,
white academics' 'idyllic and isolated discussions in the White Mountains of
New Hampshire' had been physically and ideologically insulated from escalat-
ing struggles over desegregation, community control of education, the racial
composition of the teaching force, mounting unemployment, cultural pluralism, and the meritocracy myth that 'schooling represented the surest way to
scale the social and economic ladder' (p.xi).

By the 1980s, Americans would seemingly blend elements of both progressive
models in a national meeting dubbed 'Dartmouth II' – the 1987 English Coalition
Conference (Lloyd-Jones & Lunsford, 1989). Twenty years after Dartmouth, the
English Coalition revisited the question 'What is English?' in a summer seminar that sought to redress concerns about the 1966 seminar. First, the 'English
Coalition' comprised sixty self-identified 'teachers' from the US who represented
an equal mix of primary, secondary, and college/university institutions – an
attempt to rectify how the first Dartmouth had marginalized teachers and education faculty. Second, the Coalition adopted a pedagogical vision similar to Dixon's
(1967) Growth model, but it was couched in more explicitly 'sociopolitical' terms,
such as democracy, the social, the community, and teacher autonomy. The more
social view of 'English' named at Dartmouth II included (1) a broader range of
activities beyond the literature-language-composition 'Tripod' of Dartmouth;
(2) the integration of school-based language study with language use of the home,
peer group, and community – especially for linguistic minority students; (3) understandings of how language works in society; and (4) critiques of prescriptive text
lists, prescribed curriculum, and reductive ideas of teaching and learning brought
about by standardized assessments and E.D. Hirsch's 'cultural literacy' movement
(Lloyd-Jones & Lunsford, 1989). In doing so, the English Coalition authored a
progressive vision of English teaching that both echoed and partially broke from
Dixon's (1967) Growth model. At the same time, the English Coalition did not
break new ground (Harris, 1991), and its politics were still moderate in comparison
to 'critical' and 'poststructural' alternatives to the Growth model that emerged in
Australia in the 1980s (e.g. Boomer, 1989; Mellor & Patterson, 2004).

Conclusion: English's pasts and presents

My admittedly brief and partial examinations of 1960s and 1970s publications suggests that the simple view of Dartmouth as a progressive break in the history of English teaching glosses over important struggles and multiple temporalities in English's curriculum history. The Growth model certainly provided compelling critiques of English's traditional 'cultural heritage' and 'skills' models, and Dixon (1967) clearly narrated provocative national differences that revealed a surprising conservatism among American educators of the 1960s – a conservatism explained in part by the unusual coalitions and Cold War panics that made Dartmouth possible. At the same time, American writing from the time identified historical echoes of the 1930s in Dixon (1967), which meant that the British Growth model could also be understood as (1) an important step backwards in time, (2) a model that freshened up old ideas through modern literary criticism and linguistics, (3) a politically 'moderate' and 'middle road position' for English teachers, and (4) an exclusion of more radical progressive projects predicated on social, economic, and racial equality. For me, these competing standpoints provoke important questions about the political project of Dartmouth, the Growth model, and 'progressive' English teaching more generally.

At the same time, readings of Dartmouth that focus on the Growth model/New English also overlook other historical shifts that resonate with present struggles around the teaching of English. For example, the political rationales and marriages that spawned Dartmouth in the 1960s also included:

- historically unprecedented federal interventions into state-controlled (federalist) education systems, such as the United States and Australia;
- the rise of cognitive psychologists as curriculum designers and arbiters of 'scientific' teaching practices;
- the rise of NCTE as a policy entrepreneur (Mason, 2011);
- Sputnik-era alliances of government, philanthropy, business, and science that laid groundwork for the Anglo-American model of educational 'accountability' that emerged in the 1970s under President Richard Nixon in the US and then-Secretary of Education Margaret Thatcher in England.

In this sense, the very traditional and politically conservative constructions of English that Americans offered at Dartmouth (e.g. Muller, 1967) in some respects foreshadowed some of the reform movements that would soon circulate across Anglophone countries. Those post-Sputnik relationships are not identical to today's educational policy networks and neoliberal panics about global economic competition (e.g. Rizvi & Lingard, 2010). Over the last several decades, similar networks of relations have given rise to a global reforms centered on national curriculum and national testing; standards and accountability; cognitive models of 'evidence-based' education and 'data-driven' management that re-inscribe 1960s frameworks of research evidence in education (e.g. Campbell & Stanley, 1963); psychometric constructions of 'teacher quality' and 'teacher effectiveness' that echo the late-1960s and 1970s movement to curriculum and teaching on student performance 'outcomes' and 'accountability' measures that troubled English educators in the immediate aftermath of Dartmouth (e.g. Moffett, 1972; Applebee, 1974; Squire & Britton, 1975). Key element of the education reforms that have targeted English teaching across the Anglophone world now resemble the 1960s cognitive, academic, and 'industrial' models of English teaching that Dixon (1967) critiqued and helped to displace at Dartmouth (Applebee, 1974).

In conclusion, the Dartmouth seminar resists any singular history, consensus reading, or simple narrative of progress/decline. However, English teachers and scholars can begin to unearth some of the political struggles, memories, disqualified knowledges, uneven developments, and relations of continuity and change that have not only constituted education's pasts, but also its presents and possible futures (Doecke, Turvey, & Yandell, 2016; Green, 2004). I hope that I have excavated some of these (post-)Dartmouth struggles in provocative ways that might help us to recognize the historicity of our present and the ways in which we have been positioned among the competing discourses that have shaped English teaching, for better or worse, over the last 50 years.

References

Applebee, A. N. (1974). *Tradition and reform in the teaching of English: a history*. Urbana, IL: NCTE.

Boomer, G. (1989). 'Literacy: the epic challenge beyond progressivism'. *English in Australia*, 89, 4–17.

Brass, J. (2011). 'Historicizing English pedagogy: the extension and transformation of "The Cure of Souls"'. *Pedagogy, Culture, & Society*, 19(1), 93–112.

Brass, J. (2015). 'Standards-based governance of English teaching, past, present, and future?'. *English Teaching: Practice & Critique*, 14(3), 241–259.

Brass, J., & Burns, L. D. (2011). 'Research in secondary English, 1912–2011: historical continuities and discontinuities in the NCTE imprint'. *Research in the Teaching of English*, 46(2), 171–186.

Britton, J., Burgess, A., Martin, N., McLeod A., & Rosen, H. (1975). *The Development of writing abilities, 11–18*. London: Macmillan Education for the Schools Council.

Campbell, D., & Stanley, J. (1963). *Experimental and quasi-experimental designs for research*. Chicago, IL: Rand-McNally.

Dixon, J. (1967). *Growth through English: a record based on the Dartmouth Seminar 1966*. Reading, England: NATE.

Dixon, J. (1975). *Growth through English: set in the perspective of the Seventies*. Yorkshire: Oxford University Press and NATE.

Doecke, B., Turvey, A., & Yandell, J. (2016). 'Memory/history'. *Changing English*, 23(2), 95–97.

Donlan, D. (1974). 'Backward glance at Dartmouth'. *English Education*, 5(3), 189–194.

Early, M. (1968). 'Review: *Growth through English*'. *English Journal*, 57(2), 259–261.

Emig, J. (1971). *The composing processes of twelfth graders*. Urbana: National Council of Teachers of English.

Gray, J. (2000). *Teachers at the center: a memoir of the early years of the National Writing Project*. Berkeley, CA: National Writing Project.

Green, B. (2004). '(Un)changing English – past, present, future', in B. Doecke, D. Homer, H. Nixon (eds.), *English teachers at work: narratives, counter-narratives, and arguments*: AATE/Interface & Wakefield Press.

Green, B., & Cormack, P. (2008). 'Curriculum history, 'English' and the New Education; or, installing the empire of English?'. *Pedagogy, Culture, & Society*, 16(3), 25–267.

Harris, J. (1991). 'After Dartmouth: growth and conflict in English'. *College English*, 53(6), 631–646.

Hook, J. N. (1979). *A long way together: a personal view of NCTE's first sixty-seven Years*. Urbana, IL: NCTE.

Kliebard, H. (1995). *The struggle for the American curriculum: 1893–1958*. New York: Routledge.

Lloyd-Jones, R., & Lunsford, A. A. (1989). *The English coalition conference: democracy through language*. Urbana, IL: NCTE.

Mason, C. (2011). 'The National Council of Teachers of English and federal education policy, 1958–1966'. *Dissertations*. Paper 157. http://ecommons.luc.edu/luc_diss/157.

McKenzie, C. (2017). 'Meeting the great challenge: what growth-oriented writing of the 1960s and 1970s can teach us about uniting the individualistic and social aims of English education'. *Changing English*, 24(1), 91–102.

Mellor, B., & Patterson, A. (2004). 'Poststructuralism in English classrooms: critical literacy and after'. *International Journal of Qualitative Studies in Education*, 17(1), 85–102.

Moffett, J. (1968a). *Teaching the universe of discourse*. Boston: Houghton-Mifflin.

Moffett, J. (1968b). *A student-centered language arts curriculum, grades K-13: a handbook for teachers*. Boston: Houghton Mifflin.

Moffett, J. (1972). 'Who counts?'. *English Journal*, 61(4), 571–574.

Muller, H. J. (1967). *The uses of English*. New York: Holt, Rinehart and Winston.

NCTE (1961). *The National interest and the teaching of English: a report on the status of the profession*. Champaign, IL: National Council of Teachers of English.

Rizvi, F., & Lingard, B. (2010). *Globalizing education policy*. London and New York: Routledge.

Rosenblatt, L. (1938). *Literature as exploration*. New York: Appleton-Century.

Squire, J., & Britton, J. (1975). Foreword, in J. Dixon (ed.), *Growth through English: set in the perspective of the Seventies*. Oxford: Oxford University Press.

Whitney, A. E. & Friedrich, L. (2013). 'Orientations: the legacy of the National Writing Project for the teaching of writing'. *Teachers College Record* 115, 7, 1–37.

4

THE IMPACT OF THE BLUE BOOKS PRIOR TO DARTMOUTH

Lorna Smith

> *The appropriate visible result of teaching poetry is the power and desire of the child to write poetry; if our children write verse with enjoyment, as they can and will if they are given the chance, inspectors should cease from troubling and leave us alone to achieve less assessable but more important results.*
>
> (Greening Lamborn, 1919, p.29)

One can sense this writer's frustration – the parallels with teachers' thoughts on Ofsted, the current inspection system in England, hardly need emphasising. The teacher wishes to be left alone to teach poetry, to inspire his students, his professional choices and actions respected; as Summerfield restates 50 years later, post Dartmouth, poetry in the classroom is not about cultivating poets, but forming 'more articulate, more effectively human people' (1967, p.40).

Greening Lamborn was a member of The English Association (EA), a group of teachers and scholars including FC Boas and AC Bradley established in 1906 (inspired by the Head of English at Dundee High School in Scotland) to support the development of English studies. The quotation above is taken from Greening Lamborn's essay, 'Poetry and the Child', which featured in one of the near-100 pamphlets published between 1907 and 1937 resulting from regular EA conferences. The first 15 years were particularly prolific, with around fifty pamphlets appearing on topics ranging from literary topics (e.g. *Milton and poetry* (Elton, 1908); *A Discourse on modern sibyls* (Ritchie, 1913)) to language (e.g. *What still remains to be done for the Scottish Dialects* (Grant, 1909)) and assessment (e.g. *English papers in examinations for pupils of school age in England and Wales* (Anon, 1917)) (The English Association, 1907–17). All were priced at 1 shilling and were easily available on application to the Secretary[1].

The rise of English as a curriculum subject

This intense rate of publication reflects the fact that the subject of English was becoming established in the curriculum in England. It was recognised by further education institutions: Oxford had introduced a School of English in 1893, with Cambridge following suit in 1917 (Medway et al, 2014). There was an energy and optimism, but also the feeling of a need to get things right – as English was still a new subject, there was no history of pedagogy underpinning it. Yet the developing English curriculum was clearly influenced by the work of Matthew Arnold, the famous Victorian poet and an inspector of government schools, who drew on both sides of his professional life to emphasise the necessity of all children in England (particularly the working class) being educated in English: hence, he suggests, they would have access to the 'wisdom and beauty' of English poetry and other literature and learn to question things; once inspired, they would continue to live lives seeking ever more 'wisdom and beauty' and continue after intellectual pursuits (1869, p.1).

However, it is interesting to note that the inspectors of whom Greening Lamborn is so scathing represent the body that was simultaneously actively promoting creative, child-centred practice, also in the Arnoldian tradition: The Board of Education (BoE). The BoE published a series entitled *Suggestions for the consideration of teachers and others concerned in the work of Public Elementary schools.* Bound in blue card (and, later, firmer blue hardback covers), the first was launched in 1905, the year *before* the English Association was established. There is no suggestion that the EA was inspired by these publications (hereafter 'the Blue Books'), but the coincidence of their respective foundings indicates a lively interest in education in general and English education in particular at the dawn of the twentieth century. A dominant question shared by the EA and the Blue Books was not only *what* should be taught in the subject of English, but *how?*

The EA existed primarily to support the teaching of English in grammar and independent schools, serving the elite middle class from literate homes. The Blue Books were aimed at teachers in Public Elementary schools, which served three quarters of the population – the working class. They were, according to George Sampson, the most important type of school in the country (1922). New or revised editions of the Blue Books appeared in 1912, 1923, 1925, 1927, 1935 and 1959, together with one volume, *Some suggestions for the teaching of English in secondary schools in England* (1924), devoted entirely to the one subject. The 1905 edition is a pamphlet of approximately 130 pages; the 1937 is a thick book of almost 600 pages set in a dense font. The final edition (1959) focuses on the primary age-groups only, while the others deal with pupils throughout their compulsory schooling. Although each edition is clearly a development of its predecessor(s), there is remarkable consensus in their approach and theme.

It is worth stressing that Public Elementaries educated students up to 14 years old who were not destined for grammar school or university. The schools tended to be staffed by generalists who had attended a College of Education but did not themselves have a degree. It has been suggested (Medway et al, 2014) that one might assume that children in grammar schools of the time were more able and generally better motivated, so it was less necessary for grammar school teachers to find innovative ways to teach; those teaching in a maintained school needed to find the means to inspire their students. Thus, the Blue Books emphasise a teacher's professional role, reinforcing their sense of self-worth in a hierarchical system where grammar schools were seen as superior. A message that appears in a memorandum prefacing the very first edition and reinforced in each subsequent edition (often in the same words) is that the books – as the titles themselves make plain – contain *suggestions* only: as professionals, teachers are free to practise in any way that they see fit. The purpose of the Blue Books is not to lay down 'any rigid or unthinking uniformity of method' (BoE, 1924, p.3), but to offer ideas and stimulus. The importance of teachers responding thoughtfully to the challenges of the classroom and to experiment with new approaches is stressed (BoE, 1905; 1937). Teachers are recognised as reflective and creative practitioners: the entire series is based on premise that the productivity of the learner is based on the creativity of the teacher.

The themes of the Blue Books

While a discussion on what constitutes an appropriate school curriculum develops through the Blue Books series – from the view that the curriculum is a combination of discrete subjects (BoE, 1905; 1912) to that that it is a 'unity' of topics in which the 'Three Rs' are 'best regarded as forms of skill, as means to further ends' (BoE, 1937, p.157) – English is consistently defined as the most important subject in the curriculum:

> Language is the most perfect and accurate instrument mankind has for the expression of thoughts and ideas, and the measure of our power to understand and use language is the measure of our power to receive instruction on any branch of knowledge. For this reason, if no other, the teaching of the mother tongue is the most important part of school instruction.
>
> *(BoE, 1905, p.21)*

This idea is echoed by Newbolt in his post-World War I report into England's education system. Using a biblical metaphor that would have undoubtedly resonated with the original audience, Newbolt describes the subject of English as the keystone rejected by the builders because 'the arch is too faulty to admit it' (1921, p.5): his committee saw its task was to rebuild the arch of education with the keystone of English in its central place and, as a result (and maximising the impact of the image) 'bridge social chasms which divide us' (p.6). Foreshadowing another significant English policy document, each chapter on English in the Blue Books deals with Speaking and Listening, Reading and Writing in that order – the sequence adopted by Cox when he drew up the English orders for the original National Curriculum for England and Wales over 80 years after the first Blue Book appeared (Cox, 1989) – although not necessarily under these headings.

Speaking and Listening is stated to be the most important aspect of English, good teaching providing 'not only. . . accurate *expression* for thought, but also [enrichment of] the child's vocabulary by giving him larger powers of expression and therewith a wider range of available thought' (BoE, 1912, p.21, emphasis original). New experiences in a child's life are presented as vocabulary-enriching opportunities (BoE, 1937); speech should be 'an effective instrument of understanding and thought, and hence, of communication' (BoE, 1959, p.135). The importance of the child's home language is emphasised and it is made clear that dialect should not be seen as less worthy than, but simply different to, Standard English (BoE, 1923; 1959). One version exhorts teachers to use the child's own dialect 'freely and boldly' (BoE, 1937, p.378) and recommends that a teacher should:

> seek to encourage [children's] power of vigorous and racy expression. He will realise that even slang has its place, and will try and get them to understand what that place is. In doing so, he will have frequent occasion to remind himself that language is the creation of the many and not of the few.
> *(BoE, 1937, p.391)*

Such a liberal, democratic stance is later shared by Summerfield, when he discusses the importance of 'conversation' (1968, p.23) in the English classroom.

The Blue Books' suggestions for reading encourage teachers to promote good quality literature without being too prescriptive about what constitutes 'good': a variety of canonical writers are referred to, with the implication – following Arnold and Newbolt – that exposing children to beauty will nourish them in their lives: the emphasis throughout is on teachers encouraging reading for pleasure, instilling a love of literature in a new generation and broadening their perspectives (BoE, 1912; 1927; 1937; 1959). Literature is a civilising force that develops not only children's intellectual but also emotional understanding (BoE, 1935); to 'feed' children books is also to stimulate their writing (BoE, 1959, p.164) – creativity spawning creativity. The importance of having schools furnished with ample libraries so that children can choose their own reading matter from a generous range is reiterated (BoE, 1905; 1912; 1923; 1959) and there is encouragement to include 'real' books for whole-class work, not simply those written expressly for children (the final edition citing Dr Johnson's remark that 'Babies do not want to hear about babies; they like to be told of giants and castles. . . which can stretch and stimulate their little minds' (qtd in BoE, 1959, p.168)). Literature that sparks the imagination is therefore seen as important. Several editions suggest specific texts, including *The water babies, Robinson Crusoe* and *Tom Brown's school days*. There is the warning that to try to teach Shakespeare at the Elementary stage is 'to court failure' (BoE, 1923, p.35) and that teaching Shakespeare for the sake of it is folly: teachers should be allowed to judge when (and even if) to introduce him (BoE, 1927).

In terms of writing, the Blue Books recommend that the child should have 'power to describe in his own words his own experiences, the sights and sounds, the thoughts and feelings of everyday life' (BoE, 1923, p.39), and this only when they are able to express themselves orally: 'Good written English is only more careful spoken English' (BoE, 1912, p.26); 'every oral lesson is a lesson in composition' (BoE, 1924, p.25). The authors of the 1923 edition refer to an unsourced claim by Robert Louis Stevenson that his habit of writing descriptions of everyday life was the best preparation for his own narrative writing. Writing should be 'spontaneous' (1959, p.162). It is further suggested that 'there is a point beyond which the teacher cannot pass' to ensure that the child's pleasure at '"self-expression" in language' (BoE, 1924, p.26) is not compromised and that they gain confidence; a later edition refers to the '*art* of expression' (BoE, 1937, p.352, my emphasis). The later editions contain lists of possible classroom activities, including the active modelling of writing by the teacher (BoE, 1924; 1927), even suggesting topics for writing such as describing the same scene in winter and summer. In contrast, traditional Latinate grammar lessons are not favoured: they are seen as 'valueless' as they 'tend to obscure rather than reveal thought' (BoE, 1912, p.30), while teachers should not have over-high expectations of handwriting style as that 'clogs. . . thought' (BoE, 1923, p.31).

Encouraging children to write poetry is also seen as something to be encouraged:

> Good teaching of poetry cannot fail to stimulate the creative impulse, and in literature, as in the other arts, creative work, even though of no particular merit in itself, is of great help in developing the power of critical appreciation.
>
> *(BoE, 1927, p.92)*

Clearly the authors of the Blue Books do not expect that the verse that the children write could be held up as 'poetry' in the formal sense of the term, although there is the slightly patronising point made that children's work might 'indicate real poetic feeling' (92), an idea that recurs in subsequent volumes (BoE, 1937; 1959). However, it is significant that such activities are promoted – not as an end in themselves, but because engaging in them will help pupils develop a 'sensitiveness to the poetic values' (BoE, 1927, p.92); creativity, then, is understood to be a *process* and is not reified in writing. Beyond this allusion, the term 'creative writing' is not used once across the series. However, it *is* stated that children should be allowed to write 'independently and freely' (BoE, 1923, p.31), with the topic 'factual or. . . imaginative according to a child's own gifts and interests' (BoE 195, p.162) and that 'in the hands of a good teacher, composition is an admirable means of exercising a child's imagination'; children should be able to 'invent stories. . . or to write an imaginary conversation' (BoE, 1923, p.40). The following edition builds on this theme:

> It is most desirable to exercise and quicken the genuine imaginative power in children during the period when it is naturally vigorous and fresh and while the common things of life still possess for them a romantic significance.
>
> *(BoE 1927, p.108)*

This statement is accompanied by a warning that imagination is not a synonym for inventiveness and that 'unrestrained play of the fancy and the love of make-believe' (108) hold little value: imagination for imagination's sake is not encouraged. Perhaps clarification is to be found in the subsequent edition:

> The chief criterion by which the pupils' compositions will be judged will be their truthfulness in the widest sense – the truthfulness with which they record their experiences and impressions; the accuracy with which they describe things or scenes; and the honesty that they show in stating, when called upon to do so, what they really think or feel, and not what they imagine they are called upon to think or feel.
>
> *(BoE, 1937, p.396)*

The writing should be genuine, real, un-artificial. The teacher's role is as both discussant and audience (BoE, 1959).

There are strong themes connecting the Blue Books. Even though a later edition observes that there had been 'a shift in emphasis in teaching from the subject to the child' (1937, p.7), they appear child-centred throughout; they foreground the importance of speaking and listening; they promote the exploration of language 'Language is a skill, an art, a feeling, and a doing'. . . 'In language, the selected experience of mankind is concentrated for our delight and instruction' (BoE 1937, p.350); they hold that the purpose of learning to read is to love and learn from literature; grammar is presented as subservient to the writing, grammar teaching arising naturally from writing being undertaken (BoE, 1927; 1937; 1959). They promote a broadminded, liberal approach – they welcome the use of new technologies such as the wireless and, later, television. The Conclusion to the English section of the 1937 edition is worth quoting in full:

> It is evident that the task of the English teacher is no light one. It requires an interest in children, an interest in words, and in interest in the larger world. Specialised knowledge is of less importance than such interests as these, for they can easily flower into the relevant kind of knowledge, whereas knowledge without these interests can only succeed in imprisoning the child's vital and curious mind within a mesh of facts. With such interests and aims the English teacher in the Senior School should succeed in the essentials of his task: the training of a young citizen who can speak clearly and sensibly, who can write with order and expressiveness, who can find what he wants in books, who is alive to the fullness of words, and who confronts his environment with enjoyment, with self-reliance, and with an openness to new ideas and new experiences.
>
> *(BoE, 1937, p.400)*

It is remarkable how, in many aspects, these principles pre-figure those emanating from Dartmouth.

Yet we might question the scope and reach of the Blue Book series. Although the Prefatory Note to the 1927 edition indicates that the publication had become so standard that it should be part of the 'necessary equipment' of every teacher (1927, p. 4), it seems that the messages were not generally being heeded during the publication of the series – there is little evidence their advice was acted on. Practice in the 1940s–60s was seen as 'sterile' (Medway et al, 2014, p.10); an HMI report from 1951 found 'English in both grammar and modern schools to be competent but dull' (38). One interviewee for a popular social history website describes school in the 1950s as a place where behaviour mattered more than learning; another recounts getting the slipper if he got more than three spellings wrong (Anon, BBC, 2007). John Dixon, in *Growth through English* (1967), one of the first publications post- Dartmouth, discusses the three main approaches to English teaching in England in the 1960s:

1) basic literacy teaching characterised by decontextualised language exercises;
2) the study of culturally significant literature;
3) a personal growth model, the view that creative approaches building on a student's *own* life and experiences strengthens what is innate in that individual.

The implication is that the third way was a rarity – further evidence that what was advocated in the Blue Books was not happening.

English teaching in the 1950s and 1960s

The view that English teaching was often pedestrian is supported in *Children and their primary schools*, more commonly known as the Plowden Report (1967) (hereafter the Report), commissioned by the UK Government to advise on primary education. The section on English is introduced with the comment that 'the past is still with us. . . in some schools' (1967, p.201), describing the privileging of a grammar-based approach to writing. Plowden complains that independent writing might take place only fortnightly, and then on 'prescribed topics only too frequently repeated year by year' (1967, p.218); she bemoans the teaching of poetry frequently observed, where 'at best children made individual anthologies and memorised some of the poems they chose to copy out: at worst the whole class copied a poem a week from the blackboard and poetry became little more than a writing lesson' (1967, p.216).

The Report advocates child-centred creative practice, presented as 'revolutionary' (Plowden, 1967, p.210). It is actually very much what had been at the heart of the Blue Books for over 50 years. The fact that Plowden reiterates so many of the key ideas found in the Blue Books strengthens the view that the *Suggestions* had not been widely taken up previously. For instance, Plowden restates the point emphatically made almost a decade earlier (BoE, 1959) that children learn more of language in the years before they start school than they will ever learn in the span of 4 or 5 years again. Like the Blue Books, the

Report stresses the need for rich classroom talk, states how important it is that children feel confident in speaking, and recommends that teachers should be relaxed about 'correctness' and 'accent': 'Usage is always changing and teachers must not burden their pupils with the observance of outworn conventions. Correctness should be sacrificed rather than fluency, vigour or clarity of meaning' (1967, p.211). Like the Blue Books, the Report discusses how a wide range of books should be readily available; not only that, but the books should be of good quality, not too juvenile, and that children should make their own decisions regarding the choice of reading matter so that they can learn to distinguish the 'gold from the dross' (1967, p.215). The Report even borrows the nutrition imagery of the Blue Books: children are presented as 'literary cormorants, *swallowing* all that comes within their reach' (1967, p.218). Reading will often awake new interests as well as *nourishing* existing ones' (1967, p.215) and children need '*nourishing*. . . with great poetry' (1967, p.217, my emphases). That diet should be administered by enthusiasts – 'a teacher can only share with children what he understands and likes' (1967, p.217). As in the Blue Books, where they are said to 'blunt' children's sensitivity to language (BoE, 1937, p.163), text books are to be deprecated – '[children] learn to write by writing and not by exercises in filling in missing words' (1967, p.222).

Yet perhaps it was the case that the Blue Books *did* have reach, albeit with a slow burn. While the interviewees cited above recall their 1950s schooling in rural Somerset and Hampshire respectively, in London the seeds of a movement towards child-centred English teaching had been planted. The grass-roots London Association for the Teaching of English (LATE) was established in 1947 (Gibbons, 2017), a coming together of teachers of English in the maintained sector. The energy they demonstrate post-World War II is reminiscent of the post-World War I optimism of Newbolt (1921). LATE teachers daringly taught modern as well as nineteenth-century novels, and began to publish student-friendly text books to replace the stuffy grammar books (Medway et al, 2014). LATE was instrumental in the foundation of the National Association for the Teaching of English (NATE) in 1963, providing a new opportunity for teachers from all across the country to work together. I have not found direct evidence that LATE members knew of the *Suggestions* series, but the spirit of the Blue Books breathes through their work.

Active within LATE were English professionals whose publications post-Dartmouth we celebrate but whose popularity and influence had developed over the preceding decade. Dixon was the Head of English in the experimental comprehensive, Walworth School, from 1959–65 (taking over the role from Harold Rosen) and was among the first to run a department in which English teachers collaborated with each other, shared ideas and co-developed the curriculum (Medway et al, 2014). David Holbrook was a Cambridge graduate (and student of FR Leavis) who taught in a secondary modern in Felixstowe and tutored for the Workers' Educational Association in the 1950s, before being appointed to one of the innovative Village Colleges in Cambridgeshire and given the bottom stream.

Told he could do what he liked with them (anon, 2011), he achieved more than his colleagues had ever thought possible and then used his experience to write two books that were immediately popular: *English for maturity* (1961) and *English for the rejected* (1964). Geoffrey Summerfield was the editor of the ground-breaking series of poetry anthologies for children, *Voices*, first published in the early 1960s. It is not surprising, perhaps, that when the Dartmouth Seminar invitation went out, these practitioners were among those who were keen to attend. Yet Dixon, Holbrook and Summerfield and their colleagues were not originators, nor lone thinkers. They were mouthpieces of the 'febrile activity' that was beginning to replace 40 years of 'suspended animation' in English teaching (Allen, 1973, qtd. in Medway et al, 2014, p.42).

The Blue Books' echo post-Dartmouth

As we know, publications emanating from Dartmouth promote creative teaching that seeks to enrich what pre-exists through involving students in their own learning:

> Central to [Dixon's] model was the placing of the individual learner at the heart of English and, through various processes involving language use, developing that individual.
>
> *(Goodwyn, 2011, p.70)*

This mirrors the idea that teachers have an 'interest in children, interest in words' that we saw in the 1937 Blue Book. The personal growth model became quietly influential and dominant in the following years: for instance, *Language, the learner and the school* (Barnes et al, 1969) puts the use of students' own language at the centre of their education. We can here note the 'shift' from '"taught" grammar' to '"natural grammar"' (Scott, 2003, p.104). Scott places 'taught' and 'natural' at opposite ends of the 'grammar-creativity' continuum and suggests that the move from one to another symbolised the conceptual move from 'pupil' to 'learner'.

A subtly different – although not contradictory – view is presented by Holbrook. For Holbrook, creativity is not merely an 'enriching' concept, but the very foundation, the '*basis* of our approach to English teaching as an art' (1968, p.1, emphasis original). He positions creativity and language as inextricable. Since we all use language, both for personal thought and as a means of social cohesion, creativity is necessary for social identity. Echoing Arnold (1869), he suggests that creative processes are intuitive: 'civilisation begins anew in every child' (Holbrook, 1968, p.1) and so, although to some extent it is easy for a teacher to encourage creativity as it is innate in us all, it is helpful if the teacher is aware and sympathetic, and able to cater for a child's creative needs. He argues that it is part of being human to express ourselves symbolically and, since words are symbols, English is indistinguishable from 'emotional life' (1968, p.7). Summerfield similarly does not attempt to explain the 'mystery' (1967, p.34) that is the mental creative process, but emphasises the importance of creativity for personal development: 'without the exercise of imagination we not only fail to know others but also fail to know ourselves' (1967, p.37), emphasising that such development cannot be rushed. It is the 'truthfulness in the widest sense' of the 1937 Blue Book.

Some concluding thoughts

Dartmouth is rightly remembered as championing child-centred teaching. Yet as this chapter has shown, the ideas promoted at the Seminar are *not* new – they are central to the Blue Books and retain the spirit of the Newbolt and Arnold. However, the fact that, in England at least, influential educationalists of the 1960s are remembered for presenting fresh ideas, indicates that the *Suggestions* (and other works) had been largely ignored or forgotten, the inception of LATE and NATE notwithstanding. Why?

It could have been that there were pockets of good practice but that they fell beneath the official radar (the Blue Books contained 'suggestions' only, after all, and had no overriding authority). We also know that His Majesty's Inspectorate from the 1920s–1960s did not complain about the state of English teaching (Medway et al, 2014), so there was not impetus on teachers to vary their ways.

There are two further possible reasons, perhaps more significant. One clue lies in the Plowden Report's comment on spoken language: 'whenever the matter [of accent] is discussed in the press, wide differences of opinion and strong feelings are revealed' (1967, p.211). In other words, the public was slow to warm to child-centred practice, there was pressure from traditionalists, and therefore teachers were reluctant – perhaps despite their professional instincts, and the efforts of the Board of Education and the Blue Books – to embrace it.

Secondly, the Plowden Report acknowledges that English is one of the two subjects (with Mathematics) on which the 11-plus examination is based – the ticket to grammar school. In the 1960s, only about a quarter of pupils in state-funded secondary schools in England won a grammar school place (Bolton, p.2017); doing so could be life-changing. Thus, there was pressure on teachers to prepare pupils for the 11-plus: it was 'the task-master' (Plowden, 1967, p.2). For older pupils in the secondary sector, Shayer noted 'an astonishing degree of continuity and sameness' (n.d. qtd. in Medway et al, 2014, p.42) from 1920 to 1960 in the school-leaving examinations taken at 16. These examinations consisted of 'the naming of parts. . . with little or no interest in eliciting from pupils how such units might combine to form larger functional meanings and effects' (Hall and Hewing, 2001, p.89) and so, quite simply, most teaching was geared to prepare students for such. The sage warning in the first Blue Book that external examinations 'divert the scholar' and reduce knowledge to 'competitive display. . . [which] tends to make the scholar forget or disparage the larger purposes of study' (BoE, 1905, p.9) continued to go unheeded (and, many would argue, is unheeded today).

We therefore had to wait until Dartmouth for a creative model of English teaching to be embraced. There are various possibilities that could explain why the time was then ripe: political, cultural and social.

First, a Labour government under Harold Wilson had come to power in 1964 after over a decade of Conservative rule. Wilson's government introduced the Certificate of Secondary Education (CSE) in 1965, on the back of the Newsom Report (1963), *Half our future*, aiming to enhance the prospects of 13–16 year-olds of average and below-average ability. CSE Mode 3 enabled teachers to set their own exams. There was a fresh interest in inspiring the less 'academic' and promoting their sense of self.

Next, it could be significant that it was during the 1960s that Vygotsky was read outside of the Soviet Union for the first time. His work was embraced by Britton and Rosen in UK (who were active in LATE) and Scribener and Bruner in US, so there was a new awareness that child development takes place as a socio-cultural movement through language, both spoken and written (Gibbons, 2015). The child-centred practice recommended in the Blue Books now had scientific grounding.

Thirdly, it could be that the fact that Dartmouth influenced practice in the United States which served to reconfirm and reinforce practice in England.

Thus, for a combination of causes, the personal growth approach became quietly influential and dominant in the years after Dartmouth, and a child-centred, humane style of teaching English emerged that lasted until the mid-1980s (Gibbons, 2017). Dixon, Holbrook and Summerfield would surely agree that the following quotation epitomises their collective stance, even though it was published 30 years before the Conference.

> By developing the imaginative powers of the children. . . [the teacher] is teaching them to put themselves in other people's places, to realise that there are more sides than one to every question, and that by so doing he is laying the foundation in their minds of sympathy, toleration and honest judgement.
>
> *(BoE, 1937, p.108)*

We do not know who wrote the Blue Books. Possibly the BoE inspectors who authored them were among the three school inspectors listed as being on Newbolt's committee (including Dover Wilson, the Shakespeare scholar); possibly they were members of the EA; possibly both. They sit behind their anonymity and we cannot credit them, and we can only guess who read their work. Yet it is perhaps they, as much as the famous names of the 1960s, who inspired the view of English teaching that many aspire to today.

Note

1 The history of the EA is well-documented; further detail can be found in a publication celebrating its first 100 years: *Centenary history – the English Association one hundred years on* (Baker et al., 2016).

References

Anon (2011). 'David Holbrook: obituary' *The Telegraph*, October 2011 available online at: www.telegraph.co.uk/news/obituaries/8832550/David-Holbrook.html#top [last accessed 17.10.17].

Anon (2007). 'Your fifties' *BBC website*. http://news.bbc.co.uk/2/hi/uk_news/magazine/6687549.stm [last accessed 28.10.17].

Arnold, M (1869). *Culture and anarchy* [ebook] Oxford: Oxford World's Classics.

Baker, K et al. (2016). *Centenary history – the English Association one hundred years on.*

Barnes, D et al. (1969). *Language, the learner and the school.* London: Penguin.

Board of Education (1905/1912). *Suggestions for the consideration of teachers and others concerned in the work of public elementary schools.* London: His Majesty's Stationery Office.

Board of Education (1923). *Suggestions for the consideration of teachers and others concerned in the work of public elementary schools, revised edition.* London: His Majesty's Stationary Office.

Board of Education (1924). *Some suggestions for the teaching of English in secondary schools in England.* London: His Majesty's Stationary Office.

Board of Education (1927) *Handbook of suggestions for teachers* London: HMSO.

Board of Education (1937) *Handbook of suggestions for teachers* London: HMSO.

Board of Education (1959) *Handbook of suggestions for teachers* London: HMSO.

Bolton, P (2017). *Grammar school statistics*, available online at: http://researchbriefings.parliament.uk/ResearchBriefing/Summary/SN01398 [last accessed 03.01.18].

Cox, B (1989). *English for ages 5 to 16: proposals of the Secretary of State for Education and Science and the Secretary of State for Wales.* London: Department of Education and Science and the Welsh Office.

Dixon, J (1967). *Growth through English: a report based on the Dartmouth Seminar, 1966.* OUP/National Association for the Teaching of English.

The English Association (1907–17). *Pamphlets on the teaching of English.* The English Association; available online at https://archive.org/details/pamphletsonteach00engl [last accessed 17.10.17].

The English Association (nd) Association webpages. www2.le.ac.uk/offices/english-association).

Gibbons, S (2015). 'The Importance of oracy', in Brindley, S and Marshall, B (eds.) *MasterClass in English education: transforming teaching and learning.* London: Bloomsbury.

Gibbons, S (2017). *English and its teachers: a history of policy, pedagogy and practice.* London: Routledge.

Goodwyn, A (2011). *The Expert teacher of English.* London & New York: Routledge.

Greening Lamborn (1919). 'Poetry and the child', in Morley, E (ed.) (1919) *The teaching of English in schools.* The English Association.

Hall, D and Hewings, A (2001). *Innovation in English language teaching: a reader.* Oxford: OUP.

Holbrook, D (1968). 'Creativity in the English programme', in Summerfield, G (ed.) *Creativity in English: papers relating to the Anglo-American seminar on the teaching of English (Dartmouth*

College, New Hampshire, 1966): The Dartmouth Seminar Papers. Champaign, Illinois: NCTE: 1–20.

Medway, P et al (2014). *English teachers in a postwar democracy: emerging choice in London schools 1945–65.* Basingstoke: Palgrave Macmillan.

Newbolt et al. (1921; this edition 1934). *The teaching of English in England (being the report of the Departmental Committee appointed by the President of the Board of Education to inquire into the position of English in the educational system of England).* London: HMSO.

Plowden, B et al. (1967). *Children and their primary schools: a report of the Central Advisory Council for Education (England).* London: Her Majesty's Stationery Office.

Scott, D (2003). *Curriculum studies: boundaries: subjects, assessment and evaluation.* London: Routledge.

Summerfield, G (ed.) (1968). *Creativity in English: papers relating to the Anglo-American seminar on the teaching of English (Dartmouth College, New Hampshire, 1966): The Dartmouth Seminar Papers.* Champaign, Illinois: NCTE.

5

DARTMOUTH AND PERSONAL GROWTH IN AUSTRALIA

The New South Wales and Western Australian curricula of the 1970s

Wayne Sawyer and Cal Durrant

Growth through English – and the particular view of the subject being thought through by John Dixon in his representation of the 1966 Dartmouth conference – had its key ideas taken up enthusiastically in Australia. Here we present curricula and curriculum debate from the 1970s from two Australian states (New South Wales [NSW] and Western Australia [WA]), along with writings on English that appeared in the national journal *English in Australia* in one selected year, to demonstrate the nature of vernacular inflections in Australia of what Dixon called the 'Personal Growth' model. The two curricula discussions are different and, we hope, more comprehensive because of that. Wayne has focused on the detail of the relevant NSW Years 7–10 Syllabus in the 1970s in that state and Cal has ranged more broadly over curriculum debates in WA in roughly the same period. We hope this gives readers some sense of both breadth and depth in relation to Australia's institutionalised versions of Personal Growth in the years following Dartmouth, as well as its representation in curricular debates.

The 1971 *NSW Syllabus in English for forms I-IV*

It's not an exaggeration to say that the *NSW English syllabus for forms I–IV*,[1] published in 1971, has been historically regarded as epitomising a 'Growth model'. The Syllabus was seen as revolutionary, Paul Brock calling it 'the most dramatic re-definition of junior secondary English for NSW in this century' (Nay-Brock, 1984, p.272) precisely because of this taking up of Growth approaches, with David Homer (1973, p.212) contemporaneously referring to it as 'the most carefully considered application of "growth" principles yet seen in Australia'. Later reflections on the document have rarely changed that view (e.g. Watson,

1994, p.40; Davis & Watson, 1990, p.159), with Brock (1993, p.30) later claiming it as '[t]he first "personal growth" model syllabus anywhere in the English speaking world'.

The Syllabus is famously represented by a triangular symbol, each angle of which represents one of the three elements of its overarching central phrase, *The language in use in context*. Hence one angle of the triangle represents *Language* and deals with the Syllabus' objectives for understanding and control of *usage, vocabulary, structure* and *style*. Another angle represents *Use* and deals with the Syllabus' objectives for developing skills in *writing, speaking, reading* and *listening*. The third angle represents *Context* and deals with the Syllabus' objectives for being able to understand and use language in *literature, media, personal expression* and *everyday communication*. Thus, each of the three angles are sub-divided into four areas of objectives. The twelve lines converge in the centre of the triangle, which represents 'competence', defined as the 'grasp of meaning, form and values' (NSW Secondary Schools Board, 1971, p.6–7). What, then, were its credentials for representing Growth? Firstly, the requirement 'for systematic knowledge of (linguistic or literary topics)' was removed from *the aims* of the Syllabus (but not necessarily from the course itself, which was left open to schools to design – a key distinction, as discussed below). This was because 'competence in the language in a wide variety of situations is sufficiently demanding' (NSW Secondary Schools Board, 1971, p.2). Thus, the Syllabus stressed the active *use* of language, replacing a model of pre-defined content (in fact, a systemic tradition of heavily prescribed content that included a large quantity of Latinate grammatical terminology)[2] with an 'English-as-activity' model:

> This syllabus assumes that English for twelve to sixteen year-olds should be an active pursuit: a matter of pupils developing competence by engaging in an abundance of purposeful language activities . . . For this reason, all objectives of English are stated as 'ability to *do* something'.
>
> *(NSW Secondary Schools Board, 1971, p.2)*

> This . . . represents a deliberate shift of emphasis from English as information to English as activity.
>
> *(NSW Secondary Schools Board, nd, p.6)*

Central activities were talking and writing, and the ordering of experience that these involved. This active use of language was conceived of as replacing isolated exercises on 'separate skills' of language. The Syllabus had as its aim 'to develop in pupils the utmost personal competence in using the language' and its Growth credentials are evident in such statements as 'competence . . . necessarily involv(ing) mental and emotional processes of great importance to personal development' (NSW Secondary Schools Board, 1971, p.4). Also important was the Syllabus' encouragement of an integrated approach to curriculum structure rather than a fragmented timetable.

The material of the classroom on which students brought to bear their organ-ising and learning powers had usually been literature. In *Growth through English*, Dixon wished to see other experiences valued as well, since 'one can also look at people and situations direct' (Dixon, 1975, p.54). The 1971 Syllabus widened the key 'contexts' beyond 'literature' to three others explicitly: 'the media', 'everyday communication', and 'personal expression'. 'Everyday communication' as a con-text meant placing the ability to communicate in a range of everyday situations in a position of equal importance to literary appreciation. Similarly, the importance of 'personal expression' as a 'context' gave student personal experience a key place in the classroom and the Syllabus recognised that identity was bound up with language. This exactly echoed Dixon's valuation of 'experience', as did its explicit echo of Dixon's inclusion of pupils' own work in the 'literature' of the classroom (Dixon, 1975, p.55; NSW Secondary Schools Board, 1971, p.13).

Thus, the Syllabus reflected central ideas in Dixon's book. Perhaps even more influential, however, as Wayne has written elsewhere, was the work of another Dartmouth participant, James Moffett (Sawyer, 2010a. See also Sawyer 2008, 2009, 2010b). Moffett's work in *Teaching the Universe of Discourse* explicitly sought to move 'English' from 'grammar' towards 'rhetoric' – from a focus, for example, on small units of meaning (words, sentences) to whole units of discourse, which both subsumed the operation of the smaller units and gave them a meaningful context within which to be discussed:

> Only in the largest context – the whole composition – can meaning, style, logic, or rhetoric be usefully contemplated.
>
> *(Moffett, 1968, p. 5)*

This influence is above all reflected in the Syllabus' key formulation of the nature of English in terms of:

WHO	says	WHAT	to	WHOM?
(		(		(
WHY?		HOW	with	WHAT EFFECTS

(NSW Secondary Schools Board, 1971, p.5)[3]

This formulation exactly reflects Moffett's concern with '*what* and what *for*' (Moffett, 1968, p.10) in discourse. Most importantly, Moffett specifically places this set of concerns in the context of thinking about rhetoric:

> Within the relation of the speaker to his listener lie all the issues by which we have recently enlarged the meaning of 'rhetoric'. . . Within the relation of the speaker to his subject lie all the issues of the abstractive process . . . But of course these relations are in turn related: *what* and *what for* are factors of each other.
>
> *(Moffett, 1968, p.10)*

The Chair of the Syllabus Committee, Graham Little, whose personal influence on the Syllabus was enormous (c.f. Nay-Brock, 1984, p.210), contended that 'the single most important influence upon him, immediately prior to his being appointed chairman of the Syllabus Committee in June, 1969, was his reading of Moffett's book (Nay-Brock, 1984, p.212). The key distinction between *studying* the forms of English and *using* them is one made by Moffett ('*Learning* and *learning how to* result in very different kinds of knowledge' – Moffett, 1968, p.3) and is echoed in the Syllabus' distinction between the 'ability to *do* something' and 'set knowledge about linguistic or literary topics' (NSW Secondary Schools Board, 1971, p.5). Little reported that reading Moffett

> was a kind of 'silent upon the peak of Darien' experience for me. The basic insights in this book were quite amazing to me. They were quite wonderful and I will say that the reading of it was a turning point in my whole thought
> *(Nay-Brock, 1984, Vol. II, p.53).*

Here we pick up Beavis' point that 'A revisiting of specific states' curriculum histories provides. . . a bulwark against the unproblematic. . . reintroduction of oversimplified versions of theory and curriculum' (Beavis, 2010, p.299). It is often the case that contemporary critics of Dartmouth, of the Growth model and of the latter's manifestations in systemic curricula, such as the 1971 Syllabus in NSW, are too ready to simply argue that these have roots that are individualist and Romantic and to build critique from that position, rather than reading closely what the documents are actually saying (see Sawyer, this volume, and Green and Beavis, 1996). The Syllabus's approach to language study illustrates this point. This Syllabus was expecting teachers to engage students in reading, writing, listening and speaking, in the contexts of literature, the media, everyday communication and personal expression, and the point of this was development of student language in the areas of usage, vocabulary, structure and style. A Syllabus which devoted one-third of its aims to understanding and control of usage, vocabulary, structure and style was hardly neglecting language study. Inside this Syllabus's consciously rhetorical bent, the approach to grammar is a good example of this point. The Syllabus was simply nuanced. It firstly stated that knowledge of grammatical terminology *of itself* was not the *aim* of the Syllabus, because 'the evaluation of competence is in terms of what the pupil can *do* with language, rather than what he *knows* about it in some systematic, theoretical way' (NSW Secondary Schools Board 1976, p.1). In fact, in an interview Wayne had with Graham Little in the context of his (Wayne's) writing a history of this time in NSW, Little argued that 'we could use the terminology, but . . . essentially, I didn't want meta-language to be an *objective* for a 7–10 Syllabus' (Little, 2000). Later *Notes* on the Syllabus stated that '[t]eachers are . . . free to use or not to use grammar, like any other "teaching-aid". Competence, not the use of the "aid", is the objective' (NSW Secondary Schools Board, 1976, p.1). Conscious grammatical knowledge, then, was positioned as a teaching device to be used when teachers judged this to be appropriate in their teaching context. What was rejected was not the use of grammar as a pedagogic device, but the idea that grammatical *knowledge* could stand as a proxy for linguistic *competence*:

> at no time should formal knowledge of any grammatical system or performance in formal exercises such as parsing or analysis of clauses be made part of the *evaluation of competence* in English in Years 7–10 under this syllabus.
> *(NSW Secondary Schools Board 1976, p.1, our emphasis)*

In fact, rather than neglecting the study of language, the Syllabus stressed the positive *application* of structural-linguistic knowledge in rhetorical terms:

> The objective is to develop a sense of structure in the spoken and written forms of the language. This involves:
>
> (a) Ability *to use* varying sentence patterns and *to appreciate* their influence on meaning.
> (b) Ability to *respond to and use* common indications of structure: punctuation in writing: inflexion, pause and pace in speech.
> (c) Ability *to arrange* sentences in meaningful relationships with one another and *to appreciate* the effectiveness of such relationships in others' use of language.
> (d) Ability *to discern, evaluate* and where appropriate *use* larger structural patterns.
> *(NSW Secondary Schools Board 1971, p.9, our emphases)*

As Wayne has argued elsewhere (Sawyer 2008, 2009), such an approach to English is in contradistinction to those who see the history of English as marked by a lost opportunity to have the subject focus on language and, especially, language study as rhetoric (e.g. Christie, 1993; Christie et al., 1991; Moon, 2012).

The 1970s, when this Syllabus was being implemented, were also a period of one of the most sustained media-fuelled literacy crises that Australia had ever seen. Shrill cries in features and editorials about declining literacy standards were commonly attributed to an alleged neglect of the teaching of traditional grammar. Wayne has documented this concerted media attack elsewhere in some detail (Sawyer, 2006). In NSW, much of the blame for decline was laid at the feet of the 1971 English Syllabus, which, it was argued, required no knowledge of technical terminology (Astley, 1975), lacked prescription (Williams, 1979) and reflected new ideas that had been insufficiently tested (*The Australian*, 1975), as well as 'a theory endorsed. . . by a chairman of the English Syllabus Committee' (*The Sunday Telegraph*, 1974).[4]

It is/was a caricature of Growth to suppose that there was no place in it for awareness of language.[5] The simple issue in *Growth through English* is when conscious knowledge of structure and its accompanying terminology become relevant in the exchanges between teacher and student. In terms of this Syllabus, arguing against such knowledge as a form of *assessing language competence* is far from neglecting language study. Regardless of the degree to which history might see the trans-Atlantic complementarity of Dixon and Moffett as constituting *the* Growth model in general, it is true to say that the peculiar flavour given to Growth in NSW depended heavily on qualities brought to it by Moffett:

> Moffett in one stroke had put together the two histories I was interested in: the history of mind – the idea of mind, the human faculties – and . . . rhetoric . . . Moffett put the rhetorical tradition *and* the Growth tradition together through his concept of levels of abstraction.
>
> *(Little, 2000)*

The 1971 Syllabus gave a particular and distinctive rhetorical flavour to Growth in NSW, one that is rarely acknowledged. On the other hand, some would argue that a Syllabus which aims at competence specifically in terms of usage, vocabulary, structure and style should not be thought of as a 'Growth Syllabus' at all. Perhaps this is because neither *Growth through English* nor this Syllabus are being given the credit for the nuanced approaches to language that they represent.

The Western Australian context

As in NSW, WA readily adopted a 'Personal Growth' orientation to English in the 1970s, though not necessarily as a result of direct reflection in a Syllabus, such as that in NSW from 1971. Marnie O'Neill (1992) claims that the 'new conceptualisation of English tended to be imported by academics and senior members of the Education Department of WA, rather than arising from any groundswell of teacher demand' (p.13). However, over the past four decades, different researchers have provided varying reasons for how this approach to English spread across schools throughout the state.

Dowsett (2016) has observed that key university and teachers' college English personnel in the 1960s and 1970s spent time at the London Institute of Education and returned to broadcast that experience and its accompanying knowledge amongst their own English Education students, as well as to teachers via the local English Teachers' Association. Such agencies for change in Western Australian education are not without precedent. As Ken Willis (1996) points out, just before his retirement as Inspector-General of schools in WA, Cyril Jackson appointed 'eight young men' who were committed to the 'New Education' principles of the day, based on the work of Herbart, Pestalozzi, Montessori and Froebel, to the new Claremont Training College in Perth in 1903 (p.98). Significantly, most of them had also trained and taught at the Fort Street Model School in Sydney prior to their appointment (a school in which, many years later, Graham Little taught). Presumably, the thinking behind this was that changing student-teacher attitudes and methodologies would eventually have an impact on the broader teaching cohort in the state.

Bruce Bennett (English Department, University of Western Australia [UWA]) completed his Master of Education at the London Institute of Education where he came under the influence of James Britton, Nancy Martin and Harold Rosen, among the best-known names in the 'New English' movement. Eric Carlin, who was at Churchlands Teachers' Training College and who at one time was President (and subsequently Life Member) of the English Teachers' Association of Western Australia (ETAWA), was awarded a Fellowship to the London Institute in 1970, where he 'was also influenced by the new theories and methodology of Britton and Martin who were writing influential books about the nature of teaching' (Dowsett, 2016, p.97; see Britton et al., 1975).

Marnie O'Neill (1995), on the other hand, holds the view that educational reform in WA has a history of being in direct response to Education Department initiated reports such as the Petch (1965), Dettman (Education Department of WA, 1969), Martin (Education Department of WA, 1980), McGaw (1984) and Beazley (1984) Reports. In the case of subject English, O' Neill argues that lower secondary school syllabus change since 1969 has tended to be 'the result of system-wide structural change, rather than revision within the subject area of English itself' (O'Neill, 1995, p.166). She also points out that neither UWA nor the Secondary Teachers' College (STC) were in strong positions to promote the ideals of 'Progressive' English: UWA's English Department was steeped in predominantly New Criticism or Leavisite practices, while the STC was 'not well equipped with syllabus guidelines for Achievement Certificate English; consequently, new graduates were little better informed about the new syllabus or appropriate pedagogical practices than the more experienced teachers in the schools' (p.170). Perhaps under the influence of Bennett and Carlin, amongst others, the situation had shifted by the end of the 1970s, as by 1980 Nancy Martin from the London Institute of Education was able to observe that: 'Teachers graduating since 1970 have not had to unlearn old attitudes, and are therefore more able to use their initiative and responsibility through school-based curricula and the activities of professional associations like the English Teachers' Association' (Education Department of WA, 1980, p.11).

Western Australia had up until 1971 operated under a public examination system in which individual subject curricula were driven by the previous year's Junior Certificate (Year Ten) and Leaving Certificate (Year 12) examinations. Following the Dettman Report (Education Dept of WA, 1969), the Board of Secondary Education (BSE) was established and an internally assessed Achievement Certificate was adopted to replace the Junior Certificate. The Achievement Certificate brought WA schools into line with the general democratisation of high school curricula that was occurring internationally, largely due to the post-World War II comprehensive school movement. For subject English, it presented an opportunity to move from a traditional Cultural-heritage-based literature-dominated curriculum to one more in keeping with research coming out of the

London Institute of Education and the English-as-Personal-Growth orientation at Dartmouth, at least as presented in *Growth through English* (Green 1989, p.20). As O'Neill (1995) observes, the English syllabus statement was informed by the 'ideas of language and learning, language experience, personal response to literature and the notion of a continuum between literature and life' (p.167). Student achievement was to be assessed over the first three years by 'Board-administered tests and two-yearly moderation visits by the BSE moderator in each core subject area' (O'Neill 1995, p.166), but effectively each school developed its own subject curricula, which were submitted to the BSE for approval and/or modification.

In principle, then, the possibilities offered by the Achievement Certificate meant that English teachers in WA had never had so much bureaucratic faith placed in them as professionals considered capable of making informed judgements about what their students were already able to demonstrate and of developing school-based programmes of work designed to further extend those students' individual development in all aspects of subject English. However, this very responsibility told on many English teachers. Rod Quin (1989) who was an Education Officer in the Ministry of Education at the time, recalled the pressures and frustrations felt by English teachers who were:

> being forced into the simultaneous roles of educational philosopher, curriculum writer and classroom teacher. . . the great weakness of (Achievement Certificate English) . . . was its incredible vagueness. Most teachers conceived well the general objectives of English – what we were aiming at in the long run and how to go about this in general terms – but when it came to the specifics of a programme we weren't so sure.
>
> *(p.15)*

O'Neill's (1995) summary of her reading of the WA Education Department's newsletter for secondary school English teachers, *Backchat* (Western Australia Education Department Curriculum Branch, 1900–1987), suggests that while there were 'innovative and negotiated teaching and learning experiences taking place during the late 1970s and early 1980s', they were far from being the norm (p.172). In 1980, the Martin Report (1980) reviewed Achievement Certificate English and attempted to explain how it had been problematised in WA schools for much of the previous decade:

> When the external public examination (Junior Certificate) was abolished (end of 1971 for Government schools), there was not sufficient confidence, either in the community or among teachers themselves, to do without some external measure of comparability. Consequently, in the early years of the Achievement Certificate, much emphasis was placed on comparability testing and placing students in 'correct' levels (Advanced, Intermediate or Basic). Much of the emphasis in in-service work was placed on establishing

comparable standards of written work, methods of assessment, and how to distinguish the work of a student working at Advanced level from that of one working at Intermediate or Basic level. . ..

(p.29)

As mentioned earlier, the abolition of the Junior Certificate removed a predictable external examination, which was replicated in school examinations set at the end of each term for Years 8–10. Secondly, it removed a highly structured syllabus, and replaced it with a very open guide for teachers to devise their own curricula and assessment and evaluation procedures. Most English teachers lacked any formal training in curriculum development, assessment or evaluation procedures, and for lack of anything else have continued with summative forms of assessment based either on the Junior Certificate or comparability-test models . . .

(p.33)

In general terms, the Board of Secondary Education and the assessment procedures carried out in its name have an inhibitory effect on the teaching and learning of English. The system of comparability tests, levels and grades leads to teaching directed towards assessment, with a corresponding emphasis on writing for the teacher as an examiner. It seems that as long as comparability tests are available (even on an optional basis) many schools and teachers will misuse them and shape their teaching programme towards them.

(p.37)

In the Report, Martin (Education Department of WA, 1980) quoted the Director General of Education in WA, Dr David Mossenson, lamenting the fact that the effects of the new system had run away from the aims:

I was very much involved with these confounded things from the beginning. . . I regard the Achievement Certificate as having been a progressive and worthwhile development when it occurred, and its purpose was to get a genuine comprehensive pattern going. . . But it's become formalised and its own mad momentum just continues. Comparability tests, meetings with moderators – the whole paraphernalia which was necessary to satisfy a doubting public and to allay the fears of employers ten years ago now just continues because everybody loves it. But there's no need for a whole lot of it.

(p.17)

The Martin Report proved to be a significant document in the history of English teaching in Western Australia, and while Bill Green has referred to it as being a 'fractured' document in the sense that it reflected the fractured nature of English itself at the time (Green, qtd. in Dowsett, 2016, p.116), he and Jo-Anne Reid (1986) also concede its importance as being 'the first major account in the local context of subject English, its nature and mode of functioning in the school curriculum, and the difficulties it faced in a time of general social and economic difficulty' (p.6). They also acknowledged it as being 'an exemplary instance of the common theoretical position of the "New English", and moreover, a deliberate attempt to deal more or less systematically with the relations of curriculum theory and practice as regards English classrooms' (p.6). More recently, Green (2016) has included it as one of four 'now iconic proper names' in English curriculum history, 'Dartmouth', 'Bullock' and 'Newbolt' being the other three (p.25).

According to Green (1989), Growth model English failed 'institutionally and programmatically in Western Australia', and he uses the Martin Report to support this claim (p.21). He suggests that English teachers found programming, assessment and discipline to be three constant professional problems within a Growth approach but that its 'failure' wasn't due so much to its pedagogical limitations but rather to its 'politics – its inability to move beyond its own ideological limits' (p.21). He cites the inability of the profession to 'marshall either a defence or a coherent case of its own, in the face of widespread and increasingly vocal criticism of its performance in the 1980s' (p.21).

What seems to come through quite clearly from Green's critique is that English teachers – or at least the English teaching profession in Western Australia – would appear to have 'bought into' post-Dartmouth English, both its philosophy and pedagogies, but didn't have the capacity or indeed the resolve to resist the conservative Right movement that was afoot in the space between the publication of the Martin (1980) and Beazley (1984) Reports. Green asserts that this period saw the rise of a different version of English teaching and the demise of the incumbent version in what he suggests is 'an exemplary enactment of curriculum and cultural politics' (p.20).

What rose from the Beazley Report (1984) in terms of secondary English curriculum was a very different version of what subject English was and could be. In the new Unit Curriculum, the Cultural Heritage and Personal Growth orientations were discarded and a new emphasis on functional English skills was initiated (O'Neill 1995, p.175). At first glance, this appears to be a knee-jerk reaction in Western Australia to the concerted media war waged against progressive education more broadly, and against Personal Growth orientations of English specifically. As Wayne (2006) has described, and as Green (1999) asserts, the functionalist term 'literacy' (and the apparent falling of standards *in* 'literacy') was used to persuade the broader Australian public that there was an educational crisis at hand and that previous educational/English teaching philosophies, orientations and methodologies were singularly unsuited to keeping Australia competitive in the new globalised marketplace. Green suggests that in WA, what this meant in practice was 'an increasing emphasis on *literacy* education, understood in a particular way – that is, within a renewed rhetoric of "skills" and "training" – and within this, an increasing stress on literacy *assessment*, increasingly conceived officially and in popular-public sensibility as the specific task of subject English' (p.389). By way of official endorsement, then, Unit Curriculum – enacted in 1987 – saw the end of Personal Growth orientations in secondary school English classrooms in Western Australia. The inner beliefs about their subject that secondary English teachers might have clung to is the work of a different paper.

How subject 'English' was being discussed in the professional literature of English teachers across Australia

In order to round out this picture in a small way and to place these discussions of individual states inside a national frame, we will now turn to an examination of the professional literature available to English teachers in both NSW and WA through membership of their state professional association, viz. the journal *English in Australia*. Rather than range over a number of issues of this journal, we have chosen instead to examine more closely a year when the forces described above in relation to the early 1970s in each state would have had an opportunity to take effect. The year we have chosen is 1977, the fifth year of full implementation of the NSW Syllabus, and a year midway between the Dettman and Beazley Reports in WA.

English in Australia in 1977 certainly reflects the Dartmouth 'spirit' of active language use. With language and the development of language at the centre of concerns for English, 'learning language' and 'learning about language' were often the terms in which English was discussed, (as they are, in effect, in most of *Growth through English* itself). In terms of 'learning language', *English in Australia* in 1977 included essays on:

• general language development (Halliday,1977);
• spoken language in particular (Crocker, 1977; Robinson, 1977);
• sensitivity to context in language use and for language evaluation (Crocker, 1977; Robinson, 1977).

In terms of 'learning about language', there were discussions of language in a sociolinguistic rhetorical approach, much broader than simply discussions of grammar and reflecting the inquiry-based study of language advocated in *Growth through English* itself (Dixon, 1975, p.76ff). Particular essays were on:

• studying specific aspects of language use in social contexts (Robinson, 1977);
• the even more specific use of the UK *Language in use* materials built around this approach to studying language (Halliday, 1977).

As in *Growth through English*, too ('Processes in language learning'), *English in Australia* in 1977 shows concern with the effects of class on language (Yule, 1977). Eagleson (1977) is particularly concerned to broaden teachers' perceptions of correctness – to abandon the attempt to eliminate the 'errors' of non-Standard dialects and to adopt a model that favours extending the range of the child's language types, rather than eliminating non-Standard. The stress is on Standard English as a dialect, albeit the dialect of power, and the model becomes one of 'supplementation' rather than elimination – a view argued by both Moffett (1968, p.156ff) and Dixon (1975, p.16ff).

Thus far, we think we can say that these areas of discussion in *English in Australia* reflect closely major overarching principles and concerns that are represented by *Growth through English* (and, indeed, by much of *Teaching the Universe of Discourse*). Another key issue in the journal in 1977 is literacy (Parker, 1977a, 1977b; Little, 1977). Parker's articles on literacy, in which he positions himself as a Deweyan 'progressive' – specifically not 'romantic' or 'cultural transmission' in orientation (1977a) – references the key names and ideas of Dixon's milieu: Barnes, Bullock, Britton, Wilkinson, Dixon (and Moffett). Indeed, though an academic in America, Parker had been co-researcher with Nancy Martin on the Schools Council Writing across the Curriculum project (Martin et al., 1976).

Literacy also comes under discussion in the context of the literacy crises of the mid-1970s (see Sawyer, 2006). Parker (1977a) argues that the question of 'standards' cannot be separated from one's view of education and of literacy, and that as a society adopts increasingly narrow, mechanistic views of testing, so too does its very definition of literacy become narrower, tighter and increasingly minimalist – an argument strongly reinforced by Little's (1977) then recent experience in the US, and also put forward by Eagleson (1977). The key issue here in terms of reflecting (or otherwise) a Growth orientation is not just the attitude contained in Dixon's short discussion on the narrowness of 'present' exams in *Growth through English* (p.92), but the whole approach to language development as needing to be based in 'operation', not in 'dummy runs' (Dixon, 1975, p.13) such as '"exercises" in spelling, punctuation, "correctness", comprehension and precis' (Dixon, 1975, p.128). This also relates to the always vexed question of grammar. It will be remembered that the 1971 NSW Syllabus effectively removed the study of grammatical terminology from being an *aim* or *objective* of subject English. Such knowledge could be a teaching aid – a pedagogical device – but it was not to stand in as a proxy for linguistic competence. Little himself warns here in 1977, and against the background of the 70s literacy crises, against Australia going down the American route of focusing on grammar, as manifested in small mastery steps, fill-in-the-blanks exercises and a generally pre-packaged curriculum – the very definition of 'dummy run'.

A different approach to writing based on American influences such as Donald Murray, and one that was to be profoundly significant in NSW in later years, is introduced by Walshe in 1977, when he begins to discuss writing processes. In introducing audience-response and in asking the question, 'How do real writers write?' Walshe initiates a genuine paradigm shift that was to be widely taken up in the 80s, and was to be influential in the framing of the succeeding Years 7–10 English Syllabus in NSW. His model in 1977 was that of 'Experience/Pre-Writing/Draft Writing/Re-Writing/Publication/Response' (Walshe, 1977). However, despite the linking by many of Growth and the so-called 'process writing' approaches of

Walshe, Murray, Graves and others (e.g. Christie 1993; Moon, 2012) there is no necessary or automatic link between Walshe's model and Dixon's work. Since Dixon is concerned with functions, his discussion of writing focuses far more on writing's place in shaping the understanding of experience, rather than the processes by which rhetoric is built:

> [I]n sharing experience with others man is using language to make that experience real to himself we make for ourselves a representational world, sense out to the full its ability to stand for experience as we meet it, come up against its limitations and then shoulder. . . the task of making it afresh, extending, reshaping it, and bringing into new relationships all the old elements. . .
>
> It is in the nature of language to impose system and order. . .
>
> *(Dixon, 1975, pp.6, 9)*

In fact, Britton, whose work this echoes so strongly, was later to question the very model of 'drafts and revision processes in composing' that Walshe represents here, by arguing that the model underestimates the importance of 'shaping at the point of utterance' (1980, p.61).

Not every important article being written in *English in Australia* in 1977 echoed Growth approaches, but it is fair to say that the version of English being addressed and thought through in Dixon's book on Dartmouth was being taken seriously in Australian curriculum thinking.

Conclusion

Australia in the 1970s showed great enthusiasm for the main tenets of the 'Growth model', but neither its take-up nor sustainability were uniform across the country. Western Australia took up Growth, but let it go by the mid -1980s under the influence of crisis rhetoric. NSW took it up in official curricula in 1971 and it remained a part of what has been in NSW an eclectic approach to Syllabus development, with the current K-10 Syllabus still 'enabl(ing) teachers to draw on the methods of different theoretical perspectives and models for teaching English to assist their students to achieve the syllabus outcomes at the highest levels' (BOSNSW, 2012, p.10). The professional literature as represented by *English in Australia* in 1971 strongly reflected Growth principles, though curriculum debate was already looking ahead to how other influences were to shape aspects of the subject in Australia.

Notes

1 'Forms I-IV' were then what we would refer to today as 'Years 7–10' (with students being generally 12–16 years of age). There have always been separate syllabuses for English in NSW for Years 7–10 and Years 11–12.

2 The degree of compulsion about teaching such grammar had earlier been 'modified' officially, if not in classroom practice, by an amendment of 1968 (see Nay-Brock, 1984; Watson, 1994).
3 The punctuation of this formulation is as per the Syllabus itself.
4 These latter two articles have no by-lines.
5 See, for example, the highly nuanced treatment of language in the chapter 'A question of knowledge' in *Growth through English* (Dixon, 1975. See also Sawyer's discussion of Dixon's work on this – this volume).

References

Astley, T. (1975). 'The Higher illiteracy', *The National Times*, Sept 29 to Oct 4.

The Australian (1975). 'Illiterates turned out by schools', March 3.

Beavis, C. (2010). '"A Chart for further exploration and a kind of rallying call": James Moffett and English curriculum history in Victoria', *Changing English*, 17(3), 297–307.

Beazley, K. E. (1984). *Education in Western Australia. Report of the Committee of Inquiry into Education in Western Australia.* Perth: Western Australia Government Printer.

Board of Studies, NSW (BOSNSW) (2012). *NSW syllabus for the Australian Curriculum: English K-10 syllabus*, Sydney: Board of Studies NSW. Available at: https://syllabus.nesa. nsw.edu.au/english/english-k10/.

Britton, J. (1980). 'Shaping at the point of utterance', in A. Freedman and I. Pringle (eds.) *Reinventing the rhetorical tradition*, Conway: L&S Books: 61–65.

Britton, J., Burgess, T., Martin, N., McLeod, A. and Rosen, H. (1975). *The Development of writing abilities (11–18)*. London: Macmillan.

Brock, P. (1993). 'Some reflections on teacher education programs for the prospective teacher of English in Australian secondary schools: a personal view', *English in Australia*, 106, December, 24–40.

Christie, F. (1993). 'The "Received tradition" of English teaching: the decline of rhetoric and the corruption of grammar', in B. Green (ed.) *The Insistence of the letter: literacy and curriculum theorizing*. Pittsburgh: University of Pittsburgh Press.

Christie, F., Devlin, B., Freebody, P., Luke, A., Martin, J.R., Threadgold, T. & Walton, C. (1991). *Teaching English literacy: a project of national significance on the preservice preparation of teachers for teaching English literacy – Volume 1*, Canberra: Department of Employment, Education and Training.

Crocker, W. J. (1977). 'Teaching oracy in the English programme', *English in Australia*, 39, February, 48–59.

Davis, D. & Watson, K. (1990). 'Teaching English in Australia: a personal view', in J. Britton, R. E. Shafer, & K. Watson (eds.), *Teaching and learning English worldwide*, Clevedon & Philadelphia: Multilingual Matters: 151–174.

Dixon, J. (1975, 3rd edn.). *Growth through English: set in the perspective of the Seventies*, London: Oxford.

Dowsett, P. (2016). *The History of curricular control: literary education in Western Australia, 1912–2012*, Unpublished PhD thesis: University of Western Australia.

Eagleson, R. D. (1977). 'Disadvantaged English', *English in Australia*, 39, February, 23–47.

Education Department of Western Australia (1969). *Secondary education in Western Australia* (The Dettman Report), Perth: Education Department of WA.

Education Department of Western Australia (1980). *The Martin report: what goes on in English classrooms. Case studies from government high schools in Western Australia*, Perth: Education Department of WA.

Green, B. (1989). 'Testing times? Literacy assessment and English teaching in Western Australia', *English in Australia*, 89, 18–34.

Green, B. (1999). 'Curriculum, literacy and the state: re 'Right'-ing English?', *Pedagogy, Culture & Society*, 7 (3), 385–407.

Green, B. (2016). 'Different histories? Reading Dartmouth. . . against the grain', *English in Australia*, 51(3), 25–32.

Green, B. and Beavis, C. (1996). 'Introduction: English teaching and curriculum history', in B. Green and C. Beavis (eds.) *Teaching the English subjects: essays on curriculum history and Australian schooling*, Geelong: Deakin University Press.

Green, B. and Reid, J. (1986). 'English teaching, in-service and action research: the Kewdale Project', *English in Australia*, 75(March), 4–21.

Halliday, M. A. K. (1977). 'Some thoughts on language in the middle school years', *English in Australia*, 42, November, 3–15.

Homer, D. B. (1973). *Fifty years of purpose and precept in English teaching (1921–71): an overview with special reference to the teaching of poetry in the early secondary years*, Unpublished MEd thesis: Melbourne University.

Little, G. (1977). 'Back to basics in the USA', *English in Australia*, 40, May, 20–24.

Little, G. (2000). Interview with Sawyer. September.

Martin, N, D'Arcy, P, Newton, B, and Parker, R. (1976). *Writing and learning across the curriculum, 11–16*, Upper Montclair: Boynton/ Cook.

McGaw, B. (1984). *Assessment in the upper secondary school in Western Australia (Report of the Ministerial Working Party on School Certification and Tertiary Admissions Procedures)*, Perth: Western Australian Government Printer.

Moffett, J. (1968). *Teaching the universe of discourse*. Boston: Houghton Mifflin.

Moon, B. (2012). 'Remembering rhetoric: recalling a tradition of explicit instruction in writing', *English in Australia*, 47(1), 37–52.

Nay-Brock, P. (1984). *A History of the development of the English syllabuses in NSW secondary education, 1953–1976: a continuum or a 'Series of New Beginnings'?* Unpublished PhD thesis: University of New England.

NSW Secondary Schools Board (1971). *Syllabus in English for forms I–IV*, Sydney: NSW Department of Education.

NSW Secondary Schools Board (1976). *Notes on the syllabus in English, 2: language*, Sydney: NSW Secondary Schools Board.

NSW Secondary Schools Board (nd). *Notes on the syllabus in English, 1: general bibliography and commentary*, Sydney: NSW Secondary Schools Board.

O'Neill, M. (1992). 'Contested ground: English syllabus and examination practices in Western Australia', *Curriculum Perspectives* 12(1), April, 9–22.

O'Neill, M. (1995). 'Shifting negotiations: a case study of lower secondary school English syllabuses in Western Australia', in D. S. G. Carter & M. H. O'Neill (eds.) *Case studies in educational change: an international perspective*, London: Falmer Press: 157–183.

Parker, R. B. (1977a). 'Are our standards slipping?', *English in Australia*, 40, May, 5–19.

Parker, R. B. (1977b). 'Literacy and the English teacher', *English in Australia*, 39, February, 5–22.

Petch, J. A. (1965). *A Report on the public examination system in Western Australia*, Perth: University of Western Australia.

Quin, R. (1989). 'The Challenge of the unit curriculum', *Interpretations*, 22(2).

Robinson, W. P. (1977). 'A Freedom to speak', *English in Australia*, 40, May, 25–33.

Sawyer, W. (2006). 'Just add "progressivism" and stir: how we cook up literacy crises in Australia', in B. Doecke, M. Howie and W. Sawyer (eds.) *Only connect: English teaching, schooling and community*, Kent Town, SA: AATE/Wakefield Press: 236–262.

Sawyer, W. (2008). 'English teaching in New South Wales since 1971: versions of growth?', *Changing English*, 15(3), September, 323–337.

Sawyer, W. (2009). 'Language and literature: revisiting some defining moments in the history of English', in J. Manuel, P. Brock, D. Carter and W. Sawyer (eds.) *Imagination, innovation, creativity: re-visioning English in education*, Putney: Phoenix Education: 71–86.

Sawyer, W. (2010a). 'Structuring the New English in Australia: James Moffett and English teaching in New South Wales', *Changing English*, 17(3), 285–296.

Sawyer, W. (2010b). 'Writing (in) the nation', *English in Australia*, 45(2), 7–20.

The Sunday Telegraph (1974). 'High school illiteracy', March 17.

Walshe, R. D. (1977). 'A Model to clarify the writing process', *English in Australia*, 42, November, 28–31.

Watson, K. (1994). 'English teaching in historical perspective: case study of an Australian state', in K. Watson with C. Durrant, S. Hargreaves & W. Sawyer, *English teaching in perspective in the context of the 1990s*, Rozelle: St Clair Press: 26–42.

Western Australia Education Department Curriculum Branch (1900–1987). *Backchat: a newsletter for teachers of secondary English*, Perth: Curriculum Branch.

Williams, G. (1979). 'The Great literacy debate', *The Sydney Morning Herald*, 21 August.

Willis, K. (1996). 'The Shaping of secondary English in Western Australia', in B. Green & C. Beavis (eds.) *Teaching the English subjects: essays on English curriculum history and Australian schooling*, Geelong: Deakin University Press: 96–117.

Yule, V. (1977). 'A Child's garden of WISCS and WPSSIS', *English in Australia*, 42, November, 51–59.

6

THE MANIFOLD WAYS IN WHICH LANGUAGE WORKS

The generation after Dartmouth

John Willinsky

I

I approach this Dartmouth retrospective as a Canadian school teacher and teacher educator who came of age during the 1960s and began teaching school in 1972. It would be another decade before I learned about the Anglo-American Seminar on the Teaching of English held at Dartmouth College in the summer of 1966. By that point, it seems almost trite to say, Dartmouth looked like the English teacher's San Francisco Summer of Love, which began the following year with the legendary Monterey Pop Festival. You didn't have to be there, was the general feeling, with 'flowers in your hair', because 'all across the nation. . . there's a whole generation / with a new explanation', as Scott Mackenzie sang at Monterey in the song 'San Francisco'.

In the years that followed, Dartmouth, Monterey Pop, and the Summer of Love came to be associated, beyond anything that could have been imagined at the time, with a self-conscious calling out of the moment for the generation involved and touched by these events. In the case of Dartmouth, it took the form of a professional self-awareness of the calling, as English teachers took stock of their trade and its place in the culture. The conference provided its own Monterey Pop headliners for my generation of teachers, led by James Britton and including Douglas Barnes, Basil Bernstein, Wayne Booth, John Dixon, Joshua Fishman, James Moffett, Walter Ong, Alan Purves, Connie Rosen, James Squires, and Denys Thompson.

I place myself in the generation of teachers that followed after Dartmouth, not only because I'm the age of James Britton's talented offspring Celia and Alison, who figure among the young children in his *Language and Learning*, but as I was collectively parented and schooled in the 'new explanation' offered by those at Dartmouth. Merron Chorny at the University of Calgary served as my channel to

Dartmouth, after I left school teaching and starting working in English Education at the university in 1984. Canada tended to operate at intersection of the Anglo-American exchange of educational ideas, and by at least one account, Merron was the sole Canadian 'observer' at the Dartmouth Conference (Watson, undated).[1] He maintained a strong friendship with James Britton, as well as Harold and Connie Rosen, Margaret Meek, and others. Calgary constituted Britton's 'second home', as Merron put it, when the university awarded him an honorary degree in 1977. It was in such a home, with many of his and Merron's friends dropping by a summer, that I found my footing as an English educator.

Looking back, I can see the extent to which Britton's *Language and Learning* was at the heart of Dartmouth's great appeal for me. Britton's style was that of literary essayist. His manner was informal but impassioned, rich in anecdote and dialogue; he provided lucid explanations of psychological research by Bruner, Luria, Kelly, Piaget, Vygotsky, and Winnicot. The book is anchored, however, in what philosophers – Arendt, Buber, Cassirer, and Langer – and writers – Auden, Coleridge, Dickens, Hemingway, and Wordsworth – made of language and the world. It is surely distinguished, among educational works, by an extended quote on gossip from D. H. Lawrence's *Lady Chatterly's Lover*.

Britton (1970) provides references to these sources, with almost an apology, for those who wish to 'follow the complexities', he warns in the Foreword, 'of what I simplified' (p.7). His is the writerly articulation of a literary common sense about how children come to language, learning, and literacy. That it was published as a Penguin paperback in 1970 (and a Pelican in 1972) was part of its appeal.[2] Penguins were the stock in trade for those with literary interests, at least for readers in the British Commonwealth. At a time when teacher education was in the grip of behavioral objectives and outcomes, Britton had much to offer the bookish generation of the 1960s. He made teaching the work of interested and engaged readers (of Penguins), who sought to continue the readerly conversation of their pre-teaching days.

The book was apparently one of best sellers of the Penguin Education series, which ran from 1965 to 1974, and included works by such radicals as Ivan Illich, Paulo Freire, and Paul Goodman. If anything provides a striking sense of the change between then and now, it is the passing of what might be thought of as the pulp fiction of my generation of teachers. The mix of popular paperback culture and radical educational ideas – such as Illich's desire to de-school society, Freire's pursuit of conscientization, and Goodman's howl against growing up absurd – were part of what drew my generation to teaching to be part of a larger social change.[3]

Yet in various ways, Britton's *Language and Learning* operates at a remove from the educational radicalism of Illich, Freire, and Goodman. His book is aimed at carving out a greater place for children's own language, imagination, and feeling in the classroom. He is advocating 'a view of human behavior that makes living very like learning' (p.18). It is a view (taken from the personal construct psychologist George Kelly) that contains its own mild critique of school only as it is given to setting learning apart from the rest of the child's life. He dramatizes the problem with a poem by D. J. Enright that, as he reads it, opposes the 'the language that comes from dictionaries and that teachers teach [which is] a language that takes us away from things' to the language of poets and children, which is 'the language of discovery, a language for exploring a world full of things, and a language as yet undivorced from the concrete reality of things' (p.127).

Yet Britton is careful not to leave it at the teacher-and-dictionary opposed to child-and-poet. Rather he sees, as part of his broader pedagogical hopefulness, 'the beginnings of school in a different light from that represented in the poem' (p.128). He speaks of the child entering the school as experiencing a 'continuation and refinement' in her language (p.128). This can take place as long as, he warns, learning in schools is not being treated as solely 'something you do sitting in a seat' or 'as simply an interim phase' taking place in 'the monologue of instruction' (pp.128–29, 273). Schools should encourage rather than restrict children's original, poet-like connection to language and life. Children should practice language in school, Britton recommends, as doctors practice medicine and lawyers the law; and 'not as a juggler 'practices' a new trick before he performs it' (p.130). The emphasis on authentic linguistic experiences connected to the operation of the world (if framed here in the occasionally inauthentic professional contexts of medicine and the law) was a part of Britton that I held onto in my work. But with this example of his doctors, lawyers and jugglers, Britton is not doing justice to his sense of language's different functions, which is a part of his work that I, for one, did not find as generative.

Like Louise Rosenblatt, M. A. K. Halliday, and others, Britton thought it helpful to describe the different roles that language can play in our lives. As you may recall, his particular two-sided scheme includes a 'participant' role, on the one hand, which is made up of both 'conative' and 'informative' forms of speech; then there is the opposing 'spectator' role, on the other, which includes the 'poetic' form (p.237). He also distinguishes between 'transactional' and 'expressive' speech, following a similar pattern. For example, the 'transactional speech comes when *participant* demands are made. . . to *get something done* in the world' (p.169, original italics). The spectator role, by contrast, is not about getting things done, in support of which Britton cites W. H. Auden's 'In memory of W. B. Yeats' to the effect that 'poetry makes nothing happen' (p.111).

For me, at least, making such distinctions in the use of language can obscure as much as it clarifies. After all, Auden's tribute to Yeats does some serious work on behalf of poetry and poets, which is demonstrated, as much as anything, by how Britton uses it here to make schools more welcoming of spectatorship, poetry, and expressive language.[4] Britton explains that he has 'labored the distinction [between participant and spectator roles]. . . because I believe it will prove important for a proper understanding of the manifold ways in which language works' (p.105). He is setting out these two roles for language as he fears that 'an education limited in activity to the participant role [which] is in the last analysis an attempt to produce men and women with the efficiency of machines' (p.152). His brief is, then, to create a place in the school for the juggler, or if not for the well-practiced flinging of spinning torches, then for something in which 'we work upon the world representation' rather than engage in 'problem-solving, data handling; of number work and environmental studies, scientific, historical or geographical' (p.152).

It is not that I disagree with Britton on ensuring that schools are places for both reflecting on how the world has come to be represented and for solving problems in that representation. Rather, I can see on reflection that while I wanted to work in the vein of Britton's approach to education in the company of poets, philosophers, and humanistic psychologists, I ended up taking a different approach to language and learning, a different stance on properly understanding the manifold ways in which language works, which might be more precisely put, in my case, as the ways in which language is worked. Rather than seeking to ensure that the schools did more for children finding their own voice, helping them to grow through English, whether by sitting in the bleachers or taking to the field, as spectator or participant, I pushed for something else.

While I started out following Britton's work on helping children find ways in school to express their experience of the world with all the direct and immediate sense of a poet, I came to see that we owed students something more than a chance to tell their story. It had to do with the doctors, lawyers, and jugglers, that is, with the professional, legal, and economic mechanisms by which language works as a source of power, authority, and bemusement. This became for me an extension of what Britton calls 'a proper understanding of the manifold ways in which language works', and works, in this case, as a force in their world. It included for me, after an initial run with spectator literacy, the history of publishing; the making of dictionaries; the educational legacy of imperialism; the right to access research and scholarship; and the state and status of online information. While I have written about all but the last instance elsewhere, allow me to briefly recap how they were also part of the generation that followed on Dartmouth.

II

In my final years of school teaching in the early 1980s, Ruth Fletcher taught down the hall from my classroom in a remote Northern Ontario school. First thing in the morning, Ruth would pick up a stack of blank photocopy paper, while the rest of us were waiting in line to use the machine. She was introducing her first-grade students to writing and reading, starting at the deep end with the blank page. She had dropped the basal readers from her teaching and invited her 6-year-olds to write their own readers. They started by writing and stapling together books, in a variation on the writing workshop and publishing themes of Donald Graves

(1983), Lucy Calkins (1986), and Nancy Atwell (1987). The children in her class brought their play to the page – and with great energy, excitement, and much moving about the room to share and peek. I picked up my pen and began taking notes in a thoroughly Britton-esque fashion, discovering the similarities right down to the goats, one of which had figured in Alison's transcripts in *Language and Learning* (see pages 74–76). Only with the goats in Ruth's class, it was all about the chainsaw used to shear their horns at one child's farm. The children also wrote about fish, horses, peppermints, sharks, and bombs. Their writing was exhilarating, if often laced with troubling gender divisions that included the boy's celebration of violence. The students fully realized Britton's sense of 'the value of spontaneous inventiveness' at 'the point of utterance' (1980, p.147), which is an aspect that some have felt that the writing workshop routine can drain from student's expression.[5] Britton might have also noted that Ruth's class missed out on the transactional use of language, in using language to get things down. But, then, they had started a small publishing house with its own stable of well-portfolio-ed authors in a part of the world where that had never previously happened. Ruth's class amounted to its own distinctive chapter in what I characterized as the *new literacy*, forming a tribute to Dartmouth, if with lots of room remaining for the sort of refinement and continuity of the sort that Britton recommended for the schools.[6]

The next year, I took the publishing concept on the road with an added twist. As an itinerant teacher, I was able to take middle-school students, equipped with their own compositions, through a nine-day recapitulation of the history of publishing, from the ancient Homeric traditions of oral poetry, through the illuminated manuscript of the medieval period, into the age of printing, and onto the early days of computer typography. The students saw how each publishing 'technology' involved much working of the language that resulted in carrying words, stories, and learning across great distances and in enduring ways. The students published their own poetry, which was based on the thematic and (historical) genre modeling approach of poet Kenneth Koch's *Rose Where Did You Get That Red?* (1972). With all due respect to Auden, publishing was treated as a way to make things happen in school through acts of guerrilla theatre in hallways, libraries, teacher lunchrooms, and other students' classrooms.

Once I had taken up a position at the University at Calgary, I was able to pin down a further aspect of how language works in the classroom by studying how dictionaries are made. In the course of this work, I happened in the mid-1980s to stumble upon the initial digitizing of the *Oxford English Dictionary*. This allowed a precise determination of which authors and works were cited in making the *OED* the most authoritative of dictionaries, as it rightly advertises itself. Here were the manifold ways in which a standard is created and maintained for the English language on a global scale. In *The Empire of Words*, I set out how this dictionary is a wonder of immense, and what was originally amateur, scholarship, led by the schoolteacher James Murray. It offers a history of both the language and the sensibilities and prejudices of the times during which it has been and continues to be edited. With this research, I had the opportunity to pull back the curtain on the documentation and authorization of a standard (in the English-language absence of a language academy). The dictionary is a further aspect of that 'quite unsupported claim', as Britton puts it, 'that what teachers teach is 'the language' whereas what the children use is not!' (p.132). Following Britton, I was attempting to address 'the problems of this confusing situation' in which the setting of a standard in the language comes to have such weight. Examining the publishing history and processes behind such concepts seemed preferable to proposing, as Britton does with these problems, that 'a teacher must in the end face for himself the complexities of the present social situation' associated with language (p.135). Learning about how a dictionary is assembled does not begin to resolve the complexities; it could only hope to, and perhaps in an educational way, demystify one of the pillars on which they rest.

The study of the *OED*'s vast publishing enterprise, which was initially undertaken during the heyday of the British Empire, through the turn of the twentieth century, led me to take a further step away from Dartmouth, as I considered during the 1990s the educational legacy of imperialism in our schools. In the case of English education and literature teaching, this legacy found a certain voicing in Northrop Frye's concept of the *educated imagined*, just as he was among those cited at Dartmouth in the call for a stronger disciplinary focus for English (Harris, 1991). I brought this work together in *Learning to Divide the World*, which was concerned, in the case of English education, with the particular role of the language, learning, and literature in the formation of empire, whether in the creating of an 'educated' class in India, the banishment of indigenous languages, or in Frye's literary judgment, of what set primitive nations apart from civilized ones. The making of such distinctions was also getting something done with language. It amounted to an educational transaction that was to warrant a 'civilizing' claim on the world. This Arnoldian belief in literature having this civilizing effect on students' souls is something Britton resisted in his acceptance of every child's utterance. But as John Dixon noted in his revised version of *Growth through English*, 'critics of the Dartmouth Conference have rightfully criticized the deliberations for failing to relate the teaching of English to the sociopolitical contexts in which young people live today' (p.xi). I and others had come to believe that English teaching, and schooling in general, was a part of the sociopolitical context for young people, and that teaching about this context through such artifacts as the dictionary and such concepts as civilized versus primitive created places in the curriculum to 'work upon the world representation', as Britton has it (p.152).

The one part of this imperial legacy that my interest in publishing, as well as my work in the university, put me in a position to address was an unnecessary inequality in public and global access to research and scholarship. By the closing years of the twentieth century, it seemed clear, to me at least, that the internet could make the learning represented in scholarly work far more widely available to far more people. We had long been so earnest about teaching the young to read critically and wisely, only to see them now graduating into a digital era in which everything seemed permissible except the sharing of research and scholarship (beyond the walls of well-endowed university libraries). I wanted to see what could be done to make more of this publicly funded body of research as widely available to the public as Penguin paperbacks had struck us as being in the 1970s. The project was a take on Britton's principle that 'language is an instrument; we are responsible for what we do with it' (p.276) from the perspective of our own professional practices, as scholars responsible for who has access to our work. My hope is that through this new publishing medium this learning could play a greater part in what Britton calls the 'accumulated picture of the experienced world' (p.276). Yet the emerging state of online information also led me back to English education. What counts as 'a proper understanding of the manifold ways in which language works', when so much of it works within this digital medium through deception, deceit, and derision?

III

The first thing to note in addressing current challenges in educating the young for the digital era is that personal computers and networks also had their beginnings a half-century ago, and are not so geo-psychically removed from the Summer of Love, nor so pedagogically from Dartmouth's embrace of a greater freedom of expression for children: 'We Owe it all to the Hippies', Stewart Brand, editor of the *Whole Earth Catalog* and initiator of the Whole Earth 'Lectronic Link (WELL), an early virtual community, wrote in *Time* in 1995, 'the real legacy of the sixties generation is the computer revolution'. The machines were to be a means of free and authentic expression within open communities.[7] The hopes of those innocent days have been swept aside by the dystopian online world that many feel we face today, resulting in more than a decade of polemical critique, from Andrew Keen's *The Cult of the Amateur: How Today's Internet is Killing Our Culture* in 2007 to Franklin Foer's *World Without Mind: the Existential Threat of Big Tech* in 2017. There's no question that the web is a wide world of post-fact, fake news, of click bait and sock-puppets, of spear phishing and astroturfing (grassroots manipulation strategies). Nicholas Carr's complaint in *The Shallows: What the Internet is Doing to Our Brain* picks up the key metaphor that Britton uses in critiquing the inauthenticity of learning in the schools: 'We have rejected the intellectual tradition of solitary, single-minded concentration, the ethic of what the book bestowed on us. We have cast our lot in with the juggler' (p.114).

In the title of his 2016 NCTE Presidential Address, Douglas Hesse asks 'what arts of language matter now' (2017). He speaks for many educators in giving voice to web-centric concerns over the censorship and suppression of information, and the disconnection of language from reality. The apprehensions are rooted in both the immediate politics of the current Trump presidency, and in the extent to which such demagoguery has been aided and abetted by certain elements that have taken hold of this virtual public space, whether the hoaxes, hacks, bots, and other information pretenses; or the algorithms, machine learning, and other data machinations.[8]

Of course, another side to the internet exists that speaks to its educational potential, if still marked by threats. Henry Jenkins, for example, has studied how the young have found multifaceted expressive and productive digital opportunities, which he identifies as an emerging 'participatory culture' (2009). Jenkins emphasizes how digital and networked technologies afford 'relatively low barriers to artistic expression and civic engagement, strong support for creating and sharing one's creations, and some type of informal mentorship whereby what is known by the most experienced is passed along to novices' (p.xi). Jenkins' sense of participatory culture is notable for how it cuts neatly across Britton's distinction between the spectator and participant roles in language. Jenkins is no less conscious of the challenges in educational contexts, which he characterizes as a three-fold gap, made up of a participation gap, in which not everyone has equal access to the internet; a transparency gap in which how the media shape perception is not made clear to its users; and an ethical gap concerned with standards of behavior and practice.

In light of Hesse's timely question about what arts of language matter and Jenkin's concerns, particularly around transparency and ethics, I want to conclude this retrospective with the current work that I am doing with my Stanford colleague Sam Wineburg, a professor of history education, on developing and teaching a course on the future of information. Our aim is to ensure that students do not go gentle into that good night (of reliable information); our hope is to refine the course for inclusion in teacher education programs with an eye to introducing its approach into high school classrooms as one part of a students' education in language. Although Sam and I differ in our thinking about this future, we believe our views complement each other.

Sam's approach is informed by his recent research on student's online information skills, which he has conducted with members of the Stanford History Education Group. The study involves some 7,800 students from middle school to college (as well as a number of professional historians) and has established that the vast majority of students are not readily able to determine the reliability of information from a given website: 'Spend five minutes exploring any issue – from private prisons to a tax on sugary drinks – and you'll find sites that mask their agendas alongside those that are forthcoming. We should devote our time to helping students evaluate such sites' (McGrew, Ortega, Breakstone, and Wineburg, 2017). As for what is at stake: 'If students cannot determine what is trustworthy – if they take all information at face value without considering where it comes from – democratic decision-making is imperiled'.

Again, the focus here is on how language, within a very particular domain of experience, is being actively and consciously worked for and against certain people's interests. Among Sam's illuminating examples is the minimumwage.com website, surely of relevance to high school students. It has all the trappings of authority, from a polished website to citing the *New York Times* to being sponsored by a non-profit with a .org URL. In the course of Sam's study, only six percent of college students and nine percent of high schoolers were able to determine that the website was operated by a public relations firm representing the restaurant industry.

What is at issue for Sam is the educational need to develop a level of 'civic online reasoning' by which to navigate, deliberate, and act as an informed global citizen. It involves three essential steps: '(1) identifying who's behind the information presented, (2) evaluating the evidence presented, and (3) investigating what other sources say'. Where in the past, Sam has turned to historians to learn how to help history students think like a historian, the strategies he turns to in establishing trust with online sources is the fact-checker 'at some of the nation's most prestigious news and fact-checking organizations'. What these fact checkers taught my colleague, and what we are now working on ways of teaching students, has three components to it. The first step is to be prepared to read laterally, which is to turn to other sites to read *about* the site and information in question and in that way to learn about the trustworthiness of the people and organizations behind the site.[9] A second helpful practice that Sam learned from fact-checkers is to be more discerning in handling the results of a Google or any other search engine. Rather than going with the top result or two, it is better to scan the results to get a feel for the coverage of the topic, while drawing some clues from URLs that have come up. A third recommendation is to teach students how to use Wikipedia not only for its coverage of a given topic, but to be able to turn to the references behind the information presented and to visit the Talk page for the entry, with the discussion there potentially providing further insight into reliability of information, sources, and organizations.

My approach to the future of information and this course, on the other hand, arises out of my work on improving access to research and scholarship. In Adam Gopnik's analysis of 'how the internet gets inside us', I represent something of the 'Never-Better' stance that he identifies, compared to the 'Better-Never' position (2011). That is, for me, things can seem at times to be *never better*, given what the internet can do for access to knowledge.[10] Students are able, after all, to discover and trace the flow of ideas in ways that simply were not available in high schools and many colleges previously. They have access to the look and sound of the arts on a global scale; to the controversies, then and now, over the works they're reading; to the historical background and contexts of most everything they encounter; to instructional materials on any skill or technique they wish to acquire; and to opportunities to have questions answered and to weigh in on what matters. Now, of course, all of that requires an educator's curation and caution in the face of an unsettled and unsettling world at the point of utterance, but there is little need for students to be left in the shallows.

To offer a few brief examples from this course, it includes some of the finer aspects of the specialized but publicly available search engines that will open the world of research to them, not only to add to their own understanding but that they be of better service to friends and family. For biomedical research, PubMed offers amazingly fine-grained filters, from the age of participants in a study to whether the complete study is publicly available. More generally, Google Scholar also identifies what's free to read among research and scholarship, as well as providing the means for novices to identify the high impact studies, as well as the connections among studies and ideas. As citizens of this new state of information, students are also brought up to date on gains in public access rights to research, which will prove comparable the public gain in knowledge that resulted from Gutenberg's invention, the public library movement, and the introduction of Penguins.

Students also delve into the information economy, to further facilitate their participation as consumers and producers. They consider how the subscription services, targeted advertising, and the selling of data, including information about themselves as information consumers, is affecting the quality of information. They learn about their rights as citizens to government, court, and other materials. They learn about the part played by intellectual property law in balancing the rights of creators and the public. This involves efforts to extend and facilitate the sharing of such property through the Creative Commons licensing program that operates on an international scale, as well as patent struggles over access to generic drugs in the Global South. Copyright and patents invests the use of language (and production of information) with a legal and economic status. As such, they as no less a part of how language works. Students' civic online reasoning, as much as the access to reliable sources of knowledge, will be a determining influence, we believe, on more than the future of information for generations to come.

In the half-century since Dartmouth, my own growth through English education has followed a course from the development of students' voices to something larger, civic and public, which has retained its inspiration from the stand that Britton and other Dartmouth-ians took. Britton concludes *Language and Learning* with a brief postscript entitled 'No End'. He has added it, in part, he explains, 'to place the central concerns of this book in a wider context' and language's 'place in a structure larger than itself' (p.275). It encourages me to consider how, in the intervening years, I and others have been seeking ways of contributing to that expansion of context and structure in language and learning, which, as Britton suggests, will have no end, whether with his generation, or my generation, or all of the generations – and all of the generation – to follow.

Notes

1 The original organizational 96-page program for the event lists three Canadians other than Merron as Consultants and Observers (*Anglo-American seminar on the teaching and learning of English agenda*, NCTE, September 1966). Certainly, Merron had been an organizing force for the Canadian Council of Teachers of English in 1966 and the International Steering Committee in 1971, which was to lead to the formation of the IFTE.

2 A US edition was published by the University of Miami Press 1970, with a second edition by Heinemann in 1993.

3 The challenging spirit of Freire's work, at least, has been sustained in education by those working in the area known as *critical pedagogy*, which also had a publishing presence, perhaps most notably in the Counterpoints book series by Peter Lang, edited by Shirley Steinberg and the late Joe Kincheloe, which grew to over 500 titles (and in which I published a book of essays on literacy) through the 1990s and into this decade.

4 Similarly, the child is also getting something done in the world in the course of a monologue, so common in (spectator) play, which, according to Britton's lucid account of Vygotsky, is an 'assisting activity, organizing a child's experience' (p. 59).

5 Myra Barr holds up the example of Britton's appreciation of the expressive utterance in critiquing Graves and company's belabored and potentially formulaic approach to revision and the bringing of 'journalistic' writing strategies to children (1983).

6 The influence of *Language and Learning* on my *The New Literacy* extended to a bibliographic overlap of Coleridge, Wordsworth, and Dickens, while its Dartmouth line-up encompassed Barnes, Bernstein, Britton, Dixon, Holbrook, Moffett, Ong, and Rosen.

7 In *Counterculture to Cyberculture*, Fred Turner notes how 'the new computers – particularly the 1984 Apple Macintosh – were explicitly marketed as devices one could use to tear down bureaucracies and achieve individual intellectual freedom' (2006, 103). Fred Harris observes, quoting Britton et al.'s *Development of Writing Abilities (11–18)*, that 'a similarly romantic view of the child as a 'free learner' was implied in Britton's view of intimate and expressive speech-talk that is 'as free as possible from outside demands, whether those of a task or an audience' – as a key source of most real learning' (1991, 642).

8 I would also note Hesse includes a perfectly Britton-esque critique of such common core objectives as 'write arguments to support claims in an analysis of substantive topics or texts, using valid reasoning and relevant and sufficient evidence' (CCSS.ELA-LITERACY.W.11–12.1). Hesse notes that elide writing grounded in experience and discovery, writing that renders the world to reflect and make sense, delight and console' (2017, p. 364).

9 While none of this is necessary in picking up a Penguin or Pelican paperback, I do recall that while teaching in a small town, my choice of titles was often a matter of holiday trips to the city.

10 My *never better* is opposed, by Gopnik, with those who treat the internet as it would be *better* if it had *never* existed, as reflected, for example, in Nicholas Carr's certainty that 'the depth of our thought is tied directly to the intensity of our attentiveness, [and thus] it's hard not to conclude that as we adapt to the intellectual environment of the Net our thinking becomes shallower' (cited by Gopnik, 2011).

References

Applebee, A. N. (1974). *The child's concept of story: ages two to seventeen*. Chicago, IL: University of Chicago Press.

Atwell, N. (1987). *In the middle: writing, reading, and learning with adolescents*. Upper Montclair, NJ: Boynton/Cook Publishers.

Barrs, M. (1983). 'The New orthodoxy about writing: confusing process and pedagogy'. *Language Arts*, 60(7), 829–840.

Brand, S. (1995). 'We owe it all to the hippies'. *Time*, (145)12.

Britton, J. (1970). *Language and learning*. London: Penguin.

Britton, J. (1980). 'Shaping at the point of utterance', in A. Freedman and I. Pringle (eds.), *Reinventing the rhetorical tradition*. Conway, AR: L&S Books: 61–65

Calkins, L. M. (1986). *The art of teaching writing*. Portsmouth, NH: Heinemann.

Carr, N. (2010). *The shallows: what the Internet is doing to our brain*. New York: Norton.

Dixon, J. (1967). *Growth through English: set in the perspective of the Seventies*. Oxford: Oxford University Press.

Gopnik, A. (2011). 'The Information: how the internet gets inside us', *New Yorker* Feb. 14 and 21. Retrieved from www.newyorker.com/magazine/2011/02/14/the-information.

Graves, D. (1983). *Writing: teachers and children at work* (1st ed.). Portsmouth, NH: Heinemann.

Harris, J. (1991). 'After Dartmouth: growth and conflict in English', *College English* 53(6), 631–646.

Hesse, D. (2017). 'The 2016 NCTE presidential address: what arts of language matter now?' *Research in the Teaching of English*, 51(3), 361–379.

Jenkins, H. (with Katie Clinton, Ravi Purushotma, Alice J. Robison, and Margaret Weigel). (2009). *Confronting the challenges of participatory culture: media education for the 21st century*. Cambridge, MA: MIT Press.

Koch, K. (1972). *Rose where did you get that red? Teaching great poetry to children*. New York: Vintage.

McGrew, S., Ortega, T., Breakstone, J., & Wineburg, S. (2017, Fall). 'The Challenge that's bigger than fake news: teaching students to engage in civic online reasoning', *American Educator*, 4–9.

Turner, F. (2006). *From counterculture to cyberculture: Stewart Brand, the Whole Earth Network, and the rise of digital utopianism*. Chicago, IL: University of Chicago Press.

Watson, K. (n.d.). *A Brief history of IFTE – 1966 to 1992*, International Federation for the Teaching of English, Available from https://ncte.connectedcommunity.org/ifte/history.

7

THE MANY VOICES OF DARTMOUTH

John Hodgson and Ann Harris

Introduction

The month-long seminar of English teachers from the US, UK and Canada held in Dartmouth, New Hampshire in the summer of 1966 was a notable event in the history of the teaching of English. Fifty years later, the concept of 'growth through English', enshrined in the title of John Dixon's report on the seminar, remains significant to the identity of the profession in the UK and abroad (Goodwyn, 2012). Yet the contributions of fifty delegates have been mediated to successive generations mainly through the reports written by John Dixon from the UK and Herbert J. Muller from the US. As several commentators (e.g. Daiches, 1968; Brass, 2016) have indicated, these differ widely in their approach and emphases. Dixon (1967, p.xi) acknowledges in the preface to the first edition of *Growth through English* that his report is inevitably partial: 'a simpler view from a single vantage point'. Muller explains in his introduction to *The Uses of English* (1967, p.vi) that, while he aimed to do justice to the different opinions expressed, he has 'not tried to write a wholly impersonal report'. Reflecting at the distance of a half-century on the seminar, it is natural to wonder about the provenance of these reports, and the process by which the many voices of Dartmouth were represented. What other views of Dartmouth are conceivable?

We offer here a view informed by recently available access to the two volumes of unpublished seminar papers and associated Dartmouth documents (listed in the reference section), and John Dixon's recent reflection upon the seminar and its impact (Dixon, 2017). As British teachers and researchers, members of a professional community shaped in part by *Growth through English*, we focus our attention primarily on Dixon's account rather than on Muller's; but we have tried to bring out the interplay of voices (some not present at the seminar) that produced the historical moment of Dartmouth. We begin our analysis with a brief account of the political context in the US and UK, and conclude with an assessment of the significance of Dartmouth in contemporary English education.

1966 and all that

As is well known, US government initial support for the Dartmouth seminar derived in part from the Soviet Union's apparent lead in the space race (Yuri Gagarin had orbited the Earth in 1961), which raised concerns that the West was failing to educate the coming generation. The British government, in turn, was arguably more concerned with the education of the young people whom the Newsom Report (1963) had termed 'half our future'. They comprised the greater part of the school population that (having failed the eleven-plus examination for entry to selective grammar schools) left school at fifteen without any qualification. The US government response with respect to similar concerns had been to bus socially deprived, often African-American, students across towns and cities to more affluent areas where there was ostensibly better schooling. In the UK, the Labour government required in 1965 all local educational authorities to submit proposals to end selection at eleven and to build new neighbourhood 'comprehensive' schools.

This democratic impulse was shared at Dartmouth. The record of group discussions on 'grouping' or 'streaming' students according to their perceived ability states that members of the seminar felt 'repelled' by the practice:

> [W]e are demanding a better education all round in which human beings are treated as human beings; everyone concerned with the teaching of English can help to encourage within a democracy the pursuit of excellence.
>
> *(F1, group discussion, p.15)*

While social, economic and educational segregation and deprivation existed (then as now) in many parts of the US, and had ignited the Watts riots in Los Angeles in 1965, the US government proposed no national reform of education. The UK government, on the other hand, was newly committed to provide education on an equal basis not only for 'more academic' grammar school pupils but also for those who had previously, in Holbrook's (1964, p.3) words, been 'rejected' as 'unacademic [and] unexaminable'. In 1971, the UK school leaving age was raised to sixteen for all pupils. Writing out of their personal, social and professional histories, the authors of the two reports on Dartmouth reflected contemporary concerns within these differing national contexts.

John Dixon's *Growth through English*

John Dixon's report on Dartmouth, *Growth through English* (1967), has to be understood in the light of the experience that led him to a radically democratic

Freirian (Freire, 1978) view of the purpose and mission of the English teacher. Before Dartmouth, John Dixon had taught in British schools and colleges for several years. His work at a boys' grammar school in Holloway, London, where he joined a Labour teachers' discussion group, convinced him that the comprehensive school would need 'some kind of syllabus that would work for everyone' (Dixon, 2017, p.241). In 1956, he became involved with the London Association for the Teaching of English, whose founding secretary, Guy Rogers, was Head Teacher of Walworth Comprehensive School; Dixon later joined Walworth as Head of English. There he co-wrote *Reflections*, his first classroom text, with his colleagues Simon Clements and Leslie Stratta. The title, Dixon reports, was Stratta's:

> a very good title because it was reflectiveness that Leslie kept emphasising we wanted to induct the students into, at the age of fourteen or so, to become more reflective about the experience of their social environment and lives.
>
> *(Dixon, 2017, p.245)*

Reflections (1963) and the later *Things Being Various* (1967) were not traditional classroom English texts to be worked through. The *Teacher's Book* (1967) accompanying *Things Being Various* explains:

> This is not a course book. It is a collection of experiences, and therefore there is no specific order in which to look. . . The book can provide a sort of joint explanation for the group and their teacher. . . A teacher's insight into connections will help him to suggest related material both inside the book and outside; he will judge at what point (in a discussion, a hand-back of writing. . .) to move from one extract or paragraph to a complementary or opposing passage.
>
> *(p.7)*

In whole-class discussion of topics relevant to pupils, teachers use their wider textual and experiential knowledge to encourage dialectic ('a complementary or opposing passage'). Dixon had taken from Connie and Harold Rosen 'the idea that you should talk about, you know, everyday events in their lives as a start' (Dixon, 2017, p.241) but the classroom conversation implied in *Reflections* and *Things Being Various* was not merely anecdotal. In a talk to the London Association for the Teaching of English, Simon Clements (1965) defined the aim of *Reflections* in terms of a creating a common culture, a 'sensibility which will be useful in living':

> The establishment of values is done by the children themselves in the process of *doing* and looking and reading and talking. Thus the group defines its values by talk.
>
> *(Clements, 1965)*

Clements went on to suggest the radical purpose of such discussion:

> If the kind of talk and work that goes on in a class re-defines the cultural posi-
> tion, it also re-defines the relationships within the school, and the structures
> operating within the school. This is what is happening in comprehensive
> schools and why they are confused and confusing places at present.
>
> *(Clements, 1965)*

Given his experience and vision of teaching English, it is hardly surprising that
Dixon chose to highlight 'growth' in the title of his report rather than 'skills' or
'cultural heritage', although all three models of the subject had, he states, been
widely accepted in schools on both sides of the Atlantic. This is not to suggest, as
does Harris (1991, p.631) that Dixon's account of the seminar was 'highly skewed'.
The view that language is best learned 'in operation' seems to have been generally
accepted at Dartmouth, and Dixon felt that he 'couldn't say a word' about his own
practice in teaching 'a very important ancillary side' of spelling patterns: 'nobody
had anything like that kind of story to tell' (Dixon 2017, p.247).

In the first chapter of *Growth through English*, Dixon gives an example from a
10-year old boy's diary in which, he suggests, the writer wants to make his experience real again to a sympathetic listener. As he does so, the boy's experience takes
on a meaning that he treasures. Dixon comments that this personal, tentative,
affective language should be valued in classrooms, which should be places where
pupils 'want to talk and write from impulses such as these' (Dixon, 1967, pp. 4–6).

It is hard, especially from our current perspective, to take in the radical nature of
what Dixon is proposing here. His classroom today seems a utopian space where hon-
est reflection and expression are possible. The teacher, he says (p.7), must be 'more
alert and sensitive to average pupils – more concerned with what they have to say, if
only they can realise it'. Dixon insists that he is not proposing a simple formula of 'self-
expression'. In an English classroom as he envisages it, pupils and teacher combine to
recognise all that is challenging, new, uncertain and even painful in experience. This is
evidently a very different model from that of 'skills' or 'cultural heritage', which both
imply a transmission of knowledge from teacher to pupil (p.12).

Growth through English elaborates the principles that inform the learning activities of an English classroom. Teachers need to help children discover their own
meaning through talk and writing, and to include children's stories and poems in
the literature of the classroom. Even evaluative writing about literature should be
tentative and leave room for connections with personal experience. The study of
language similarly involves the affective as well as the cognitive. Pupils should be
freed of disabling misconceptions about the 'correctness' of dialect forms, and can
learn from both linguistic and literary disciplines ways of organising their experience in the act of reading, speaking and writing. Progression in English will live in
new forms of organising experience and in additional refinement or complexity.

In line with the discovery mode of classroom discourse that his book generally advocates, Dixon reports that the Dartmouth seminar advocated a unitary

rather than fragmented approach to the English activities of drama, talk, reading and writing.

> The more active a part pupils are given, the more difficult to predict all they will find and uncover; thus the need for a flexible teaching strategy rather than rigid lesson plans, and for teachers confidently able to move with a class for instance from reading [Gorki's] *My Childhood* to discussing old people they know or acting encounters of youth and age.
>
> *(Dixon, 1967, p.33)*

What unifies these classroom activities is the theme of human experience on which drama, talk, reading and writing centre. Teachers organise activities in the hope of effecting insight into experience. In his 2017 interview, Dixon makes clear that this 'experience' can be mediated in various forms:

> If you're interested in the kind of English that (say) *Reflections* represented, and in working class development through English (and more than working class development). . . then it was inevitable that you get into the fringes of Sociology, Psychology, Anthropology. In other words, other human stories told in different ways.
>
> *(Dixon, 2017, p.250)*

This emphasis on experience clearly privileges the content of written or spoken communication rather than its form. There is no specific suggestion in *Reflections* or *Growth through English* that work should include analysis of such features as genre, literary form, medium or mode. Even the mass media, according to Clements (1965), should be approached 'as we approach literature – in a spirit of exploration'.

Herbert Muller's *The Uses of English*

The author of the US report on Dartmouth, Herbert J. Muller, taught English at Cornell and Purdue Universities, and in 1959 was named Distinguished Professor of English and Government at Indiana University. His career, like Dixon's, attests to a spirit of broad intellectual inquiry (Carter et al., 1980). He published a number of interdisciplinary works, and was one of the signatories to the *Humanist Manifesto II* (AHA, 1973). As David Daiches (1968, p.219) has noted, Muller's title *The Uses of English* implies a rather more utilitarian view of the subject than Dixon's *Growth through English* – although Muller's subheadings, variously, *A blueprint for a new direction in the teaching of English in the Anglo-American countries* and *Guidelines for the teaching of English from the Anglo-American conference at Dartmouth College*, suggest he did have aspiration for the ideas included within the report. Muller, however, unlike Dixon, did not seek a synthesis in his version of events but rather chose to highlight the range and variety of perspectives, including his own:

> I should emphasize all these issues are highly debatable (a gentle way of say-
> ing controversial – a word frightening to some Americans) and that I am not
> in fact uncommitted or free from bias. Naturally I have tried to do justice
> to the different opinions expressed, but I have not tried to write a wholly
> impersonal report.
>
> *(Muller, 1967, p.vi)*

This was at least in part because:

> [T]he disagreements grew out of the complexity of the problems besetting
> the profession. This report might be justified if it gives readers nothing but a
> fuller awareness of the complexities.
>
> *(Muller, 1967, p.9)*

Reflecting on 'what is English?', Muller viewed the subject as being in a 'state
of hopeless confusion' and referred to English teaching as being 'not a profession but a predicament' (p.4). He acknowledged that some of the disagreements
in Dartmouth stemmed from the differences between the American and British
'educational systems, traditions and problems' (p.11). Nonetheless, his book represents the seminar discussions under themes that concerned Dartmouth more
broadly. Like Dixon, he discusses democracy in the classroom; the development and growth of the child; 'good' English; writing, talking and other issues.
Overall, Muller's book supports Dixon's consensus on key issues, most notably
the agreement that literature in the classroom should include television and children's writing. His conclusions, although acknowledging 'confusion' (p.171) to
the 'bitter end', were more positive than might have been inferred from the
initial discussion. As he noted in the final chapter: 'Fluidity is after all a healthier
state than stagnation' (p.171) – although he could not resist observing that the
seminar was: 'not bolstered by optimism over the prospects of its recommendations being acted on promptly and decisively' (p.172). 'External factors' had
'haunted' every discussion, and Muller admitted that 'the System and behind it
Society' undermined some of the ambient utopian zeal (p.172). In Muller's view,
the British were somewhat naive in their aspirations for a growth and workshop
subject; the American experience had suggested that the acquisition of skills,
knowledge and understanding would remain paramount; yet:

> the British were saying what most needs to be said in our technocratic soci-
> ety. They were defending the all-important human values that are being
> neglected in the interests of economy and efficiency.
>
> *(Muller, 1967, p.176)*

His final comment, however, reinforced his pragmatism in an all too utilitarian
way:

English as the seminar proposed it to be taught would be more liberal and humane than English as it is taught in most schools, but it would also be riskier, possibly unsettling, certainly less likely to turn out students well-adjusted to a highly commercialised society devoted to efficiency and affluence. Readers might ask themselves: are they willing as taxpayers willing to foot the bills for better English teaching of English? Do they as parents really want their children to become developed individuals with minds of their own?

(Muller, 1967, p.187)

While many of us might give a resounding yes to the final question, Muller's view of the role of education in a 'highly commercialized society' has a depressing resonance today.

The many voices of Dartmouth

As we suggest in the Introduction to this chapter, Dixon and Muller's very different reports cannot fully represent the many voices of Dartmouth. In this section, we explore the unpublished conference materials and consider several of the Working Papers and accounts of delegate discussions, relating these where possible to the published reports discussed above.

At Dartmouth, the different working groups addressed what were perceived as key concerns in English teaching at the time. Working Party 1 started with the fundamental question: 'What is English?', which in itself provided a range of responses and opportunities for discussion and contention. Albert Kitzhaber in his initial address positioned the subject as 'central in education' (WP1, p.1) and yet in a 'chaotic' state of 'confusion and a lack of identity' (WP1, p.4). While choosing not to suggest answers himself, 'since it is not my responsibility to do so but that of the seminar as a whole' (WP1, p.9), he established a challenging agenda. Douglas Barnes responded to this by celebrating the multifaceted and diverse nature of English, and acknowledging that 'The discussion papers imply conceptual frameworks each of which supplies a completely different answer to this question' (A1, p.1). James Britton in his response was even more forceful: 'I can see no possibility of defining English, or, if that is putting it too strongly, I can see no useful way of defining it without considering its place in the total structure' (A1, p.2). The question, Britton declared, 'assumes that English is something, and it makes the very large assumption that if we find out what it is, it follows that this is what the English teacher should be teaching'. Britton suggested strongly that delegates should rephrase the question, 'and not say "What is English?" but, more simply, "What ought English teachers to be doing?"' (A1, pp.5–6). The seminar had been divided into multinational groups addressing each of the key topics; each, however, came back to 'What is English?', although the group assigned to this pondered its validity as a topic.

Addressing the question: 'What is continuity in English teaching?' (WP2, pp.1–27), Frank Whitehead argued that it was not possible to derive a rational sequence for the teaching of English, as there is no agreement as to the nature of its internal structure and the emphasis would be on knowledge as opposed to use. In view of the largely unconscious nature of linguistic development, the evidence points to a flexible teaching strategy in which the teacher's wider perspectives nudge pupils along the directions in which they are already moving. The growing child will adapt their vocabulary, accent, syntax and style to different audiences and contacts, and learn to vary the mode or register of their writing. As the young person turns to literature appropriate to their stage of development, the teacher will draw on a sound sense of literary values, and help the pupil to develop contextual knowledge about the author and the time in which they wrote.

It is evident from the seminar papers, which contain not only Whitehead's paper but also an eighteen-page record of discussion (B3), that Whitehead's contribution was a significant element in the seminar proceedings. Its rejection of an anthropological approach to literary themes and forms would have appealed to the thirteen representatives of 'Cambridge English' (Gibbons, 2017, p.20), while its approach to nurturing children's natural development in language use, contextual awareness and reading maturity will have appealed to the professional experience of most, if not all, of the delegates. It is, we think, equally easy to see why Dixon chose not to foreground Whitehead's developmental sequence in his presentation of growth through English. It comes from a different world of discourse than Dixon's democratic classroom.

As Whitehead's discussant, Berenice Christenson drew attention to the importance of 'an interdisciplinary approach to teaching of English, combining knowledge of the human growth and development with an understanding of the use of the English language' (PS 2, pp.3–4). In discussion, John Dixon asked provocatively 'Was it common ground within the group that we were not concerned with a line or model?' (B3, p.4), but delegates moved on to debate a presentation by James Moffett:

> The emphasis, in the search for continuity, should be placed on the discourse of the student – on the progression in his modes of depicting and organizing experience.
>
> *(Moffett, E2, p.1)*

Ways of thinking and modes of discourse interact, Moffett argued, in the child's verbal development:

> The various narratives. . . (and the term is meant to include all the chronological genres, plays and narrative poems as well as myths, tales, fables, etc.) may offer a continuum of cognitive and verbal growth.
>
> *(Moffett, E2)*

Moffett's ideas on continuity do not seem (from the papers) to have provoked as much discussion as Whitehead's, but they were prescient, as will be indicated in the final section of this chapter.

Working Paper 3, 'English: one road or many?', by Wallace Douglas, elicited much debate around streaming and segregation; it reached what Muller calls a 'startling consensus' by 'unanimously condemn(ing) the practice' (Muller, 1967, p.27). This was surprising because then (as now) streaming is a polemical topic. Muller himself was not, however, won over, stating in *Uses*: 'It seems to me clearly undesirable to do away with all groupings under present conditions' (Muller, 1967, p.33). The key phrase here, however, is 'under present conditions', and both the British and the North Americans advocated better environmental and working conditions that would allow greater flexibility in pedagogy and practice. It wasn't so much 'one road or many' as 'one way and many' (Muller, 1967, p.33). Harold Rosen was later to highlight what was happening at Dartmouth when he asserted: 'Dialogue inside grows out of dialogue with others. This is how society penetrates our thinking' (Dixon, 1967, p.14).

Denys Thompson's Working Paper 4 introduced discussion of the nature of knowledge and proficiency in English by arguing that external pressures in both the US and the UK produced similar effects: 'a distortion of the curriculum, a pseudo-content, a fragmentation of a unified subject into separate skills'. In the best UK primary schools, Thompson declared, doubtless with the anticipated findings of the Plowden Report (1967) in mind: 'English is not separately taught as a subject; it is an activity which pervades the lives of children in and out of school; it is inseparable from their own experiences and social relationships'. Knowledge and proficiency in English develop pupils' capacity in the various language modes through a rich experience of talk, reading and writing; they are not developed the discrete testing of language 'skills', which Thompson blamed for the current situation:

> (Examinations) exert an extremely powerful influence in determining the English curriculum of many schools, and they kill much of the joy that can be had in learning and teaching.
>
> *(WP4, p.3)*

In his paper on creativity in the English classroom, David Holbrook offered a response to mechanical teaching and testing. Reiterating his colleagues, he emphasised the value of experience and its place in English and in writing:

> What we are concerned with in English, essentially, is literacy in its deepest and widest sense – the capacity to use words to deal with inner and outer experience.
>
> *(SGP3, p.2)*

In Holbrook's approach, creativity often seemed identified with personal writing, a view supported by Miriam Wilt in her paper on how children learn English:

> Children will find many ways to tell their stories. . . Let him tell where he is in this mainstream of life and learning. Listen to the songs he sings. . .
>
> *(SGP4, p.7)*

Much of the discussion around creativity fed into what Dixon was able to explore in *Growth through English*, a society in which not only children's voices were valued but where every voice could be heard. Holbrook had seen creativity in this radical and unsettling way:

> One last important point: since creativity is an uncertain and often disturbing activity, it can only be done in a school in which there is courageous and liberal minded approval of its value and worth. . . . Is our society yet capable of tolerating the open sympathy creativity demands?
>
> *(SGP3, p.16)*

For Muller, however, this account of creativity was problematic. While recognising that Holbrook claimed a rarefied notion of 'creative living', Muller feared that, in the hands of 'ordinary teachers', creative writing would become 'another assignment that may oppress youngsters, especially the diffident ones' (Muller, 1967, p.117).

Working Paper 5, 'Standards and Attitudes', by Albert Marckhardt, was a reflective account of the value of linguistics to the English teacher. Marckhardt declared that a grounding in linguistics should demonstrate 'that the concept of original sin, linguistically speaking, is untenable; children are not born with an innate tendency towards multiple negation or the lack of agreement between subject and verb'. It should also, Marckhardt suggested, encourage the teacher to find a way of teaching the standard forms 'without stigmatising those which represent the folk speech of the community' (WP5, p.25). Discussion of Marckhardt's paper and those appended to it showed a balanced apprehension amongst the participants of the largely unconscious and cultural processes of language learning and of the teacher's need to intervene in a way that supports the pupil's growth. Miriam Wilt suggested:

> One of the most intimate possessions of a person is his dialect. . . The identification of the child with his community and his relationship to it must be protected.
>
> *(SGP4, p.5)*

In the secondary school, she argued, the explicit study of language becomes urgent; but the only important aspect that concerns us is: 'Does the study of language help us to use it more effectively?' As Wilt herself admitted, there was room at the seminar for some difference of opinion on this. She clarified the question by suggesting that language study should make explicit what is already in operational use or subject to direct observation (S1, p.5). Discussion tended to accept this definition but to doubt the use or efficacy of current practice in teaching English language, which, according to Harold Rosen, suggested that 'language is a matter of yes–no questions, and not a matter of more–less, partly–partly, questions' (S2, p.2) James Britton addressed this by recognising the value of creative and imaginative experiential writing:

Whenever a student writes successfully he shapes the experience and he also gets a bit better at doing so next time. . . He has shaped experience – entered into and altered and shaped experience – and also improved his skill, his ability to read difficult passages. Now we have consistently given our attention to the second of these and ignored the first.

(A1, p.9)

Dixon picked up this point when he wrote in *Growth through English* (1967, p.11) that the majority of the seminar valued the kind of language knowledge that helped pupils perceive themselves as the organisers of their experience.

After Dartmouth

When John Dixon came to write the concluding chapter of the second edition of *Growth through English*, 'In the perspective of the seventies' (1975), the political and social tensions of the preceding 9 years inflected his account. After the student rebellions of the late sixties, the power relationships of the classroom and institutions needed to be addressed. Learners may be 'born free but [they] are everywhere in chains', he wrote, and 'the social models built into us consistently pressurise and distort' the attempts to create productive relationships (Dixon, 1975, p.111–112). If the social relationships of the classroom then appeared increasingly problematic, language also appeared less of a transparent window on experience. Dixon asked at this late stage (p.113) what he termed an elementary question: what processes of selection and organisation are going on, and what constraints are inevitably imposed, when we try to get experience into words?

In response to this question, Dixon returned to James Moffett's contribution to Dartmouth and extended the account of this given in the first edition of *Growth through English*. Moffett's later *Teaching the Universe of Discourse* (1968) elaborates ideas about the social origins of language and thought (reminiscent of Bakhtin [1981]) that may have offered Dixon a bridge between his sense of the primacy of individual pupil experience and realisation that 'development is always within social structures and that you've got to look at the interaction between the two' (Dixon, 2017, p.251):

> If schools wish to influence how students think and speak, they must take account of all the language contexts which have determined how the individual already thinks and speaks, then create a new language community that will induce what is missing.
>
> *(Moffett, 1968, p.69)*

Dixon was also attracted by Moffett's theory of the various levels of abstraction in which experience is handled (Dixon, 1975, p.114). In the final chapter of the 1975 edition of *Growth through English*, Dixon described a progression in pupils' thinking and writing from 'living through' to 'written with hindsight', and declared that

English is 'centrally concerned with the elementary levels of abstracting from experience, with enacting and narrating'. The need to grapple with experience in these ways was, he wrote, 'not simply child's play, but a challenge for life' (Dixon, 1975, p.117). Moffett's ideas influenced the London Institute of Education's thinking about writing in the following decade (Britton et al., 1975), and his holistic view of the relation of English to the curriculum – the intuition that in a sense English *was* the whole curriculum – was taken up by writers such as Peter Medway (see, for example, Medway, 2005) who have developed the philosophy of English teaching in the years since Dartmouth.

Dartmouth was prescient in many ways. The participants shared much common ground in their debates on the language of the child, the concepts of continuity and creativity, the place of linguistics in the curriculum, and the significance of technology in the development of the subject (which we have not had space to outline here). They all wished to ensure that English teaching and learning would produce expressive and democratic individuals. Many of the voices even admitted the importance of examinations and the enduring desire of stakeholders, government, employers and parents for an educational environment that produced young people capable of 'accurate' English. What those voices at Dartmouth could not have imagined was the political and economic circumstances that would drive the educational agenda into the twenty-first century. In *Growth through English*, John Dixon created a blueprint for the English teaching of the 1970s, but there was an inevitable backlash. Dixon has shared his own reflections on time passing (Dixon, 2017) and has acknowledged some elements of the first edition of *Growth through English* that have been especially tested by time. In darker moments, we may well think that Muller's questioning at the end of *The Uses of English* whether this new radical 'workshop' English was suited to 'a highly commercialised society devoted to efficiency and affluence' (Muller, 1967, p.187) was prophetic of the neo-liberal agenda which currently dominates the 'results-based' educational systems of both the US and the UK. However that may be, Dixon's *Growth through English* articulated a genuine synthesis of the Dartmouth debates that remains an inspiration to those many teachers who still believe in a practice of English teaching that aims to develop children's language for personal growth and democratic progress.

References

AHA (1973). *Humanist manifesto II.* https://americanhumanist.org/what-is-humanism/manifesto2/ (accessed 2 January 2018).
Bakhtin, M. (1981). *The Dialogic imagination.* Austin: University of Texas Press.
Britton, J., Burgess, T., Martin, N., McLeod, A., Rosen, H. (1975). *The Development of writing abilities (11–18).* London: Macmillan.
Brass, J. (2016). 'Re-reading Dartmouth: an American perspective', *English in Australia,* 51(3).
Carter, B., Gaither, M., and Gray, D. (1980). Memorial resolution: Herbert Joseph Muller'. *Bloomington Faculty Council Circular BO8–1981.* Bloomington, IN: University of Indiana. http://webapp1.dlib.indiana.edu/bfc/view?docId=B08–1981 (accessed 2 January 2018).

Clements, S. (1965). *'Reflections and after': an examination of the role and relevance of the Walworth English Course, and of our future needs in the education of the adolescent.* Reported by Nancy Martin. Talk to autumn conference of the London Association for the Teaching of English, 16–18 October 1965.

Clements, S., Dixon, J. and Stratta, L. (1963). *Reflections.* Oxford: Oxford University Press.

Clements, S., Dixon, J. and Stratta, L. (1967). *Things being various.* Oxford: Oxford University Press.

Clements, S., Dixon, J. & Stratta, L. (1967). *Things being various – teacher's book.* London: OUP.

Daiches, D (1968). 'Dartmouth questions on teaching English', *Universities Quarterly*, 22(2), 217–228.

Dixon, J. (1967). *Growth through English.* Oxford: Oxford University Press.

Dixon, J. (1975). *Growth through English: set in the perspectives of the Seventies.* Oxford: Oxford University Press.

Dixon, J. (2017). 'A conversation with John Dixon. Edited by John Hodgson'. *English in Education* 51(3), 238–254.

Freire, P. (1978). *The Pedagogy of the oppressed.* New York: Seabury Press.

Gibbons, S. (2017). *English and its teachers: a history of policy, pedagogy and practice.* London: Routledge.

Goodwyn, A. (2012). 'One size fits all: the increasing standardisation of English teachers' work in England', *English Teaching Practice and Critique*, 11(4)

Harris, J. (1991). 'After Dartmouth: growth and conflict in English', *College English* 53(6), 631–646.

Holbrook, D. (1964). *English for the rejected: training literacy in the lower streams of the secondary school.* Cambridge: Cambridge University Press.

Medway, P. (2005). 'Literacy and the idea of English', *Changing English*, 12, 19–29. Published online: 21 Oct 2010.

Moffett, J. (1968). *Teaching the universe of discourse.* Boston: Houghton Mufflin.

Muller, H. (1967). *The Uses of English: a blueprint for a new direction in the teaching of English in the Anglo-American countries.* New York: Holt Rinehart and Wilson.

Newsom, J. (1963). *Half our future: a report of the Central Advisory Council for Education* (England). London: HMSO.

Plowden, B. (1967). *Children and their primary schools: a report of the Central Advisory Council for Education (England).* Bridget Plowden, Chair. London: Her Majesty's Stationery Office.

Cited unpublished papers from Dartmouth conference

WP1: Working Party Paper 1: *What is English?* (Albert Kitzhaber)

A1: Response to Working Party Paper 1 (Douglas Barnes, Chair; James Britton, discussant)

WP2: Working Party Paper 2: *What is continuity in English teaching?* (Frank Whitehead)

PS2: Response to Working Party Paper 2: Plenary Session 2 (Berenice Christensen, discussant)

B3: Response to Working Party Paper 2: Record of Group Discussion

E2: Response to Working Party Paper 2: *Toward a model of continuity* (James Moffett)

WP3: Working Party Paper 3: *English: one road or many? Some historical reflections* (Wallace Douglas)

F1: Group discussion

WP4: Working Party Paper 4: *Knowledge and proficiency in English* (Denys Thompson)

WP5: Working Party Paper 5: *Standards and attitudes* (Albert A. Marckwardt)

I1: Response to Working Party Paper 5
SGP2: Study Group Paper 2: *Drama in English teaching* (Douglas Barnes)
SGP3: Study Group Paper 3: *Creativity in the English classroom* (David Holbrook)
SGP4: Study Group Paper 4: *How does a child learn English?* (Miriam E. Wilt)
S1: How Children Learn English I (Miriam E. Wilt)
S3: How Children Learn English II (Harold Rosen)
SGP5: Study Group Paper 5: *Response to literature* (James Britton)

PART II

Dartmouth today

Why it still matters

8

FROM PERSONAL GROWTH (1966) TO PERSONAL GROWTH AND SOCIAL AGENCY (2016) – PROPOSING AN INVIGORATED MODEL FOR THE 21ST CENTURY

Andrew Goodwyn

Introduction

The Personal Growth (PG) model, as outlined by John Dixon in 1967 and developed from his contribution to the Dartmouth Seminar, is unquestionably still recognisable to English teachers, remaining aligned to their philosophy of teaching English. This chapter traces a key element in the history of PG and explores present continuities traceable to Dartmouth in 1966, and defines an invigorated PG model to embrace twenty-first-century life and to take English forward into the future. Dixon himself never offered a concise definition; however, one historically significant attempt to do this (perhaps the first?) was produced in the *Cox Report*, the document that defined the first National Curriculum in English (NCE) in England in 1989. In focusing on a key historical moment, the UK's *Cox Report* in 1989, almost half way between 1966 and the time of writing, this chapter addresses the continuities and developments stemming from Dixon, being indicative of how subject English has expanded and changed over those 50 years. This analysis of Cox is followed by a briefer commentary on the most recent NCE, in 2013, as an example of official policies that have demonstrated increasing discontinuity with PG, leading to a complete disjunction.

Since 1966, amongst many extraordinary societal changes, perhaps the most profound, especially for young people, has been the growing presence of technology in everyday life and its affordances, which, whatever may be some negative elements, provide much greater potential agency to the individual. The emergence of this paradigm change is very present in Cox. However, this disruptive moment in 2013 of a new NCE and new examination regime provokes a re-examination of PG as the consistently key model for English teachers, now ready to be updated and expanded, drawing on the increasing importance of the Cultural Analysis model. Using contemporary Critical Realist theories of identity, Personal Growth is invigorated to include a broader conceptualisation of an *omniculture*, a prototype model is offered as *Personal Growth and Social/Cultural Agency*, an emancipatory concept to align with signs of radical progressivism in young people.

The Personal Growth (PG) model as articulated by John Dixon in 1966 has now had over 50 years of both influence and contestation. His book, *Growth through English* (1967) is famously a report of the Dartmouth Seminar, the reference point for this volume, a forum in which the purpose of English as a school subject was debated by its leading figures from the UK and USA. His more considered text, the 3rd edition in 1975 (Dixon, 1975), clearly revises some of his thinking between those dates (Goodwyn, 2016) and quietly takes into account some of the US think-ing that he mostly rejected in 1967 (see Goodwyn, 2017). However, his opening chapter, providing the rationale for PG, was not revised; and he never offered a short definition of the phrase PG itself. He did remark later, indicating his belief that PG would need revising:

> Is a new model for education struggling to emerge, just at the point when we have spelt out for ourselves the fuller implications of a model based on personal growth? Very well. The limits of the present model will be reached, that is certain, and thus a new model will be needed to transcend its descriptive power – and in so doing to redirect our attention to life as it really is.
>
> *(Quoted (but not attributed) in Allen, 1980, p.4)*

There is no question that if we are to 'look at life as it really is' now, then we must acknowledge that the societal environment in which the subject English is taught has changed remarkably since 1966, perhaps most extraordinarily in terms of how culture exists and is mediated to audiences and individuals, with the role of the internet being the most profound and all-encompassing example. Equally, since Dixon's time of writing, factors such as globalisation, rapid immigration flows leading to new modes of ethnic diversity, and an intensifying neoliberal form of capitalism, have had huge impacts on nation states. One impact of these seismic shifts towards globalisation, paradoxically if viewed on the surface, has been a resur-gence of nationalistic and religious intensities, and these movements are certainly affecting schools and teachers. However, much of this intensity seems to come from the conservative concerns of aging populations, with the examples of Brexit in the UK, Putin's ascendance in a rampant Russia and the election of Trump in the USA. It is important to reflect on the fact that the Dartmouth Seminar was funded by the US government because of the Cold War, and its fear that its education system was falling behind that of 'The Soviets'; the progressive PG model of English that emerged was certainly an unintended consequence. There are many clichés about 'the 60s', but rolled together they stem from a recognition that thinking, certainly in 'the West', began to change, despite the opposition of the establishment; young people began to refuse to conform. Something of that kind seems to be happening in the second decade of the twenty-first century. This chapter therefore draws on the history of the subject but as a resource to contemplate and energise its future in times of some resurgence of radical thinking.

Most young people did not vote for Brexit or for Trump; we can only speculate about Russia. Certainly in England, the focus of this chapter, there are real signs that the young increasingly reject neoliberalism and its greed for the natural resources of the planet, and they are turning to a politics of radical optimism. They want new (although they are actually old) ideas. John Dewey might have a wry smile on his face. I suggest young people are not buying into neoliberal nationalism and certainly partly, perhaps mostly, because their enveloping 24-hour culture, so bewildering and threatening to the materially safe elders of the tribe, gives them unparalleled access to all forms of culture and information and to the diverse and multifarious identities of humans around the globe, reminding them that we are all alike. Simultaneously, of course, this flood of information also includes 'Fake News' and many absurdities generated on social media. As always, but with more urgency, English teachers have a vital emancipatory role in developing critical literacy in their students. Subject English has been through many phases[1] of evolution and elsewhere I argue for seven – and that now is still the period of Phase 6: *Building the Panopticon, the coming of control, conformity and self-regulation*, but that phase 7 may be developing, see below (Goodwyn, 2018).

I argue here that we may now need to conceptualise that in 'developed' (and developing) societies, there is a pervasive 'omniculture' available to (almost) all young people (whether they choose from it or not, it is there) and this both challenges and strengthens individual agency to an extent unthinkable in 1966. I use omniculture as a term with two complementary emphases. Firstly, as an umbrella term for all types of culture, rejecting the concept of the traditional spectrum of popular to serious or high to low. This 'spectrum' notion has played a significant part in the history of English teaching, with figures such as F.R. Leavis famously intoning the need to oppose the popular and to 'discriminate and resist'. However, his famous dictum was appropriated by later figures from cultural and media studies who renamed it 'innoculation theory' and considered Leavis an unwitting parent to Media Studies. *Growth through English* has only passing concerns with popular culture in any 'mass media' sense (the term of the time) except in its advocacy for English teaching having local relevance to the lives of young people in their living experience of community.

Omniculture, secondly, is adopted, as it is more often used, as an alternative to multiculturalism, as:

> Omniculturalism is not just a combination of assimilation and multiculturalism policies. First, unlike assimilation and multiculturalism as practiced so

far, omniculturalism is founded upon human universals established through empirical research. Second, in omniculturalism policy there is a strong bias to socialize citizens to give priority to human universals, and to only secondarily attend to intergroup differences.

(Moghaddam, 2012, p.317)

The term 'multicultural' has a powerful semantic presence in the history of English teaching worldwide, and the concept played a valuable role in the formation, for example, of the first National Curriculum for English in England in 1989 (DES, 1989; see also Brian Cox's two books which document the design of the first NCE and the political struggles that surrounded that work). However, as a term, it seems to have become problematic – even discredited. Therefore, I adopt the term 'omniculturalism' as a helpful conceptualisation partly to counter the inherent racism in these negative, nationalistic and neoliberal times. I will also argue that these changes in what can be defined as an omnicultural society for young people, do not reduce the value of the fundamental elements of PG. In essence they highlight how important PG's continuities from figures such as Dewey remain (Goodwyn, 2016), with their clear definition of humanity as a reflective and emancipatory species with individual agency and responsibility in the real world, emphasising human commonalities.

In his opening pages Dixon famously described English (Dixon, 1975, p.1) as a 'quicksilver amongst metals – mobile, living and elusive. Its conflicting emphases challenge us today to look for a new, coherent definition'. One might feel that the 'coherence' of subject English remains elusive. I will argue for a form of ideological coherence whilst accepting that definitions of the subject, and what it encompasses, will always be ideologically contested. Dixon was very clear that two models he, and the Seminar participants, identified as powerful in 1966 needed to be reinterpreted; they were 'skills' and 'cultural heritage' and he argues that a model of language in operation will reposition those models with PG. The focus here is to consider how at least one curriculum context, England, reveals continuities and evolutions in these three models, and especially the primary place of PG.

A great has deal happened to subject English in the UK between 1966 and 2018. Between 1967 and 1989, I would argue that PG became a pervasive part of English teaching in England. I would also argue that many teachers embraced popular culture as the establishment of Media Education (Goodwyn, 1992a) clearly demonstrates, and that recognising cultural diversity (multiculturalism) had become a normative element in English. The date 1989 is a kind of watershed, with the publication of the very first NCE and where the first concise definition of PG occurs in the *Cox Report* (DES, 1989), the document written to justify and introduce the first National Curriculum for English; at that time it was reasonable to speak of *the UK*; in 2013, it becomes specifically *England*. The authorship of this definition is never stated and by implication can be considered to be the Cox Committee (see Cox, 1991). As a historic moment, the 1989 NCE, deserves close attention, occurring as it does almost half way between the Dartmouth seminar and its 50th anniversary.

In terms of the formative ideologies of English teaching, the *Cox Report* does not compare to Dartmouth in relation to generative thinking. However, it is a document with real intellectual importance – something obscured now perhaps because it had such political resonance as the first NCE to be prescribed in the 'English-speaking' world. Since then most such countries (notably the USA) have moved – or are moving – in a similar, more nationally prescriptive direction (see for example, Zancanella and Moore, 2014) and with Australia certainly formulating an NC of its own, although at the time of writing still not fully articulated.

The Cox models of English: the prominence of Personal Growth, the rise of Cultural Analysis

There is no space here for a fulsome account of the genesis of the National Curriculum in England. Accounts are available (Goodwyn, 2005, 2010, 2011) including that of the key author of the Report, Brian Cox (Cox, 1991; N.B. there are no page numbers in the original, just paragraph numerals). The focus in this section will be on the five models put forward, connecting three of them to Dixon's ideas and examining the two others as examples of new, important thinking. PG appears as one model amongst five and they are all introduced as follows under the heading 'The role of English in the curriculum':

> 2.20 It is possible to identify within the English teaching profession a number of different views of the subject. We list them here, though we stress that they are not the only possible views, they are not sharply distinguishable, and they are certainly not mutually exclusive.
>
> *(DES, 1989)*

No attempt is made to explain where these models came from and there is no evidence that at any point the committee conducted any research to determine if English teachers recognised and aligned with these views of the subject. After presenting the models the committee added two paragraphs of comment. It is worth quoting these in full because they clearly reveal continuities in the 'quicksilver' subject but also its expanding remit. The omniculture is emerging:

> 2.26 Some of these views look inwards: either in the sense of developing the individual child or in the sense of developing English as a separate school subject. Other views look outwards: they are concerned with helping the child with the needs of language elsewhere in the curriculum, or in the outside world of work. Alternatively, they are concerned with passing on the culture from one generation to the next, and with critically understanding what that culture consists of. Another distinction is that some of the approaches concern essentially the child's developing use of language, whereas others concern the knowledge about language and literature required of an informed and educated citizen in a democratic society.

2.27 Teachers of English will differ in the weight they give to each of these views of the subject. Indeed, some differentiation will derive directly from the stage children have reached at school: for example, the 'adult needs' view is more relevant to the later years of compulsory schooling than to the primary years. Some aspects of 'cultural analysis' are also more relevant to older children. However, aspects of media education are also important for children in the primary phase, because they can be influenced by the conventions and assumptions of mass media, and should learn to recognise this.

(DES, 1989)

These comments make clear some continuities with Dixon, especially the emphasis on the individual child's developing use of language, and equally reveal a new emphasis in 'cultural analysis' on mass media and critical understandings, including developing these understandings in primary-aged pupils. These paragraphs also posit a more agentive individual who is engaging with culture but critically and is a nascent 'informed and educated citizen in a democratic society'.

The document then presents the five models, and the first provided was:

2.21 A 'personal growth' view focuses on the child: it emphasises the relationship between language and learning in the individual child, and the role of literature in developing children's imaginative and aesthetic lives.

The placing of PG as first was, perhaps accidentally, exactly right, see below, as it is certainly the 'number 1' model for English teachers (Goodwyn, 1992a, 2010, 2016, Goodwyn and Findlay, 1999). There is therefore, in the 1989 NCE, a foregrounded, strong continuity with *Growth through English*.

The continuity with Dixon is further strengthened with the appearance of Adult Needs, an updated version of his skills model, which he saw as a form of basic literacy (Dixon, p.2). He saw this model as having been achieved through provision of universal literacy, however by 1966, it had become a problem to him as a form of practice leading to drilling and mechanistic exercises.

2.22 An 'adult needs' view focuses on communication outside the school: it emphasises the responsibility of English teachers to prepare children for the language demands of adult life, including the workplace, in a fast-changing world. Children need to learn to deal with the day-to-day demands of spoken language and of print; they also need to be able to write clearly, appropriately and effectively.

(DES, 1989)

This Cox definition is clearly much broader and more emancipatory than a simplistic 'skills' model and touches presciently on a 'fast-changing world'. Dixon's additional chapter in the 1975 edition is very much focused on communication and a recognition that there is much more to adult needs than 'skills'.

The third continuity – even in name – is Cultural Heritage:

> 2.23 A 'cultural heritage' view emphasises the responsibility of schools to lead children to an appreciation of those works of literature that have been widely regarded as amongst the finest in the language.
>
> *(DES, 1989)*

Dixon might well have argued (as would I) that this statement was not an updated version, still treating culture as a 'given' (Dixon, p.3) and ignoring the living culture that the individual child brings actively into the classroom. The student is here very passive, being 'lead' and is not critical, instead needing to appreciate texts that are the 'finest'; here we feel the spectrum concept of culture with this model actually more like a ladder, focused on only the top of culture, the 'high' end.

Dixon's original argument was that these two 'old' models in 'skills' and 'heritage' were outmoded and needed superseding by PG, and so his report was fundamentally a manifesto to dislodge them. However, it is not clear whether Dixon expected the 'old' models to continue in some form or to disappear entirely. The Cox committee simply places them beside the other two, implying, though never stating, equal status by saying, they are 'different views of the subject', just qualifying slightly their age relatedness in the prefacing comments above, 2:26 and 2:27.

Their fourth model was cross-curricular:

> 2.24 A 'cross-curricular' view focuses on the school: it emphasises that all teachers (of English and of other subjects) have a responsibility to help children with the language demands of different subjects on the school curriculum: otherwise areas of the curriculum may be closed to them. In England, English is different from other school subjects, in that it is both a subject and a medium of instruction for other subjects.
>
> *(DES, 1989)*

This model derives from the Bullock Report of 1975, which argued for *A Language for Life* (DES, 1975). However, this has never been a model *of subject English* and research proved conclusively (Goodwyn, 1992b) that English teachers saw this as emphatically the responsibility of other subject teachers. There is material here for another chapter about whether this rejection is a somewhat complacent elision of the issue in English of literary knowledge and its terminology. Importantly this 'rejection' was repeated later in England when, for similar reasons, English teachers rejected being called 'Literacy' teachers in the early twentieth century (for an account see Goodwyn and Fuller, 2011).

What was accepted by English teachers was the fifth and 'new' model, Cultural Analysis (CA):

> 2.25 A 'cultural analysis' view emphasises the role of English in helping chil-dren towards a critical understanding of the world and cultural environment

in which they live. Children should know about the processes by which meanings are conveyed, and about the ways in which print and other media carry values.

(DES, 1989)

There are some passing mentions of popular culture in *Growth through English*, but there is very little attention to popular culture in the numerous Dartmouth papers, it was simply not a priority at that time. This is partly surprising because the Dartmouth conference was attended by many students of F.R. Leavis, including Denys Thompson. Thompson's book, jointly authored with Leavis, *Culture and Environment* (1933) is generally seen as a seminal text in the development of cultural, later media, studies. Thompson was later the editor of *Discrimination and Popular Culture* (1964) a key text that came out of the national conference sponsored by the National Union of Teachers in 1960. The year 1964 also saw the establishment by Richard Hoggart of the landmark Centre for Cultural Studies at Birmingham University (see Hilliard, 2012). These developments help explain the emergence of Cultural Analysis in 1989 and a link to the later emergence of Critical Literacy, especially in Australia.

By 1988 the world, as stated above, had changed dramatically from 1966. Just before the *Cox Report* was produced a very different report, the *Kingman Report* (DES, 1988) was published. Its remit was to consider the place of *Knowledge about Language* in English teaching; what happened to that report is another story in itself. For our current purpose, one of its statements, approvingly quoted by the Cox committee was:

> Round the city of Caxton, the electronic suburbs are rising. To the language of books is added the language of television and radio, . . . the processed codes of the computer. As the shapes of literacy multiply, so our dependence on language increases.
>
> (Kingman, 1988, 2:7)

A key continuity is that this quotation heads the chapter (nine) entitled 'Media education and information technology', which intelligently argues that these areas of knowledge should be a part of English teaching and this is the acknowledgement of a truly fundamental change, towards the omniculture.

The *Cox Report* is a very interesting piece of curricular (and political) history, and the 'turn' towards acknowledging 'multi literacies' is signalled by Chapter Nine and the new model of Cultural Analysis, legitimising the place of Media Education in the curriculum (Goodwyn, 1992a) and its struggle to secure a 'home'. In England there was a vigorous debate about whether Media Education should be embedded within English (Goodwyn, 1992a, 2004) or cross-curricular (BFI, 1989) or a separate subject called either Media Studies or Cultural Studies. However, research at the time (Goodwyn, 1992b) made it clear that PG, not CA, was the key model for English teachers and they saw PG strongly infused in the first NCE.

This NCE did emerge from a kind of consensus in a period I have categorised elsewhere as 1980–1992 *English in harmonious practice* (see Goodwyn, 2018).

This author felt strongly in 1989 both that the 5 models were all important, but not equally important, to English teachers, and that the ideology of this first NCE was broadly in line with good practice in teaching English. An investigation to check this conviction was born out through a survey of serving teachers in 1990, which demonstrated that the first NCE was broadly welcomed, that PG was the key model, and that cross-curricular was seen as a necessary model but for other subject teachers. The other three models were 'equal second'. What might be seen as most striking about this latter finding was that Cultural Analysis was already judged by teachers to be as important as Cultural Heritage and Adult Needs. This innovative research was the beginning of numerous projects, spanning 25 years, investigating the relationship between new NCE versions and the ideology of English teachers. This work has been extensively published elsewhere, so to sum-marise some broad movements, revealed by that research:

- The NCE, with each revision, becomes increasingly unaligned to the ideol-ogy of English teachers – the most distant point (so far) is 2013;
- PG has retained its pre-eminence for English teachers;
- Cultural Heritage decreases in importance, increasingly reverting, in its official prescription, to that 'given' and elite form that Dixon rejected in 1966;
- However, teaching literature remains central to English teachers, this is a mix-ture of canonical and contemporary texts;
- Textual choice remains concerned with reflecting a diverse society with a number of heritages and including 'popular' twentieth-century texts from the English-speaking world, such as the USA and Australia;
- CA has become the second most important model for English teachers and the gradual inclusion of media education in the NCE, between 1989 to 2012, was generally welcomed.

Since 1989, there have been two broad periods, one overarching and one very specific, of curriculum change. The first, 1989–20013, although marked by sev-eral versions of the NCE, saw a steady broadening of subject English to include Media Education – itself increasingly broadening to encompass digital literacy as multi-modality became pervasive (Goodwyn, 2004). The research showed teachers maintaining PG as their priority but with CA steadily becoming the second most important model and with Cultural Heritage (at least as defined officially) steadily declining in importance.

There was a kind of sub-period, 1997–2007, within this broader movement: the National Literacy Strategy, a massive policy intervention (Goodwyn and Fuller, 2011) fundamentally aimed at primary teaching but developing a second-ary strand, *The Framework for English* from 2000–2007, during which, English teachers rejected being called English AND Literacy teachers, profoundly reject-ing the conceptualisation of the Framework (Goodwyn and Fuller, 2011) not least because it was not student centred as with PG, but instead very teacher and content oriented, with much scripted teaching and prescriptive in-service training. The continuity with Dixon and PG remains clear throughout the period and CA is steadily growing in importance.

The new curriculum period begins in 2013 (and continues) as the latest version of the NCE (2013) has simply evicted all references to the kinds of focus put forward in CA. It is also heavily marked by being content-driven and by prescribing a very narrow version of cultural heritage, essentially solely the English literary canon. The specifications for the GCSE examinations (key national examinations for 16 year-olds) also define Literature as deriving solely from the English literature 'tradition'. This shift to the fossilised traditional view of cultural heritage is exactly what Dixon was aiming to dislodge in 1966 and it is made more dramatic by the diminution of emphasis on Speaking and Listening and the reintroduction of terminal examinations with no course work of any kind (see the Department for Education website for current NCE documentation, DfE, 2018).

The steady distancing of the ideology of the NCE, especially the period of the Framework, from the ideology of teachers leads finally to a proposal for a new model of English that 'updates' but does not reject or abandon PG; indeed contemporary research evidence (Goodwyn, 2016) remains strong that PG stays central.

Critical Realism and nascent agency

What PG needs currently is strengthening and broadening, especially when curricular changes are so antipathetical, certainly in England, to the ideology of English teaching. I propose a twenty-first-century model of PG. This must be here a necessarily brief introduction to an argument needing far more depth and development. Although Dixon's model was conceived during late Modernism it was very much in the spirit of the Sixties, with its emphasis on a democratic classroom with no deference towards elite culture. It was very much conceptualised as a Deweyan project, insisting that English valued each individual's experience and that the English classroom was the place to share experiences. It has comfortably survived the inroads of Postmodernism.

During the last quarter of the twentieth century, Critical Realism has become a force in social science theory (see Collier, 1994; Archer, Bhaskar, Collier, Lawson and Norrie, 1998; Cruickshank, 2003) and has superseded – rather as Dixon argued PG should – these two older movements of Modernism and Postmodernism. Both these movements had definitions of the self, identity and humanity. Here I draw on Archer's model of the emerging mature social agent (Archer, 2003a) to argue for a new version of PG. Archer's Critical Realist model rejects 'Modernist man' as 'Homo Economicus' and a 'completely impoverished model of man'. Equally, postmodernist humans are just a 'grammatical fiction', 'a person is not a natural object, but a cultural artefact'. Archer argues for a far more robust and resilient model of humanity and of the individual. I will summarise key strands of Archer's thinking and relate these to PG and its origins, particularly in the work of Dewey. There is an absolutely direct line from Dewey, through Dixon and on to Archer, focusing on the individual as an active and reflexive agent. For a fully developed insight into Archer's thinking, readers are referred to her trilogy of books (Archer, 2003a, 2007, 2012).

Key elements from Archer (2003b) about the reflective agent can be summarised as follows:

- We have 'selfhood – a continuous sense of self – a reflexive self-consciousness';
- There is a 'universal sense of self' and an 'evolving sense of self' for the individual';
- 'personal identity is a matter of what we care about in the world' (p.19);
- 'our social identities are made under conditions that are not of our making';
- There are three orders of reality – the natural, the practical and the social. We need a modus vivendi to survive and thrive;
- The process of reflection is conducted as an inner conversation as we decide how and what to be in the external world. It is an 'unseen moral life' monitoring our fundamental concerns;
- Social identity can only be a sub set (large or small) of personal identity because we have a continuous sense of self that interacts with a changing social environment;
- Personal identity and social identity exist in a dialectical relationship;
- The mature agent is active and reflexive – and enacts social reproduction (the status quo) but can also be part of transformation, that is, being emancipated and emancipatory.

(p.20)

Archer also discusses the importance of the nascent personal identity of the young as they determine where to act (or be acted upon) by social reality. In this particular chapter and throughout her trilogy she analyses developed societies as in a state of morphogenesis, partly caused by the affordances of the new modes of culture enabled by the internet and individualised computer access.

In the spirit of Dixon's model, I offer an attempt at, perhaps best considered a prototype of, an expanded PG, attempting to retain its Deweyan qualities (Dewey, 1997, 1980, 2011) but invigorated for a twenty-first-century environment and omniculture, and emphasising the nascent agency of the emergent individual following from Archer's outline. I must emphasise that this model still only focuses specifically on the role of subject English, most clearly signalled in the reference to literature:

A 'personal growth and social agency' model is an emancipatory view of English and focuses on developing nascent and maturing individual agents, constantly fostering their growing critical powers. It emphasises the relationship between language and learning in developing reflexive individuals; it enables stimulating interactions with the omniculture, especially literature. It develops the social, imaginative and aesthetic lives of children and young people.

This 'prototype' provides continuity with Dixon with its emphasis on PG in the Deweyan sense and on the fundamental relationship between language and learning, of which literature is a key element. It then stresses the importance of agency and criticality in the maturing individual. The culture here is the omniculture that is the environment for all young people in a developed society. This 'prototype' subsumes any 'Romantic' notions of the artist, something critics often cite as an indulgent weakness in PG (see Hunter, 1988, 1991; Reid, 2004) by following Critical Realism and clarifying that the 'personal' is that which is at the heart of reflexive and critical agency in all humans, and offers emancipatory potential in the social world.

This invigorated model is proposed at a time when younger generations, the students who are also future English teachers, are yearning for new ways forward beyond neoliberalism. Perhaps the 2020s may have some of the radical power of the 1960s, as neoliberal and conservative religious forces and the super-rich are seen by the young as literally blocking their futures and endangering the planet itself. In England the term 'education system' no longer applies, as neoliberal policies have marketized schooling and marginalised local authorities, ironically reducing the grip of the NCE, which applies to less than half of schools. Simultaneously, the assessment system has attempted to reinforce the power of canonical English literary heritage. Somewhere in this chaotic and disputative scenario, new opportunities are emerging for English to regain its emancipatory force and for students to jointly enable growth through English. Perhaps the phase I have called 'Building the Panopticon, the coming of control, conformity and self-regulation', has almost ended and perhaps we may now enter a truly new phase, in harmony with young people's radical aspirations, 'Emancipation, agency and social justice for all' (Goodwyn, 2018).

Note

1 These 'phases' come from my attempt to capture the ontology of English as a school subject (Goodwyn, 2018) from its nineteenth-century origins to the present day, I have therefore coined them as:- 1: Ennobling the vernacular; 2: Conventions and conditions; 3: Culturing the citizenry; 4: Growth through Language – 1954 to 1989; 5: English in harmonious practice; 6: Building the Panopticon, the coming of control, conformity and self-regulation; and 7: Emancipation, agency and social justice.

References

Allan, D. (1980). *English teaching since 1965: how much growth?*, London: Heinemann Educational.

Archer, M. S. (2003a). *Structure, agency and the internal conversation*, Cambridge: Cambridge University Press.

Archer, M. S. (2003b). 'The Private life of the social agent: what difference does it make?' in Cruickshank, J. (ed.) *Critical realism: the difference it makes*, London: Routledge.

Archer, M. S. (2007). *The reflexive imperative in late modernity*, Cambridge: Cambridge University Press.

Archer, M. S. (2012). *Making our way through the world: human reflexivity and social mobility*, Cambridge: Cambridge University Press.

Archer, M., Bhaskar, R., Collier, A., Lawson, T. and Norrie, A. (eds.). (1998). *Critical realism: essential readings*, London, Routledge.

Bazalgette, C. (1989). *Primary media education: a curriculum statement*, London: The British Film Institute.

Bullock, A. (1975). *A language for life*, (known as The Bullock Report), London: HMSO.

Collier, A. (1994). *Critical realism: an introduction to Roy Bhaskar's philosophy*, London: Verso.

Cox, B. (1991). *Cox on Cox: an English curriculum for the 1990s*, London: Hodder and Stoughton.

Cox, B. (1992). *The Great Betrayal: memoirs of a life in Education*, London: Chapmans.

Cruickshank, J. (ed.) (2003). *Critical realism: the difference it makes*, London: Routledge.

Department for Education (2018). *National curriculum in England.* www.gov.uk/government/publications/national-curriculum-in-england-english-programmes-of-study.

DES (1988). *Knowledge about language*, London: HMSO.

DES (1989). *English for ages 5–16*, London: HMSO.

Dewey, J. (1980 edition). *Art as experience*, New York: Perigee Books.

Dewey, J. (1997). *Experience and education*, New York: Simon and Schuster.

Dewey, J. (2011 edition). *Democracy and education*, Milton Keynes: Simon and Brown.

Dixon, J. (1975). *Growth through English: set in the perspective of the Seventies.* Oxford: Oxford University Press.

Goodwyn, A. (1992a). *English teaching and media education*, Buckingham: Open University Press.

Goodwyn, A. (1992b). 'Theoretical models of English teaching', *English in Education*, 26(3), Autumn, 4–10.

Goodwyn, A. (2004). *English teaching and moving image*, London: Routledge Falmer.

Goodwyn, A. (2005). 'A framework for English? Or a vehicle for literacy? English teaching in England in the age of the Strategy', *English Teaching, Practice and Critique*, 3(3), January, 16–28.

Goodwyn, A., (2010). *The expert teacher of English*, London: Routledge Falmer.

Goodwyn, A. (2011). 'The impact of the framework for English: teachers' struggle against "informed prescription"', in Goodwyn, A and Fuller, C. (eds.), *The great literacy debate*, London: Routledge Falmer.

Goodwyn, A. (2012). 'One size fits all: the increasing standardisation of English teachers' work in England,' *English Teaching, Practice and Critique*, 11(4), 36–53.

Goodwyn, A. (2016). 'Still growing after all these years? The resilience of the "Personal Growth model of English" in England and also internationally', *English Teaching, Practice and Critique*, 15(2), 7–21.

Goodwyn, A. (2018, forthcoming) 'The origins and adaptations of English as a school subject', in Hall, C. & Wicaksono, R. (eds.). *Ontologies of English: reconceptualising the language for learning, teaching, and assessment*, Cambridge: Cambridge University Press.

Goodwyn, A., Durrant. C and Reid, L (eds.) (2014). *International perspectives on the teaching of English in a globalised world*, London: Routledge.

Goodwyn, A., and Findlay, K. (1999). 'The Cox Models revisited: English Teacher's views of their subject and the National Curriculum', *English in Education*, 33(2), Summer, 19–31.

Goodwyn, A., Fox, D. and Zancanella, D. (1993). *Theoretical models of English: a comparison of the beliefs of English teachers in the UK and the US*, The Language in Education Conference, The University of East Anglia.

Goodwyn, A and Fuller, C., (2011). *The great literacy debate*, London: Routledge Falmer.

Hilliard, C. (2012). *English as a vocation: the Scrutiny movement*, Oxford: Oxford University Press.

Hunter, I. (1987). 'Culture, education, English: building "the principal scene of the real life of children"', *Economy and Society*, 16, 568–88.

Hunter, I. (1988). *Culture and government: the emergence of literary education.* London: Macmillan.

Hunter, I. (1991). 'Learning in the literature lesson: the limits of the aesthetic personality'. in Luke, A and Baker, C (eds.), *Towards a critical sociology of reading pedagogy*, Amsterdam: John Benjamin.

Moghaddam, F. M. (2012). 'The Omnicultural imperative', *Culture & Psychology* 18(3), 304–330.

Reid, I. (2004). *Wordsworth and the formation of English studies*, London: Ashgate.

Thompson, D. (ed.) (1964). *Discrimination and popular culture*, Harmondsworth: Penguin.

Zancanella, D. and Moore, M. (2014). 'The Origins and ominous future of the US Common Core Standards in English language arts', in, Goodwyn, A., Durrant. C and Reid, L (eds.) *International perspectives on the teaching of English in a globalised world*, London: Routledge.

9

DARTMOUTH'S GROWTH MODEL RECONCEIVED FROM A SOCIAL PERSPECTIVE

Peter Smagorinsky

The Summer of 1966. . . I was 13 years old, about to enter ninth grade at Thomas A. Edison High School in Alexandria, Virginia. Needless to say, I was quite oblivious to the Anglo-American conference scheduled for Dartmouth, NH, that summer. I was oblivious to things in general, like most kids about to make the transition from junior high to high school. It was one of several new experiences that I was having at that time. My seventh-grade year at Mark Twain Junior High School had been the first time I'd ever attended school with an African American, when federally-ordered integration of Virginia schools placed a single Black student in the historically White school for the first time.

Latinx? There was no such thing at the time that I knew of. First, there were simply no people of any color but White in my school or neighborhood, both segregated by law. Before my junior year in high school, my father's career moved us to New Jersey, where schools had long been integrated and there were a small number of Puerto Rican families. I knew about them from *West Side Story*. But they lived more in cities, while we lived in the college town of Princeton.

And the x in Latinx, representing a trans population? This was the *Mad Men* era, when simply being lesbian or gay would have been inadmissible. The world was monochromatic and mostly monocultural, by tradition and by design. None of this celebration of diversity that later overcame some pockets of society. In a way, the world was overtly structured the way it is now covertly practiced, with schools and society designed to benefit and privilege people acculturated to some form of a European society's practices.

For eighth grade my parents put me in a private school in hopes of awakening me intellectually, something I had never managed on my own. My year at Ascension Academy for eighth grade did make me look like a student, attired in coat and tie every day, but barely changed my shabby study habits. In the summer of 1966, they gave up and re-enrolled me in the public school system, where I continued on my journey to the professoriate. My ability to float through classes as a student and still get into a series of good colleges is no doubt evidence of what we call White Privilege: My missteps never really cost me much.

The year 1966 was a key point in the history surrounding the Dartmouth Conference. Woodstock and Flower Power had not yet arrived; we were still listening to the British Invasion bands and Motown, at least among White people, the only people I was allowed to meet. The Establishment, soon to become villainized, was alive and well throughout institutions built following the Second World War, during a great era of prosperity and expansion, for us Whites at least. Unbeknownst to me and my 13-year-old sensibilities, however, movements toward Civil Rights were afoot among African Americans, Native Americans, and women against those very institutions that invested power in monied White men. The Vietnam War was getting increasingly costly and questionable, in terms of money and lives and purpose, and was in the process of becoming implicated in the general unrest over inequity. As many songs of the era asserted, the soldiers sent to fight across the world were people of color and lower socioeconomic classes; they weren't, to quote one song, no fortunate sons (Creedence Clearwater Revival, 1969).

Dartmouth was a good fit for the times. It was established with a revolutionary intent: to map out the future of English studies across the Anglo world and its colonial heritage, to break the shackles of establishment thinking. Dartmouth's thematic core came in its resistance to the predominant teacher-and-text-centered tradition – the establishment of all establishments, the authority of canonical texts – that dominated schools at the time and that has pulled off a stunning revival in the Common Core curriculum and standards that have reinstituted the technically-oriented, text-bound values of New Criticism. Dartmouth and its key products (e.g., Dixon, 1975) helped to shift emphasis from the text to the learner's development, making the student the center of the curriculum rather than historical modes of writing, the canonical texts that embody them, and the teacher's authoritative, deliberate brokerage of that curriculum to students whose task was to align themselves with its values.

Dartmouth's influence helped lead to the founding of the National Writing Project in 1974, renewed attention to Rosenblatt's reader-centered approach to teaching literature, a shift in attention from learning product to learning process, the acceptance of linguistic variation for those whose home languages departed from textbook conventions (Conference on College Composition and Communication, 1974), and other changes designed to break down the edifice of establishment schooling and make schools more student-centered and aligned with the progressive, democratic, transactional ideas of John Dewey.

Known as the British 'growth model', this approach asserted that the purpose of engagement with an English curriculum was to promote the personal growth of individual learners. Dixon (1975/1967) and his British colleagues argued that emphasizing texts, rather than learners' engagement with them, did not contribute to their personal growth trajectories. Rather, all students were expected to grow at the same rate using the same materials toward the same outcome. This idea of standardization of curriculum and instruction to produce a single sort of student product was rejected, even as the policy pendulum has now swung back mightily to reinforce them at government-imposed levels.

Dixon's (1975/1967) account of the 1960s could easily pass for a present-day critique. Right- and left-wing populism has gripped England's media and, following the Brexit referendum, the UK is falling out of the EU; and President Trump has attempted to institute a Muslim travel ban and believes that a wall on the Mexican border is feasible – environmentally, economically and as a barrier to entry. Dixon's description of societies during times of rapid change could well describe the US presidential election of 2016:

> there is a tendency to panic, to define an external curriculum – a system into which teacher and pupil must fit – instead of helping teachers, in departments and larger groups, to define for themselves the order and sequence that underlies their best work
>
> *(p.84).*

This fear in the face of change tends to produce various forms of nativism, including reversions to 'traditional values' favored by members of the dominant culture, who feel threatened that their place atop the social world might be jeopardized by diverse perspectives and viewpoints. As Dixon might say, there is then a tendency to panic and impose a centralized, externally-produced curriculum. Such initiatives as 'character education', for instance, often are undertaken during social upheavals as a way to return to some quaint notion of lost values, even when those values were firmly situated in the sort of segregated society in which I grew up (Smagorinsky & Taxel, 2004, 2005). Rather than celebrating diversity and cultivating individual growth trajectories, these programs are designed to homogenize students into a single cultural disposition, as embodied by Hirsch's (1987) proposal of a shared knowledge base that he argues is quintessentially American.

The fiftieth anniversary of Dartmouth comes at a time remarkably like those of 1966. To Dixon (1975/1967), the predominant authoritarian approach to teaching, no doubt like authoritarian conceptions of governance in general, produced:

> an uneasy dualism in English teaching. Literature itself tended to be treated as a given, a ready-made structure that we imitate and a content that is handed over to us. And this attitude infected composition and all work in language. There was a fatal inattention to the processes involved in such everyday activities as talking and thinking things over, writing a diary or a letter home, even enjoying a TV play. Discussion was virtually ignored, as we know to our cost today on both sides of the Atlantic. In other words, the part of the map that relates a man's[1] language to his experience was largely unexplored.

(Think of the trivial essay topics that still result from this ignorance.) The purposes and pressures that language serves tended to be reduced to a simple formula—a lump sum view of inheritance.

(p.4)

This sense of a proper education places assimilation to a cultural heritage at the center of curriculum and instruction; and some people's cultural heritages were more equal than others. In today's world, this inequity is evident in the overwhelmingly White, Anglo-Saxon orientation of both the curriculum – which is remarkably stable and little different from what Applebee (1993) found a quarter-century ago – and the manner in which curriculum materials and instructional guides are built on assumptions that subtly impose the values of the White *status quo* and discourage any critical look at societal inequity that might discomfort those for whom school is already a secure place (Berchini, 2016). Meanwhile, texts from outside this established set of materials and practices have been excoriated for allegedly undermining academic rigor, destroying American culture, and rotting the core of society (e.g., Stotsky, 1999).

In reaction against the skills and cultural heritage approaches to teaching English, the Dartmouth participants proposed a curriculum based on personal growth, outlined by Dixon (1975/1967) as follows:

- Authentic discussion, rather than teacher-orchestrated and -dominated talk, should drive daily classroom life, where students talk to one another (not just the teacher) concerning things they care about. These discussions should involve expressive or exploratory talk in which the process of talking leads to new insights as what Applebee (1981) called 'a tool for exploring a subject' to help 'generate new ideas 'at the point of utterance'' (p.100). This speech may also be halting, partial, and nonlinear as the speaker works through ideas while thinking out loud.
- Just as spoken speech should take on an exploratory, expressive character, so should writing, potentially allowing a process of discovery. Writing should involve new thinking and not simply record someone else's approved information. Students' writing should not be confined to the analytic and informational, but should include informal, creative, and hybrid genres. This exploratory dimension shifts attention from received to constructed knowledge, from product to process.
- Students' personal experiences should play a central role in their education, from the topics of their writing to their infusion of meaning into the texts they read, allowing them to serve 'as the vital core of English work' (Dixon, 1975, p.48). An experiential emphasis in turn suggests that the emotional lives of students should be involved in learning, a departure from the tenets of New Criticism that view readers' emotions as impediments to their quest to discern the author's intentions.
- Teachers should be less defenders of their own cultural heritage and more open to students' diverse orientations, including their linguistic patterns and the perspectives that accompany them. By listening to students instead of

conceiving of them as a captive audience, teachers can pick up on students' emerging feelings and ideas, and in turn use that understanding to raise thematic possibilities and connections.

- To Dixon (1975/1966), 'a teacher's art lies in taking a pupil where he is interested and in some sense sharing with him the search for new possibilities' (p.86). Teachers thus do not dominate the direction of learning and the materials that support those top-down goals. Rather, they follow individual children's chosen pathways and help them along the way without throwing them off their own preferred course.

- School ought to provide abundant opportunities for students to engage in drama, conceived here as the personal enactment of textual knowledge rather than the formal performance of theater. In classroom drama, students' talk 'differs from other talk in three ways: movement and gesture play a larger part in the expression of meaning; a group working together upon an improvisation needs more deliberately and consciously to collaborate. . .; the narrative framework allows for repetition and provides a unity that enables the action more easily to take on symbolic status' (Dixon, 1975/1967, p.37).

Dartmouth, then, was situated in a time and place that called for a particular anti-authoritarian response. The schools of the early 1960s represented the *status quo*, stifling students' free expression and force-fitting them all into the same academic mold, one that bracketed out their personal knowledge and engaged them in the study and recitation of established, formal facts and figures. The British congregation offered in response the growth model, which shifted attention to learners, albeit as acultural individuals constructing their own personal worlds outside the influence of coercive adults. By the time I began my senior year at Princeton High School in 1969 – where the students were heavily influenced by the aggressive political action of Princeton University students, a stunning contrast from the sports-oriented culture of my Northern Virginia roots – these values had begun to infiltrate US classrooms through more open-ended writing, free expression of anti-establishment values, assertions by disenfranchised cultural and racial groups of their constitutional rights, shifts in strict dress and grooming codes toward more individual forms of expression, demands for equal rights by women (but not nearly yet for LGBTQ+ people), and other meaningful forms of social action that had not before been a central part of public education.

Toward a more social understanding of human development

As I have reviewed, the more things change, the more they remain the same. The times and teaching profession have changed (Pasternak, Caughlan, Hallman, Renzi, & Rush, 2017). Yet current world events have brought about a renewal of xenophobia, the specter of cultural deterioration, racism, misogyny, homophobia, and other fears. This environment of anxiety has produced a circling of the cultural wagons and a reinstitution of authoritarian politics and education as a way to hold society to the traditions of those who have historically held power. This effort to standardize education is easily evident in efforts to develop a national curriculum in the spuriously named, centrally-developed Common Core State Standards, to make standardized testing the driver of curriculum and instruction, to reduce the effects of multicultural education, and to keep the barbarians from the gates by making school policies represent the values of those who have historically controlled schools: White, upper- and middle-class men of limited cultural exposure.

The goal of removing the shackles of tradition led the Dartmouth participants to defy the establishment by encouraging young people to 'doing your own thing'. This individualistic conception assumed that people, by nature, are good and kind, and that they will seek a personal direction for their learning without taking up other people's space and resources. This Rousseauian conception of students as noble savages viewed pupils as innocently constructing worlds of their own, independent of cultural mediation and teachers' authoritarian direction, and without pursuing their goals at the expense of other people's needs.

This assumption has proven wrong on several counts. First, people are not as altruistic as the progressive ideal would suggest. Among the greatest menaces to school safety is bullying (Goodstein, 2013), a form of abuse that is modeled daily for them by adults, and often rewarded. Racism, xenophobia, misogyny, and homophobia are rampant throughout society and schools. The competitive structure of school encourages cheating and other dirty play for advancement in academics and college choice (ABC News, 2017). Romantics such as Kohn (2011) believe that schools should simply trust kids to let their goodness and inquiry for knowledge emerge. However, such assumptions appear to work best in specialized, fee-driven environments such as Montessori schools. There is little evidence to support the idea that such a plan would ever succeed on a large scale across the range of public schools. Many blame capitalism's competitive values for society's cruelty (Martin, Houston, McLaren, & Suoranta, 2010). Many more point to Finland as the epitome of possibility for humane schooling that produces a respected teaching force and high-achieving set of students, no doubt overlooking the possibility that Finland's system values equality more than excellence (Partanen, 2011) as part of its socialistic orientation, along with providing good health care and other public services that require a degree of taxation and sacrifice that Americans will not make.

The Dartmouth conference valorized personal growth without attention to the social responsibilities that accompany growing and participating in a society. The British participants endorsed an individually-oriented personal growth approach as an educational end in itself. In their Foreword to the 3rd edition of Dixon's *Growth through English*, Dartmouth participants James Squire and James Britton (1975) see 'the impact of the Dartmouth ideas—perhaps the Dartmouth ideal—in the enterprise of individuals' (p.x). The developmental view of student-centered education outlined by Dixon, they say, suggests that 'self-discovery through language and in self-expression, with writing to realize oneself, has occupied the attention of teachers' since the book's original 1967 publication (p.xvii). The subject of English comprises 'the sum total of the planned and unplanned experiences through language by means of which a child gains control of himself and his relations with the surrounding world' (p.xviii). These relations are always gratifying and harmonious. They are also byproducts of realizing oneself, which should become the central occupation of school.

My concern with the assumption that personal growth and realization are the primary purpose of education comes from the fact that the personal growth curves of individuals often come at the expense of the goals and growth of others. The absence of attention to this fact has led, I think, to a Romantic conception of the individual student in much educational writing since. By elevating the individual's growth as the object of education, the Dartmouth tradition has embraced an ideal that is virtually impossible to achieve except under the most rarified of conditions, those in which young people are not only free of conscious malicious intent, but do not subconsciously impose their values and priorities on those around them in the process of seeking to meet their own goals.

When I wrote about Dixon (1975/1967) for *English Journal* (2002) upon rediscovering the book roughly 35 years after its initial publication, I was both impressed with its focus on human development and bothered by its Romantic assumptions about the societally-unfettered, noble character of the individual. As a teacher, I had seen both tremendous possibility for youth and a good bit of meanness. In that article, I reviewed a set of experiences from my own classroom teaching that involved misogyny and other hateful forms of conduct that emerged during students' open-ended opportunities for expression and meaning-construction. Their own acculturation to broader societal values prevented my classroom from becoming an idyllic respite from society. Rather, as other researchers have discovered, when left to their own devices, my students would often jockey for power and positioning at one another's expense (Finders, 1997; Lewis, 1997).

As a result, I had to manage a balance between authority and freedom. I could not tolerate male students who treated female students with disrespect or social violence, and had to impose rules that forbade such action. While helping each student find a pathway in life, I had to make sure that they did not run others off their own roads. Whether they were deliberately mean or engaged in what are now called unintentional microaggressions against others – at the time, using the term 'gay' as a universally pejorative term was among them – I made efforts to teach a form of respect that their own natural inclinations had not yet provided them. Simply allowing each to pursue a personal pathway, I learned, opened the door to forms of abuse that I found far less savory than my imposition of social rules on the group dynamics.

My article focused on my own classroom experiences, connected to the outside world through misogynist popular culture. What I could not see from the limited vantage point of my classroom was the deep structure of the school system itself and its artifacts. Their engrained presence advantaged those whose own families and communities were aligned with the mores inscribed in the school's disciplinary code, dress code, demands for academic language, reliance on specific speech genres and social languages, topic preferences, historical perspectives, conceptions of scientific knowledge, and other axioms that guided people through the day. Schools prefer certain types of people to others, and ignoring this fact can lead to discriminatory practices that are punitive toward those who come with other forms of socialization and acculturation. Schools also prefer certain forms of knowledge over others, accentuating formal, abstract, impersonal understandings over knowledge gained through everyday experience outside school.

Berchini's (2016) study of how a textbook publisher's teacher's manual shapes teachers' leading of discussions illustrates how cultural values become insinuated unconsciously into everyday teaching and learning. As she notes, the curriculum materials provided through the *Prentice Hall literature* series that she studied 'frames and represents [the short story] 'The White Umbrella' and, consequently, directs teachers' subsequent application of its content in a way that mutes the multicultural themes that [Chinese-American author Gish] Jen foregrounds in the short story' (pp.55-56). Her careful analysis of a classroom episode admirably does not pathologize the teacher's conduct of the lesson, a common problem in Critical Whiteness Studies from the 'first-wave' in which awkward teachers are called out as racists for having difficulty addressing racism in discussions. Rather, she looks at the deep structure of the curriculum to see how teachers are guided toward uncontroversial discussion topics and how they suggest that teachers point students toward literary technique and relatively trivial story elements that bypass sensitive topics. The curriculum, then, is built to bypass topics that might engage students emotionally and intellectually because they might also invite controversy and conflict. This reinforcement of the *status quo* minimizes opportunities for students to engage in important social critique, the deconstruction of inequity, the reconstruction of more equitable possibilities, and the design of authentic social action (Jones, 2006).

Remarkably, when students are emotionally disengaged from school, they do not learn skills that later in life they take up with gusto. In a dissertation-in-progress at The University of Georgia, Darren Rhym is studying interviews of rappers reflecting on what they learned in their secondary school English classes that helped develop their poetic and expressive abilities. The simple answer: not much. In fact, some of his participants had extremely high absentee rates in school because they were so alienated from the curriculum, where they saw virtually nothing that represented their culture or life experiences. As Darren puts it, these highly agile and fluent language users tuned out of school because they did not see their own stories told there. Only later when taking up rapping did they find a medium through which they could relate the experiences of themselves and their communities.

Once that possibility became real to them, they began to take language study quite seriously, going to clubs to study rap techniques, learning about figurative language, and generally taking literary arts seriously. Unlike in school, as described by Berchini (2016), their rap expression did not avoid difficult social issues, but rather embraced them. Unlike school instruction grounded in New Criticism's technical emphasis and discouragement of personal meaning-making, the rappers foreground meaning and seek techniques that amplify its expression. Long after high school, the rappers in his study found a reason to engage with poetic expression, because they began to see it as a means for telling stories that their schools had not allowed in the curriculum.

Discussion

In this chapter I have questioned a major theme of the Dartmouth Conference, that being its focus on individual pathways of development liberated from the shackles of tradition, authority, and culture. My reading of sociocultural theory (e.g., Vygotsky, 1987) has led me away from individualistic notions of thinking and acting grounded in both Piagetian developmental psychology and cognitive psychology's focus on internal mentation. Rather, I see human development as socially mediated and meaning-making to be, not independent of social influence but profoundly shaped by sociocultural mediation (Smagorinsky, 2001), from local classroom practices to school policies to curricular structure to societal conflicts.

It's important, then, to avoid the pitfall of viewing schooling in terms of the binary of teacher-centered and student-centered instruction. This emphasis, among other problems, isolates teachers from their social contexts and makes them blameworthy for problems originating well outside schools and classrooms. If the promise of Dartmouth's attention to personal growth is to be realized, appropriate developmental theories that take into account the mediated nature of human development need to be understood at the immediate, social levels and at the deeper cultural, historical, and systemic levels. With such attention, a more realistic and socially inclusive notion of how schools can foster a nation of responsible citizens may become more possible.

Note

1 I retain Dixon's use of masculine language, the norm at the time, yet indicative of the masculine orientation of the Dartmouth participation roster and the authority structure of the profession, which is now more properly balanced along gender lines.

References

ABC News. (2017, April 29). 'A Cheating crisis in America's schools'. New York: Author. Retrieved June 8, 2017 from http://abcnews.go.com/Primetime/story?id=132376&page=1.

Applebee, A. N. (1981). *Writing in the secondary school: English and the content areas* (NCTE Research Report No. 21). Urbana, IL: National Council of Teachers of English.

Applebee, A. N. (1993). *Literature in the secondary school: studies of curriculum and instruction in the United States.* Urbana, IL: National Council of Teachers of English. Retrieved from http://files.eric.ed.gov/fulltext/ED357370.pdf.

Berchini, C. (2016). 'Curriculum matters: the Common Core, authors of color, and inclusion for inclusion's sake'. *Journal of Adolescent & Adult Literacy,* 60(1), 55–62.

Conference on College Composition and Communication. (1974). *Students' right to their own language.* Urbana, IL: Author. Retrieved from www.ncte.org/library/NCTEFiles/Groups/CCCC/NewSRTOL.pdf.

Creedence Clearwater Revival. (1969). 'Fortunate son'. On *Willie and the poor boys.* Berkeley, CA: Fantasy Records.

Dixon, J. (1975/1967). *Growth through English: set in the perspective of the Seventies* (3rd ed.). Yorkshire: National Association for the Teaching of English.

Finders, M. J. (1997). *Just girls: hidden literacies and life in junior high.* New York: Teachers College Press.

Goodstein, P. K. (2013). *How to stop bullying in classrooms and schools: use social architecture to prevent, lessen and end bullying.* New York: Routledge.

Hirsch, E. D. (1987). *Cultural literacy: what every American should know.* Boston, MA: Houghton Mifflin.

Jones, S. (2006). *Girls, social class, and literacy: what teachers can do to make a difference.* Portsmouth, NH: Heinemann.

Kohn, A. (2011). *Feel-bad education and other contrarian essays on children & schooling.* Boston, MA: Beacon Press.

Lewis, C. (1997). 'The Social drama of literature discussions in a fifth/sixth-grade classroom'. *Research in the Teaching of English,* 31, 163–204.

Martin, G., Houston, D., McLaren, P., & Suoranta, J. (eds.) (2010). *Havoc of capitalism: educating for social and environmental justice.* Boston, MA: Sense Publishers.

Partanen, A. (2011). 'What Americans keep ignoring about Finland's school success'. *The Atlantic.* Dec. 29. Retrieved from www.theatlantic.com/national/archive/2011/12/what-americans-keep-ignoring-about-finlands-school-success/250564/.

Pasternak, D., Caughlan, S., Hallman, H., Renzi, L., & Rush, L. (2017). *Secondary English teacher education in the United States: a historical and current analysis.* London: Bloomsbury.

Smagorinsky, P. (2001). 'If meaning is constructed, what is it made from? Toward a cultural theory of reading'. *Review of Educational Research,* 71, 133–169. Retrieved from www.petersmagorinsky.net/About/PDF/RER/RER2001.pdf.

Smagorinsky, P. (2002). '*Growth through English* revisited'. *English Journal,* 91(6), 23–29. Retrieved from www.petersmagorinsky.net/About/PDF/EJ/EJ0916Growth.pdf.

Smagorinsky, P., & Taxel, J. (2004). 'The Discourse of character education: ideology and politics in the proposal and award of federal grants'. *Journal of Research in Character Education,* 2(2), 113–140. Retrieved from www.petersmagorinsky.net/About/PDF/JRCE/JRCE2004.pdf.

Smagorinsky, P., & Taxel, J. (2005). *The Discourse of character education: culture wars in the classroom.* Mahwah, NJ: Erlbaum.

Squire, J., & Britton, J. (1975/1967). Foreword, in J. Dixon, *Growth through English: set in the perspective of the Seventies* (3rd ed.) Yorkshire: National Association for the Teaching of English: vii–xviii.

Stotsky, S. (1999). *Losing our language: how multicultural classroom instruction is undermining our children's ability to read, write, and reason.* New York: The Free Press.

Vygotsky, L. S. (1987). 'Thinking and speech', in L. S. Vygotsky, *Collected works* (Vol. 1) (R. Rieber & A. Carton, eds.; N. Minick, Trans.). New York: Plenum: 39–285.

10

THE STATUS AND RELEVANCE OF THE GROWTH MODEL FOR A NEW GENERATION OF ENGLISH TEACHERS IN NEW SOUTH WALES, AUSTRALIA

Jacqueline Manuel and Don Carter

Introduction

The Dartmouth Conference of 1966 is widely recognised as a watershed moment in the history of English as a subject in schools. It seeded pioneering conceptualisations of the subject that found fertile ground in educational contexts across the globe (Brock, 1984a, 1984b; Sawyer, 2008, 2009) – particularly in New South Wales (NSW), Australia. The re-visioning of English, initially set out in John Dixon's *Growth through English* (1967/1975), was at the heart of the transformation of the NSW junior secondary English Syllabus in 1971 (cf. Brock, 1984a, 1984b, 1993, 2009; Sawyer, 2008, 2010). Homer (1973) described this syllabus as 'the most carefully considered application of "growth" principles yet seen in Australia' (p.212), while two decades later Brock maintained that it was 'the first "personal growth" model syllabus anywhere in the English-speaking world' (1993, p.30): it was 'suffused with the spirit of what has been called the "new English"' (1984a, p.204). According to Sawyer, '[c]ommentators on the Syllabus have generally agreed that it was: (1) a "revolutionary" document, certainly within NSW itself and (2) an institutionalised manifestation of the "growth model"' (2010, p.288).

The installation of the Growth model in the 1971 Syllabus and the persistence of its hallmark principles have been well documented in research and scholarship (Brock, 1984a, 1993, 2009; Sawyer, 2008, 2009, 2010; Watson, 1994). It is likely that those who completed their secondary education in NSW from the 1970s on and then chose to become teachers of English, carried with them an amalgam of formative 'epistemic assumptions' (Reid, 2002, p.32) about the subject, teaching, and student learning that in some measure inscribed the legacy of Growth. While the inheritances of Dartmouth encoded in the NSW junior secondary English curriculum have been extensively historicised, 'there has been very little "real world" research which investigates the actual views of English teachers about models of English and their preferences and beliefs' (Goodwyn, 2016, p.7). Goodwyn's observation holds for English teachers in NSW – especially those who have recently entered the profession.

The intention of this chapter then, is to address an identified gap in the research by reporting on aspects of an empirical study with 22 early-career English teachers in NSW. We were curious about the extent to which new teachers' values and beliefs about the subject, students, pedagogy and syllabus materials disclosed an allegiance to certain tenets of the Growth model that continue to find expression in the English curriculum in NSW. To gauge the currency and significance of Growth, we invited teachers to rank its status for them in relation to other recognised approaches to English teaching that are manifested in both junior and senior secondary English syllabuses in NSW.

In addition, we sought to ascertain the degree of alignment or dissonance between new teachers' philosophy and 'subject paradigm' (Ball, 1983) and that apparent in the official syllabus documents they are required to implement. Are new teachers' values, beliefs and conceptualisation of English reflected, affirmed, disrupted or challenged by constructions of the subject in the syllabus and the pragmatic classroom-based demands of the enacted curriculum? For a new generation of English teachers entering the profession, does Growth continue to speak to their sense of self and their vision as educators, 50 years on from Dartmouth? If so, what features of this model possess an enduring appeal and why? And what are the implications of this for English teachers' ability to realise their philosophical and pedagogical preferences?

Background and context

Both Brock (1984a, 1984b, 1993, 2009) and Sawyer (2008, 2009, 2010) have provided thorough analyses of the confluence of historical, theoretical, situational and educational forces that gave rise to the Dartmouth-inspired 1971 junior secondary English syllabus. Their work in the field has contributed not only to a deep understanding of the lineage of junior secondary English in NSW. It has also charted the stream of Growth originating in the 1971 syllabus and flowing through subsequent versions. This scholarship has traced a persistent attachment to certain Growth principles, each of which has proven remarkably durable over time. These include:

- the integrated design of the syllabus that replaced the more atomised representation of English as the discrete study of language and literature as a body of knowledge to be transmitted by the teacher and acquired by the student;
- the positioning of students as active users of language and participatory meaning-makers whose lived experience, language, imagination, social context and

interactions constitute the foundation for the development of their personal and social identity (cf. Brock, 1993; Sawyer, 2010);

- English-as-activity with an emphasis on the processes of using language in context, displacing prior orthodoxies of English-as-content or a body of knowledge (about language and literature) (Brock, 1984a, p.216; Sawyer, 2008, p.324);
- the continuity and interdependence of the language modes of writing, reading, speaking, and listening (and later, viewing and representing);
- a broader definition of what constitutes the 'content' of the subject, with literature (including the student's own creations, contemporary and popular texts, media and film) regarded as part of the 'shared store of experience' (Dixon, 1975, p.43) and aesthetic capital to 'inform our encounters with life as a form of spectating on life. . . bringing order and composure to our inner selves' (p.54); and
- a conceptualisation of English as an emancipatory, democratising project in pursuit of social justice and individual and collective agency (Goodwyn, 2016).

We are not proposing that these principles account for the entirety of the complex matrix of philosophical, ideological, political and cultural ideas that differentiates the Growth model from other approaches to English education in schools. Rather, they have remained prominent in NSW junior secondary English syllabuses and for the purposes of this study, they represent what is understood as Growth in the context of NSW English teaching and learning.

The study

During 2016, data were gathered from 22 secondary school English teachers in NSW who had been teaching for between 1 and 4 years. The study was conducted via an online structured questionnaire. Participation was voluntary and all responses were anonymous. The questionnaire contained 26 items: the first five items were questions seeking demographic and profiling information about the participant's gender, age, length of service, current role, school postcode/setting, employment status and subjects taught. The remainder of the questionnaire contained items seeking teachers' views on a range of matters including: their values and beliefs about the purpose of English; their theoretical and pedagogical preferences; the impact of regulatory and accountability requirements; national and local standardised testing programs; levels of motivations and satisfaction with teaching; and career intentions.

The majority of items were multiple choice questions, allowing for internal multiple responses. Most of the question types were based on a Likert rating scale, with the option of 'other' responses and an open field for comment. Responses were analysed using an inductive, iterative approach (Creswell, 2013) in order to apprehend general trends.

Participants

In the research sample of 22 early-career secondary English teachers, 20 were female and 2 were male. The average age of this sample was 31.[1] All participants completed their secondary schooling and their Initial Teacher Education (ITE) in NSW. Of the 22 participants:

- 18 were teaching in full-time positions in a secondary school; one was teaching in a full-time temporary position; and three were working in a casual (supply) capacity. No participants were teaching part-time.
- 11 were in their first year of teaching; eight in their second year of teaching; two in their third year of teaching; and one was in her fourth year of teaching.

Conceptual framework: models of English and their relevance to teachers' 'subject paradigm'

The Cox Report (DES, 1989) set out five theoretical perspectives – or models – that were considered to be instantiated to a greater or lesser degree in the range of approaches to English as a subject in schools, namely: Personal Growth, Cultural Heritage, Cultural Analysis, Adult Needs and Cross-Curricular. Although the Cox Report was produced in the context of curriculum reforms in England at the time, the models described in the Report have since gained more widespread utility as a shorthand means of classifying the theoretical, pedagogical and ideo-logical emphases in English curriculum documents. The models are frequently cited in research in the fields of English teacher education and curriculum, par-ticularly in England and Australia (Goodwyn and Findlay, 1999; Goodwyn, 2016; Marshall, 2000).

For the present study, we adapted the Cox models to serve as a conceptual framework for interpreting teachers' preferred 'subject paradigm' (Ball, 1983). To reflect the emphases in the English curriculum in NSW, the Critical Literacy model was included in the framework, replacing the Cross-Curricular model since the latter has been less explicit in syllabus materials until recently (NESA, 2014). The Critical Literacy model, along with the other four identified by Cox, has been evident in NSW junior secondary English syllabuses at some point dur-ing the past four to five decades. All participants in the study, because of their own secondary schooling and ITE, were familiar with the assumptions and theoretical orientations of each model.

Applying this conceptual framework, we asked teachers to rank the models according to:

- each model's relevance to their own philosophy of teaching, beliefs and values;
- the perceived presence of the model in the current junior secondary English syllabus;

- the perceived presence of the model in the current senior secondary English syllabus; and
- the model most evident in their classroom teaching.

As Goodwyn and Findlay (1999) point out, the Cox models 'were put forward, without evidence, as being of equal status and of equal value' (p.20) when in fact, the relative prominence of each model in a syllabus and in classroom practice is contingent on a constellation of complex and mutable factors, including the beliefs, values and predilections of the individual teacher.

Findings

In the following discussion we report on participants' responses to selected items that are directly relevant to determining the relative influence and status of Growth for new teachers of English in NSW.

The purpose of English as a subject in the curriculum

Integral to the decision to teach a particular subject are beliefs about that subject's purpose in the curriculum (cf. Heinz, 2015; Lindqvist and Nordanger, 2016) and its perceived affordances for the individual teacher, students and society more broadly. More than 90 percent of early-career teachers in this study identified a 'love of English as a subject' and 'making a difference in people's lives' as the chief motivational factors in their decision to teach. Both factors gesture towards the kind of altruism characteristic of the discourses of Growth. This altruism was pronounced in participants' responses to a series of statements about the purpose of English as a subject. An overwhelming majority rated the following as 'very important' on a five-point scale ranging from 'very important' to 'not important':

- Build students' knowledge and understanding of themselves and the world;
- Teach for critical thinking;
- Develop students' social and interpersonal skills;
- Encourage students' self-expression through language;
- Develop capacities for reflection;
- Articulate personal values, beliefs and ethics and recognise others';
- Inspire a love of learning;
- Develop students' creative and imaginative capacities;
- Support self-realisation through using language and the study of literature;
- Develop principles of social justice;
- Develop students' autonomy and self-direction.

Immediately apparent in this cluster of statements is the overriding theme of students' personal growth through language and interaction as a defining purpose of the subject. Together, these statements encompass the emblematic tropes of the Growth model. What is striking here is the high value participants assigned not only to the development of students as autonomous, imaginative, ethical, skilled and reflective learners, but also to the development of students as active, social beings attuned to the purpose of their own learning, their personal aspirations, and the contexts they both inhabit and observe. The purpose of English as a vehicle for 'self-cultivation' – resonating with the German idea of 'Bildung' that envisions education as the development and refinement of the self – is balanced by the equally strong emphasis participants placed on the social, cultural and ethical dimensions of teaching and learning in English.

From their responses, it is clear that teachers continue to subscribe to the view that the purpose of English is far more expansive than merely the development of functional literacy and preparation for work. English is conceptualised as the curricular site for advancing students' intellectual, affective, critical, ethical, imaginative and creative capacities through their meaningful immersion in integrated language and textual experiences. Encoded in this conceptualisation are the familiar principles of Growth, especially two basic principles advocated by Moffett (an American Dartmouth participant, though better known in England and Australia than in the US for his specific work in secondary English curriculum) in *Teaching the Universe of Discourse* (1968) – both of which have been foundational to the NSW junior secondary English syllabus since 1971. The first is that a curriculum should 'centre on the learner as producer and manipulator of symbols' (p.32). The second is that the curriculum should pursue as its aim the 'growth of the whole human being', which can be achieved only through a process founded on 'a new integration of learning' (p.18).

Teachers' perspectives on the relevance of models of English

A series of items in the questionnaire was intended to elicit teachers' beliefs about: the relevance of models of English to their philosophy; the perceived presence of the models in contemporary junior secondary and senior secondary syllabus documents; and the model/s most influential in their classroom practice. The results set out in Table 10.1 provide a comparative snapshot of the overall ranking of each model according to each questionnaire item.

For more than 90 percent of participants, the Growth model was cited as the most 'highly relevant' and 'relevant' to their philosophy of teaching, beliefs and values. Critical Literacy and Cultural Analysis were identified as 'highly relevant' and 'relevant' by more than 70 percent of participants, while Skills and Adult Needs and Cultural Heritage models were 'highly relevant' and 'relevant' to around 50 percent of participants. This finding is not surprising, considering the Growth principles of valuing a student's language and experiences and the study of literature and other texts (such as, for example, film and media)

TABLE 10.1 Comparison of teachers' ranking of models

Rank	Rank according to its relevance to the teacher's philosophy, beliefs and values	Rank according to how teachers see the model reflected in the junior secondary English syllabus	Rank according to how teachers see the model reflected in the senior secondary English syllabus	Rank according to how teachers see the model reflected in their classroom teaching
1	Growth	Growth	Critical Literacy	Critical Literacy
2	Critical Literacy	Cultural Analysis	Cultural Heritage	Growth
3	Cultural Analysis	Critical Literacy	Cultural Analysis	Cultural Heritage
4	Skills and Adult Needs	Skills and Adult Needs	Growth	Cultural Analysis
5	Cultural Heritage	Cultural Heritage	Skills and Adult Needs	Skills and Adult Needs

have been explicit in NSW junior secondary English syllabuses since the 1970s (Brock, 1993; Sawyer, 2009). Similarly, the priority given to Critical Literacy and Cultural Analysis models reflects the presence of these in NSW junior secondary English syllabuses since the late 1990s.

Although an overwhelming majority of teachers reported the strongest affinity with the Growth model – providing evidence of its continued salience and priority status for teachers' 'subject paradigm' – each model was recognised and regarded as relevant to some extent for all participants. No participant reported any single model as 'not relevant' to their philosophy. This finding underlines the informed eclecticism of English teachers' theoretical and pedagogical allegiances and illustrates the tendency to exercise professional agency by 'bower-birding' elements of a range of models in constructing their 'subject paradigm'. It also supports Goodwyn and Findlay's (1999) argument that 'the cultural view of language and literature is potentially consonant with a Personal Growth ideal, since it places pupils' cultural experience and resources on the agenda' (p.27).

The Cultural Heritage model was viewed as the least relevant to participants' philosophy, beliefs and values, and the least prominent model apparent in the junior secondary syllabus. It was, however, perceived by more than 80 percent of teachers to be the most 'clearly prominent' and 'prominent' model informing the senior secondary English syllabus. The Growth model – with its core tenet of student-centred teaching and learning – was perceived to be only minimally evident in the senior secondary syllabus. Participants' ranking of models perceived to be more pronounced in the senior syllabus reflects the historically embedded prescribed study of traditional canonical literary forms and the more tightly-regulated, exam-focused, content-driven and product-oriented nature of teaching and learning in the senior years (Manuel and Brock, 2003; Manuel and Carter, 2016).

When asked about the models that were most relevant to, and evident in, participants' classroom teaching (Column 4, Table 10.1), the Growth model was ranked second in priority, closely behind Critical Literacy. Teachers reported a high degree of alignment between their preferred 'subject paradigm' (Column 1, Table 10.1) and the pedagogical choices implemented in their day-to-day practice.

Of interest in this comparison of responses was the consistently low ranking of the Skills and Adult Needs model. While participants identified the need to 'teach basic skills' as one of the purposes of the subject, this model was less influential than each of the other models listed in this question. As Brock (1984a) and Sawyer (2008) have noted, the NSW junior secondary syllabus of 1971, and successive versions, rejected the traditional skills-oriented model of English that focused on the explicit teaching of grammar and knowledge *about* language in favour of an approach to language-in-use-in-context, extolled by Dixon, Moffett, Britton and other key figures from the post-Dartmouth period.

Two further observations can be made about responses to these items. First, English teachers in this sample did not ascribe equal value and status to each model in their own philosophy of teaching and in their classroom practice. The Growth model was the dominant influence on teachers' conceptualisation of the subject, and was ranked as only marginally less significant than Critical Literacy in teachers' classroom practice. Second, the responses exposed a palpable tension between teachers' preferred model of English and that most prominent in the senior secondary English syllabus.

Factors enabling and impeding the realisation of teacher's philosophy, beliefs and values

Research has shown that the extent to which a teacher's philosophy, beliefs and values are affirmed in their daily working lives is positively correlated with greater levels of commitment, performance and longevity in the profession (Day, 2012; Gu and Day, 2007; Heinz, 2015). Similarly, a teacher's sense of professional agency and self-efficacy along with their capacity to exercise professional autonomy is directly implicated in overall work satisfaction, motivation and engagement (Mason and Matas, 2015). For these reasons, we sought to identify the factors that may enable or impede the realisation of teachers' internalised 'subject paradigm' – which the results from earlier questionnaire items confirmed is predominantly Growth-based. The questionnaire items designed to gather data on these factors listed a series of statements about values and beliefs, and about agency and autonomy.

Around half of participants agreed that:

- their 'values as a teacher have not been challenged by colleagues or the system' they work in;
- their 'beliefs about (themselves) as a teacher are affirmed in (their) work';
- they have 'been able to maintain their ideals'; and
- are 'well supported by colleagues'.

A considerable proportion, however, expressed ambivalence or disagreed that they had maintained their values, beliefs, and ideals or experienced affirmation and support from colleagues. Of specific concern was the percentage who conveyed that their values have been challenged by colleagues or the system (50 percent).

In response to indicators of professional agency and autonomy, more than three-quarters of participants agreed that they: 'participate in decision-making that impacts on' their classroom practice; 'have the freedom to make choices about the literature' they teach in junior secondary English; 'have opportunities to develop programs, units of work and resources'; and enjoy 'professional autonomy in deciding on the pedagogical approaches' implemented in the classroom in junior secondary English. In terms of their sense of self-efficacy, the overwhelming majority of participants believed that they are 'making a difference' as teachers.

The key enabling factors in maintaining teachers' values and beliefs and thereby contributing to their sense of agency, motivation, enthusiasm and work satisfaction were:

- a love of literature and the scope to shape the nature of teaching and learning in the junior secondary years;
- the rewards that flow from engaging students and witnessing their development;
- validation from colleagues; and
- the latitude afforded by the junior secondary English syllabus to enact their preferred 'subject paradigm' and pedagogy.

While the majority of participants identified these aspects of their work that served to strengthen their commitment and fortify their professional identity, they expressed equally candid views about the factors that impede, threaten or disrupt their 'subject paradigm'. Foremost amongst these was the far-reaching effects of external examinations, testing regimes and the heightened impact of government regulatory and accountability systems. The final external leaving credential examination, the Higher School Certificate, was considered by participants to be especially constraining, with all participants agreeing that the examination not only 'drives the way teaching occurs in HSC English': 'if there were no HSC exam, I would approach the teaching of literature in Year 12 differently'.

Participants reported that the pressure on teachers – and students – to perform in high-stakes tests radically skews the purpose and pedagogy of English in the senior years. These responses resonate with Australian and international research into standardised testing, which concludes that faced with a programme of regular, high-stakes testing, teachers increasingly 'teach to the test' (Au, 2001; Jones, 2007; Thompson and Harbaugh, 2013) leading to an emphasis on teacher-centred instruction (Au, 2001; Thompson and Harbaugh, 2013), and thus seriously compromising a central tenet of Growth: student-centred teaching and learning.

Similarly, teachers lamented the other 'casualty' in these high-stakes examinations: the marginalisation and devaluing of imaginative writing, which sits at the core of a Growth-oriented paradigm of English. As one participant observed:

Stage 6 (years 11 and 12) students are more interested in being taught whatever the magic formula for a good mark in the creative component of the exam is than they are in learning about creative writing in a general sense.

Another participant encapsulated the views of many that imaginative and creative writing is considered by senior secondary students as 'irrelevant or (as) wasting time'. Students will only undertake such writing when it is a compulsory component of assessment. Otherwise, the imaginative and creative dimensions of English are 'largely ignored'.

Conclusion

This small-scale study included the aim of understanding early-career English teachers' perspectives on the status and relevance of the Growth model, relative to the other recognised models of English in schools. More than 50 years on from the revolutionary paradigm shift generated by the Dartmouth Seminar, the findings presented here confirm the persistence, resilience and indeed, the normative, status of the Growth model in shaping NSW English teachers' philosophy, values and beliefs about their work and identity. The centrality of Growth to participants' 'subject paradigm' bespeaks the enduring appeal of its ideology, discourses, tenets and vision, even in the face of momentous cultural, social, educational and technological transformations that have occurred since 1966.

While the Growth model can be seen to represent the centre of gravity for these contemporary teachers' conceptualisation of the subject and their professional identity, the findings have also shed light on the tendency for teachers to deliberately amalgamate elements from a range of models in constructing and adapting their 'subject paradigm'. The models, in this sense, are perceived to be more compatible than they are hermetic or dichotomous. What is clear, however, is that teachers do not regard the models as equally relevant or ideologically neutral.

For around half of the 90 percent of teachers who identified Growth as the most compelling and influential model, there was a substantial degree of coherence between their values and beliefs, the theoretical and pedagogical nature of the junior secondary English syllabus, and their approach to teaching in the junior secondary years. Although these teachers could enact and sustain their Growth-based philosophy in the context of teaching junior secondary English, the high-stakes exam-driven senior secondary syllabus – with its emphasis on Cultural Heritage – figured as one of the greatest challenges to their 'subject paradigm', along with a lack of support and validation from colleagues and the system within which they worked.

Around half of the participants reported that their initial values and beliefs had been significantly compromised and had not been supported and affirmed by colleagues. Those who indicated that their beliefs about the subject did not cohere with the conceptualisations of English evident in official curriculum documents or those espoused by colleagues were those who also expressed:

- greater levels of dissatisfaction with their work;
- concerns about the constraining impact of syllabus requirements and examination imperatives on their teaching of literature;
- uncertain or equivocal views about their efficacy and professional agency; and
- strong reservations about their career futures.

This finding suggests that for the teachers in this sample, their investment in teaching as a career diminished when their philosophy, values and beliefs were seen to be undermined by extrinsic, institutional or other factors. Conversely, when teachers' 'subject paradigm' was validated through the capacity to exercise agency and autonomous professional judgements in their teaching, and through a perceived congruence between their philosophy and curriculum documents, they reported greater levels of work satisfaction, motivation and intention to continue in their career.

Although it was beyond the scope of this study to probe more fully the reasons for teachers' steadfast attachment to the filaments of Growth, the findings prompt some speculative interpretations. It is arguable that the conceptualisation of English as 'the meeting point of experience, language and society' (Dixon, 1975, p.85) continues to speak most powerfully to the altruism and idealism of those who are motivated to teach English in order to make a difference to individual lives and to the quality of society more broadly: to play a role in enabling young people to find meaning in, and make choices about, the kind of life they are living and are to live.

In an educational context dominated by a culture of measurement, competition, compliance, techno-rationalism and the marginalisation of the arts and humanities, English remains one of the few sites in the school curriculum where individuals – in relationship with each other – interpret, enlarge and make sense of their worlds through language and story. The 'humanising' discourses of Growth, with their tropes of possibility and hope, may reverberate even more intensely for a new generation of teachers whose motivation to enter the profession includes the desire to push back against the tide of dehumanising neo-liberal agendas. Ultimately, what has emerged from this study is evidence of the remarkable durability of the spirit, vision and legacy of the Growth model for NSW early-career English teachers – more than half a century on from its genesis during the Dartmouth Seminar of 1966.

Note

1 The slightly higher than expected average age of the sample can be attributed to the inclusion of participants who were mature-age and career-change entrants into teaching. There was an over-representation of female teachers in this sample.

References

Au, W. (2011). 'Teaching under the new Taylorism: high-stakes testing and the standardisation of the 21st century curriculum', *Journal of Curriculum Studies*, 43(1), 25–45.

Ball, S. J. (1983). 'A subject of privilege: English and the school curriculum 1906–35', in M. Hammersley and A. Hargreaves (eds.) *Curriculum practice: some sociological case studies*, London and New York: The Falmer Press: 61–88.

Brock, P. (1984a). *A history of the development of the English syllabuses in NSW secondary education, 1953–1976: a continuum or a 'series of new beginnings'?* PhD Thesis, Armidale: University of New England.

Brock, P. (1984b). 'Changes in the English syllabus in New South Wales, Australia: can any American echoes be heard?' *The English Journal*, 73(3), 52–58.

Brock, P. (1993). 'Some reflections on teacher education programs for the prospective teacher of English in Australian secondary schools: a personal view', *English in Australia*, 106, 24–40.

Brock, P. (2009). 'The value of literature and language in contemporary education: a personal perspective'. in J. Manuel, P. Brock, D. Carter, and W. Sawyer (eds.) *Imagination, innovation, creativity: re-visioning English in education*, Sydney: Phoenix Education: 28–41.

Creswell, J. (2013). *Qualitative inquiry* (3rd ed.). Thousand Oaks: Sage Publications.

Day, C. (2012). 'New lives of teachers', *Teacher Education Quarterly*, Winter, 7–26.

Department of Education and Science (1989). *The Cox Report: English for ages 5–16*, London: Her Majesty's Stationery Office.

Dixon, J. (1967). *Growth through English*, Oxford: Oxford University Press.

Dixon, J. (1975). *Growth through English: set in the perspective of the Seventies.* (3rd ed). Oxford: Oxford University Press.

Goodwyn, A. (2016). 'Still growing after all these years? The resilience of the "Personal Growth model of English" in England and also internationally', *English Teaching, Practice and Critique*, 15(1), 7–21.

Goodwyn, A. and Findlay, K. (1999). 'The Cox Models revisited: English teachers' views of their subject and the National Curriculum', *English in Education*, 33(2), 19–31.

Gu, Q. and Day, C. (2007). 'Teachers' resilience: a necessary condition for effectiveness', *Teaching and Teacher Education*, 23, 1302–1316.

Heinz, M. (2015). 'Why choose teaching? An international review of empirical studies exploring student teachers' career motivations and levels of commitment to teaching', *Educational Research and Evaluation*, 21(3), 258–297.

Homer, D. B. (1973). *Fifty years of purpose and precept in English teaching (1921–71): an overview with special reference to the teaching of poetry in the early secondary years.* Unpublished MEd thesis. Melbourne: Melbourne University.

Jones, B. (2007). 'The unintended outcomes of high-stakes testing', *Journal of Applied School Psychology*, 23(2), 65–86.

Lindqvist, P. and Nordanger, U. K. (2016). 'Already elsewhere: a study of (skilled) teachers' choice to leave teaching', *Teaching and Teacher Education*, 54, 88–97.

Manuel, J. and Brock, P.(2003). '"W(h)ither the place of literature?": two momentous reforms in the NSW senior secondary English curriculum', *English in Australia*, 136, 15–26.

Manuel, J. and Carter, D. (2016). 'Sustaining hope and possibility: early-career English teachers' perspectives on their first years of teaching', *English in Australia*, 51(1), 91–103.

Marshall, B. (2000). *English teachers: the unofficial guide – researching the philosophies of English teachers*, London: Routledge.

Mason, S. and Matas, C. P.(2015). 'Teacher attrition and retention research in Australia: towards a new theoretical framework', *Australian Journal of Teacher Education*, 40(11), 44–66.

Moffett, J. (1968). *Teaching the universe of discourse.* Boston: Houghton Mifflin.

New South Wales Education Standards Authority (NESA) (2014). *NSW English K-10 Syllabus.* Retrieved 10 July 2015 from www.boardofstudies.nsw.edu.au/syllabuses/.

Reid, I. (2002). 'Wordsworth institutionalized: the shaping of an educational ideology', *History of Education*, 31(1), 15–37.

Sawyer, W. (2008). 'English teaching in New South Wales since 1971: versions of growth?' *Changing English*, 15(3), 323–37.

Sawyer, W. (2009). 'The Growth Model of English', in S. Gannon, M. Howie, and W. Sawyer (eds.) *Charged with meaning*, Putney: Phoenix Education: 19–30.

Sawyer, W. (2010). 'Structuring the New English in Australia: James Moffett and English teaching in New South Wales', *Changing English: Studies in Culture and Education*, 17(3), 285–296.

Thompson, G. and Harbaugh, A.G. (2013). 'A preliminary analysis of teacher perceptions of the effects of NAPLAN on pedagogy and curriculum', *Australian Educational Researcher in Education*, 40(3), 299–314.

Watson, K. (1994). 'English teaching in historical perspective: case study of an Australian state' in K. Watson, C. Durrant, S. Hargreaves, and W. Sawyer (eds.) *English teaching in perspective: in the context of the 1990s*, Rozelle: St Clair Press: 26–42.

11

GROWING THE NATION

The influence of Dartmouth on the teaching of literature in subject English in Australia

Larissa McLean Davies, Lucy Buzacott and Susan K. Martin

Introduction

It is hard to imagine any subject English classroom in the Anglophone world that does not continue to be impacted by the model of personal growth that was developed through the month-long Dartmouth Conference in 1966 and explored through Dixon's now famous book *Growth through English* (Dixon 1969, 1975). The importance of the Dartmouth conference, and the influence of Dixon's book, are evident through the ways in which English teachers across continents, even those who were in their infancy when Dixon published his first edition, subscribe to the notion that students' personal growth is core business to subject English (Goodwyn, 2017; Dowsett, 2016). The question 'What is English', which was central to, but not able to be satisfactorily answered at the Dartmouth conference, remains an elusive obsession for those involved in the teaching, research and scholarship of English as a school subject (Evans, 1993; Medway 1990; Durrant, 2004). However, there is both tacit and explicit agreement that the individual growth of learners through and with texts is a major aspect of the subject as it is taught throughout the world (Reid, 2003; Tarpey, 2016).

This is not to say that the legacy of Dartmouth, as it is enacted across continents, remains uncontested, or that notions of growth in English are unproblematic or static (Green, 2016; Smagorinsky, 2002). Rather, understanding the ways in which subject English has been infiltrated by central aspects of what Reid calls 'the growth enterprise' (2016, p.11) in particular national contexts assists us to understand contemporary challenges and points of tension for the teaching of English, and prompts us to consider what growth through English might look like in a globalised world. In this chapter, we will turn specific attention to the Australian context and, drawing on curriculum documents and recent research into the teaching of literature in secondary schools, will consider the ways in which personal growth approaches have impacted and continue to impact, on pedagogy and practice. We will explore some of the tensions that exist for teachers and curriculum and policy writers as they negotiate contemporary possibilities of 'growth through English' in the context of the teaching of literature in Australia. We will contend that the unquestioned presence of British and American canonical literature in late twentieth and early twenty-first century articulations of subject English in Australia, and the distinctions made in curriculum and practice between student growth and national cultural knowledge and understanding, reveals the ideological complexity of applying personal growth approaches in post-colonial contexts. Exploring the implications of these tensions for the future teaching of literature in subject English, we will conclude this chapter by outlining considerations for a model of growth that is sustainable and generative in the twenty-first century in a post-colonial, pluralistic national context.

Part I: growth and the teaching of literature in subject English in Australia

The fiftieth anniversary of the Dartmouth Conference was marked with various conferences, special editions of journals, and other key publications (including this book), in all parts of the Anglophone world (Dowsett, 2016; '50th Anniversary Dartmouth', n.d.). Australia was no exception to this: a seminar was held in conjunction with the national conference in 2016, and a special edition of the national journal, *English in Australia*, was inspired by this seminar (Volume 51 number 3, 2016). This is particularly interesting, given that there were no Australians present at the 1966 Dartmouth event. As Ian Reid notes, participation was confined to select groups from Britain and North America, meaning that Australians, even those old enough to have attended, experience Dartmouth 'through reports by people who took part – reports in the form of books, conference papers, and other impure residues of their subjective experiences' (Reid 2016, p.12). Yet, despite their absence from the North American conference, Australian teachers and teacher educators were keen to explore Dixon's notions of learner-centred English. The level of interest in, and commitment to, the arguments advanced by Dixon and colleagues at Dartmouth by Australian teachers and subject English scholars and researchers is reflected in Dixon's significant engagement with Australian colleagues. This includes his opening address to the 1973 VATE Conference, which was followed by a publication produced by the Curriculum and Research Branch of the Education Department of Victoria titled *John Dixon in Australia* and his involvement in the combined International Federation of the Teaching of English/Australian Association for the Teaching of English Conference held in Sydney, Australia in 1980. As Reid recounts, there were over 800 participants in this conference, and three-quarters of them were Australians (2016, p.12). Indeed, Dixon has continued to have a close relationship with English teaching in Australia, and with Australian teacher educators and scholars, through contributions to the national journal into the new century (see for example Dixon, 2003 and the most recent Dartmouth anniversary edition of *English in Australia*, 2016).

While there was not unequivocal support for the growth model in Australia in the years following Dartmouth (Reid, 2016) it is fair to say that there was far greater support for Dixon's model of English, representing the British position, than the North American preference for more traditional literary analysis and formal skills championed by Herbert J. Muller (1967). The enthusiasm for the growth model in Australia can be understood as motivated by the new narrative of English teaching offered by Dartmouth that resonated with the zeitgeist in Australia at the end of the 1960s. Dixon conceived the English classroom as a place where processes 'combine together to help or hinder individual growth' identifying these moments as the 'concerns of English in its widest sense' (1975, p.70). Consequently, he argued that teachers should privilege classroom encounters that were of 'personal importance to pupils' (Dixon, 1975, p.51), and advocated for pupils to have the opportunity to 'explore aspects of their immediate lives' (Dixon, 1975, p.55) through subject English. These ideas resonated with, and arguably influenced, the work of renowned Australian educator and scholar, Garth Boomer, whose advocacy for teaching and for students to negotiate the English curriculum (Boomer, 1992; Green, 1999), like the growth movement more broadly, has had a profound impact on the teaching of English in Australia (Dowsett, 2016; Green, 2016).

However, while the enthusiasm for the British approach to growth through English can be understood in terms of its resonance with the priorities of English teachers in the southern hemisphere in the 1970s, the allegiance to this approach in Australia is arguably also inextricably connected to Australia's colonial history and its political alliance with Britain. As Bill Green and Phil Cormack have explained, a key part of the project of English in Australia, since its inception in the nineteenth century, was to 'become British' (Green and Cormack, 2008). This resulted, as Wayne Sawyer has observed, in Australia (and Australian English teachers) largely inhabiting the 'British "zone" of the English education world' throughout the twentieth century (Sawyer et al., 2016, p.40). As we have argued elsewhere, this political history has often resulted in practices and approaches in subject English in Australia that reveal a tacit but tenacious and uncontested imperial allegiance (McLean Davies, 2011; McLean Davies et al., 2017). Thus, there is a level of irony in Australia adopting a model that Dixon and his supporters conceived as a turn away from heritage approaches, and ongoing tension in the competing and intersecting colonial and emancipatory motivations for growth in English in Australia. This lends an additional nuance to Reid's claim that the popularity of the growth model in Australian was 'not always accompanied by a detailed knowledge of what it supposedly meant' (2016, p.12).

This complexity is exacerbated when one turns attention to the teaching of literature, and in particular, to considerations of Australian literature, as it is enacted within and alongside the approaches advocated by Dixon and his colleagues. It is fair to say, at the outset, that in *Growth through English* literature was not Dixon's primary concern.

Indeed, he laments the approach to literature which he perceives has led teachers away from genuine dialogue with students and the capacity to honour their experiences:

> By re-emphasizing the text, the heritage model confirmed the average teacher in his attention to the written word (the point of strength in his training) as against the spoken word (the pupil's strength). It confirmed him too in presenting experience (of reality and the self). But in doing so it set up tensions that have brought about its own collapse and a major reinterpretation of its noble aims.
>
> (*Dixon, 1975, p.3*)

In seeking to offer an alternative approach, as John Yandell notes, Dixon conceived students as the producers of literature rather than simply the receivers of culture (Yandell, 2016). Yet, while Dixon clearly imagines a different relationship between texts and readers to that which had characterised English teaching prior to the 1960s, it would be inaccurate to suggest that in rejecting the heritage approach, he is also rejecting the place of literature in English, or, more to the point, the place of British literature in the education of British citizens. Throughout his book, Dixon cites no less than 31 literary works: 26 of the authors concerned are from the United Kingdom, 30 are men and only one is by a woman (Bronte's *Jane Eyre*). Further, only three texts (Ellison's *Going to the Territory*, Berger's *A Fortunate Man* and Blyth's *Akenfield*) are published after 1961. Clearly, the issue for Dixon is not that the literary works need to be changed, or even that the definition of literature should be expanded (a point he does raise belatedly in his introduction to the 1975 edition of *Growth through English*), but rather that the pedagogy associated with these texts requires radical revision. Although Dixon criticises the idea that '[t]hrough literature all that was best in national thought and feeling could be handed onto a generation that knew largely slums and economic depression' (1975, p.3) and argues instead for the vital 'interplay between [the student's] personal world and the world of the writer' (1975, p.3), he uncritically accepts the canonical selection of texts routinely set for study.

While Dixon appears either to assume that student personal growth is unmediated by the cultural specificities of texts, or conversely accepts that textual experience is 'naturally' facilitated by a canonical corpus, Richard Squire and colleagues, who report on the activities of the Dartmouth literature working group (Squire, 1968), are more specific about the role of literature in offering particular access to cultural experience. In *Response to literature: Papers Relating to the Anglo-American Seminar on the Teaching of English at Dartmouth College*, text contributors blur the line Dixon advances between heritage and growth models (Sawyer et al., 2016, pp.42–45). This is evident throughout the collection, and is captured clearly in the contribution of D.W. Harding, eminent British psychologist and literary critic and leader of the working group, who writes:

> Most values are culturally derived; at their best, they are the currency given to the adjustments to experience of most sensitive members of society. Thus,

in entering into the 'virtual experience' of influential works of literature a
child is offered a flow and recoil of sympathies that accords with the culture
pattern in which he is growing up.

(Harding 1968, p.12.)

It is clear, therefore, that by choosing as exemplar certain traditional authors and
texts, Dixon, Harding, Squires and colleagues actually reinforce the role of heritage
in subject English. Of the 50 times a text or author is mentioned, 45 are male, with
only five references to female authors or texts (*Jane Eyre* makes another appearance
here alongside Louisa May Alcott's *Little men*, Johanna Spyri's *Heidi* and two mentions of George Eliot's *Silas Marner*). Texts and authors from the United Kingdom
dominate, with 34 of the 50 listed hailing from this region, although the United
States with 13 references, does feature more prominently than in Dixon's text,
which is understandable, as members of the Literature Working Group spanned
both sides of the Atlantic Ocean.

Given Australia's political history, it is perhaps unsurprising that, just as the British
and North American literary canons remain central and unproblematised in the work
of Dixon, and essential for Squire and colleagues, in the Australian application of
personal growth approaches in the 1970s, canonical British texts also remained key
to this enterprise. This resulted in the radical curriculum aims embodied by a growth
approach being paradoxically mobilised, for Australian students, through texts which
for the most part represented a British-centric view of cultural heritage. An example
for the mid-1970s from the State of Victoria serves to illustrate this point. As we
have noted, John Dixon was the keynote speaker at the Victorian Association for the
Teaching of English in 1973, and it is clear that his work has influenced the 1976
Higher School Certificate (HSC) syllabus, which advised teachers that:

> The first object in studying [the set] books should be to grasp as fully as
> possible, and to assess, whatever each book or group of books adds to our
> understanding – or our capacity to understand – ourselves and the world.
> No doubt literary questions about how each book does so will arise in
> the course of reading and discussion; nevertheless, these questions should
> be subordinate.

(VUSEB, 1975, p.187)

The texts set for these students, unlike those tacitly recommended by Dixon and
Squire a decade earlier, show some consciousness of temporality: there are 28 texts
on this list, and 10 of these had been published in the previous decade (ALIAS, 2018).

However, while a range of social contexts are represented, only four of the
texts set for study are by Australians (and only four are by women, and two of
these about men – Brodie's *The Devil drives* (1968) and Kael's *The Citizen Kane
book* (1971). There are none by Australian women). Conversely, 14 of the texts
are by British authors, and a further seven by authors from North America.
'Growth' for Australian students, whist filled with potential, thus involved clear

movement towards an imperial centre. The texts are divided into seven groups of four and teachers were required to select one of these groups of texts to be the focus for the year. It is interesting to note that the four Australian texts are distributed across only two of the groups, thus rendering it less likely for students to encounter an Australian text as they negotiate the interplay between the self and the world. Indeed, some students would have somewhat paradoxically encountered Australia at a distance through Dickens' novel *Great expectations*, which was set for study as part of 'Group 4'. As we have noted previously, *Great expectations* featured strongly on syllabuses across Australia from 1948, and this arguably had 'implications for national identity and consciousness' (Martin and McLean Davies, 2017 p.245). In this novel, as we have observed, 'Australia is depicted as a place of deprivation while the real business of life takes place in England' (Martin and McLean Davies, 2017, p.245); indeed, it is in the northern hemisphere, in this novel, that growth and development take place. We are not suggesting that 'growth through English' should be limited to local literary experiences, it is clearly desirable to culturally and aesthetically expand the worlds a student has access to; however, we *are* pointing to the paradoxical disconnection between an overt pedagogical preference for growth through English, the marginalisation of Australian literature, and the enduring nature of a heritage approach in Australia through the setting and examination (see Teese, 2013) of British or North American texts. It will be useful to provide a brief overview of the status of the teaching of national literatures in order to better explain the conditions that have led to this complex context.

Part 2: Australian literature in curriculum and practice – reconsidering growth

Australian literature has always had a precarious existence within the national textual ecosystem. As literary scholar Ken Gelder has asserted, Australian literature is perennially perceived as fragile or in crisis (Gelder, 2013). From the 1940s, when Australian literature was routinely denounced by senior academics in Australian universities (Doecke et al., 2011; McLean Davies, 2011), the national literature in Australia has required advocacy in order to be included systematically and in a sustained way on secondary and tertiary English courses. As we and others have argued, this can be primarily attributed to Australia's colonial history, and the links between subject English and English subjectivity (McLean Davies et al., 2013; Martin and McLean Davies, 2017; McLean Davies and Buzacott, 2018; Green and Cormack, 2008). Writing in 1989, Ken Gelder and Paul Salzman observed that the previous 18 years had 'seen a massive increase in the production of Australian fiction' and a 'new efficiency in the packaging, promotion and circulation of that fiction' (Gelder and Salzman, 1989, p.1). They acknowledge that this was significantly impacted by Federal Government funding made available from the early 1970s and distributed through the Commonwealth Literary Fund and the newly established Literature Board (Gelder and Salzman, 1989, pp.1–2). Gelder and Salzman note that between

'1973 and 1974, the Literature Board supported the publication of 54 works of fiction; by 1986, the number had increased to over 200' (Gelder and Salzman, 1989, p.2).

Yet, as was revealed in our discussion of the 1976 Victorian Higher School Certificate (HSC) text list, despite this considerable increase in the production and profile of Australian literature, the works set for study at this time were predominantly not Australian. Indeed, it is important to note that the dominance of British and American texts in subject English has been maintained despite these significant increases in Australian publishing, the expansion of definitions of Australian literature, and the growing presence of writers' festivals and other related cultural activities over the past 50 years. This is illustrated through an examination of the Analysis of Literature in Australian Schools (ALIAS) database, the product of a research project led by Tim Dolin and John Yiannakis which houses text lists from senior years' English curricula in the states of Victoria, Western Australia, South Australia, Tasmania, and New South Wales from 1945–2005. Using this database, we have identified that between 1966–2005 (from the year of Dartmouth to the last date available in the database) the texts most set across these States of Australia were: *The crucible* (appears 132 times), *Tess of the D'Urbervilles* (appears 115 times), *Hamlet* (appears 109 times) and *The Adventures of Huckleberry Finn* (appears 106 times).

Thus, while Australian texts have been increasingly set for study in subject English since the 1970s by education department panels and examination boards, the discretion available to teachers, the greater rewards available to students who write on canonical texts (Teese, 2013), and 'Magwitch Madness' (McLean Davies, 2011) – a desire for textual return to the imperial centre – has meant that Australian literature has not achieved the unconscious and uncritical status of British or American canonical literature. This was addressed, with other perceived 'problems' of English in 2008, when Australia launched its first national curriculum. Like all curricula, this document can be read more broadly as responding to what was politically understood to be the issues of practice requiring remediation. In this case, the perceived issues included the lack of explicit teaching of grammar and in particular phonics, and an increasingly diffused approach to texts, which did not adequately emphasise the centrality of the work of literature, and in particular, national literatures, in the formation of the student as local and global citizen. In response to these identified issues, *The Australian Curriculum: English (AC: E)* conceived a new architecture and organisation of subject English. While curricula around Australia had, for at least two decades previously, arranged the subject according to the language modes – reading and viewing, speaking and listening, and writing and producing (or similar) – the *AC: E* organises the curriculum into three strands: Language, Literature and Literacy (ACARA, 2018). In addition to 'returning' Literature to the centre of subject English, this curriculum has also mandated the study of Australian literature at each year level (from the first year of Primary school (Foundation – 5 years old) to the final year of compulsory education (Year 10 – 16 years old).

The rationale section of the *AC: E* reveals the curriculum writers negotiating understandings of literature in English, bringing heritage and growth models into a different dialogue, and attempting to reframe what might constitute these categories:

> There are many different ways to engage with literature, ranging from personal preferences for literature to the way in which texts reflect the context of culture and situation in which they are created. The appreciation of literature in one or more of these ways provides students with access to mediated experiences and truths that support and challenge the development of individual identity. Through engagement with literature, students learn about themselves, each other and the world.
>
> *(ACARA, 2018, pp.6–7)*

While 'personal preferences' and 'cultural context' are initially presented as distinct reasons for literary study, these approaches come together for the overall purpose of individual personal growth and identity development for individuals in their local and globalised contexts. These links between heritage and growth are further explored in a later statement:

> *The Australian Curriculum: English. . .* helps students to engage imaginatively and critically with literature to expand the scope of their experience. Aboriginal and Torres Strait Islander Peoples have contributed to Australian society and to its contemporary literature and its literary heritage through their distinctive ways of representing and communicating knowledge, traditions and experience. *The Australian Curriculum: English* values, respects and explores this contribution. It also emphasises Australia's links to Asia.
>
> *(ACARA, 2018, p.4)*

It is worth noting that there are several notions of experience and heritage explicitly and implicitly conveyed here. Students will have opportunity for expanded experience through literature. This will be made possible through engaging with Aboriginal and Torres Strait Islander texts, which in turn reflect a different national experience. This point is taken up further in the following paragraph, in a statement that is repeated in the preface material for each of the Year levels covered in the curriculum:

> The range of literary texts for Foundation to Year 10 comprises Australian literature, including the oral narrative traditions of Aboriginal and Torres Strait Islander Peoples, as well as the contemporary literature of these two cultural groups, and classic and contemporary world literature, including texts from and about Asia.
>
> *(ACARA, 2018, p.7)*

The listing of Australian literature, and specifically Indigenous literatures at the start of this statement can be understood as a deliberate attempt to recalibrate what has, by default, come to constitute literary range. In this paradigm, students benefit from engagement with literature on local and global levels and from a rich range of literary texts which will constitute the interplay between personal experience and the narratives (fiction and nonfiction) of others.

On one level, this recalibration of heritage in the *AC: E* can be seen as a social justice intervention that attempts to break with the imperial legacy of 'growth' that has endured, as we have discussed, in subject English in Australia. On another level, though, this historical and cultural acknowledgment of what constitutes 'heritage' and 'experience' in Australia has the effect of othering Indigenous peoples and students. Indeed, it appears that the curriculum is addressed to non-Indigenous students who will benefit from having their world expanded in this way. Indigenous students, conversely, are not specifically addressed, and remain rhetorically 'other' in the curriculum, while they are at the same time the source of the expansion of heritage possibilities. 'Growth' for these students is not imagined in the curriculum, perhaps because notions of personal growth, with their imperial overlay, continue to be the cause of much pain and suffering in a society where colonisation remains a strong and present legacy.

An analysis of the content of the curriculum across the Year levels reveals that while Australian literature broadly understood is identified as central to the subject English in the opening sections of the *AC: E*, this category is not used in the content descriptions, beyond the statement about the range of texts to be included, which we have cited above. In short, the links between the local and global that are imagined in the opening statements about literature are not supported by the detail. With regard to Australian literature, it is only Aboriginal and Torres Strait Islander texts that are referred to specifically in the suggested content and approaches for each year level, and these references, as intimated above, serve to remind the non-Indigenous student of the 'otherness' of Indigenous peoples and their experiences. These references, which have been undoubtedly provided with good intentions, and with the view to incorporating Indigenous texts in subject English, where they have not always been taken up, are often written in such a way as to render the experiences alien. In Year 8, for example, under the category 'Literature and context', teachers are encouraged to 'explore the ways that ideas and viewpoints in literary texts drawn from different historical, social and cultural contexts may reflect or challenge the values of individuals or groups'. This point is elaborated in the following ways: students can 'investigate texts about Aboriginal and Torres Strait Islander history from different sources and explaining different viewpoints' and 'compare attitudes and ideas in texts drawn from contexts that are different from students' own' (ACARA, 2018, p.136). What is being suggested here is not so much a new understanding of growth, but rather, a revised approach to heritage. Personal growth, despite the initial promise of the curriculum rationale, is not explicitly linked to a widening of students' reading practices.

This resonates with the findings of a pilot study into the teaching of Australian literature which we conducted in 2016, some 8 years after the implementation of the *AC: E*. Supported by the Copyright Agency Cultural Fund, we explored the setting and uses of literature in subject English following the curriculum mandate to include Australian literature at each level. The project had two major components, a preliminary national survey of teachers' attitudes and reported practices, which elicited 210 responses nationwide, and workshops with teachers held in Victoria (see McLean Davies et al., 2017). Drawing on the responses to two key questions, we will briefly discuss the ways articulations and commitments to the growth approach impact on attitudes towards the teaching of Australian literature. The enduring nature of individual personal growth in understandings of the teaching of literature in English in Australia is reflected in answers to Question 10, which asked respondents to rank the factors that contribute to their selection of Australian texts. The options were: canonical Australian literature; gender; genre; literary challenge; national identity issues; relevance to student cohort; representation of indigenous Australians; representation of migrant experience; teacher knowledge of the text; and other. Significantly, 105 of the 135 respondents to this question identified that 'relevance to the student cohort' was the most significant factor influencing their text selection practices. By contrast, 41 respondents considered the 'representation of Indigenous Australians' to be significant factor, and a further 37 considered both the representation of migrant experience and national identity issues to be significant factors when selecting Australian texts. The focus on relevance and engagement is reflected in Question 9, where respondents listed five Australian texts they had taught. The most listed text was Craig Silvey's *Jasper Jones*, a novel which is set in a fictional Australian country town, where the protagonist, white middle-class Charlie Bucktin comes of age through his encounters with the social outcast Aboriginal youth Jasper Jones, his first (white) girlfriend Eliza, and his Vietnamese friend Jeffrey Lu. Made into a popular film, this award-winning book acknowledges the prejudice and diversity of Australian communities; however, it also tells a story of diversity through the eyes of one who remains privileged by and through the dominant culture. It might be regarded as a 'safe' textual choice, enabling identification with, and access to, an implied reader-student perceived at some level to be white, middle class, and probably male. Access to the 'other' world is through the primary protagonist. The film, directed by acclaimed Indigenous film maker Rachel Perkins, may unsettle these lines of affective identification. Combined with a charter to provide 'relevant' texts for students, we can see how a generative understanding of growth, which would seek to unsettle stereotypes and reimagine community, may not be achieved unless this popular book is supplemented with less safe, alternative narratives.

Conclusion

In this chapter, we have explored the enduring nature of a personal growth approach to subject English in Australia, and showed the ways in which this approach, both in its initial conception by Dixon and his colleagues, and as it has been appropriated in and for an Australian, post-colonial context, did not forsake cultural heritage. A growth approach heralded a new way of thinking about the purpose of subject English, and the agency of students, but neither in its original formulation, nor in its Antipodian rendering, has 'growth through English' moved substantially beyond canonical texts. In his paper 'Literary experience and literature teaching since the Growth Model', Reid argues that what Dixon 'dismissed as a cultural heritage model is not beyond redemption if literature teaching can bring to it a more politically aware understanding of culture and heritage' (2016, p.16). Our analysis of the *AC: E* showed an attempt to bring about a politically aware understanding of heritage, but also revealed the limitations of this approach, and an unintentional 'othering' of Indigenous Australians, despite efforts to expand students' understandings of national cultures. This confirms Tim Dolin's observation, that 'literature as cultural heritage is fundamentally at odds with the student-centred personal growth agenda at the heart of subject English' (2016, p.347). Given this, it seems that what is needed in a twenty-first-century version of growth through English is not only a revised understanding of cultural heritage, as Reid suggests, but also movement beyond a somewhat singular focus on the needs of individuals. Peter Smagorinsky writes that in Dixons' model 'personal growth is valorised without attention to the social responsibilities that accompany growing and participating in a society' and that 'the personal growth curves of individuals often come at the expense of the goals and growth of others' (2002, p.26). It is this challenge, to consider growth at the level of community, nation and world, and the range of literary texts that need to be mobilised to support this, on which we need to focus attention when, like the Dartmouth participants before us, we respond to the question 'What is English?' in 2018.

References

'50th Anniversary Dartmouth Institute and Conference'. (nd). Retrieved from: https://dartmouthwritinginstitute.wordpress.com/the-conference/.

Alcott, L.M. (1871). *Little men*. London: Puffin Books.

Analysis of Literature in Australian Schools database (ALIAS). (2018). www.australiacommonreader.com/syllabus. Web. 22 March 2018.

Australian Curriculum, Assessment and Reporting Authority (ACARA). (2018). *The Australian curriculum: English*. Accessed 21 March 2018 www.australiancurriculum.edu.au/f-10-curriculum/english/.

Berger, J. (1967). *A fortunate man*. London: Pantheon.

Blythe, R. (1969). *Akenfield*. London: Akadine Press.

Boomer, G. (1992). 'Negotiating the curriculum'. in Boomer, G., Lester, N., Onore, C. and Cook, J. (eds.), *Negotiating the curriculum: educating for the 21st Century*. London: Falmer: 4–13.

Brodie, F. M. (1967). *The Devil drives: a life of Sir Richard Burton*. London: W.W. Norton.

Bronte, C. (1847). *Jane Eyre*. London: Wordsworth Editions.

Dickens, C. (1861). *Great expectations*. London: Penguin Classics.

Dixon, J. (1969). *Growth through English*. London: National Association for the Teaching of English.

Dixon, J. (1975). *Growth through English: set in the perspective of the Seventies*. Yorkshire: National Association for the Teaching of English.

Dixon, J. (2003). 'Two steps forward; one – or two – steps back? Reflections on Dartmouth 1966'. *English in Australia*, 136(Autumn), 85–86.

Doecke, B., McLean Davies, L. and Mead, P. (2011). 'National imaginings and classroom conversations: past and present debates about teaching Australian literature', in Doecke, B.,

McLean Davies, L. and Mead, P. (eds.), *Teaching Australian literature: from classroom conversations to national imaginings.* Adelaide: AATE Interface Series: 1–16.

Dolin, T. (2016). 'Literature's ghosts: cultural heritage and cultural analysis in subject English'. in Dolin, T., Jones, J. & Dowsett, P. (eds.), *Required reading: literature in Australian schools since 1945,* Melbourne: Monash University Publishing: 339–358.

Dowsett, P. (2016). 'Revisiting Dartmouth – 50 years on'. *English in Australia.* 51(3), 2–4.

Durrant, C. (2004). 'English teaching: profession or predicament?' *English in Australia,* 141, 6–8.

Eliot, G. (1861). *Silas Marner.* London: Beka Book.

Ellison, R. (1976). *Going to the territory.* New York: Vintage.

Evans, C. (1993). *English people: the experience of teaching and learning English in British universities.* Milton Keynes: Open University Press.

Gelder, K. (2013). 'Recovering Australian popular fiction: towards the end of Australian literature'. *Journal of the Association for the Study of Australian Literature,* 112–120. Accessed 21 March 2018 https://openjournals.library.sydney.edu.au/index.php/JASAL/article/view/9597/9487.

Gelder, K. and Salzman, P. (1989). *The new diversity: Australian fiction 1970–88.* Melbourne: McPhee Gribble.

Goodwyn, A. (2017). 'From Personal Growth (1966) to Personal Growth and Social Agency (2016) – proposing an invigorated model for the 21st century'. *English in Australia.* 52(1), 66–73.

Green, B. (1999). *Designs on learning: essays on curriculum and teaching by Garth Boomer.* Deakin West, ACT: ACSA.

Green, B. (2016). 'Different histories? Reading Dartmouth. . . against the grain'. *English in Australia.* 51(3), 25–32.

Green, B. and Cormack, P. (2008). 'Curriculum history, "English" and the New Education; or, installing the Empire of English?'. *Pedagogy, Culture and Society,* 15(3), 253–267.

Harding, D. (1968). 'The Report of the study group', in Squire, J.R. (ed.), *Response to literature: papers relating to the Anglo-American seminar on the teaching of English at Dartmouth College, New Hampshire 1966.* Champaign: National Council of Teachers of English.

Hardy, T. (1892). *Tess of the D'Urbervilles.* London: Penguin Classics.

Kael, P.(1971). *The Citizen Kane book.* New York: Little, Brown and Company.

Martin S.K. and McLean Davies, L. (2017). 'What the Dickens: exploring the role of canonical texts in mediating national identity in subject English in Australia', in Dolin, T., Jones, J. and Dowsett, P. (eds.), *Required reading: literature in Australian schools since 1945.* Melbourne: Monash University Press: 238–260.

McLean Davies, L. (2011). 'Magwitch madness: archive fever and the teaching of Australian literature in subject English', in Doecke, B., McLean Davies, L., Mead, P. (eds.), *Teaching Australian literature: from classroom conversations to national imaginings.* Kent Town: AATE/Wakefield Press: 129–152.

McLean Davies, L. and Buzacott, L. (in press 2018). 'Re-forming the nation: curriculum, text selection and Asian literature in subject English in Australia', in Loh, C.E., Choo, S., and Beavis, C. (eds.), *Literature education in the Asia-Pacific: policies, practices and perspectives in global times.* London: Routledge.

McLean Davies, L., Doecke, B. and Mead, P. (2013). 'Reading the local and global: teaching literature in secondary schools in Australia'. *Changing English,* 20(3), 224–240.

McLean Davies, L., Martin, S. and Buzacott, L. (2017). 'Worldly reading: teaching Australian literature in the twenty-first century'. *English in Australia.* 52(3), 21–30.

Medway, P. (1990). 'Into the Sixties: English and English society at a time of change', in Goodson, I.F. and Medway, P. (eds.), *Bringing English to order: the history and politics of a school subject.* London, New York and Philadelphia: The Falmer Press: 1–46.

Miller, A. (1953). *The crucible.* New York: Penguin Classics.

Muller, H. J. (1967). *The uses of English: guidelines for the teaching of English from the Anglo-American conference at Dartmouth College.* New York: Holt, Rinehart and Winston.

Reid, I. (2003). 'The persistent pedagogy of "Growth"', in Doecke, B., Homer, D. and Nixon, H. (eds.), *English teachers at work: narratives, counter-narratives and arguments.* Kent Town: AATE/Wakefield Press: 97–108.

Reid, I. (2016). 'Literary experience and literature teaching since the Growth Model', *English in Australia*, 51(3), 11–18.

Sawyer, W., McLean Davies, L., Gannon, S. and Dowsett, P. (2016) 'Mid-Atlantic crossings: some texts that emerged from Dartmouth'. *English in Australia*, 51(3), 40–51.

Shakespeare, W. (1609). *Hamlet.* London: Folger Library.

Silvey, C. (2009). *Jasper Jones.* Melbourne: Allen & Unwin.

Smagorinsky, P. (2002). '*Growth through English* revisited'. *The English Journal*, 91(6), 23–29.

Spyri, J. (1880). *Heidi.* London: Little Girl Press.

Squire, J.R. (1968). *Response to literature: papers relating to the Anglo-American seminar on the teaching of English at Dartmouth College, New Hampshire 1966.* Champaign: National Council of Teachers of English.

Tarpey, P. (2016). '"Fire burn and cauldron bubble": what are the conjectural effects on English teacher professional memories, identities and narratives'. *Changing English*, 23(1), 77–93.

Teese, R. (2013). *Academic success and social power: examinations and inequality.* Sydney: Australian Scholarly Publishing.

Twain, M. (1884). *The Adventures of Huckleberry Finn.* New York: Bantam Classics.

Victorian Universities and Schools Examination Board (VUSEB). (1975). *Handbook of directions and prescriptions for 1976.* Melbourne: VUSEB.

Yandell, J. (2016). 'Growth and the category of experience'. *English in Australia*, 51(3), 19–24.

12

LANGUAGE AND EXPERIENCE

Re-reading *Growth through English*

Brenton Doecke and John Yandell

Introduction

This essay takes John Dixon's *Growth through English* as a prompt to revisit the question of the relationship between language and experience. For Dixon, a consciousness of that relationship is at the heart of English curriculum and pedagogy, requiring sensitivity on the part of teachers to attempts by their students to give meaning to their experiences through language and the other semiotic resources available to them. To be sensitive to that struggle is to acknowledge the struggle we all face – teachers and pupils alike – when creating representations of our experiences in order to achieve a sense of our identities and an understanding of the world we hold in common.

We are mindful that such a reading of *Growth through English* goes against the grain of accepted accounts of 'personal growth' pedagogy. Dixon's work has been subject to a number of critical readings that ascribe to him a narrow focus on the individual pupil and an equally narrow focus on language as personal expression. This emphasis has supposedly been at the expense of any recognition of how people use language for social purposes. Frances Christie, for example, has argued repeatedly that the 'growth model' presupposes 'an essentially romantic notion of the individual' (Christie, 1991, p.77; Christie, nd; Christie and Macken-Horarik, 2007, p.162) that privileges middle class students. Those students might be eager to express their experiences of the world through personal writing of the kind that Dixon values, but children from socially disadvantaged communities require support in the form of explicit instruction as to how language works for them to communicate effectively. And in order for such children to overcome their social disadvantage, teachers need to do more than encourage them to write stories about their personal experiences. Their job, rather, should be to scaffold their students into the 'powerful' genres that constitute the realms of public discourse (cf. Cope and Kalantzis, 1993, p.6; Locke, 2015; Martin et al., nd; Christie et al., 1991).

We seek to challenge such readings of 'personal growth' pedagogy and the binaries with which they operate. For Dixon, 'experience' is not a private space to be cherished that only finds expression in writing of a narrowly personal kind. Dixon's understanding of 'experience' is predicated, rather, on an understanding of language as mediating between the private realm of the 'self' and the public realms that people negotiate each day, between the 'personal' and the 'social', between 'inner' and 'outer', between 'thought' and 'word'. These words echo Vygotsky (1987 [1934]) and Vološinov (1986 [1929]), who both emphasise the role that language plays in the relationships and activities in which people engage in their daily lives. Yet for both theorists this recognition of language as a social phenomenon gives rise to an equally important recognition of the need to explore how, through language, individuals become conscious of themselves and the world in which they find themselves and so begin to play an active role in the life that is happening around them. Indeed, Vološinov explains the impetus behind his work as arising from this insight into the significance of language as it is felt personally, as a part of an individual's growing awareness of 'self'. Although 'the reality of the word, as is true of any sign, resides between individuals', a word is also a phenomenon of inner life or an individual's consciousness (p.14).

The distinctive quality of *Growth through English* derives from the way Dixon is able to show through his careful analyses of students' writing how they use language to negotiate a relationship between the 'personal' and the 'social' as they experience it. He thus provides a framework for a culturally sensitive pedagogy that understands classrooms as vitally important sites for enacting a social democracy more responsive and more accountable than that which we and our students tend to encounter in the world beyond the classroom.

Beyond 'models' of English

The opening chapter of *Growth through English* famously heralds 'personal growth' as a new model of English that has displaced the previous models of 'skills' and 'cultural heritage'. Dixon presents this as an 'historical' perspective, associating the focus on 'skills' with an era of rapid industrialisation 'when initial literacy was the prime demand' (Dixon, 1972 [1967], p.1), while the 'cultural heritage' model had its apotheosis in the Newbolt Report of 1921 (p.3). Dixon's strategy is clearly to promote 'personal growth', and in so doing he allows the question of the adequacy of this representation of the history of English teaching to go begging – any attentive reading of the Newbolt Report, for example, shows it to be a multifaceted document that resists being labelled simply as promoting a 'heritage model' (see Doecke and Mead, 2017; Doecke, 2017; Departmental Committee, Board of Education, 1938 [1921]). Dixon is hardly the first person to ring out the old and ring in the new – educational reforms are typically announced as opening up a bright new future that sweeps aside a benighted past – but the schema he presents in the opening pages of *Growth through English* has none the less posed a serious obstacle to attempts to think about our history as English teachers in a reflexive way that might enhance our capacity to grapple with the complexities of the present. Subsequent advocates of educational reform have found it easy to repeat Dixon's litany of 'models' of English, merely extending the list by adding their own model as embodying the newest and best approach to the teaching of English (cf. Reid, 2003, p.98), with the result that 'personal growth' has itself been vulnerable to the same broad brushstroke treatment that Dixon metes out to 'skills' and 'cultural heritage'.

The challenge is to re-read *Growth through English* attentively in order to engage with the language of the text as it unfolds in the course of Dixon's argument. Not that the debates surrounding *Growth through English* can be resolved through a close reading that is somehow truer to the original text than the summary judgements made by the commentators we have been considering. Our epigraph is meant to signal, rather, that any re-reading is always part of a continuing dialogue in which we should try to be mindful of what we ourselves are bringing to the conversation. We need to cultivate an awareness of all that mediates our reading of *Growth through English*, trying to imagine the historical conditions to which Dixon was responding before judging his views and values. Such an historically reflexive stance also includes reflecting on the ideological assumptions that shape our own reading of the text.

For us the abiding significance of *Growth through English* does not lie in its account of changing models of English. A few pages in and Dixon puts this programmatic schema behind him to focus on entries from the diary of a 10-year-old boy in order to explore the complexities of reading and responding to students' writing. But his analysis amounts to more than an illustration of 'personal growth' pedagogy, and the diary can be read as a text in its own right:

> 1st April. Rainy with sunny periods. After breakfast I went to get some newts. I got a large jar, washed it and put a stone in it, then went to poplar pond with a stone and a tin . . ..
>
> 2nd April. Very rainy dull and wet. Today I made a fishing net, not to catch fish but newts. I caught six. I picked out the ones I thought best. . . There were lots of newts in the pond today. I daresay they like this kind of weather. . .

Although Dixon proceeds to show why he finds this text interesting, the richly concrete detail of the entries – they tell of the boy's efforts to catch newts, his failure one day and his success the next – invites readers to gauge their own responses to the writing without necessarily subscribing to the terms of Dixon's analysis. Indeed, the question that motivates Dixon's analysis is: 'What, as English teachers, can we learn from such an extract?' (p.5). Even though Dixon is arguing the value of a particular lens for exploring this text's features, by posing this question he is also giving the diary an independent status as a focus for our attention. He thereby acknowledges that no one can pretend to have the last word about this text, that it is not something that can be pinned down in any analysis of it. We would certainly not be doing it justice if we were to fall back on the kind of judgments that teachers have traditionally made by giving it a mark and a summary comment at the bottom of the page. The standpoint that we are invited to share, rather, is that of English teachers who are committed to observing the language of their students 'in operation from day to day' (p.4), who try to remain open to new insights that their students' uses of language make available to them, even insights that might cause them to 'modify' their preconceptions about the nature of language (p.4). English teachers are thus encouraged to bring all their knowledge of language and literature to bear on their engagement with their pupils in classroom settings, but this is not to suppose that they have nothing else to learn through their exchanges with them.

This standpoint, involving a disposition to learn from the language and experiences that children bring to school, is not unique to Dixon – we might consider Marjorie Hourd's analysis of the writing her students produced in her classes during the 1930s and 1940s (Hourd, 1968 [1949]). Nor is this a practice that has completely fallen into disuse since the time that Dixon first wrote his account of Dartmouth – we might think of how students' writing is featured in studies such as *The Development of Writing Abilities (11–18)* (Britton et al., 1975) or Peter Medway's *Finding a Language* (Medway, 1980) or Brian Johnston's *Assessing English* (Johnston, 1987 [1983]) or Dixon and Stratta's exploration of the role of storytelling in students' writing in *Writing Narrative – and Beyond* (Dixon and Stratta, 1986). With colleagues we have ourselves tried to follow Dixon's example when writing accounts of English teachers' work in classrooms in Australia and England (Yandell, 2014; Yandell and Brady, 2016; Doecke and McClenaghan, 2011; Doecke and McClenaghan, 2009). Yet the fact remains that our current policy environment is one characterised by the imposition of forms of accountability that demand teachers continually judge their students' writing against certain pre-defined 'outcomes' that supposedly demonstrate the acquisition of skills that are taken to be the defining properties of effective writers. It is therefore timely for English teachers to consider what they might learn from students' writing by suspending the criteria they habitually employ and recognising that even the most modest sample of student writing is open to interpretation (cf. Sawyer, 2005, p.141).

To see students as writers, to treat their work as worthy of careful and serious reading, reflects a particular understanding of the way language mediates our sense of self in relation to others and our capacity to know and to act within the world around us. This, in turn, reflects a particular understanding about the nature of knowledge (who has it) and experience (its value) which positions teachers and students differently from the hierarchical structures that have historically characterised schooling in capitalist society. The promise of 'personal growth' pedagogy lies in the way it provides the foundations on which to enact more humane, socially responsible, democratic pedagogic relationships. Or perhaps we should say: *begin* to enact. For Dixon's stance in *Growth through English* is a tentative and exploratory one, despite his rhetoric about ringing in the new in the opening pages of his book. The essential modesty of his claims about 'personal growth' is evident in both the original volume and the revised version published in 1975

(subtitled 'Set in the perspective of the Seventies'), where his diffidence about
making claims for the socially emancipatory potential of 'personal growth' is echoed by James Squire and James Britton, two other prominent contributors to the
Dartmouth Seminar, who in their Foreword to the new edition sound a warning
about the threat posed by government attempts at 'intervention in the educational
process' in the form of 'back to basics' and a growing emphasis on 'accountability'
through standardised testing (Squire and Britton, 1975, p.xii).

It is as though at the very moment of the publication of *Growth through English*,
system-wide educational reforms emphasising narrow forms of 'accountability'
and 'efficiency' were in train that would prevent 'personal growth' pedagogy
from ever being fully implemented. For Squire and Britton, this increasing
focus on 'holding schools and teachers accountable for what pupils learn' (p.xii)
is symptomatic of the 'widespread economic and social dislocation' that had
occurred since the Dartmouth Seminar, including 'the crisis in values in the
United States accelerated by growing rejection of the Viet Nam conflict and
the revolt of students on campus and in schools' (p.xi), which had prompted
governments to take measures in order to stifle dissent. Dixon himself, in a
concluding chapter to this new edition, remarks that his own perspective has
changed since Dartmouth, but that this change is not one that can be 'confined to English teaching', which is 'just one microcosm of a far wider struggle'
(Dixon, 1975 [1967], p.111). He then goes on to refer to the 'uneasy wakening'
he has experienced that has forced him to confront 'the dilemmas of coercive
authority and inescapable subordination', bringing him to 'recognize again and
again how prone the teacher is to use language to dominate and constrict'
(p.111), a lesson that he has learnt not only by watching other teachers in action
but through monitoring his own exchanges with students. He recognises, in
short, that whatever his intentions might be as an educator (intentions that he
powerfully articulates in *Growth through English*), his practices as a teacher are
also a function of the institutional setting in which he is operating, producing
contradictions with which he continues to struggle.

We are brought to contemplate, in short, a vision of a critically aware pedagogy that raises larger questions than the value or otherwise of particular models
of English teaching, which remain, after all, mere abstractions in relation to the
concrete particularities of classroom life. English teachers need to reflect on how
their professional practice might be mediated by larger social and economic contexts beyond the immediacy of everyday life in school. Any affirmation of the
promise of 'growth pedagogy' or for that matter any new approach to teaching
and learning demands, simultaneously, a recognition of the ways schools operate to reproduce the inequalities of capitalist society. This is not to deny the
need for teachers to remain actively committed to making schools sites for the
achievement of social democracy. For all the reified structures arrayed against
teachers and their pupils, it remains vitally important to seize those moments of
communication and insight within classrooms that 'personal growth' pedagogy
highlights. To borrow from Raymond Williams, 'growth pedagogy' is one of

'the many forms of opposition and struggle' against the 'hegemonic process' that schools in capitalist society attempt to impose. (Williams, 1977, p.113)

Teachers can hardly turn away from their ethical responsibility to be fully responsive to the efforts by their students to make sense of their lives and the society in which they live through writing personal narratives about their experiences.

That said, it remains the case that the critiques of 'personal growth' made to promote alternative models of English have been characterised by a loss of historical memory that has obscured the insights made available through the samples of students' writing that Dixon analyses in the course of his argument. The issue turns on the impulse to classify pieces of writing in order to judge whether they satisfy certain criteria. As James Britton and his collaborators observe at the beginning of *The Development of Writing Abilities (11–18)*, 'we classify at our peril': 'even the lightest touch of the classifier's hand is likely to induce us to see members of a class as more alike than they actually are, and items from different classes as less alike than they actually are' (Britton et al., 1975, p.1; cf. Doecke and McClenaghan, 2009). To become obsessed with classifying a piece of student writing is to risk failing to recognise, let alone appreciate, its distinctive features as a text and the desires invested in it. But the fact is that the flexibility of judgment that Britton and his collaborators see as integral to the work of English teachers has been undermined by the very kind of mentality that they caution against. We are thinking especially of the expectation that students should produce writing that accords with the requirements specified for particular text types or genres, writing that is shaped by and assessed according to a set of pre-specified criteria.

Language, experience, reification

We have said enough to indicate that the history of English curriculum and pedagogy in the post-war period can hardly be represented in the form of a series of 'models' of English. An historical imagination requires us to trace how the beliefs and practices associated with any particular pedagogy might have intersected with larger social and economic developments. This is not to say that we should treat those models as merely a reflection of those developments (as in that form of Marxist analysis that reduces the superstructure to a mere epiphenomenon of the economic base). The task, rather, is to gauge their ideological character as responses on the part of educators to the circumstances with which they were faced. We can then make a judgment about the adequacy or otherwise of those responses to the challenges posed by a specific historical moment, which includes identifying the social interests they served. This is as distinct from the rationale that the historical actors might give for their actions. The proponents of Systemic Functional Linguistics, for example, are no doubt sincere when they claim that their aim is to provide students with an explicit knowledge of 'powerful' genres that will enable them to overcome their social disadvantage. Yet it is only necessary to ask how they define the place of 'human beings in the world' (to borrow again words from Raymond Williams, 1977, p.21), to sense that the ideological work they are performing may be the opposite of what they intend.

To tease out the ideological nature of so-called 'genre' pedagogy, we shall look at an analysis of students' writing that Jim Martin, Frances Christie and Joan Rothery presented in the early 1980s, when they first emerged as prominent players in debates about language and literacy education. Their treatment of the following sample of student writing also serves to show how their approach differs from the way that John Dixon uses students' texts. We shall present only a small excerpt of the text, which was published originally by Brian Gray as part of a 1985 Conference Proceedings (see Gray, 1986, pp.198–199, Martin et al., nd, p.72):

> All the things are on the table. We will use them to make toast. There is honey, vegemite, peanut butter, bread, margarine, jam, a knife, a plate and a toaster. We are ready to make toast. Kevin is getting two slices of bread out of the packet. Then he puts the bread in the toaster. . . .Kevin watches the bread inside the toaster cooking. It is still white. The toast came popping out . . . .

As with the diary entries about collecting newts, such writing, at this distance in time, is intriguing for the traces it offers of lives and circumstances that are otherwise inaccessible to us. Samples of children's writing almost invariably provide insights into the way children and adolescents inhabit the present, enabling us to sense how their expectations shape their engagement with the world around them. Yet if the excitement of this bunch of kids preparing breakfast is imbued with the poignancy of a moment that is now irretrievably in the past, the verdict that Martin, Christie and Rothery deliver about the quality of this text has all the gravity of a life sentence. We are told that 'this kind of writing is not functional in our culture' (Martin et al., nd, p.72). This is because 'generically speaking it is neither recount (i.e. what we did), nor procedure (i.e. how to do something)', which they illustrate by pointing to the confusion of tenses within the text, and the fact that it reads largely like 'running commentary', which is 'spoken, not written down' (p.72).

Such judgements reflect an inability on the part of educators to evaluate a text on terms other than those that conform to their preconceptions as to the form that a piece of writing should take. Their condemnation of the text is all the more perplexing for their refusal to recognise its value as a joint composition featuring the use of the first person plural that typically combines photographs and sentences in an effort to represent the joy of this fleeting moment: of being together, of making toast and spreading it with vegemite, peanut butter or jam. We suspect that most English teachers have at some stage facilitated the creation of texts of this kind, involving the juxtaposition of photographs and language in an effort to represent a special moment that the class has shared together. Brian Gray, who originally used this text, included the photos alongside the written language, thus providing a stronger sense of its context and function, though he also struggles to grant it legitimacy, claiming that 'such texts waste the opportunity to extend the literacy competence of the children through exposure to models of factual texts which deal with the generalisation of information' (Gray, 1986, p.200).

That this text was actually produced by Indigenous students in a school in the Northern Territory makes the judgment that it is 'not functional in our culture' even more disturbing. Gray sketches this context in his paper, although, as we have just indicated, this knowledge does nothing to modify his own judgment about the 'confused nature' of the text (Gray, 1986, p.197). Later in the paper, he does at least provide samples of written texts that arise out of bilingual programs, admitting to feeling challenged by the fact that they display generic features deriving from traditional culture that do not correspond to any accepted 'text model' in English (p.205).

This early example of analysis of student writing by leading proponents of genre pedagogy shows that they are doing more than advocating the value of a body of linguistic knowledge that might be imported into English classrooms which would otherwise be organised along familiar lines. Fundamental to the understanding of language that underpins *Growth through English* is a recognition that schools and classrooms provide children and adolescents with an opportunity to engage in meaningful communication with one another. This is to say that classrooms are constituted by the social relationships enacted within them, where language and other semiotic resources play a crucial role in enabling people to get along together and to learn from and with each other. This notion of the classroom as a social space where students engage in purposeful communication reflects a fundamentally different understanding of the way language mediates our experience and our relationships with one another to that which is being advocated by genre theorists.

There are many paradoxes here, not least the way genre theorists claim to anchor language within society in contradistinction to the view of language as personal expression that they ascribe to Dixon's work. In an early exchange with Dixon, Christie sees herself as restoring a proper focus on language as a social phenomenon, arguing that a child's individuality 'is constantly shaped in the endless processes of interaction with others. . . created, negotiated and sustained in social experience' (Christie, nd, pp.29–30). It seems unlikely that Dixon would disagree with this proposition – he always analyses a student's text as arising out of the social context of the classroom, as the product of continuing interaction and negotiation with others who occupy that space, and hence as a quintessentially social phenomenon, like all language. Christie, however, persists in constructing his stance as reflecting what she sees as a Romantic focus on the individual, picking up a reference that he makes to 'classroom genres' as 'mind-forg'd manacles' (Dixon, nd, p.9) as showing that 'it is Blake's sense of the individual' that 'lies in Dixon's work' (Christie, nd, p.30). Quoting David Butt, she contends that 'to understand human communication, one begins in the community system and arrives at the individual; not the other way round' (p.30).

Such a view posits language as something external to students, as a set of conventions to which they must conform. Leaving aside the question of the validity or otherwise of Christie's characterisation of Dixon's standpoint, she is advocating a definition of language that Vološinov characterises as 'abstract objectivism' (p.45), where the focus is less on the way people actually use language to achieve social purposes than on the construction of a system at a remove from the interactions in which people engage in their daily lives. That this system is posed as comprehending the richly diverse exchanges of everyday life only underlines its abstract and reified character, for no definition of language can ultimately contain that diversity, or, for that matter, provide a framework in which teachers and their pupils might participate in and learn from the linguistically mediated social interactions that are a feature of classroom life. For all Christie's claims to swing our attention from the individual to the social, the social space of the classroom is elided. The 'social' in genre theory exists only as a reified concept of society that exists beyond the classroom. The classroom itself is seen not as a social space in which people use language for authentic purposes, but merely a site for formal language exercises at a remove from the language and experience of students – the very kind of exercises that Dixon criticises in *Growth through English*.

And it is not only the 'social' that disappears in genre theory, but the social world of students as they each *personally* experience it. The first-person representations of experience that are a feature of *Growth through English* can all be read as linguistic investigations into the relationship between 'I' and the social world that is implied by grammatical person. Genre theorists typically treat such writing as examples of what they call 'recount' – it is symptomatic of their ideological standpoint that they reify a verb into a class of things to which all children's stories must conform. For genre theorists, 'recounts' are characteristic of an early stage of writing development that is superseded by the more 'powerful' genres of public discourse, such as factual writing and reasoned argument. Captive to an ideology that crudely asserts the primacy of the system over the individual, they have no capacity to appreciate the multiple ways in which people might occupy the first person and thus begin to use language in order to understand both self and the world. As Adriana Cavarero argues, autobiography always emerges out of a self that 'belongs to the world, in the relational and contextual form of self-exposure to others' (Cavarero, 2000, p.36; Kottman, 2000, p.xvii; cf. Doecke and McClenaghan, 2011, p.72). A first-person account of experience always involves a degree of reflexivity, a sense that this is the world as 'I' am experiencing it through my relationships with the people around me.

Language and experience as the content of English

Growth through English is an attempt to affirm the complexity of human experience against its continuing devaluation in capitalist society. It might thus be compared with other contemporaneous attempts to treat students' experiences and their struggles, to render those experiences into words as the content of English – such as James Britton's insistence that educators should 'begin from where the children are' (Britton, 1976/ 1970, p.134), or Harold Rosen's efforts to conceptualise 'the whole school curriculum' in terms of 'its narrative possibilities' (Rosen, nd, p.19). But such work, as Rosen shows, is also a product of larger literary and philosophical traditions that have emerged in response to the reified structures and forms of consciousness of capitalist society. We might think of the socially critical stance of the English Romantic poets (cf. Williams, 1971/1958, pp.48–64), as well as significant moments of cultural critique in the twentieth century, such as Walter Benjamin's reflections on the fate of human experience and storytelling vis-à-vis the horror of mechanised warfare during the First World War (see Benjamin, 1973/ 1970).

By using the word 'reified' to characterise the forms of knowledge typically 'handed over by the teacher' (Dixon, 1975 [1967], p.11), including the bodies of knowledge associated with linguistics and literary studies, Dixon explicitly locates his work within this tradition of social critique. He is protesting against the way schools socialise students into a sense of their place within society by confronting them with 'things' with which they can make no personal connection. School knowledge can have no lasting significance for students unless they can connect it with their own lives. Ultimately it only has significance as part of a social process that involves continually interpreting and reinterpreting the phenomena of every-day life as we make the world and ourselves anew each day. As common cultural resources, as representations of human experience, both literary studies and linguistics usefully provide 'frames of reference' (p.80) for teachers and their pupils as they interpret and respond to what they say to one another in classroom settings. But the focus, according to Dixon, should be on the knowledge that 'may arise from pupils learning as well as teachers instructing' (p.73), on the knowledge that students might make their own through engaging in meaningful communication with one another and reflecting on such exchanges.

To participate consciously in that process of meaning making is in itself a crucial dimension of students' experience as Dixon conceives it. He is not sub-stituting students' 'experience' for 'knowledge' (conceived in the conventional sense of disciplines such as linguistics or literary studies) but inviting us to radi-cally reconceptualise knowledge as inherently social in nature, as embodying conversations in which we might all join. This is to think of social relationships and intellectual exchange as inextricably bound up with one another (cf. Barnes, 1992/1975, p.145). Part and parcel of this conception is a recognition that entry into such exchanges is crucially a personal experience, a matter of recognising that these issues matter to 'me'. You are taking a step towards making sense of the world and the social relationships in which you find yourself, both on your terms (how 'I' see the world) and in negotiation with others who share this world and this life – and this language – with you (how 'they' see the world, involving reflection on why 'they' might see it differently.)

Dixon, in short, is far from advocating some kind of uncritical valorisation of the immediacy of students' everyday experiences or of life in their local com-munities. Nor should his insistence on seeing students as writers be construed as a denial of the value of a literary heritage, understood as a set of cultural resources for meaning-making on which everyone can draw. The word 'experience', as it is used in *Growth through English*, always has a divided character, naming both the experiences on which students draw when they read and write and talk and listen to one another within classroom settings and – crucially – something that they make 'real' to themselves through the language they choose in an effort to represent and share their experiences and insights (p.6) with one another. It is in this sense that the work they do might be equated with the work of creative writers and other cultural workers, for all writing is an inquiry into the meaning-making potential of language.

But the point is that this inquiry begins with how 'I' experience the world in which 'I' find myself. And 'I' continually return to this starting point, not with a sense of defeat, as though 'I' have gone nowhere, but because each attempt to write in the first person opens up new dimensions, new knowledge about who 'I' am. With his long-time collaborator, Leslie Stratta, Dixon shows how 'stories about ourselves' might provide the foundations of an English curriculum (Dixon and Stratta, 1986), presenting analyses of first-person narratives in the same spirit that he exemplifies in *Growth through English*. The point of this book is that such a focus on personal narratives is more than a matter of 'cherishing private souls' (p.15, p.25), that stories open up possibilities for generalisation and argument that might prompt students to 'move beyond first-hand experience' (p.58) in order to explore other types of writing and dimensions of the world. Yet such writing is not something to be transcended on a journey to higher levels of abstraction, but continues to provide an opportunity to explore who 'I' am, how others see 'me', and whether 'I' accept the version of 'my' identity that 'they' ascribe to 'me'.

References

Barnes, D. (1992 [1975]). *From communication to curriculum*, 2nd edn., Portsmouth, NH: Boyton/Cook.

Benjamin, W. (1973 [1970]). 'The storyteller: reflections on the works of Nikolai Leskov', in Benjamin, W. (ed.), *Illuminations*, with an Introduction by, H. Arendt, translated, H. Zohn, London: Fontana: 83–110.

Britton, J. (1976/[1970]). *Language and learning*, Harmondsworth: Penguin.

Britton, J., Burgess, T., Martin, M., McLeod, A. and Rosen, H. (1975). *The development of writing abilities (11–18)*, London and Basingstoke: Macmillan Education.

Cavarero, A. (2000/ [1997]). *Relating narratives: stories and selfhood*, trans, with Introduction by P. A. Kottman, London and New York: Routledge.

Christie, F. (nd). 'Genres as choice', in Reid, I. (ed.), *The place of genre in learning: current debates*, Typereader Publications no.1, Centre for Studies in Literary Education: Deakin University: 22–34.

Christie, F. (1991). 'The "Received Tradition" of English teaching: the decline of rhetoric and the corruption of grammar', in Green, B. (ed.), *The insistence of the letter*. London: Routledge.

Christie, F., Devlin, B., Freebody, P., Luke, A., Martin, J.R., Threadgold, T. and Walton, C. (1991). *Teaching English literacy: a project of national significance on the preservice preparation of teachers for teaching English literacy*, Canberra: Department of Employment Education and Training.

Christie, F. and Macken-Horarik, M. (2007). 'Building verticality in subject English', in Christie, F. and Martin. J.R. (eds.), *Language, knowledge and pedagogy: functional linguistics and sociological perspectives*. London: Continuum.

Cope, B. and Kalantzis, M. (eds.) (1993). *The powers of literacy: a genre approach to teaching writing*, London: The Falmer Press.

Departmental Committee, Board of Education. (1938 [1921]). *The Teaching of English in England*, London: His Majesty's Stationery Office. [The Newbolt Report]

Dixon, J. (1972 [1967]). *Growth through English: a report based on the Dartmouth Seminar 1966*, Huddersfield: National Association for the Teaching of English/Oxford University Press.

Dixon, J. (1975[1967]). *Growth through English: set in the perspective of the Seventies*, 3rd edition, London: Oxford University Press.

Dixon, J. (nd). 'The Question of genre', in Reid, I. (ed.), *The place of genre in learning: current debates,* Typereader Publications no.1, Centre for Studies in Literary Education: Deakin University: 9–22.

Dixon, J. and Stratta, L. (1986). *Writing narrative – and beyond*, Ottawa: The Canadian Council of Teachers of English.

Doecke, B. (2017). 'What kind of "knowledge" is English? (Re-reading the Newbolt Report)', *Changing English*, 24(3), 230–245.

Doecke, B. and McClenaghan, D. (2009). 'The content of students' writing', in Beard, R., Myhill, D., Riley, J. and Nystrand, M. (eds.), *The SAGE handbook of writing development*, London: SAGE: 374–386.

Doecke, B. and McClenaghan, D. (2011). *Confronting practice: classroom investigations into language and learning.* Putney: Phoenix Education.

Doecke, B. and Mead, P. (2017). 'English and the knowledge question', *Pedagogy, Culture & Society,* DOI: 10.1080/14681366.2017.1380691:http://dx.doi.org/10.1080/14681366.2017.1380691.

Gray, B. (1986). 'Aboriginal education: some implications of genre for literacy development', in Painter, C. and Martin, J.R. (eds.), *Writing to mean: teaching genres across the curriculum: papers and workshop reports from the 'Writing to Mean' conference, University of Sydney, May 1985.* Occasional Papers, Number 9: 188–208.

Hourd, M.L. (1968 [1949]). *The education of the poetic spirit: a study of children's expression in the English lesson.* London: Heinemann.

Johnston, B. (1987 [1983]). *Assessing English: helping students reflect on their work*, Milton Keynes: Open University Press.

Kottman, P. A. (2000). 'Translator's introduction', in A. Cavarero, *Relating narratives: stories and selfhood*, trans, with Introduction by. P.A. Kottman, London and New York: Routledge: pp.vii–xxxi.

Locke, T. (2015). 'Paradigms of English', in Marshall, B. and Brindley, S. (eds.), *MasterClass in English education: transforming teaching and learning*, London: Bloomsbury: 16–28.

Martin, J. R., Christie, F. and Rothery, J. (nd). 'Social processes in education: a reply to Sawyer and Watson (and others)', in Reid, I. (ed.), *The Place of genre in learning: current debates,* Typereader Publications no.1, Centre for Studies in Literary Education: Deakin University: 8–82.

Medway, P. (1980). *Finding a language: autonomy and learning in school*, London: Chameleon Books.

Reid, I. (2003). 'The persistent pedagogy of "Growth"', in Doecke, B., Homer, D. and Nixon, H. (eds.), *English teachers at work: narratives, counter narratives and arguments*, Kent Town, South Australia: Wakefield Press/Australian Association for the Teaching of English: 97–108.

Rosen, H. (nd). *Stories and meanings*, Kettering: National Association for the Teaching of English.

Sawyer, W. (2005). 'Becoming a new New Critic: assessing student writing', in Doecke, B. and Parr, G. (eds.), *Writing=learning*. Kent Town: AATE/Wakefield Press: 129–145.

Squire, J. and Britton, (1975). 'Foreword', in Dixon, J. *Growth through English: set in the perspective of the Seventies*, 3rd edn., London: Oxford University Press: vii–xviii.

Vološinov, V.N. (1986 [1929]). *Marxism and the philosophy of language*, trans. Matejka, L. and Titinik, I.R., Cambridge, Mass. and London: Harvard University Press.

Vygotsky, L. (1987 [1934]). *Thought and language*, trans. newly revised and edited by Kozulin, A., Cambridge and London: MIT Press.

Williams, R. (1971[1958]). *Culture and society: 1780–1950*, Harmondsworth: Penguin.

Williams, R. (1977). *Marxism and literature*, Oxford: Oxford University Press.

Yandell, J. (2014). *The social construction of meaning: reading literature in urban English classrooms*, London and New York: Routledge.

Yandell, J. and Brady, M. (2016). 'English and the politics of knowledge', *English in Education*, 50(1), 44–59.

PART III

Reflections

But for the future

13

W(H)ITHER MEDIA IN ENGLISH?

Steve Connolly

*Round the city of Caxton, the electronic suburbs are rising. To the language of books is added
the language of television and radio, the elliptical demotic of the telephone, the processed codes
of the computer. As the shapes of literacy multiply, so our dependence on language increases.*
                                                                          Kingman (1988, p.8)

This quote from the Kingman Report, commissioned by the UK government in
1988 as an 'Inquiry into the teaching of English' seems startlingly prescient when
read some 30 years later. For Kingman, the need to establish the nature and substance of a version of curricular English prior to the development of a national
curriculum that included the study of media texts was almost taken for granted.
What kind of future did English have as a subject if it could not accept that the idea
of texts had moved beyond the limits of the printed word? Such a question makes
a clear connection with the Dartmouth seminar and its outcomes, postulating as it
does the idea of both personal and societal growth and development (Dixon, 1975).
In 1966, there was no internet, no mobile phone; even in the US, television was
in its infancy, and the digital media environment of the early twenty-first century
was unimaginable; but the spirit of Dartmouth, especially the dimension presented
by Dixon, was to centre English in the life-worlds of all young people. That is still
what English teachers aspire to for all their twenty-first-century students.

   At the time of writing however, the study of media texts within the UK English
curriculum has all but disappeared, with the enlightened optimism expressed by
Kingman and those who developed the original version of the National Curriculum
in the late 1980's apparently forgotten in a rush to return to more 'traditional' interpretation of the subject. This chapter intends to give a historical perspective to the
study of media texts within English curricula, by both reflecting on the way that
this study is conceived of in global terms, and then, more specifically using the UK
as an example of the way that the study of media texts has been characterised in the

English subject curriculum and its relationship to that subject, from the inception of the National Curriculum in 1988 to its most recent manifestation in 2014. In this time period, the place of the study of media texts of all types (print, moving image and digital) within subject English has shifted considerably, from being seen as an integral part of modern curricular versions of the subject, externally assessed and fundamentally connected to traditional conceptions of reading and writing to something much less significant. As a consequence, then, the chapter has two key aims; first, to examine how the study of media texts has been and is conceived by a National Curriculum for English – both in the UK and further afield; and second, to analyse some of the reasons for changes in these conceptions, in an attempt to explain why the current version of the National Curriculum has expunged the study of media texts from within English.

Theoretical and methodological frameworks

This chapter borrows from a range of research methods in order to examine the documents and discourses which surround subject English both in terms of the NC in England and in other countries. These approaches can, for the purposes of this study, be broadly grouped into two categories: documentary research and discourse analyses. These methods are used primarily because there are many hundreds of documents in both the UK National Archives and the public domain that consti-tute both the National Curriculum itself and the work that went into its creation. Consequently, they need to be analysed both as documents in their own right, but also because they make particular uses of language, which form part of the discourse around media within English. It is notable that the legacy of Dartmouth exists in two books discussed in this volume, those of Dixon (1975) and Muller (1967), whilst the rest of the material exists in simple document form, stored in ERIC, not in a specialist archive.

Educational historians such as Gary McCulloch, suggest that when researching documents there are four 'well established rules that apply. . . and these are gener-ally discussed in terms of *authenticity, reliability, meaning and theorisation*' (McCulloch, 2004, p.42). Within this chapter, the first two rules can be broadly accepted as being, in some senses, unproblematic. All the documents analysed in the three sections below are produced by government departments, teacher organisations or academic departments. For such bodies, authenticity and reliability are significant benchmarks – whatever members of the public may think – and it is most unlikely that such documents will be inauthentic or unreliable. As McCulloch goes on to comment, they will normally be 'housed in public archives, well-guarded and meticulously catalogued' (p.43).

It is the third of these two rules that lead to the need for a further theoretical framework, however. Establishing the meanings (both surface and underlying) of these documents and their implications requires a research method which allows for a closer scrutiny of the language and presentation they contain. Consequently, a rudimentary discourse analysis, of the kind developed by Norman Fairclough

(2001) is employed to give some insight into the way that the curriculum might be interpreted and theorised. This kind of discourse analysis owes a good deal to the social theory of Jurgen Habermas, who put forward the idea, in his seminal work *The Theory of Communicative Action*, that discourse, far from simply being about language and the utterances that constitute it, is more a means of regulating social behaviour and the conflicts that arise in it (Habermas, 1987). For Fairclough and others, such an analysis is a way of understanding not only what the text says and what that means, but also how the text is used to enact power in society. As a consequence, then, one of the tasks of this chapter is to examine (admittedly in quite an introductory way) what the status of media texts within English curricula can tell us about various power dynamics; between students and teachers, teachers and governments and governments and their electorates.

The international context – media in global English curricula

A number of countries around the world who have adopted the idea of a National Curriculum have a clear place for the study of media texts within that structure. Perhaps the two which most clearly present contrasting ways in which this positioning might occur in the Anglophone world are the National Curricula of Australia and New Zealand. In the New Zealand English curriculum, reading media texts is seen as being of absolutely equal status to any other kind of printed or spoken text. The initial introduction to the English 'Learning Area' in the curriculum document clear states that

> In English, students study, use, and enjoy language and literature communicated orally, visually, or in writing.
>
> *(Ministry of Education, 2007, p.18)*

From the outset here, the use of the word 'visually' implies the idea that not all the texts that students will encounter – either in terms of making or viewing – will be printed word texts. The curriculum document goes on to suggest that young people studying English in New Zealand need to:

> be effective oral, written, and visual communicators who are able to think critically and. . . learn to deconstruct and critically interrogate texts in order to understand the power of language to enrich and shape their own and others' lives.
>
> *(Ministry of Education, 2007, p.18)*

It is interesting to note here how the curriculum explicitly links effective communication with deconstruction. While one cannot know how this statement is actually enacted in every school in New Zealand, the document carries a strong sense of a 'parity of texts', where notions of cultural and textual value are worked through by the student in cooperation with the teacher, rather than imposed. Concomitantly, there is no prescriptive content underlying this curriculum framework. This lack of prescription, along with the explicit inclusion of the words 'oral' and 'visual', suggests that modes of communication have a similar parity. This encourages both teachers and students to see media texts (alongside others) as having a status within English. While, as Rata acknowledges (2017), this lack of prescription can present some problems, it is not a quality apparent in the most recent version of the English National Curriculum for English.

The Australian NC for English – at least for Secondary schools – provides an interesting contrast to both the New Zealand and English frameworks. Here, there is a great deal of specificity, with examples given of what students should be learning in three different strands – Language, Literature and Literacy. It is fascinating in itself to see the curriculum organised on these lines rather than in terms of Speaking, Reading and Writing as in the UK, but such delineation does allow for some clear guidelines about where media texts might be positioned within the English classroom. A closer look at the Year 9 Literacy strand, for example, illustrates exactly what Australian students are expected to be able to do with media texts, requiring that students:

> Analyse how the construction and interpretation of texts, including media texts, can be influenced by cultural perspectives and other texts.
>
> *(ACARA, 2017, p.21)*

The curriculum document goes on to identify a number of ways in which this analysis might be carried out, including:

- *comparing perspectives represented in texts from different times and places, including texts drawn from popular culture;*
- *identifying, comparing and creating relationships between texts (including novels, illustrated stories, social issue cartoons, documentaries, multimodal texts).*

> *(ACARA, 2017, p.21)*

For some teachers, such prescription might be unhelpful. Aside from the issue of how this analysis and identification might actually work in classroom practice – an accusation that can be levelled at many curriculum documents – for some professionals, such examples might be deemed unnecessary or worse still patronising. However, whatever professional position the teacher chooses to take up, it is likely that they will prefer either the less prescriptive New Zealand approach or the more prescriptive Australian one. In terms of the study of media texts within English, it does not matter, because both curricula, implicitly or explicitly, accept the integrality of their study.

These two examples can be augmented by many others (The Netherlands, Spain, USA, etc.) – where the study of media texts has a place within the teaching of English and other subjects. While these countries may not have positioned this teaching through a National Curriculum, such prevalence makes it all the more mystifying that in England, such study appears to have been all but abandoned.

The National Curriculum in England 2014 – whither media?

The 2014 version of England's National Curriculum contains no mention of media, moving image, multimodal or even news texts. There are one or two brief mentions of culture in relation to reading and writing, but these appear to be (largely) about the cultural contexts of what the curriculum documents call 'literary tradition'. As discussed below, previous versions of the NC saw media and moving image texts as an integral part of the English curriculum, particularly in the way that they were conceived as being a gateway to other cultures and texts (more of which below).

So how did this situation arise? How did the UK move from a position in which the study of media texts was seen as an essential part of English to one in where such study was considered so unimportant as to not be mentioned? Part of the answer to this question is cultural and ideological and will be discussed further below, but part of it is simply in some ways about political happenstance. In 2010, a General Election brought a coalition government to power in the UK, and the incoming Secretary of State for Education (Michael Gove) made it very clear that the new government was going to be marked by a range of reforms, many of which were explicitly positioned as returning education in the UK to a more traditional place. These reforms were introduced via a white paper – the first stage of the law and policy-making process in the UK – entitled *The Importance of Teaching* (DFE, 2010). This document, widely believed to have been largely authored by Gove personally, spoke of the need to return to 'traditional subject disciplines' (p.42), 'blazer and tie uniforms, prefects and house systems' (p.37) and 'rigour and high standards' (p.37). Aside from the significant detail that many of these phenomena had been in evidence in UK schools prior to the arrival of the new government, the document was clearly designed to set a tone; to differentiate its educational agenda from that of its predecessor. For Gove, widely seen in both political and educational circles as an ideologically-driven neo-liberal, there needed to be a clear line drawn between the educational past and the future, and this line would be established by a new National Curriculum. A more in-depth analysis of the reasons that lie behind this return to tradition, and how it specifically pertains to media education is offered by David Buckingham (2017) and may be of particular use for readers unfamiliar with the UK context.

The Importance of Teaching promised that teachers would be consulted about the proposed curriculum – drafts of which were made available at the start of 2013, and a consultation duly took place. Respondents were simply asked if they had any comments about the draft curriculum as a whole, and then if they had any comments on specific subjects, such as English. A number of organisations, most notably the National Association for the Teaching of English (NATE, 2013) and the English and Media Centre (EMC, 2013) responded, pointing out the absence of any reference to media, multimodal or moving image texts in the curriculum. The English and Media Centre's response described this absence as a 'glaring omission', pointing out that:

A curriculum for the 21st Century that does not mention the media, or the many different ways in which people produce, encounter and critically read digital and visual texts, is one which fails to prepare pupils for important aspects of English in the real world.

(EMC, 2013, p.1)

The summary report on the consultation (DFE, 2013) did not acknowledge these concerns, or indeed, many of the concerns raised about the English curriculum as a whole. The entire set of responses regarding the English curriculum – of which there were nearly four hundred – was summarised in five bullet points (Spoken English, Grammar, The Absence of Drama, The Primary English Curriculum and the Structure of the Proposals). It was becoming very clear to many interested parties that not only was the study of media texts being excluded from the curriculum for English, but also that the aforementioned curriculum was being redrawn in very narrow terms, and that the new curriculum, with its lists of grammar and 'representative Romantic poetry' was building some clear ideological foundations – namely, that it would equate ideas of literary heritage with rigour.

The final draft of the NC (DFE, 2014) appeared to be very similar to the original proposals, at least in the sense that there was no place for the study of media texts within English. It is worth pointing out here that for some schools this was not a problem, either because they welcomed the return to a more traditional curriculum, or because they were academies (in the UK, these are state funded schools that are virtually completely autonomous and are not bound by the national curriculum), or because some more adventurous practitioners interpreted the absence of advice as a signal to do whatever they wanted to (Grahame, 2012). However, there was the sense that harder times were coming for English teachers who wanted to make the study of the media an integral part of their classroom work. Further reforms to GCSE English and English Literature, which replaced coursework with Controlled Assessment and then lengthy closed-book exams focusing on pre-twentieth-century literature and poetry, reinforced this sense further.

Media in English: the National Curriculum in England 1988–2010

So if that is now, what was then? There are more than thirty separate files in the UK National Archives pertaining to the development of the English component of the original National Curriculum published in 1989. Each of these thirty files contains hundreds of pages of documents, many of which relate to the English Working Group established in order to consult on and devise the curriculum. A good proportion of these many thousands of pages are devoted to the place of media in that English curriculum. There are minutes of meetings, submissions from School Inspectors, teachers, academics and civil servants, position papers, conference proceedings and hand-written notes from ministers to their underlings, many of which consider the role of media texts in the English curriculum alongside literature and language.

A book chapter cannot really do justice to this rich vein of educational history, but it is possible to give an initial sense of the way that media featured in English during this 22-year period by considering three different sets of documents. These are

a) Submissions to the English Working Group –or EWG – whose task it was to come up with the framework that would form the basis of the English Curriculum from 1990 onwards;

b) The final report of the EWG, *English Ages 5–16*, commonly referred to as the Cox Report;

c) The finished version of the 1990 NC and subsequent revisions of it in 1993, 1995 and 2007.

The nature of the published consultation and curriculum documents means that b) and c) are relatively easy to summarise briefly, and an attempt to do so, alongside an analysis of these documents, is included below. However, the group of documents that form a) is much more extensive and the discussion presented here can, for reasons of space, constitute only a relatively selective analysis of the evidence provided by them. In effect, there are a handful of examples, included here to illustrate the kinds of discussion that were undertaken in order to establish the role of media in the English curriculum. It is hoped that a more expansive interrogation of these documents will be carried out in future.

Submissions to the EWG

The National Curriculum English Working Group was established in the Spring of 1988 in the wake of the Kingman Report, an enquiry into the teaching of English in British (as they were at the time) schools. Kingman had looked forward to the development of a common curriculum for English and the institution of the EWG was part of a wider move by the UK government to develop a National Curriculum. The EWG was headed by Professor Brian Cox, who was Pro-Vice Chancellor and Professor of English Literature at the University of Manchester. The group was expected to produce a report which would form the basis of the National Curriculum for English and was composed of a number of senior teachers, academics, inspectors and teacher educators (the writer Roald Dahl was also originally a member of the group, but resigned midway through the groups' deliberations) who met across a number of weekends throughout 1988. They discussed the potential content of the NC for English and, very aware that their work would be the basis for that curriculum document, took care to organise their final report into sections that they thought would reflect the breadth of English as a subject. Consequently, not only Media, but also Drama, Knowledge About Language, SEN and Equal Opportunities all made an appearance.

Many submissions were made to the EWG, both from individuals concerned about the form and content of the finished curriculum and other interested groups of teachers. There were also some extensive discussions about individual topics, which were minuted by the civil servants in attendance. In terms of media education, both these types of document reveal a great deal about the importance and status of media within English. Some of the submissions made, with the benefit of 30 years' distance, might be viewed as being elicited from the 'usual suspects' within British media education (Cary Bazalgette, David Buckingham, the fledgling subject association for media – TEAME, Len Masterman and many others) but what is most revealing about the whole process is the time and space they were afforded to press their case for the importance of Media within English. Similarly, it is clear that many of these contributors were approaching the fundamental connections between media texts and literary texts from a wide variety of viewpoints. In their submission David Buckingham and Philip Drummond of the IOE (TNA; ED282/85/2) suggested that:

> It can be argued that it will be precisely through the mass media that children will receive their most powerful social experiences of written and spoken language. At the same time, verbal language forms but one component of the broader 'audio-visual' language which characterises media texts, and which in turn requires a broader notion of audio-visual literacy.
>
> *(Buckingham and Drummond, 1988)*

For Buckingham and Drummond, the relationship between media and the English curriculum is a sociolinguistic one; for students' language and literacy to develop, they must be exposed to written and spoken language, and this exposure will occur through the media. This view makes for an interesting contrast with the contribution submitted by Len Masterman, for whom the connection is more between texts and cultural value.

> . . .the history of media education within our schools has been, to a large extent, a history of the changing meanings of discrimination, a concept inflected and stretched finally to breaking point by attempts to apply it to the media.
>
> *(Masterman, 1988, p.2)*

For this particular researcher, what is striking here is the tacit acknowledgement in the documents gathered and retained that there are a range of views about the relationship between English and media and that they are all essential elements in thinking about what was, at the time, a new curriculum. A word such as 'discrimination' here, with all its Leavisite connotations, has a resonance for teachers today. When they read sections of the 2014 NC which refer to 'high-quality, classic literature' (DFE, 2014) some may wonder, as Masterman implies, who is doing the discriminating and who is defining what 'high quality' means.

In some respects, these submissions are what we might expect from consultation processes. Academics and teachers always have strong views on the nature of curricula. What is more surprising perhaps is the role of the inspectorate, revealed by a closer look at the minutes of the EWG. For the purposes of this chapter, the most interesting of these is the record of an EWG meeting held 23rd June 1988 (TNA; NC/EWG88) which was addressed by James Learmonth, then a member of Her Majesty' Inspectorate for Schools (HMI) and latterly an academic at Canterbury Christ Church University. Learmonth was a former headteacher who had a career-long interest in media education (Bolas, 2007), and the minutes record him giving a summary of the state of media education in English schools at the time, and then identifying what he saw as the priorities for media within English. These were firstly, 'the development of a curricular framework for media studies' and secondly, what Learmonth refers to as 'institutionalising the work'. It would appear that what he means here is that at the time of the meeting, media education generally relies upon the efforts of a small hardcore group of teachers and that their ideas and practices, which need to be incorporated into the national curriculum and other structures in order to make them truly effective. For Learmonth, it is clear that 'institutionalising' here is not a negative term, but rather one that legitimises what those teachers are doing. After Learmonth's presentation, there is a wide-ranging discussion, recorded in the minutes, about the ways that the EWG might formalise this institutionalising process. It is interesting to note here that the minutes of this meeting never suggest anything other than the idea that Learmonth – despite having the dual role of regulator and policymaker – is a collaborator in the process of devising the curriculum, operating within John Dixon's 'spirit of Dartmouth' (see below). Teachers today might wonder if such a meeting of minds would be possible in contexts where relationships of this kind are often more antagonistic. These are just a small number of examples of documents which form part of the deliberations of the EWG. However, they do give a small insight into a process which suggests that those involved really saw a significant role for the study of media texts within English, and as will be suggested below, these deliberations led to a reasonably significant role for that study in future versions of the curriculum. These deliberations in and of themselves evoke 'the spirit of Dartmouth'; John Dixon's belief in the democratic participation of teachers (Dixon, 2009) is manifest in these documents and the ideas expressed within them.

The final report of the EWG

When the Cox Report was finally published in March 1989, quite a lot of this deliberation was captured and a broad consensus was evident in the chapter devoted to media in English. This three-page section of the report highlighted a tension still evident in media education today, in that the final third of it considered the sometimes-vexed relationship between English, Media and Information Technology, but the first two pages do capture the critical, cultural and creative relationships that exist between the two areas of study. In prefacing the chapter of the report with the quote from Kingman recalled at the start of this chapter, the EWG was emphasising the way that both 'the media' and technology had to have a relationship with English in the new curriculum, and a closer analysis of the chapter bears this out. Early on in the chapter, the report makes a cultural argument not unlike the one made by Len Masterman in his submission to the group:

> Television and film form substantial parts of pupils' experience out of school and teachers need to take this into account. Pupils should have the opportunity to apply their critical faculties to these major parts of contemporary culture.
>
> *(DES, 1989, p.103)*

For the EWG then, concepts of criticality and culture make a natural connection with literary texts, suggesting that there is room for both 'heritage' and 'cultural studies' models of the English curriculum. However, the report also acknowledges the kind of socio-linguistic connection made by Buckingham and Drummond's submission:

> Media education, like drama, deals with fundamental aspects of language, interpretation and meaning. It is therefore consonant with the aims of English teaching. In fact, media education has often developed in a very explicit way concepts which are of general importance in English. These include selection (of information, viewpoint, etc.), editing, author, audience, medium, genre, stereotype, etc.
>
> *(DES, 1989, p.103)*

The language used in this acknowledgement might be characterised as post-structuralist in its tone (suggested by words such as 'interpretation' and 'meaning') and indeed it is clear that for the EWG, the linguistic and analytical act of deconstructing texts is a significant aspect of the English curriculum. In effect, the 2014 curriculum is probably a rejection of the importance of these ideas – an attempt to return to a period in which structure and agency were not things that English teachers concerned themselves with. This return to a reductivist, absolutist view of the subject – in which a spirit of inquiry is replaced by an over-emphasis on factual knowledge – is presented and defended by statements which suggest that such an emphasis is necessary because 'standards' have fallen. These kinds of (admittedly contested) value-claim, return the debate about the English curriculum to the immediate aftermath of the Cox Report, in which ideological entrenchment on both sides of the argument replaces a considered dialogue about where English teaching should go in the twenty-first century.

Interestingly, much of the detail and intention of the EWG's report regarding media in English did not make it in to the final published National Curriculum, much to the chagrin of both Professor Cox himself and the rest of the EWG. In an extraordinary move, Kenneth Baker, then Secretary of State for Education, decided to publish the last three chapters of the report (which contained the recommendations of the group) before the preceding 14, where the complex detail and argument about the curriculum was laid out. While this was obviously not all to do with disliking the parts of the report that were to do with media education, it did send a signal that both Baker and the government he was part of were not going to accept the EWG's advice verbatim.

The National Curriculum – 1990, 1995, 1999, 2007

In the 20-year period from 1990–2010, the National Curriculum programmes of study, both for English and other subjects underwent a number of re-writes. These 'versions' of the original 1990 curriculum came about as a result of a number of different factors. For example, teacher dissatisfaction with the original programmes of study (POS) led the government to appoint Sir Ron Dearing to review them and this in turn led to the 1995 version of the curriculum. Space does not permit a full account of these decisions and revisions here, but suffice to say there was a fair amount of political wrangling about the content of the programmes (Byers, 1994). In the case of the study of media within English, it is interesting to look at the language used, and the way that it evolves as time progresses. This evolution is, I would suggest, indicative of a number of phenomena that could be observed in this period, perhaps most notably the convergence of media and print texts in new technological forms and the fact that more English teachers were teaching Media Studies alongside their main subject discipline.

It is interesting to note that, as in the original submission of the EWG, there are references to media texts which appear throughout the programmes of study for Speaking and Listening, Reading and Writing. In the writing POS, for example, teachers are often encouraged to get students to write scripts for television and film. However, it is in the Reading programmes of study that use of media texts is most clearly identified, and so this analysis focuses on the way that these are presented.

In the original 1990 version of the National Curriculum, the Reading POS suggests that:

> Pupils should be introduced to a range of media texts and be encouraged to consider their purpose, text and intended audience.
>
> *(DES, 1990, p.32)*

This paragraph of advice is preceded by a longer paragraph which refers to, amongst other things, developing 'powers of discrimination' when considering a range of media texts (DES, 1990, p.32). These two short paragraphs at least capture some flavour of the discussions of the EWG, in that both directly and indirectly reflect ideas about purpose and audience, cultural awareness and an ability to connect issues of literacy with the mass media.

However, by the time the revised 1995 curriculum is published these two paragraphs become condensed into one:

> Pupils should be introduced to a wide range of media e.g. magazines, newspapers, radio, television, film. They should be given opportunities to analyse and evaluate such material, which should be of high quality and represent a range of forms and purposes, and different structural and presentational devices.
>
> *(DFE, 1995, p.20)*

Note here, the origins of the phrase 'of high quality', which recurs in a different context in the 2014 version of the NC in relation to literary text. There is no use of such a phrase in the original EWG report, or indeed in many of the submissions to the EWG, and as such, one may suspect that it has been inserted by other means;

it does perhaps demonstrate that Cox was right to see his report as unpopular with the politicians reading it.

When the curriculum was revised again, in 1999, there were some further developments from a media texts point of view. Most notable of these was the clear acknowledgement of the difference between print and moving image texts. The Reading POS was extended from its 1995 wording to reflect this.

> Pupils should be taught:
>
> a)   *How meaning is conveyed in texts that include print, images and sometimes sounds*
> b)   *How choice of form, layout and presentation contribute to effect (for example; font, caption, illustration in printed text; sequencing, framing, soundtrack in moving image text)*
> c)   *How the nature of and purpose of media products influence content and meaning (for example; selection of stories for front page or news broadcast)*
> d)   *How audiences and readers choose and respond to media.*
>
> *(DFEE, 1999; p.35)*

Media Studies teachers will probably be the first to note that this curricular guidance effectively asks English teachers to cover three of the four key concepts used in their subject (Media Language, Representation and Audience) and there is tacit acknowledgement here that for at least some teachers, the subject silos of English and Media Studies are converging around a third subject – what Julian McDougall has suggested we might just call 'Text' (McDougall, 2006). While this was probably not the case for all teachers interpreting the National Curriculum guidance, it meant at least that all students were being exposed to a range of media texts in English, because exam boards introduced compulsory Reading assessments which involved media texts at GCSE level in English. This state of affairs broadly remained unchanged from 1999 to 2010. The wording of the POS highlighted above is largely consistent in the 1999 and 2004 revisions of the curriculum. Perhaps most interestingly of all in the final iteration of the NC prior to the change of government, published in 2007. The Reading POS for KS3 uses the term 'text' in an interchangeable way throughout the curriculum guidance:

Reading for meaning

> Pupils should be able to:
>
> a)   *recognise and discuss different interpretations of texts, justifying their own views on what they read and see, and supporting them with evidence*
>
> [. . .]

g)   understand how audiences and readers choose and respond to texts

h)   understand how the nature and purpose of texts influences the selection of content and its meanings

i)   understand how meaning is created through the combination of words, images and sounds in multimodal text

(QCA, 2007)

Here, reading and seeing are the same thing. No distinction is made between printed, visual or multimodal text and the use of a word like multimodality suggests that implicit in the construction of the curriculum is the idea that in the twenty-first century, language and literacy are heavily reliant upon the successful encounter between the student and texts, which do not necessarily only occur in the printed mode. This final pre-2010 version of the English Curriculum is moving towards (if not already at) a point at which the media and printed texts are fully integrated with each other within the subject. There can be little doubt that the subsequent changes to the NC, post-2010, are designed to 'turn back the clock' to an idea of English that excludes such integration on the grounds that near-mythical, pre-NC versions of the subject were somehow better or more worthwhile.

Conclusions

While this analysis of a set of apparently obscure documents in an archive in London might seem to reveal a peculiarly English set of problems, the sense of what has been lost from the curriculum points towards more global concerns. It is possible to see the excision of media texts from school English as part of a wider set of trends: the focus on mechanistic drill-based methods of teaching writing in the US, established by the Common Core State Standards (Peel, 2017); the demand for a national phonics screening check in Australia; some of the objections to the liberal ideological tone of the New Zealand curriculum. All of these phenomena hint at an abandonment of the growth model of English cultivated by the UK contingent present at Dartmouth in 1966.

There are however, a number of voices set in opposition to both the newest version of the curriculum and the way it appears to be part of a wider global trend towards a more conservative and less growth-orientated version of English, most notably those behind the series of documents entitled *Curriculum and Assessment in English 3 to 19: a Better Plan* (Richmond et al., 2016b). These reports identify a number of deficiencies in the 2014 NC and suggest an alternative model that might be adopted in its place. While the authors acknowledge that their ideas will be at odds with legislators, they go out of their way to stress that in the twenty-first century it seems at best remiss, and at worst, illogical to exclude the study of media texts from the English Curriculum.

A particular blind spot in the new orders, across the piece, is the almost total absence of any recognition that in the second decade of the 21st century the children and young people in our schools are surrounded by electronic and digital media.

(Richmond et al., 2016a)

The authors proffer an alternative curriculum (Richmond et al., 2016b) which puts the reading and writing of media texts at its heart, alongside a clear sense of developing students as critical readers. Their view gives a good deal of consideration to what a sophisticated, mature English curriculum has the potential to look like. One other important point that they make is about the abandonment of 'the principle of general entitlement' (Richmond et al., 2016a, p.19): because of legislation in the UK which effectively frees certain schools (broadly those described as academies) from any obligation to deliver the National Curriculum it seems pointless in having one at all. As David Buckingham has pointed out, writing in relation to the position of media education generally, this is part of a wider paradox in which there is both greater centralised control of education but also greater deference to the free market (Buckingham, 2017) With such a 'paradoxical politics' (p.1) at play it is hardly surprising that there is an illogicality present in the current English curriculum.

Importantly, these voices hark back to the ideas present in the original Dartmouth seminar. John Dixon, writing in 1975, nearly a decade after the gathering, suggested that the shifting ground of culture and its relationship with English as a subject might produce the kind of knee-jerk reaction that the 2014 NC has come to resemble:

Under such pressures there is a tendency to panic, to define an external curriculum-a system into which teacher and pupil must fit-instead of helping teachers, in departments and larger groups, to define for themselves the order and sequence that underlies their best work. There was considerable agreement at the Seminar that such panic measures were to be avoided.

(Dixon, 1975, p.137)

Here then, is a salient reminder of how far English teaching has come since Dartmouth, not only in the way that teachers have continued to reflect and act in the best interests of their students, but also in the way that they have attempted to make their subject best serve those interests. This thing that they do – teaching English – which includes exploring the way that media texts communicate meaning, is far too significant to be left to the fantastical whims of politicians, and as such requires that they keep hold of things that both those colleagues at Dartmouth, and those people who were involved in the development of the original National Curriculum, articulated as being central to the study of English.

References

ACARA – Australian Curriculum Assessment and Reporting Authority (2017). *The Australian curriculum.* Sydney: ACARA.

Bolas, T. (2009). *Screen education: from film appreciation to media studies*. Fishponds: Bristol Intellect.

Buckingham, D. (2017). 'The strangulation of media studies' available online at www.academia.edu/34424271/The_Strangulation_of_Media_Studies.

Buckingham, D. & Drummond, P. (1988). 'English and Media Studies in the National Curriculum: a submission to the National Curriculum English Working Group', identified in The National Archives. NC/EWG (88)3.

Byers, R. (1994). 'The Dearing review of the National Curriculum'. *British Journal of Special Education*, 21, 92–96.

Cox, B. (1991). *Cox on Cox: an English curriculum for the 1990s*. London: Hodder & Stoughton

Department for Education & Science (1990). *English in the National Curriculum*. HMSO: London.

Department for Education & Science (1989). *The Cox Report: English for ages 5–16*. HMSO: London.

Department for Education (1995). *English in the National Curriculum*. HMSO: London

Department for Education (2010). *The importance of teaching*. London: DFE.

Department for Education (2014). *National Curriculum in England: English programmes of study*. London: DFE.

Department for Education and Employment/QCA (1999). *The National Curriculum for England: English*. HMSO: London.

Department for Education (2013). *Reforming the national curriculum in England: summary report of the July to August 2013 consultation on the new programmes of study and attainment targets from September 2014*, London: Department for Education.

Dixon, J. (1975). *Growth through English: set in the perspective of the Seventies*. Oxford. NATE/OUP.

Dixon, J. (2009). 'English renewed: visions of English among teachers of 1966', *English In Education*, 43(3), 241–250.

EMC (2013). 'Initial thoughts on theKS3 consultation – a discussion document', *English and Media Centre*. Available online at www.englishandmedia.co.uk.

Fairclough, N. (2001). *Language and power*. Harlow: Longman.

Gibbons, S. (2013). 'The Draft National Curriculum for English: a response', NATE. Available online at www.nate.org.uk/index.php?page=85&mail=215

Grahame, J. (2012). '5. Future of Film and Media Education', Media Education Association AGM Minutes. Available online at www.themea.org.uk/archive/page/5/

Habermas, J. (1987). *The theory of communicative action*. Cambridge: Polity.

Kingman, J. C. (1988). Report of the committee of inquiry into the teaching of English language: appointed by the Secretary of State under the chairmanship of Sir John Kingman, March 1988. London: HMSO.

Masterman, L. (1988). 'Should Media Studies be integrated into the main English Curriculum or remain relatively separate?' identified in The National Archives. NC/EWG (88), 39.

McCulloch, G. (2004). *Documentary research: in education, history and the social sciences*. London: Routledge Falmer.

McDougall, J. (2006). *The media teachers book*. London: Hodder Arnold.

Ministry of Education (2007). *The New Zealand curriculum*. Learning Media Limited: Wellington.

Muller, H. J. (1967). *The uses of English*. New York: Holt, Reinhart & Winston.

Peel, A. (2017). 'Complicating canons: a critical literacy challenge to common core assessment', *Literacy*, 51(2), 104.

Qualifications and Curriculum Authority (2007). *English programme of study for key stage 3 and attainment targets*. Available online at http://webarchive.nationalarchives.gov.uk/20100

209103209/http://curriculum.qcda.gov.uk/uploads/QCA-07-3332-pEnglish3_tcm8-399.pdf.

Richmond, J., Burn, A., Goddard A., Dougill, P., Raleigh, M., & Traves, P. (2016a). *Curriculum and assessment in English 3 To 19: a better plan – the National Curriculum for English from 2015*. UKLA/NATE/NAAE: Leicester.

Richmond, J., Burn, A., Goddard A., Dougill, P., Raleigh, M., & Traves, P. (2016b). *Curriculum and assessment in English 3 to 19: a better plan – the essentials of English*. UKLA/NATE/NAAE: Leicester.

The National Archives. ED 183/100. National Curriculum: English Working Group; establishment and terms of reference for the Group; first and second reports, on primary and secondary English.

The National Archives. ED 282/85 National Curriculum: English Working Group; agenda and papers.

The National Archives. NC/EWG88 4th. Minutes of the 4th Meeting of the English Working Group held at Elizabeth House on Thursday 23rd June 1988.

14

BACK TO THE FUTURE

The restoration of canon and the backlash against multiculturalism in secondary English curricula

Lesley Nelson-Addy, Nicole Dingwall, Victoria Elliott and Ian Thompson

Introduction

Questions of what constitutes culture have frequently sparked controversy and arguments about the validity and composition of English curricula. In particular, the selection of literary texts as cultural and historical artefacts for use in English lessons in increasingly diverse classrooms involves choices about both cultural values and cultural representation. As Eagleton (2016) reminds us, culture is one of the most complex words in the English language and may variously be taken to mean:

> (1) A body of artistic and intellectual work; (2) a process of spiritual and intellectual development; (3) the values, customs, beliefs and symbolic practices by which men and women live; or (4) a whole way of life.
>
> *(Eagleton 2016:1)*

The history of English Literature as a subject has at various times embraced at least the first three of these definitions and at other times has conflated them. The personal growth model of English that came to dominate the teaching of English in schools after Dartmouth in both the United Kingdom (UK) and the United States (US) drew heavily on the concept of relevance to young people's lives. John Dixon (1967) captured the mood of Dartmouth in *Growth through English* when he argued that:

> In English, pupils meet to share their encounters with life, and to do this effectively they move freely between dialogue and monologue between talk, drama and writing; and literature, by bringing new voices into the classroom, adds to the store of shared experience. Each pupil takes from the store what he

can and what he needs. In so doing he learns to use language to build his own representational world and works to make this fit reality as he experiences it.

(p. 13)

The growing awareness of the social nature of learning that involves a plurality of voices from which pupils make meaning of the world in the classroom led in time to a wealth of 'multicultural' texts entering the English classroom (Gibbons, 2017) which challenged traditional Leavis-influenced conceptions of the literary canon. Of course, the framing of texts as being 'from other cultures' or even 'multiple cultures' has been seen as problematic (Rogers, 2015) in terms of both the ways students understand them and some teachers frame issues of diversity for the English classroom. Rogers (2015) noted that the separation of 'other cultures' from literary heritage from an English anthology to prepare pupils for examinations at age 16 (Northern Examinations and Assessment Board, 1998) only served to remind and entrench the notion that multiculturalism was an outlier to English literature and that 'otherness' is a concept based on race in grouping together black or South Asian authors, and so ignoring other categories such as social class, geographical context or gender. Nevertheless, at least not all texts read in schools were by dead, white, Victorian males. As Goodwyn (2016) argues in revisiting Dartmouth, conceptions of personal growth need to be seen in the context of developing the social agency needed to fully participate in literature classroom discussions and analysis.

However, in recent years curriculum reform in both the UK and the US in favour of cultural literacy and core knowledge has led to a reduction in multicultural texts in English and a backlash against multiculturalism in the curriculum in general (see for example the status of Mexican-American studies in Arizona) and in society. In England, in particular, this is seen through the renaissance of the (largely) dead, white, male canon for statutory study at 14–16, following the reforms to examinations in 2015 led by former Secretary of State for Education, Michael Gove.

In this chapter we address the problematic relationship between questions of social equity involving the effective teaching of a literary canon to enable academic success and the moral issues around the increasingly monocultural or white, male and middle-class cultural perspectives of these texts, which potentially exclude the interests and experiences of a diversity of learners. We draw on the reflections and practice of an experienced local teacher working in an inner-city context, and her position as a black woman teaching a largely white curriculum (Nelson-Addy), to explore the moral and ethical dilemmas surrounding the teaching of canon and of multicultural texts 50 years after Dartmouth and look towards the future for teaching literature in diverse societies.

Culture, multiculturalism and literary texts

Culture as a term is currently highly politically charged in both the UK and the US. Trump's 'culture wars' and some Brexit rhetoric have exposed the rift between conceptions of a shared national culture and the culture of diversity. What lies behind many historical and contemporary concerns about the meaning of culture and literary texts is the tension between what is culturally consumed and culturally valued. For example, the authors of this chapter have lively disagreements over whether J. K. Rowling's *Harry Potter* series represents quality literature. Yet for any of us involved in the initial teacher education in the subject of English to claim that these texts are not culturally important for the current generation of trainee teachers of English would be patently absurd, when a good proportion of trainee teachers each year on the PGCE course in our own institution cite them as the root of their passion for English. Whether this inspiration will be the same in 20 years we cannot tell because culture, unlike some GCSE exam board syllabi, does not stand still. If one agrees with the definition of the identity of human culture as 'constant creations, re-creations and negotiations of imaginary boundaries' (Benhabib 2002:8) then one might argue that the curriculum ought to embrace texts that appeal to this diversity rather than to the single projected voice of the typically white and predominantly male canon.

Previously, Thompson (2015) has argued that English teachers need both to understand the diverse cultural worlds of their pupils and to develop pedagogical skills if they are to involve or re-engage students in making meaning of the complex and contradictory cultural worlds of English. English as a subject is concerned with the understanding of language use in a wide variety of literary and linguistic forms as well as their cultural reception, although definitions of what constitutes a culture remain highly contested. In using the term 'culture' in this chapter we refer not only to the explicit or implicit cultural understandings embedded within literate practices but also to the cultural and historical practices that shape the production, reception, and understanding of literary texts.

Culture also has a highly political and class-based dimension. Said (1993) pointed out both the hybrid and heterogeneous nature of all cultures, as well as the tendency for dominant cultures to impose their particular form of cultures on the oppressed. For example, various aspects of dominant European culture played a part in the imposition of ideas involved in imperialism. Holborow (1999) points out that the politics and practice of slavery stole both people's freedom and brutally suppressed their language. Thus, although non-white writers in English are 'multicultural' they are nevertheless forced to use and perhaps subvert the language of empire. Eddo-Lodge (2017) also highlights how the absence of Black British history (race is generally read and discussed from the US perspective) is also a way for the curriculum to impose the views of the dominant class. Students are therefore reading these cultural texts from a decontextualised position and are thus exposed to a variety of texts that they may never fully relate to or understand.

In fact, the term 'multiculturalism' is attacked in the UK not just by those on the right with their inherent fear and hatred of the other but some on the left who view the term as attempting to normalise and thus excuse the consequences of oppression (McCallum 2012). Some politicians use the term 'multiculturalism' in a positive sense in order to celebrate the various cultural identities across the UK, yet others deploy the term to effectively segregate ethnic groups when making political decisions or statements. Another difficulty arises with the use of the collective terms 'multicultural' and 'other cultures' used to refer to texts written by British people (by birth or naturalised status), alongside people who desire to explore experience through their native country's perspective. Should British writers be termed 'other cultures', especially when Irish, Scottish and Welsh writers are grouped with other English writers? Equally, should all authors of 'other cultures' be grouped together, ignoring important differences in these authors' cultural identities, ethnicity, gender or social class?

In the US and New Zealand, the concept of culturally responsive pedagogy or practice (e.g. Gay, 2010; Bishop, 2008; Villegas and Lucas, 2007) is often preferred to multiculturalism whereas intercultural (e.g. Rosen, passim.) is a term sometimes used in the UK. These pedagogical practices involve the celebration of the positive and fluid aspects of culture rather than a focus on deficit models, by providing content that is meaningful to students and receptive to the heterogeneity of cultural experience (Paris and Alim, 2014). At the same time, from a cultural-historical perspective Gutierrez, Zitlali Morales and Martinez (2009) have pointed out that the language use of terms such as cultural and ethnic 'diversity' or 'at risk' and 'underachieving' learners are not neutral in the practices of literacy learning. These terms can reinforce deficit models where the dominant culture is seen as 'normal' and other cultures as 'diverse' or not normal. Cultural-historical and sociocultural perspectives argue the need to draw on the heterogeneous cultural repertoires from a range of communities. For example, Lee's (2007) cultural modelling work on cultural repertoires of practice and Moll's (2001) work on funds of knowledge in literate practices both draw on the resources of pupils from nondominant groups. Similarly, Gutierrez's (2008) work highlights the need to focus on the third spaces created by focusing on forms of literacy that forefront students' sociohistorical lives rather than traditional academic conceptions.

The backlash against 'multicultural' texts

The twenty-first century has seen a widespread backlash in policy and practice against both multiculturalism and diversity in the UK, Europe and the United States (Vertovec and Wessendorf, 2015). A 2010 law in Arizona banned courses that promoted ethnic solidarity. This led to the closure of Mexican-American Studies courses throughout the state in schools and colleges; in particular, a well-known course in the Tucson Unified School District was targeted for removal. Subsequently Cabrera, Milem, Jaquette and Marx (2014) used achievement data in Arizona from 2008–11 to demonstrate that taking Mexican-American Studies courses was strongly associated with an increased likelihood not only of passing the Arizona standardised test in 10th grade but also of graduating from high school. This was particularly, but not exclusively, true of Mexican-American students, who not only tended to come from lower prior attainment and lower socio-economic backgrounds, but to have a number of other characteristics which are normally associated with lower attainment. This is an unusually clear empirical demonstration of the way in which a representative curriculum can increase attainment across the board, especially among those who see themselves represented in this way.

In England, Gove's reforms of the GCSE English Literature curriculum were symptomatic of the backlash against the use of 'multicultural' texts. In early speeches justifying his reforms, Gove (2013a) complained that only 1% of GCSE students answered an exam question on a pre-1900 novel, with the implication that when it comes to literature, the older the better. As Sarah Olive (2013) has pointed out, the authors praised by Gove in one speech had been dead for an average of 206 years. The prioritising of older texts has clear implications for the erasure of non-white authors from the curriculum (and potentially non-male, although this does not seem to have come to pass (Elliott, 2017)). The accompanying change to the poetry guidance, to representative Romantic poetry and war poetry, from 'poetry from other cultures' has effectively removed non-white and non-British authors from the GCSE curriculum altogether. We have as teachers and teacher educators all noted the washback effect which this has had on the lower school curriculum, as departments focus on preparing younger students for the pre-1900 texts they will encounter in the unseen sections of the examination at age 16, reducing the multicultural and modern content delivered in English. This is true, too, of debates about text choices in higher education. For example, a University of Cambridge student in 2017 wrote an open letter to the university, signed by other students, requesting that there be an attempt to incorporate the presences of black, minority and ethnic authors on the English literature syllabus. The attack by the right-wing press on the student's letter against an all-white university literary curriculum shows the perfidious nature of the dominant culture (see Okundaye, 2017).

Performativity and the narrowness of the curriculum

The accountability of schools sees high-stake testing placing pressure on teachers. The exam now becomes the focus of the curriculum rather the content and development of knowledge beyond the curriculum. The curriculum becomes prescribed in order to enable students to recall information for the examinations. In England, the four GCSE exams boards between them give the choice of eight Shakespeare plays and eight British-authored nineteenth-century novels. Although the range of post-1914 prose and drama is broader there is still only a choice of 12 texts. As for non-white British or Irish authors, the range of texts is very narrow, with Meera Syal's *Anita and me* included in all four specifications and Kazuo Ishiguro's *Never let me go* in three. Nichols and Berliner (2009) note that Campbell's law comes into play in this situation as both the social indicator and those who use it become tainted; in this case the exam and the teacher, the latter now teaches to the narrowness of the curriculum and does not have the space to move beyond the constraints of the curriculum.

The canon, knowledge and a moral dilemma

The positioning of canonical literature teaching both as a moral imperative (Pike, 2014) and as an exercise in Britishness in government rhetoric (Elliott, 2014) raises issues relating to the teaching of the canon in a country where there is not an established canon of non-white authors (in contrast, for example, to the African-American novelists widely taught in the US), and in which class is still a dominant issue in the education system. Canonical literature is promoted as a means of acquiring 'cultural capital' linked to 'social mobility' (and therefore to not teach it is an immoral decision, which makes teachers 'enemies of promise' as Gove (2013b) framed it). This view suggests that without the benefit of reading Shakespeare amongst other canonical texts, students from low socio-economic backgrounds will not have the knowledge to achieve in the school or social environment (Coles, 2013); the teaching of Shakespeare could be a 'chance of liberat[ing] our poorest children from the shadow of ignorance and the chains of dependency' (Gove, 2010). As Gay (2010) has argued, the broadening of the canon to include, for example, more women and writers from ethnic minorities is often criticised by those who argue that this act dilutes or corrodes mainstream academic knowledge. This attack on diversity has often been veiled in the guise of equal opportunity (Banks, 1993) as in Hirsch's (1988) concept of 'cultural literacy' as a shared body of cultural knowledge and assumptions within a national language. This version of 'cultural literacy' is both influential in English curricula in both the UK and the US and highly problematic in the context of diversity. Yet the amount of 'cultural literacy' required even to access and to analyse the set texts in the GCSE examinations exposes and produces further problems of equity. The removal of representation of non-white, non-middle-class voices from the curriculum produces another ethical dilemma for teachers who believe in the need for such representation: should they use the earlier years of secondary school to supply this lack, or is that doing a disservice to the very students who need more experience with canonical texts in order to access the examination curriculum?

However, the canon that Gove claimed was every 'child's birthright' does tend to ignore the cultural background of many pupils that the curriculum is supposed to give a chance to. Williams (1977) describes processes such as the making of a canon as a selective tradition, 'a version of the past which is intended to connect with and ratify the present' (p. 116). It is also intended to promote a particular form of knowledge about both culture and history. Young and Muller (2013) highlight the divide between the inequitable 'knowledge of the powerful' and 'powerful knowledge' (p. 229) that can be used to challenge the hegemony of the powerful. If the dominant culture of the politicians remains the preeminent knowledge in the curriculum, how do students from non-white backgrounds access the canon? We cannot assume that their lack of knowledge of this particular culture is a failure (Mullican, 1991) particularly as they have other valid funds of knowledge (Moll et al., 1992) that they could draw on. The failure in this case would not be with the students but with the curriculum and a narrow conception of a static national culture and its essential literary texts. Indeed, Doecke and Mead (2017) take issue with Young's (2008) definition of knowledge from the perspective of the subject of English by arguing that it privileges prepositional knowledge at the expense of the interpretive approach endemic to literary studies. Likewise, Yandell (2015) critiques the idea of knowledge in English as a static entity by arguing that knowledge has its birth and life in social activity. Responding to literary texts from this stance becomes a question of recontextualising concepts encountered in both everyday and classroom experiences.

The moral dilemma in practice

Should teachers of English solely deconstruct literary texts and equip students with the skills to negotiate the examination process or do teachers have a moral and ethical duty to engage young people with the complex social, historical and cultural processes that shape literary reception and understanding? How do teachers' own conceptions of culture affect their pedagogical choices? Do they teach the canon or subvert it, and what are the consequences of this for their students? In order to illustrate our argument on this moral dilemma we present here the first-person account of one of the authors, Nelson-Addy, a black teacher of English literature working in the state secondary school sector in England.

As a British-born Black woman of Ghanaian descent I acknowledge that I am unable to address all of the nuances of this 'multicultural' discussion. However, I will use my experiences as a teacher to address some of the gaps in education that we, as teachers and teacher educators, could do well to close.

Before I explore my experiences with GCSE students (aged 14–16) and the new English Language and Literature AQA specifications, I want to address the fact that there are still challenges at KS3 level (11–14 year-old students). For example, as a Department Lead on Year 9 curriculum and progress, I question whether addressing the students' contemporary experiences and the questions they might have based on their present, personal social experience through literature may lead to better results in the future, as opposed to spending the year of study focusing on 'high-brow' literature in preparation for their GCSEs.

Presently, the classroom has the potential to be one of the safest places to dispel one's ignorance of the experience of ethnically marginalised groups. From my experience, with the growth of social media, secondary students are becoming more aware of the differences in racial experiences. However, these students are usually exposed to the stark differences between the races or the racial tension more specifically experienced in America. This focus on America is misleading for British students. It is therefore our duty as educators to allow students to be privy to the racial experiences portrayed in British literature.

The contextual background of each text should be considered while texts are being debated, analysed and discussed within the classroom. The first GCSE AQA English Language Paper 1 exam sat by students in Summer 2016, to conclude 2 years of study, included an unseen extract by Katherine Mansfield from her short story 'The Tiredness of Rosabel'. The final question on the paper was: 'A student said, 'This part of the story, set in the hat shop, shows that the red-haired girl has many advantages in life, and I think Rosabel is right to be angry'. To what extent do you agree?'. The exam board's indicative standard suggested students wrote this to receive the highest mark:

She has wealth, beauty and happiness, all characteristics of a privileged lifestyle, and the writer's use of colour to describe her – 'beautiful red hair and a white skin and eyes the colour of that green ribbon shot with gold' — implies she is also radiant, vivacious and exotic.

Insensitively placing an unseen text that has the potential for racist readings in a summative exam is problematic because we are unable to address the inherent ignorance within it in relation to the correlation between wealth, whiteness and beauty, thus, reinforcing the inferiority of other races and social groups. Thus, these texts should be discussed within the classroom space, outside of the examination pressure, so students are able to discuss the context of the writer, text and the time further. The ambiguity of this discursive question in relation to 'many advantages' begins to encompass 'white skin' as an advantage. Perhaps the AQA was focused on the socio-economic divide explored in the extract, but it is short-sighted to suggest the racial ideas expressed here will go unnoticed by the student, and they may even subliminally reinforce racist ideas.

In order to truly establish a sense of variety of texts, we should seek further literary representations of the ethnic involvement in British history, in addition to the same recycled, isolated rap-style poems like 'Half-Caste' and 'Checkin' out mi History' by John Agard that have been included in the GCSE English Literature poetry anthologies since 2004. For example, World War One literature is still being taught from the perspective of our white officer poets Owen and Sassoon, but we have failed to include the sepoy voice or poems that may have been written by or about the British West Indies Regiment (BWIR) (Eddo-Lodge, 2017). Exploration of this perspective begins to provide a more holistic understanding of Britain. Following this, there is also a question of whether texts from a variety of cultures should be heavily focused on their efforts to 'integrate' within the British white norms or whether we should seek literature that deals with one's experience of growing up, being in love or relating with people at home or at school — just everyday common experiences that do not strive to highlight the differences or the efforts to be treated equally.

An incident that occurred while I was teaching a selection of poetry for the GCSE examination highlights both the possibilities and the dilemmas for teachers in addressing diversity. I asked students to read all of the poems in the anthology first and select the top three poems they preferred. Even though there was another British-born black student in the class, a black male student, who had moved to this country during primary school, seemed to connect with 'Checkin Out Mi History' by John Agard the most. This poem explores the anger and frustration felt by a black male speaker, who is confronted with the Eurocentric history syllabus. At the end of the lesson, I was intrigued to know why he was so adamant about this poem being the only one he really wanted to study. Firstly, the student strongly agreed with the views expressed in the poem and found its free-verse form empowering. He later told me that if we did not explore the text together in class, he was willing to work on it independently at home. This is only one example of the current determination among young people who may be seeking for some cultural representations of their own thoughts, feelings and experiences. They seem to also be in search of opportunities to explore them within the classroom space.

Despite this tangible student interest, I am still left with the dilemma: is it right to spend the time it would take to explore the depths of a poem like 'Checkin Out Mi History' by John Agard or 'Tissue' by Imtiaz Dharker from the Power and Conflict *collection or 'Singh Song' by Daljit Nagra from the* Love and Relationships *collection when:*

1. *Some teachers predict that these poems would be too difficult and therefore do not teach them to the students. The AQA GCSE English literature poetry exam involves a thematic question with reference to an unannotated, printed copy of a named poem from the collection and the student has to select another poem of their choice to make comparisons. So that the examination is accessible to all students, some teachers believe that the exam board would not print these poems in the paper.*

2. *These poems' contextual backgrounds are starkly different to the cluster of other poems within the collection. For example, the* Power and Conflict *collection has a cluster of seven poems that all focus on the effects of war.*

3. *The layers of contextual references and ideas involved in the process of understanding these poems should not really be crammed into two lessons in year 10 or 11 (aged 14–16) – students should be exploring these ideas across the curriculum, across all school years.*

4. *The concept of cultural and racial identity has the potential to be a foreign one to students who were born and raised in this country with no real challenges to their own national status. Most of the cultural poems chosen for school study deal with this concept of cultural identity in relation to their similarities and differences to the dominant culture.*

Concluding remarks

Nelson-Addy's account highlights the dilemma involved in achieving a balance between the classroom as a potential for social agency and the need for young people to be offered the opportunities that may be afforded by exam success. The removal of representation of non-white, non-middle-class voices from the curriculum produces another ethical dilemma for teachers who believe in the need for such representation: should they use the earlier years of secondary school to supply this lack, or is that doing a disservice to the very students who need more experience with canonical texts in order to access the examination curriculum? What is clear from Nelson-Addy's account is a strong sense of her knowing the potential power of learning from exploring texts that have a strong resonance with young people's personal experiences, whilst at the same time she worries about the curricula pressures of the impending exam.

Nelson-Addy's reflections suggest the moral imperative for a 'multi' or 'inter' cultural discussion of literary texts. Claiming that 'cultural capital' enables 'social mobility' is superficial as this discourse ignores issues such as race, gender and social class. A wider cultural representation of authors not only benefits those who then see themselves in the texts before them, but also society as a whole, providing for a more empathetic and balanced understanding of the people who make up the population of the UK or the US. In addition, the studying of a wider variety of literary genres and styles from writers from different cultures allows opportunities for classroom explorations of what constitutes prejudice of 'the other'.

Of course, the moral balance needs to be struck between personal life opportunities as represented by exam success and the potential for social agency (Goodwyn, 2016). Yet these potential polarities are not necessarily mutually exclusive. For example, Lee (2007) in her work in the US using a cultural modelling approach found that students developed their tacit knowledge of signifying cultural practices in literary texts when they were provided with cultural data sets that exemplified both interpretive problems of understanding tone and meaning as well as complex and dynamic figurative language. Through analysing a range of texts such as rap music, poetry and 'canonical' African-American literary texts the students developed the needed navigational tools for reinterpreting both new and canonical literature. In other words, curriculum choices that provide a wider variety of literary genres and styles from writers from different cultures can help students become both critical and culturally responsive interpreters of literature who are more likely to do well in examinations. Rather than going 'back to the future' through narrow canonical specifications, a reconceptualisation of the cultural, historical and social importance of studying, analysing and even valuing literary texts that was so celebrated at Dartmouth now involves a wider literary representation of the lived experiences of our diverse student population.

References

Banks, J. A. (1993) 'The canon debate, knowledge construction, and multicultural Education', *Educational Researcher*, 22(5), 4–14.

Benhabib, S. (2002) *The claims of culture: equality and diversity in the global era*, Princeton University Press: Princeton, NJ and Oxford.

Bishop R. (2008). 'Te Kotahitanga: Kaupapa Māori in mainstream classrooms', in Denzin, N. K., Lincoln, Y. S., Tuhiwai Smith, L. (eds.), *Handbook of critical and indigenous methodologies*, Thousand Oaks, CA: Sage: 439–458.

Cabrera, N. L., Milem, J. F., Jaquette, O. and Marx, R. W. (2014) 'Missing the (student achievement) forest for all the (political) trees: empiricism and the Mexican American studies controversy in Tucson', *American Educational Research Journal*, 51(6),1084–1118.

Coles, J. (2013) 'Every child's birthright? Democratic entitlement and the role of canonical literature in the English National Curriculum', *The Curriculum Journal*, 21(1), 50–66.

Dixon, J. (1967) *Growth through English*. Oxford: Oxford University Press.

Doecke, B. and Mead, P. (2017) 'English and the knowledge question', *Pedagogy, Culture and Society*, DOI: 10.1080/14681366.2017.1380691

Eagleton, T. (2000) *The idea of culture*. Oxford: Blackwell Publishers.

Eagleton, T. (2016) *Culture*. New Haven and London: Yale University Press.

Eddo-Lodge, R. (2017) *Why I'm no longer talking to white people about race*. London: Bloomsbury.

Elliott, V. (2014) 'The treasure house of a nation? Literary heritage, curriculum and devolution in Scotland and England in the twenty-first century', *The Curriculum Journal*. 25(2), 282–300.

Elliott, V. (2017) 'What does a good one look like? Marking A level English scripts in relation to others', *English in Education*, 51(1), 58–75.

Gay, G. (2010) *Culturally responsive teaching: theory, research, and practice*. New York: Teachers College Press.

Gibbons, S. (2017) *English and its teachers: a history of policy, pedagogy and practice*. London: Routledge.

Goodwyn, A. (2016) 'Still growing after all these years? The resilience of the "Personal Growth model of English" in England and also internationally', *English Teaching: Practice and Critique*, 15(1), 7–21.

Gove, M. (2010) 'All pupils will learn our island story'. Speech retrieved from http://conservative-speeches.sayit.mysociety.org/speech/601441.

Gove, M. (2013a). *What does it mean to be an educated person?* Speech presented at Brighton College, Brighton. Retrieved from www.politics.co.uk/comment-analysis/2013/05/09/michael-gove-s-anti-mr-men-speech-in-full.

Gove, M. (2013b) 'I refuse to surrender to the Marxist teachers hell-bent on destroying our schools' *The Daily Mail*. Retrieved from www.dailymail.co.uk/debate/article-2298146/I-refuse-surrender-Marxist-teachers-hell-bent-destroying-schools-Education-Secretary-berates-new-enemies-promise-opposing-plans.html.

Gutierrez, K. D. (2008) 'Developing a sociocritical literacy in the third space', *Reading Research Quarterly*, 43(2), 148–164.

Gutierrez, K. D., Zitlali Morales, P. and Martinez, D. C. (2009) 'Re-mediating literacy: culture, difference and learning for students from nondominant communities', *Review of Research in Education*, 33(1), 212–24.

Hirsch, E. D. (1988) *Cultural literacy: what every American needs to know*. New York: Random House.

Holborow, M. (1999) *The politics of English*. London: Sage Publications.

Lee, C. D. (2007) *Culture, literacy, and learning: taking bloom in the midst of the whirlwind*. New York: Teachers College Press.

McCallum, A. (2012) *Creativity and learning in Secondary English Teaching for a creative classroom*. Routledge Oxford.

Moll, L. C. (2001) 'The Diversity of schooling: a cultural–historical approach', in M. de la Luz Reyes and J. J. Halcón (eds.), *The best for our children: critical perspectives on literacy for Latino children*. New York: Teachers College Press: 13–28.

Moll, L. C., Amanti, C., Neff, D., and Gonzalez, N. (1992) 'Funds of knowledge for teaching: using a qualitative approach to connect homes to classrooms', *Theory into Practice*, 31(2), 132–141.

Mullican, J. S. (1991) 'Whose cultural literacy: whose culture? whose literacy?' *English Education*, 23(4), 244 –250.

Nichols, S. L. and Berliner, D. C. (2009) 'The inevitable corruption of indicators and educators through high-stakes testing', *Education Policy Research University*, Arizona State University.

Okundaye, J. O. (2017) 'The "decolonise" Cambridge row is yet another attack on students of colour'. *The Guardian* October 2017. Retrieved from www.theguardian.com/commentisfree/2017/oct/25/decolonise-cambridge-university-row-attack-students-colour-lola-olufemi-curriculums.

Olive, S. E. (2013) 'A Great tradition?: Shakespeare in the national curriculum', *Alluvium*, 2(1), 1–2.

Paris, D. and Alim, S. (2014) 'What are we seeking to sustain through culturally sustaining pedagogy? A Loving critique forward', *Harvard Educational Review*, 84(1), 85–100.

Pike, M. A. (2014) *Ethical English: teaching and learning in English as spiritual, moral and religious education*. London: Bloomsbury.

Rogers, A. (2015) 'Crossing "other cultures"? Reading Tatamkhulu Afrika's "Nothing's Changed" in the NEAB Anthology', *English in Education*, 49(1), 80–93.

Rosen, M. (2013) 'Culture vs interculture (re 'In our Time@ BBC Radio 4)' http://michaelrosenblog.blogspot.co.uk/2013/01/culture-vs-interculture-re-in-our-time.html Retrieved 16/10/2017.

Said, E. W. (1993) *Culture and imperialism*. London: Chatto and Windus.

Thompson, I. (2015) 'Communication, culture, and conceptual learning: task design in the English classroom', in I. Thompson (ed.) *Designing tasks in Secondary education: enhancing subject understanding and student engagement*. London and New York: Routledge.

Williams, R. (1977) *Marxism and literature*. Oxford: Oxford University Press.

Vertovec, S. and Wessendorf, S. (2015) 'Assessing the backlash against multiculturalism in Europe', in Vertovec, S. and Wessendorf, S. (eds.) *Multiculturalism backlash: European discourses, policies and practices*, London: Routledge, 1–31.

Villegas, A. and Lucas, T. (2007) 'Responding to changing demographics: the culturally responsive teacher', *Educational Leadership*, 64(6), 28–33.

Yandell, J. (2015) 'Growth and the category of experience', *English in Australia*, 51(3), 19–24.

Yandell, J. (2017) 'Knowledge, English and the formation of teachers', *Pedagogy, Culture and Society*, 25(4), 583–599.

Young, M. (2008) *Bringing knowledge back in: from social constructivism to social realism in the sociology of education*. London: Routledge.

Young, M. and Muller, J. (2013) 'On the powers of powerful knowledge', *Review of Education*, 1(3), 229–250.

15

FINDING AND KEEPING POETRY

Sue Dymoke

I was honoured to give the Harold Rosen Memorial Lecture at NATE's 2016 research symposium celebrating 50 years after Dartmouth. When preparing to give that keynote I revisited certain aspects of my English education between the ages of 5 and 18 years in the 1960s and 70s, and recalled some of the teachers in whose care my development as a literate, numerate and creative learner was entrusted in order to try to understand their significance for my development as a poet and poetry teacher. In focusing on this formative period, the following chapter explores the nature of language and personal growth (Dixon, 1967, p.1) which were central elements of the original month-long seminar held in 1966 at Dartmouth College in New Hampshire, USA. It reflects on how poetry came to be such a key influence on my learning, teaching and writing and what lessons might be drawn from these experiences to inform future pedagogical practice or research in the field. In doing so, the chapter refers to previously published research on drafting, reading and performing poetry, poetic identity, poetry pedagogy and spoken word to consider how young people can find and keep poetry for themselves in ways that will continue to enrich them throughout their adult lives.

My poetry discoveries began in the summer of 1969 or, to be more precise, just before the historic first moon landing on Monday 21st July 1969. At some point during the weeks of anticipation leading up to Armstrong's 'one small step for man . . . one giant leap for mankind', I wrote the poem below.

The moon is dark and silent
and always still.
There are rocks upon her surface
like a hill.
There are craters and sand there.
Beware astronaut beware.

I was 7 years old. It is the first and only piece of writing that I can remember completing at Infant school. I have previously commented that the composition of this poem may not be of a particularly high quality but, for me, it marked a hugely significant moment which continues to have resonance today (Dymoke, 2003). What I am interested to consider here is how I came to write it and how I came to find poetry.

The Saturday after Armstrong's bouncy walk across the alien surface my Infant school days were coming to an end. Mum and Dad bought me my first dictionary, the *Oxford Concise*. I covered it in sticky back plastic and carried to school. In the years that followed, the monikers of almost all the teachers in whose classes I was most happy were inscribed there. Even now their signatures send me straight back to their classrooms, language labs, netball courts, stages and domestic science rooms.

Mrs Sharma was my Reception class teacher. Her brilliant red and orange saris shimmered along the corridor. She read us 5-year-olds wonderful stories and poems from a thick, well-thumbed book during wet playtimes. Miss Acker taught us italic handwriting and thought that the curls of my fffffs were never ever neat enough. Mrs James was one of my Junior school teachers. Nature was what drove her. She was a huge exponent of the great outdoors as a stimulus for writing. We were forever on field trips and nature walks, sketching, jotting, peering through magnifying glasses and binoculars. Thanks to her I experienced, at 8 years of age, the early morning beauty of a misty bluebell wood, learned to identify birdsong, beetles and different varieties of wildflowers. Because of her I wrote and published poems in local magazines. She made the vital connection between nature and writing and forged an enticing path for me to follow.

For a long time I have tried to make sense of how and why I was taught in the particular way I was and why I responded with such enthusiasm. As a result of their teaching – not just their English teaching – I became Edward Lear's Runcible Spoon in our Junior school play (*The Owl and the Pussycat went to See*), listened in awe to *Under Milk Wood*, savoured Portia's unstrained 'quality of mercy', enjoyed the language of algebra and quadratic equations, puzzled over T. S. Eliot's mysterious voices in 'Journey of the Magi' and always strove to perfect a fast serve on the tennis court. But I want to concentrate on two teachers – one from Infant school and one from Secondary school. Between them, they encapsulate so much about my finding of poetry and my personal growth through language.

Poetry at Infant school

In *Growth through English*, John Dixon comments:

> It has taken the Infant Schools, in their work with five-to-seven-year-olds, to prove that a new and complex relationship is possible between the 'skill' elements and the broader processes that prompt a child to use language in the first place.
>
> *(Dixon, 1967, p.2)*

He also writes of the need for all pupils to be empowered through their exploration of language to gain greater independence. In doing so, they will be enabled to take on a new role as spectator and consequently 'enter into and share in the work of the mature artist and thinker' (Dixon, 1967, p.31). Dixon cites the example, from Holbrook's controversially titled *English for the Rejected*, of 'Joan', a young woman of low IQ who had previously been condemned by her primary school as having 'no originality or imagination' (Holbrook, 1964, p.54) and yet wrote a poem about her yearning for a little yellow bird that 'flew in to the golden yellow sun' (p.54). Interestingly, Joan's poem was composed during an examination at the end of her first year of Secondary school. Given the Hirschian (1987) model of knowledge acquisition that underpins the literacy/English testing endured by twenty-first-century school students in England, it is almost impossible to imagine such a creative act occurring in an examination now.

Dixon notes that creative work such as Joan's gives educators permission or a 'new right to talk about the creative potentialities of all children' (1967, p.27). This sense of permission is one that I would explore much later in doctoral research on poetry teaching in Secondary schools. Some of my case study English teachers acknowledged how children of all abilities could reach high levels of achievement with poetry and could produce jewel-like phrases as a result of the accessibility, 'honesty and . . . economy' of language that poetry writing activities offered them (Dymoke, 2001, p.36).

It occurs to me that, in the same period as the Dartmouth Seminar, my Infant school headteacher was striving to create an inclusive school community where pupils, parents, and teachers were made to feel part of a shared learning conversation, in which all were encouraged to recognise young people's creative potential and achievements. In the late 1960s, Rosemary Clayfield was the newly appointed Headteacher of Letchmore Road School in Stevenage, a fast-expanding New Town in southeast England. She had arrived shortly after I had first started school. In later life she became Rosemary Davis, an emeritus Professor at the Institute of Education, University College, London. She is the first of the teachers who has had such an influence on my personal growth through English.

Professor Davis noted that during her training (at Goldsmiths College, University of London and the Laban Centre in the early fifties) she had learned a practical, activity-based approach to teaching the curriculum in which art, drama and music were integral elements (Dymoke, 2016, p.28). Poetry featured very regularly in my Infant school life. We heard poems in assemblies. We brought them alive through painting, dance and drama. We connected them with science and the world outside. We listened to poems when rain speckled our classroom's high windows at playtime. We wrote poems. We longed to borrow poetry books from the 'cupboard with its scarlet-ribboned key' (Dymoke, 1987, p.6). We also read poems on the ever-changing poetry noticeboard in the corridor outside our Headteacher's office. Poems written by Rossetti, Stevenson and Walter de la Mare. Poems by other pupils, including my moon poem. In reading this poem with hindsight I can see the influence of de la Mare's 'Silver' in terms of atmosphere, some aspects of word choice and the feminisation of the Moon as she 'walks the night in her silver shoon' (de la Mare, 1958, p.106). However, in structure, rhyme scheme and voice my piece is very different. My moon is an ominous place, riven with risk, uncertainty and mystery for the astronauts. One could argue that the unknown silent surface I describe anticipates not only what Armstrong and Aldrin would find there but the uncertain challenges of the blank page on which I was writing a poem for the first time.

Poetry as a legitimate act

I have subsequently learned that all pupils in the final year Infants class were given a choice about how we could respond to the Apollo 11 mission. Writing a poem was just one choice along with story-telling, painting, drawing and other creative options. Apparently I was the only pupil who wrote a poem. However, having made my choice, my abiding memory of the moon poem is not the act of writing it – if only I could remember that – but the way others responded to the piece, the life it would lead after it had been written. I know that my class teacher, Mrs Buckingham, liked it and showed it to her colleagues. I know that the Headteacher, who had herself initiated the whole creative moon project, pinned it to the noticeboard near the main entrance where it seemed to stay for some time. I also know that it was photocopied and displayed somewhere outside school for teachers and advisors to read. All of those small events served as a vital and early affirmation that it was okay for me to take a risk and choose to write poetry. They signalled that it was legitimate to be 'spectator . . . an attentive immersed onlooker' (Dixon, 1967, p.29) and to explore an event beyond my own lived experience – a trip to the moon – something and somewhere that had been discussed, dreamed about and imagined for the whole of that summer term. It was also okay to voice fears about the dangers that might lurk on the moon surface and to issue a warning to three astronauts whom I would never meet and who were highly unlikely to ever read my poem. Infant school teachers gave me the freedom to express myself as I wished, and poetry gave me even more freedom in return. In years to come these were experiences that would become central to my own philosophy of English teaching.

I once heard novelist Pat Barker urging writers to go into writing 'wanting to surprise yourself because if you can't do that then no-one else will be surprised by what you write'. Her comments echo poet Stephen Dunn's maxim: 'your poem effectively begins at the first moment you've surprised or startled yourself' (Dunn, 2001, p.137). I love the element of risk implied in their guidance: you are going out into the unknown in your writing, exploring unknown headspace, or, as *Star Trek*'s Captain James T. Kirk would say, 'strange new worlds. . . new life and new civilisations, to boldly go where no [one] has gone before', and that is exciting. Children and adults who are learning to write continually need to experience this thrilling sense of mission and discovery when they write. That is what so many of my school experiences gave me.

Poetry at Secondary school

The second major influence on my growth through English was Richard Wallace, an English teacher at The Barclay School, a state Secondary comprehensive school in Stevenage. He taught me between the ages eleven to thirteen and sixteen to eighteen. The activities he chose, his wealth of poetic knowledge and the quality of his written feedback enabled me to learn how to develop my writing and deepen my knowledge and understanding of poetry. This learning would, years later, feed directly into how I would go on to teach poetry in Secondary English classrooms.

With his wild wispy hair and flared checked trousers, Mr Wallace cut a gangly figure. To inspire us he blew bubbles in the classroom, set fire to things, made us collect new cool words, write ballads and shape poems, haiku and even shorter pieces. Another student's poem:

Gone.

She left me.

This was the piece I was most envious of. I think it stunned us all with its economy.

Through serious fun our English teacher helped us to find (after Ted Hughes) our own inner 'thought fox(es)' (1957, p.14) and experience the joy of how poetry can make you think – an aspect of poetry teaching which is acknowledged as fundamental (Ofsted, 2007). Looking back over the poetry he introduced us to I am amazed at what we covered in the junior years of Secondary school. It ranged from *Beowulf* to Elizabeth Jennings, Shakespeare to Roger McGough, Robert Browning to Stevie Smith. The connection between listening, reading and writing was ever-present. Mr Wallace used poems as models for writing but always gave us choices and the freedom to use these as loosely as we wished. 'My Bus Conductor' by Roger McGough was one such poem. It led me to write a poem about my grandfather who worked on the railways his whole life until 'the whistle blew and the last station faded away'.

Poetry experiences

Mr Wallace firmly believes in E.M. Forster's instruction in *Howards End* (a novel partially set in my home town): 'only connect the prose and the passion and both will be exalted' (1941, p.188). He achieved this by creating a context for sharing poetry together, tapping into events in his students' own lives and creating new experiences. The latter might involve seeing where Keats coughed up blood in his Hampstead home or by picking blackberries in the scruffy bit of the school car park, staining fingers with Heaney's 'summer's blood' (1966, p.20).

Mr Wallace is a huge fan of Thomas Hardy's writing. I discovered his novels in our school library when I was twelve and can still see the smile on my teacher's face when I told him I had just borrowed *Far From the Madding Crowd*. Immediately he began to quote the novel's opening:

When Farmer Oak smiled the corners of his mouth spread till they were
within an unimportant distance of his ears . . .

(Hardy, 1942, p.1)

However, it was to be Hardy's poetry that made the greatest impression on me.
Most memorable was our group's visit to Thomas Hardy's cottage in Higher
Bockhampton, Dorset. Hardy's poem 'The Self Unseeing' sends a shiver down
my spine even now. Part of me is forever there in that cottage with our teacher
standing in the doorway reading the poem and us silently, waiting for the 'dead
feet' (166) to walk in.

Richard Wallace completed his English degree and initial teacher education in
London in the early 1970s, with Harold Rosen as one of his examiners. He remembers little about these experiences except that, like many teachers of his generation,
he learned a great deal of poetry during his undergraduate years and drew on this
poetry store in his teaching. This is so different from many new pre-service teachers
today, who may have avoided optional poetry modules in their degrees and need
considerable subject knowledge support (Dymoke, 2009).

Access to secondary discourse

I come from a working-class family. My parents both left school at the age of 14.
Dad read us *Winnie the Pooh* and *Treasure Island* at bedtime. Mum avoided reading
(and writing) unless it involved deciphering knitting patterns or recipes. Neither
of them read poetry for pleasure, although Dad did chuckle over some of Pooh's
hums and Mum could recite John Masefield's poem 'Cargoes', which she had had
to learn by heart at school. Although not literary people, they knew the value of
learning. They made sure I joined the library as soon as I was old enough and I am
eternally grateful for that. They indulged my requests for a typewriter and books
as birthday presents. One year I spent book tokens on the beautifully illustrated
Louis Untermeyer's *Golden Treasury of Poetry* (1969), which remains a favourite
companion. Here I first discovered May Swenson's ravishing 'Was Worm' with
its dazzling compressed imagery of the larva released from its swaddling: 'Now,
tiny sequin coat/peacock bright . . .' (73). The day before I gave the 2016 lecture
I came across Beryl Hales' writer's shed miniature (Figure 15.1), which was exhib-
ited in our neighbourhood's art week. By coincidence Untermeyer's anthology
was one of her favourite poetry books, too, and it formed the shed's base. I am
struck by the significance of this: it seems symbolise how a foundation of reading
poetry underpins writing poetry.

I went to three ordinary neighbourhood state schools. Increasingly, however,
I realise that my school experiences were extraordinary. James Gee notes that, 'if
you have no access to the social practice, you don't get in the Discourse, you don't
have it' (Gee, 2015, p.168). The greater the distance that exists between one's
primary discourse – the discourse of home and family – and other, secondary, discourses, the greater the challenge there will be to perform effectively within that

FIGURE 15.1 Beryl Hales, 'Writer's Shed' (2016)

new discourse. For some poets, such as Seamus Heaney, poetry was embedded within the home culture (Heaney, 1980). Not all young people are so fortunate. My teachers opened the door for me to a secondary discourse in that they enabled me to find poetry for myself, to recognise the marvellous economy, precision and distillation of language, to go on finding it beyond the classroom and to keep it close in my head and on the page ever after.

Spoken word

When carrying out external evaluation and research work in London schools with Spoken Word educators and secondary students I have witnessed at first-hand how Spoken Word can give young people opportunities to engage with the genre as a secondary discourse in ways that are less alien to their own contexts. The Spoken Word subgenre empowers them to draw on language and experiences of their primary discourse (namely, home life, personal history, social context and idiolect) as they are striving to make sense of themselves and carve out their identity. The 11- to 18-year-olds whose words and performances I read and heard were coming to terms with aspects of emotional literacy through their writing. They wrote about: their identity, origins and journeys; arguments with friends and family; suffering and loss of loved ones; dislocation and learning. For example:

> My city weeps in shadows and longs for kites that
> will not fly in its sullen helicopter skies. (Yr 11 student)

> I'm gonna learn to play the game
> I'm trying to bounce from the bottom to the top of the league …
> Not a wasteman that lives in a wasteland. (Yr 7 student)

> I am made of words beyond silence. (Yr 12 student)

The writing processes that these young people engaged in not only validated these topics as legitimate subjects for poetry but, in doing so, they offered their young writers a route into membership of a community of writers and a chance to participate in a new secondary discourse with greater confidence and sense of purpose (Dymoke, 2017).

The line 'I am made of words beyond silence', is from a long poem, written and performed by a 17-year-old female student at an evening showcase event in her school. These words exemplify Ann Haas Dyson's view that Spoken Word contains within it 'experienced worlds awaiting articulation' (Dyson, 2005, p.152). The young woman sees language as a vital element of what makes her who she is. Within the measured simplicity of her language there is a strong statement of intent: these words have given her a voice, one with which she can overcome silence and tell her stories to anyone who will listen. One which, now found, is hers for the keeping.

Poetry in initial teacher education

How, therefore, can today's teachers help students to find and keep poetry beyond school, at a time when their work is framed by neo-liberal discourses and account-ancy models of learning (Dymoke, 2016)? All teachers need support to develop their confidence as creative readers and writers, to draw on the different identities and writing practices that constitute who they are (Dymoke and Spiro, 2017). This cannot be achieved without careful allocation of time – a precious resource within intensive, time-poor courses. Beginning teachers especially need to learn to struggle with words on the page, to trust their peers to critique and support their endeavours. They also need to establish what Benyon calls a 'pedagogy of permission' (2015, p.179) to experiment with a set of writing practices and social interventions which they could adapt and use with their own classes. One way of initiating such a process is through a portfolio approach. For example, each year we require our University of Leicester English pre-service teachers to produce a writing portfolio of new work – finished pieces, work critiqued by readers of their choice and work in progress – in a range of genres and media. We give them opportunities to write in different places, including our lovely botanical gardens, the New Walk museum, providing both visual and written stimulus to provoke their ideas and choices.

Finding poetry

One writing practice I always use with new and experienced teachers is found poetry. Monica Prendergast describes this as 'the imaginative appropriation and reconstruction of already existing texts' (2006, p.369). In its most straightforward form, found poetry involves selecting a piece of prose (such as junk mail, a news article, a set of instructions), breaking that text into new lines or extracting words and phrases to create a poem. It could also involve collaging and combining language from several texts or using verbatim texts. The language is already provided so the writer can concentrate on creative use of cut and paste to find 'beauty in the unexpected' (Manhire, 2009, p.8). The range of subjects and sources for found poetry is endless. Digital technology affords opportunities for writers to cast their nets widely for suitable texts. In 2015, my group's forays into found poetry included: writing a poem about pop star Madonna's fall from grace at a music awards ceremony (sourced from tweets); a piece about dementia (using blog and website extracts); a valedictory poem for a tutor (drawn from a tutor's emails to a student), and a series of haiku about the ups and downs of teacher life (composed from Facebook status updates). At the end of the course, one Newly Qualified Teacher identified found poetry as her 'best' teaching discovery of the year (Dymoke, 2016, p.69).

An initial inspiration for my keynote lecture was the traditional phrase:

Finders keepers

Losers weepers

In their ground-breaking research on the language and lore of school children (first published in the 1950s) Iona and Peter Opie identified that this phrase was widely used. They also comment on phrases spoken by two children when they happened to speak the same words simultaneously. In Alton, Hampshire each child would 'touch wood' and name a poet. If this happened elsewhere children would link pinky fingers, make a silent wish and name a poet. If they lived in London or Edinburgh the poet should NOT be Shakespeare or Burns 'not Shakespeare because Shakespeare spears the wish; not Burns because he burns it (Opie, 1977, p.334). The two poets usually named were Keats and Shelley. It would be fascinating to know if this phrase still exists anywhere in the UK or the world today (and whether Keats and Shelley's names are spoken). Let us hope that somewhere, children have found new poets and that Zephaniah and Agard, or Nichols and Kay, Dharker and Nagra, or Duffy and Rosen are named and wished for. Let us also hope that they realise these poets are ordinary people like them, people who can make the ordinary become extraordinary through their writing.

Keeping poetry

The moon still holds a fascination for me (*Moon at the Park and Ride* was my second full poetry collection) and personal poetry discoveries continue. In most cases these are of single-authored collections rather than single poems, which are so often the limited experience of those studying poetry in school (Dymoke, 2012b). In the last eighteen months I have enjoyed fine work by writers including Nancy Campbell, Helen Dunmore, the Foyle Young Poets of the Year, Nancy Gaffield, Alice Oswald, Jan Wagner and Cliff Yates, along with *Rain Won't* by Kenji Miyazawa, one of Japan's foremost twentieth-century poets, and the magnificent poem 'Hermit Crab' written by Peter Porter in the last year of his life, in which he contemplates 'this shell I soon must leave' (2015, p. 53).

The poet Audre Lorde insists:

> poetry is not a luxury it is a vital necessity of our existence . . . Poetry is the way we help give name to the nameless so that it can be thought.
>
> *(1977, p.419)*

I agree that it is an essential element of self-expression and our spiritual lives. We should weep to think so many young people could be turned off poetry and that some might, as Michael Rosen puts it in his provocative 'Bear Grylls' poem 'die of poetry' (2015, p.212) because of their examination experiences. If they do then they will lose touch with its strength and beauty.

John Dixon emphasises how students and teachers need to 'work together to keep language alive and, in doing so, to enrich and diversify personal growth' (1967, p.13). I have been fortunate to connect with poetry through so many different means. Teachers first sowed the seed of my interest. They helped me to locate it as a desirable destination. I firmly believe it is our responsibility as a teaching profession to ensure that all our students and future teachers are similarly enabled and equipped to go on finding, choosing, writing, keeping and making poetry happen for themselves for the rest of their lives.

An earlier version of this chapter first appeared in Teaching English, *Autumn 2016, Issue 12.*

References

Benyon, E. (2015) 'Engaging invisible pupils through creative writing' in S. Dymoke, M. Barrs, A. Lambirth and A. Wilson (eds.) *Making poetry happen: transforming the poetry classroom.* London: Bloomsbury: 173–180.

Campbell, N. (2015) *Disko Bay.* London: Enitharmon Press.

Dixon, J. (1967) *Growth through English.* Huddersfield: NATE; NCTE and ML.

Dunn, S. (2001) *Walking light: memoirs and essays on poetry* (2nd edition). Rochester, New York: BOA Editions.

Dunmore, H. (2017) *Inside the wave.* Hexham: Bloodaxe Books.

Dymoke, S. (1987) 'Reading matters', in *A Sort of clingfilm.* Huddersfield: Wide Skirt Press.

Dymoke, S. (2001) 'Taking poetry off its pedestal: the place of poetry writing in an assessment-driven curriculum'. *English in Education* 35(3), 32–41.

Dymoke, S. (2003) *Drafting and assessing poetry.* London: Sage/Paul Chapman.

Dymoke, S. (2009) *Teaching English texts 11–18.* London: Continuum.

Dymoke, S. (2012a) *Moon at the park and ride*. Nottingham: Shoestring Press.

Dymoke, S. (2012b) 'Poetry is an unfamiliar text: locating poetry in Secondary English classrooms in New Zealand and England during a period of curriculum change'. *Changing English Studies in Reading and Culture*, 19 (4) 395–410.

Dymoke, S. (2016) 'Integrating poetry-focused digital technology within a literacy teacher education course', in C. Kosnik, S. White, C. Beck, B. Marshall, A. Lin Goodwin and J. Murray (eds.) *Building bridges: rethinking literacy teacher education in a digital era*. Rotterdam: Sense Publications: 59–76.

Dymoke, S. (2016) 'It all began with the Moon . . . finding and keeping poetry', *Teaching English*, 12, 27–32.

Dymoke, S. (2017) 'Poetry is not a special club': how has an introduction to the secondary discourse of spoken word made poetry a memorable learning experience for young people?' *Oxford Review of Education* 43(2), 225–241.

Dymoke, S. and Spiro, J. (2017) 'Poet-academics and academic-poets: writing identities, practices and experiences within the Academy'. *Writing in Practice*, 3, March,.

Eliot, T.S. (1969) 'Journey of the Magi', in *The complete poems & plays of T. S. Eliot*. London: Faber & Faber.

Forster, E.M. (1941) *Howards end*. London: Penguin Books.

Gee, J. P. (2015) *Social linguistics and literacies: ideology in discourses* (5th Edition). London: Routledge.

Gaffield, N. (2016) *Meridian*. Hunstanton: Oystercatcher.

Hardy, T. (1942) *Far from the madding crowd*. London: Macmillan.

Hardy, T. (1976) 'The Self unseeing', in *The complete poems*. London: Macmillan.

Heaney, S. (1966) 'Blackberry picking', in *Death of a naturalist*. London: Faber & Faber.

Heaney, S. (1980) *Preoccupations: selected prose 1968–1978*. New York: Farrar, Straus & Giroux.

Hirsch, E. (1987) *Cultural literacy: what every American needs to know*. Boston: Houghton Mifflin.

Holbrook, D. (1964) *English for the rejected*. Cambridge: Cambridge University Press.

Hughes, T. (1957) 'The thought fox', in *The hawk in the rain*. London: Faber & Faber.

Lorde, A. (1977) 'Poetry is not a luxury', in Lorde, A. (1984) *Sister Outsider: essay and speeches*. Trumansburg, NY: The Crossing Press.

De la Mare, W. (1958) 'Silver', in *Peacock pie*. London: Faber & Faber.

Manhire, B. (2009) 'Unconsidered trifles: the writer as thief', *English in Aotearoa*, October, 6–14.

Masefield, J. (1939) 'Cargoes', in A. Quiller-Couch (ed.) *The Oxford book of English verse 1250–1918*. Oxford: Oxford University Press.

McGough, R. (1967) 'My bus conductor', in *Penguin modern poets 10: The Mersey Sound. Adrian Henri, Roger McGough. Brian Patten*. London: Penguin Books.

Milne, A. A. (1965) *Winnie-the-Pooh*. London: Methuen.

Miyazawa, K. (2013) *Rain won't*. A. Binard (Trans.), K. Yamamura (Illus.) Tokyo: Imajinsha.

Ofsted (2007) *The teaching of poetry in schools*. London: HMSO.

Opie, I. and P. (1977) *The Lore and Language of Schoolchildren*. St. Albans: Granada Publishing Ltd.

Oswald, A. (2016) *Falling awake*. London: Jonathan Cape.

The Poetry Society (2016) *Foyle Young Poets of the Year anthology: the wolves of normality*. London: The Poetry Society.

Porter, P. (2015) 'Hermit crab', in *Chorale at the crossing*. London: Pan Macmillan.

Prendergast, M. (2006) 'Found poetry as literature review: research poems on audience and performance'. *Qualitative Inquiry*, 12(2), 369–388.

Rosen, M. (2015) 'Bear Grylls', in *Don't mention the children*. Ripon: Smokestack Books.

Stevenson, R. L. (2000) *Treasure Island*. London: Penguin.

Thomas, D. (1954) *Under Milk Wood*. London: J.M. Dent & Sons.

Untermeyer, L. (ed.) (1969) *The golden treasury of poetry*. London: Collins.

Wagner, J. (2015) *Self portrait with a swarm of bees*. Todmorden: Arc Publications.

Wood, D. & Ruskin, S. (1970) *The Owl and the Pussycat went to see*. London: Samuel French.

Yates, C. (2016) *Jam*. Sheffield: Smith Doorstop.

16

READING FOR PLEASURE IN ENGLISH CLASS

Developing reading dispositions and identities in a digital society

Joanne O'Mara and Catherine Beavis

Halloween has recently made its way into the Australian celebration calendar, at least into some enclaves of inner and middle suburban Melbourne. In Jo's local area, the celebration centres around the local primary school. This year her witchly self, her ghostly daughter, her son as Frodo from *The Lord of the Rings*, and many others from the community joined together to collect lollies and celebrate the pleasures of the characters they took on from fictive texts: from traditional horror texts, popular culture texts and literary fiction texts. Jo was struck by the number of characters represented from popular fiction. A friend from the local school Parents and Friends' Association book club was dressed as Offred, from *The Handmaid's Tale*, by Margaret Atwood. This was one of the books they read in 2017, a year where dystopian fiction sales skyrocketed, and HBO produced a mini-series of the Atwood novel, as these worlds seemed to represent the present more truthfully than realism. As Jo went to leave her friend's house, Offred pressed a candy into Jo's hand and whispered into her ear, 'Under His eye'. Jo left, giggling with the pleasure and delight of the reference, and of the chance as a middle-aged woman to play dress-ups.

In revisiting the legacy of the Dartmouth conference and Dixon's work (1967) for this chapter, we were drawn to the impact that the personal growth movement had on the promotion of wide reading programmes in English to promote reading for pleasure in the 1970s and 1980s. Manuel's ongoing and extensive work in surveying young people's reading practices and preferences highlights the decline in time given over to reading for pleasure in classrooms, as well as the need to re-focus our attention on the significance of reading in the lives of young people (Manuel, 2012; Manuel and Robinson, 2002; Manuel and Carter, 2015). Manuel and Carter (2015) write:

While it is evident that opportunities for reading for pleasure are increasingly threatened and diminished by the imperatives associated with high-stakes testing, it is equally evident that time spent reading for pleasure directly correlates with reading proficiency and reading achievement, including performance in reading tests and assessments.

(p.126)

Likewise, Krashen, through an ongoing set of systematic reviews of large-scale literacy data and literature reviews (e.g. Krashen, 2011), argues strongly for the importance of free, voluntary reading. He has condensed the pedagogical implications of his work into a set of simple directions for policy makers, school leadership, teachers and parents: '. . .read to young children with a focus on the story; provide access to interesting reading; give students time to read; and allow them to self-select their own reading material' (Krashen et al., 2017: 83).

In this chapter we locate the pleasures of reading in our own histories, dispositions and identities as life-long readers of fiction – as students, teachers, teacher educators and readers in the community – and examine our histories and stories for what we might learn about facilitating the reading of print texts as an enjoyable and valued activity for young people. In doing this, we argue for wide reading programmes as one aspect of personalised learning in the English classroom, recognising the importance of valuing the texts young people read, and we call for the broadening of the range of texts and ways of studying text that we make available to young people. As personalised learning, we argue for both student choice and teacher direction in wide reading sessions. We note that enjoyment is linked not just to success, but to purpose and identity. If we are in a post-typographic era, as Merchant (2015) suggests, what does this mean for books and reading in English classes, and what might these pleasures be?

Developing an early passion and disposition for reading

As passionate readers, we both have strong memories of early reading, and the pleasures of reading fiction have stayed with us. When Catherine was a child she looked forward every year for a 'package from England' of several gold-leafed hardback volumes to be shared amongst the family. One of her earliest memories is of her mother standing by the ironing board in the earth-floored laundry at the back of the house, telling her stories – fairy stories – that in later years reappeared in the form of large and beautifully illustrated tales from Perault and others. There were always books as presents, with books publicly associated with luxury, leisure and pleasure. Books were treats and rewards, read legitimately, read walking to school, read under the desk, in sand dunes on summer holidays, by the fire in winter. Jo has similar memories. Her mother is also a passionate reader, and read to her from an early age. She remembers books at birthdays and Christmas, and the thrill of reading as much as she could from every shelf in the library. For both of us, reading was both an adult-sanctioned activity and a sneaky furtive pleasure.

Catherine recalls reading furtively by torchlight under the blankets after lights out. Jo sat on the toilet for hours after she was supposed to be asleep, reading page after page of the latest novel. The layout of Jo's house helped her escape from adult eyes, her occupation of the 'third bedroom' meaning she was located well away from the central business district of the home and could escape, unnoticed, for hours at a time. Catherine would read a book as she performed piano practice scales, and later as an adult, on the regulatory treadmill at the gym. At the Catholic primary school Jo went to in the 70s, the desks were made of wood and the bench seats were joined to them. There was a gap near the top of the desk crafted perfectly to slide an open novel, and sneakily read during class, an eye positioned to read the board quickly if her name was called. We love Germaine Greer's description of her dangerous, furtive reading practices:

> I read under the sheets but not by the light of a battery torch, which I had no money to buy. I pinched candle ends from the parish church and burned them in bed, a recollection that makes me shudder. My front hair still stands up in a crinkly quiff from being regularly singed.
>
> *(2015: 174)*

We have noted, year after year after year, that our pre-service Secondary English teachers, most with majors or sub-majors in Literature themselves, have similar stories of the many pleasures of reading fiction that they have held from childhood. We suspect that you, dear reader, may also have a similar disposition, but hope your illegitimate reading was with torches or in the toilet rather than under the smoky embers of stolen votive candle ends. Reading, like other language forms, is a social practice and for passionate readers, purposeful and enjoyable. It is not surprising that people like us have ended up becoming English teachers. As English teachers, our concern is to create the conditions to encourage all of our students to read and to enjoy reading literary fiction and other texts.

Research again and again shows the strong, but unsurprising, relationship between literacy achievement and the enjoyment of reading (Warsop, 2014; Clark and Rumbold, 2006; Krashen and Mason, 2017; Thomson et al, 2013; Sullivan and Brown, 2013). Research studies have consistently shown that sustained silent reading increases reading ability and vocabulary more than other teaching methods (Krashen and Mason, 2017). This relationship is so strong that reading for pleasure is now measured in the OECD PISA tests of students (OECD, 2010). The evidence that emerges from PISA is that there is a strong link between the incidence and intensity of reading practices, reading motivation and reading proficiency among adults (Statistics Canada, 2000). The 2009 PISA Report stated that, 'Students who are highly engaged and are effective learners are most likely to be proficient readers and proficient readers are also those students that are most engaged and interested in reading' (OECD, 2010: 27).

Subversive texts and *readicide*

In Margaret Atwood's evocative essay on the pleasures of reading she describes learning to read before school, and her parents ordering an original *Grimm's Fairy Tales* by mail, 'unaware that it would contain so many red-hot shoes, barrels full of nails, and mangled bodies' (2015: 167). She writes:

> My parents were worried that all the skeletons and gouged-out eyes in Grimm's would warp my mind. Perhaps they did, although Bruno Bettelheim has since claimed that this sort of thing was good for me. In any case I devoured these stories, and a number of them have been with me ever since.
>
> *(pp. 167–168)*

Of her early school experiences, Atwood writes, 'The school readers, the notorious milk-and-water *Dick and Jane* series, did not have much to offer me after *Grimm's*. See Jane Run, indeed' (p.168).

At primary school in the 1970s, Jo was a product of the 'scientific' approach to reading. The big box of Scientific Reading Association (SRA) cards, the centre of our language and literacy curriculum, sat at the front of the classroom, accompanied by the gratefully received antidote of books borrowed from a visit to the school library every fortnight. SRA cards offered the 1970s version of personalised learning, colour coded through from shallows of aqua to the dizzying heights of purple, the top colour and my personal favourite. Each card began with a short piece of graded text, fiction and non-fiction, then a series of questions—multiple-choice comprehension, short answers, and putting words into full sentences. Outside of class, and under my desk, my reading was very exciting. I was consuming books as fast as I could get my eyes on them. Year after year, more SRA cards would appear on the front desk, the biggest thrill being the chance to get out of your seat to change the card over. When I was in Grade 5, with the end of the box in sight, I asked my teacher, what happened when children finished all of the cards. She told me that anyone who finished could spend the SRA time reading in the library. Thus began my race to become *that* child. In a few weeks I completed every card, and then every day was sent to the library to spend time with Mrs Fallon, the librarian. This continued throughout all of Grade 6 as well. It was wonderful. I, joined later by others who had been through the box, would be given all of the new acquisitions to read. We read them and wrote short reviews which were displayed around the library: *Carrie's War, Tuck Everlasting* and *A Wrinkle in Time*.

Gallagher (2009) coined the term 'readicide' to describe the 'systematic killing of the love of reading' (p.2). Too often we have met young people who have learnt that they cannot read, or that it is not for them. Manuel (2012) considers how readicide might be happening in the Australian context, mounting an argument around the pressures put onto teachers by standardised testing. She notes the ways that the testing regimes impact upon students' 'holistic achievement as readers, their appetite for reading, and their proclivity for the kinds of enjoyment, satisfaction and pleasure offered by the experience of reading' (p.47). Manuel also critiques the consequences of reading pedagogy created by a high stakes environment for students who struggle with the literacy demands of the curriculum, describing that they 'have internalised images of themselves as inadequate readers, have experienced repeated "failure" in formal schooling contexts, and for whom reading holds little value or significance' (p.48). We have seen this in our own work with schools and teachers – in particular, the ways in which English teachers describe how Education Departments pressurise school leadership to improve results, which almost always ends up with a more reductive curriculum being put in place (O'Mara, 2014). This high-stakes testing regime rarely results in schools timetabling more time for reading for pleasure and working to create a positive culture around reading.

Promoting reading for pleasure through a wide reading programme

We have both been highly influenced by the earlier work of Margaret Gill and Gillian Barnsley in our understandings of ways of promoting reading for pleasure through wide reading programmes. Catherine taught with Gillian and Margaret at Rusden Teachers' College (later Victoria College, then Deakin University), where Jo was a student in the 1980s, Catherine going on to do a PhD with Margaret on literature teaching when Margaret moved to Monash University (Beavis 1996, 1998, 2000, 2001). Margaret and Gillian's deep insights, knowledge, critical eyes and enthusiasm permeate our approach to, and thinking about, how we might go about promoting reading for pleasure in contemporary classrooms and times.

A central component in promoting reading for pleasure in the English curriculum has been the inclusion of 'wide reading' programmes alongside those texts set for whole-class study. Wide reading programmes have an important role to play within the contemporary push for personalised learning across the curriculum. Reading for pleasure opens up and widens out opportunities for students' reading – both the texts they already read and know, and ones yet to be discovered. As a rule, wide reading programmes focus on print texts, and are about 'the book', and the particular affordances and pleasures offered by 'the world told' through the page (Kress, 2003). Valuing the texts young people read, and creating a culture of reading in the classroom, has much to offer. Opening up the ways of studying texts made available to young people can enrich and extend their reading repertoires and strengths, and open up new avenues and capabilities. Reading texts of one's choice for pleasure epitomises personalised learning. Central here are both student choice and teacher direction, framed by a relationship of mutual respect between teachers and students for each other's reading choices. Other elements essential to success include giving wide reading programmes their own time allocation and being focused on enjoyment and enabling student choice. It is also important that teachers work with their students to know their reading preferences and expand their textual encounters, and that a working system for keeping track of each reader's choices and progress is implemented (that does not entail intrusive accountability demands or testing).

Making time to read as a valued activity within the curriculum

Secondary schools are not generally places where students (or teachers) have much sense of leisure or free time. In the 'crowded curriculum' there is little space for activities undertaken for their own sake, or simply because they are enjoyable. For many students, their out-of-school lives are similarly under pressure, particularly as they move up the school, from the competing demands of part-time work, extra-curricular, social and homework activities. Time is in short supply. The sustained reading of any text requires time, to allow readers to immerse themselves in the world of the text, and to lean into that anticipated pleasure of reading a good book. Typically, by contrast, time is more likely to be given to writing a response to what has been read, than to the reading itself, and there is a tendency to value writing about the text more highly than the act of reading it. Further, readers read at different paces, and the same reader reads at different paces at different times, slowing down to savour or re-read, speeding up to get past a boring bit or when the action is gripping and fast-paced. By creating time in the weekly timetable for students and teachers to slow down, 'switch off' and read, the school signals to students that reading is a valued and valuable activity. It gives students a chance to encounter new books, to get 'hooked' into the activity, and to read enough of the book, and, if we are lucky, for them to want to read on. It gives teachers a chance to read with their students, to position themselves as readers, and to share books that they love, in order to help students expand their reading choices.

Schools running a wide reading program will typically allocate an hour a week to reading for pleasure, and there are different ways of organising this time. Sometimes the reading period is not taken out of English, but implemented across the school as one period a week or perhaps 10–15 minutes every day. For programmes such as these, not just students, but all teachers and office staff may be asked to 'Drop everything and read', to model for everyone the school's commitment to reading. Jo worked at a school where one hour per week of English class time was devoted to reading for pleasure as sustained silent reading. Teachers could decide whether they did 10 minutes every lesson, usually at the beginning, or ran the programme for a whole lesson in the library. Jo found the important thing was that she was also reading, and that the reading was done individually, so that everyone had a chance to become immersed in their book. Aligned with this, she would devote other time in class to discuss the reading – both her own reading, and what students were reading. This would often be open time, where students could move around the room, and talk to others in an informal way about their reading choices. Without some formal allocation of class time, a wide reading programme at junior and middle years is unlikely to succeed.

Enjoyment, student choice and access to books

The establishment of an informal class library based on student choice provides easy access to books in the classroom. In Year 7, as class librarian, Catherine shopped for the class library with her teacher (one book per child) with funds provided from the school budget. In the mid-80s, when Jo was on teaching practice at Huntingdale Technical School she went shopping to a local bookshop with Val Kent and her English class. Each student in the class chose a book for the class library. The students gathered in a group at the back of the bookshop, and Val reviewed the choices with them. They agreed as a class on a set of books, and these were purchased with money from the school budget. In both of these examples, the school created a class library of adolescent fiction in addition to the school library collection. Such libraries, informal and chosen by students, provide a casual borrowing experience and a way in which students can easily access a range of books that others in the class recommend and have read. This access helps to build a culture of valuing reading and books in the classroom and builds the question, 'What are you reading?' into class relationships.

A genuine wide reading programme offers students informed choice, but ultimately respects the decisions students make. Groups of texts are often specified or recommended, and the teacher might 'tempt' students to choose one book or another through reading the opening paragraph or 'selling' it in other ways. Mackey (2014) framed choosing a book as 'a paramount skill often neglected in schools' (p.521). The English teacher is in a strong position to develop text selection skills in her students, to open up new texts and possibilities, and to entice students into new reading worlds. This can be one of the greatest strengths and pleasures of a wide reading programme, for teachers and students alike. At the same time, however, heavy-handed coercion to 'choose' a specific text will most likely result on the student's part in a grudging reading (if a reading happens at all), turning wide reading into a lifeless activity.

The *Children's Choice* project (Bunbury, 1995), an historical review of reading preferences of Australian children since 1929, found at the time of writing that although children were reading widely for leisure, their English teachers and school librarians were having minimal influence on their choice and very little of the reading done at school, or for school purposes, was enjoyed. At the present time, with school library budgets often divided between technology purchases and books, a demise in the numbers of dedicated teacher-librarian positions in schools, and the increased emphasis on external standardised testing, we suspect this trajectory continues. The teaching practices of English classrooms tend to systematically privilege some students, some texts, and some ways of reading, over others. For many students, particularly boys, but also students of minority ethnic populations, rural students and students living in poverty, school expectations and curriculum marginalise their interests and fail to recognise or value literacy abilities which don't conform to dominant norms (Alloway et al, 2002; Alloway et al, 2003; Cloonan et al, 2014; Freebody et al, 2001, Pennycook, 2017).

Developing a culture of reading

If we want the reading of print texts to be an enjoyable, and hence valued, activity for all students, we need to create a culture of reading, encouraging students to select their own reading materials. For some classrooms, this may mean broadening both the texts that might be brought into the English/literacy classroom, and the ways we approach them. Even then, we need to take care. Context shapes meaning, and this is nowhere more true than when it comes to reading in school. The simple act of just bringing a text into English can have the effect of flattening it into one more school text, stripping it of its furtive pleasure and clandestine appeal by making it become a teacher-sanctioned text. We need to explicitly take care to avoid deadening effects such as these.

Mutual respect is the key to all good teaching, and much easier to say than to achieve. Amongst other things, in the wide reading context, it entails the sort of reciprocity in which if a student is prepared to read one of 'your' texts, you need to be prepared to read thoughtfully something he or she thinks is wonderful. Wide reading programmes modelled on adult book clubs and other reading practices such as mutual recommendation are part of creating a reading climate, as is scope for students to reject books or to be able to talk about what they don't like, as well as about what they do. In all this, as Tucker (2009: 297) notes:

> The tricky bit is still the creation of a reading environment which encourages trust, experimentation, risk taking and sharing, among the myriad of other subtle factors in the classroom learning ecology. However, this is the stuff of good English teaching in all areas of the curriculum. The crucial development in a wide reading classroom is the elimination of fakery, plagiarism and hypocrisy.

A working system for keeping track of students' reading

In an ideal classroom, there would be no reporting back on wide reading other than record-keeping and the enthusiastic 'selling' of good books by students to other students. In a climate where accountability is unavoidable, wide reading programmes need to find ways to keep track of students' reading and to provide for 'response' in ways that, hopefully, do not overwhelm the original reading experience. In the UK, many schools use a software programme called Accelerated Reader, which aims to 'inspire a love of reading while monitoring progress and attainment' (Renaissance Learning Inc., 2017). Students read a book of their choice, then take a quiz on it to check understanding, then receive feedback. Far from 'inspiring a love of reading', this level of testing and surveillance of students' reading, the competition it evokes, and the ways the system itself is designed around reading levels, rather than about individuals demonstrating ebbs and flows in their practices and preferences, is counterproductive, potentially harmful and limiting. Topping (2015) analysed some of the enormous amount of data from this system to investigate students' reading preferences in relation to their reading levels. He found that students had a wide range of 'reading levels' in their choices, and made a series of recommendations including:

> Moves by central government to prescribe a list of approved books that children should have read by the time they reach a certain age are at best useless

and at worst damaging to reading standards. Such moves have been a regular feature with governments of all political colors since the introduction of the national curriculum in the UK (a prescribed curriculum for all schools in the country). What should be happening is that teachers and librarians should be trusted to listen to children.

(p.385)

We recommend students keeping their own log, either physical or digital, which could be as simple as a series of front cover photographs on an image-collecting site such as *Instagram* or *Pinterest* (which is how one of Jo's book groups keeps track of what they have read). Some schools have class reading blogs, to which individual students contribute reviews and rankings. Some libraries have provision and facility for young people to join reading groups. A good example of an institution that is listening to young people is our state library, the State Library of Victoria (SLV). They run a website for young people about books they like to read. This site, *Inside a Dog* (named from a quote attributed to Groucho Marx, 'Outside of a dog, a book is a man's best friend. Inside a dog, it's too dark to read'), is 'all about books, by young people for young people' (SLV, nd). Young people can upload reviews of books they have read, vote on books and join/create book clubs. It is a great place for recording reading – both what young readers have read and what they want to read – and its free, open, accessible nature is in direct contrast to the proprietary Accelerated Reader. Whatever approach teachers take to recording reading, it is important that it does not take away the freedom of choice and the pleasures – that it is not burdensome, but adds to the experience and development of young people's identities as readers.

What might the place of reading for pleasure be in the digital society?

The pleasures of the material book are immense, and, as we have noted, we have both enjoyed them throughout our lives. Jo has a set of Victorian books she began collecting as a child when her grandfather gave her a hardback copy of Andersen's tales from the late 1880s that had belonged to his older sister. This was a particularly prized gift, as his sister died as a child, and this was one of her few possessions. Catherine enjoys the feel of the physical book and the smell, the pleasure of pages, but Jo reads almost all her fiction now on a digital device, preferring the backlighting, the lightness and the ability to, finally, read in bed with the light off.

Reading pioneer Frank Smith wrote of 'twelve easy ways to make learning to read hard, and one difficult way to make it easy' (Smith, 1983). Reading in context, for meaning, makes reading easy. Making reading enjoyable begins and continues that way. All too often, we have found, young people have learnt that they can't read rather than learning *to* read. Other young people have learnt that they don't like reading. In our research with young people and digital games, we have seen again and again that when you make a space in the classroom for texts students feel passionate about, you create opportunities for developing the pleasure of reading. In one school we worked with, Year 9 English students moved across the textual platforms of books and computer games in their study of the fantasy genre. As the teachers explained:

> Previously, the students had studied archetypes in a unit of work designed by. . . one of the Year 9 English teachers. . . They had also examined the stages of the quest narrative. . . and were asked to apply the knowledge gained from both to a text already on the Year 9 booklist – Tolkien's *The Fellowship of the Ring*. Students read and discussed selected passages and watched the film version, while also investigating the wide use of archetypes and the quest narrative in print media and film. Lastly, as an introduction to our computer games unit, we took all our Year 9 students to ACMI's *Game On* exhibition.
>
> *(McNeice et al, 2012)*

Being open to students' interest in the game and the film led to study of the fantasy genre more broadly, and the exploration and discussion of narrative computer games and classic fantasy fiction. The 10-year-old boy dressed as Frodo at Halloween already has a stake in a broad and open study such as this.

Throughout this chapter, we note that the pleasures of reading – the enjoyment – is linked not just to success as a reader, but to purpose and identity. Krashen et al., (2017) use the term 'compelling comprehensible input', arguing that reading which is compelling and can be understood, 'is an important part to full literacy development, full language acquisition, finding one's true interests, and developing the competence to pursue these interests' (p.87). If we want the reading of print texts to be an enjoyable, compelling and valued activity for all students, we need to change and broaden both the texts that might be brought into the English/literacy classroom, the place we make and the ways we approach texts and reading in the English curriculum.

References

Alloway, N., Freebody, Gilbert, P. and Muspratt, S. (2002) *Boys, literacy and schooling: expanding the repertoires of practice*, Canberra: Commonwealth Department of Education, Science and Training.

Alloway, N., Gilbert, P. and Henderson, R. (2003) 'Boys performing English', *Gender and Education* 15(4), 351–364.

Atwood, M. (2015) 'The pleasure of reading', in A. Fraser and V. Gray (eds.) *The Pleasure of reading: 43 writers on the discovery of reading and the books that inspired them*, London: Bloomsbury: 167–173.

Beavis, C. (1996) 'Changing constructions: literature, "text" and English teaching in Victoria – an historical account', in B. Green and C. Beavis (eds.) *Teaching the English subjects: essays on English curriculum history and Australian schooling*, Geelong: Deakin University Press: 15–39.

Beavis, C. (1998) 'Constructing the subject: literature teachers and curriculum change', Unpublished PhD thesis: Monash University.

Beavis, C. (2000) '"What I really like now. . . " Renewal and curriculum change in literature teaching', *English in Australia*, 127–128, May, 51–59.

Beavis, C. (2001) '"It makes you realise, really, just how deep your subtext is": literature, discourse and curriculum change', *Research in the Teaching of English* 36(1), 38–63.

Bunbury, R. M. (ed.) (1995) *Children's choice: reading at home or at school* Geelong: Deakin University Press.

Clark, C., and Rumbold, K. (2006) *Reading for pleasure: a research overview* (no city) National Literacy Trust.

Cloonan, A., O'Mara, J. and Ohi, S. (2014) 'Supporting intercultural engagement in literacy education', in B. Doecke, G. Auld and M. Wells (eds.) *Becoming a teacher of language and literacy*, Port Melbourne: Cambridge University Press: 83–98.

Dixon, J. (1967) *Growth through English*. Reading: National Association for the Teaching of English.

Freebody, P., Dwyer, B and Muspratt, S. (2001) *Difference, silence, and textual practice: studies in critical literacy*. Cresskill, N.J.: Hampton Press.

Gallagher, K. (2009) *How schools are killing reading and what you can do about it*, Portland: Stenhouse.

Greer, G. (2015) 'The pleasure of reading', in A. Fraser and V. Gray (eds.) *The Pleasure of reading: 43 writers on the discovery of reading and the books that inspired them*, London: Bloomsbury: 174–181.

Krashen, S. (2011) *Free voluntary reading*, Santa Barbara: ABC-Clio.

Krashen, S. and Mason, B. (2017) 'Sustained silent reading in foreign language education: an update', *Turkish Online Journal of English Language Teaching*, 2(2), 70–73.

Krashen, S., Lee, S. and Lao, C. (2017) *Comprehensible and compelling: the causes and effects of free voluntary reading*. Santa Barbara: ABC-Clio.

Kress, G. (2003) 'Interpretation or design? From the world told to the world seen', in M. Styles and E. Bearne (eds.) *Art, narrative and childhood*, Stoke on Trent: Trentham Books: 137–153.

Mackey, M. (2014) 'Learning to choose', *Journal of Adolescent and Adult Literacy*, 57(7), 521–526.

Manuel, J. (2012) 'Teenagers and reading: factors that shape the quality of teenagers' reading lives', *English in Australia* 47(2),45–57.

Manuel, J. and Carter, D. (2015) 'Current and historical perspectives on Australian teenagers' reading practices and preferences', *Australian Journal of Language and Literacy*, 38(2), 115–128.

Manuel, J. and Robinson, D. (2002) 'What are teenagers reading? The findings of a survey of teenagers' reading choices and the implications of these for English teachers' classroom practice', *English in Australia*, 135, 69–78.

Merchant, G. (2015) 'Keep taking the tablets: iPads, story apps and early literacy', *Australian Journal of Language and Literacy* 38(1), 3–11.

McNeice, L., Smith, A. and Robison, T. (2012) 'Computer games, archetypes and the quest narrative: computer games as texts in the Year 9 English classroom', in C. Beavis, J. O'Mara and L. McNeice (eds.) *Digital games: literacy in action*, Kent Town: Wakefield Press.

O'Mara, J. (2014) 'Closing the emergency facility: moving schools from literacy triage to better literacy outcomes', *English Teaching: Practice and Critique*, 13(1), 8–23.

OECD (2010) *PISA 2009 results: learning to learn – student engagement, strategies and practices* (Vol. III), Paris: OECD Publishing.

Pennycook, A. (2017) 'Translanguaging and semiotic assemblages', *International Journal of Multilingualism* 14(3), 269–282.

Renaissance Learning (2017) Accelerated Reader. Available at: http://renaissance.com.au/practice/accelerated-reader/.

Smith, F. (1983) *Essays into literacy: selected papers and some afterthoughts.* London: Heinemann Education.

State Library of Victoria (SLV) (nd) *Inside a dog.* Available at: https://insideadog.com.au.

Statistics Canada (2000) *Literacy in the information age: final report of the international adult literacy durvey.* Paris: OECD Publishing.

Sullivan, A., and Brown, M. (2013) 'Social inequalities in cognitive scores at age 16: the role of reading', *CLS Working Paper 2013/10.* London: Centre for Longitudinal Studies.

Thomson, S., Hillman, K. and L De Bortoli, L. (2013) *A teacher's guide to PISA reading literacy.* Camberwell: ACER.

Topping, K. (2015) 'Fiction and non-fiction reading and comprehension in preferred books' *Reading Psychology* 36(4), 350–387.

Tucker, E. (2009) 'Wide reading', in S. Gannon, M. Howie and W. Sawyer (eds.) *Charged with meaning*, Putney: Phoenix Education: 295–299.

Warsop, A. M-L. (2014) '"Why has she stopped reading?" The case for supporting reading for pleasure in secondary schools', Unpublished PhD thesis: University of East Anglia.

17

CULTURALLY SUSTAINING PEDAGOGY AND THE PROBLEM OF POVERTY

From cultural identity to political subjectivity

Todd DeStigter

Introduction: changing the story

'My dad tells me that if you don't do nothing in life, you would just be a bum.' Martín and I sat in the back of his English classroom, just a few weeks before the end of the school year.[1]

'Hm,' I said, and Martín continued:

'You know, my dad finished high school, but he lived in a small town in Mexico, in Michoacán. There were, I think, eight brothers and sisters. And my grandpa was really hard on my dad and uncles and aunts. But there's one thing that we learned from my grandpa, and my dad told me after my grandpa passed away. He told me that, 'Los cortos nunca llegaron al cielo.''

'Wait, a 'corto'? Doesn't that mean 'short'?' I asked. 'So, short people never arrived at or reached the sky? That's a little. . . insensitive, don't you think?'

'Well, yeah, a 'corto' would be 'short',' Martín said. 'But in Spanish we have so many sayings. And this one can mean, like, if somebody doesn't do nothing in their life, they won't reach for their goal. If you're not ambitious, then you're a 'corto.' And then you won't reach for what you're going to do. And it's funny because it's true.'

'Oh, okay,' I said, 'So what about the summer; do you have plans?'

'I'm actually trying to find a job. I've tried so many places, but there's nothing. I've tried Best Buy, I've tried Bed Bath and Beyond, I've tried Home Depot. I think they're completely full because there are so many people who are applying.'

Although I'm pretty sure that Martín had never heard of the 1966 Dartmouth Conference, that he and I were even having this conversation was largely the result of the shift the Conference initiated in English teaching from a focus on subject matter to process-oriented and student-centered learning. Further, this new interest in students and the contexts of their learning established the rationale for my having encountered Martín in the first place, for we had met during my three semesters of ethnographic research in Tejada High, a Chicago public school where over 95% of the roughly 1,400 students are Mexican or Mexican-American and eligible for free lunch. I had entered Tejada High to explore the results of a new policy requiring all members of the senior class – including special education students and English language learners – to take a full year of Advanced Placement Language and Composition. This initiative, I thought, was consistent with what I already knew to be the school's aggressive neoliberal reform policies, and so the story I anticipated telling was how such policies were dismissive of the students' languages and cultures. The students, however, told me a different story. Besides Martín's account of the bleak job prospects that threatened to make him look like a 'corto', students spoke of working long hours after school at car washes and retail clothing stores. They told me of bill collectors calling their houses at dinnertime and of their inability to afford college. In sum, the dominant leitmotif of their stories was the corrosive anxiety that comes from being poor.

Among the recent manifestations of the Dartmouth Conference's turning away from an exclusive focus on texts to the ways in which meaning is created in transaction with students' lived experiences has been the rise of Culturally Sustaining Pedagogy (CSP), or, more recently, Culturally Sustaining/Revitalizing Pedagogy (CSRP). As Django Paris and H. Samy Alim (2017) have explained, 'CSP seeks to perpetuate and foster – to sustain – linguistic, literate, and cultural pluralism as part of schooling for positive social transformation' (p.1). This pedagogical 'stance' has enjoyed such an enthusiastic response among teachers and researchers that Michael Domínguez (2017) is justified to call the rapid ascendance of CSP a 'paradigm shift in education' (p.225). However, precisely because the Dartmouth Conference taught me to pay attention to students, the stories of Martín and his classmates challenged me to think hard about how educators can sustain students' cultures while also working *not* to sustain something that is too often part of those cultures – namely, poverty. Moreover, as Peter Smagorinsky (2002) has noted, while the Dartmouth Conference initiated an important shift in ELA teaching from 'teacher-and-text-centered' curricula to a focus on students' lived experience and priorities, this valorization of individual students' 'personal growth' downplays what Smagorinsky calls 'the social responsibilities that accompany growing and participating in a society' (p.26). In Smagorinsky's view, it is thus up to teachers adopt and yet extend the recommendations of Dartmouth to include 'a more social view of teaching and learning' (p.26). Therefore, in what follows I'll take a 'social view' of the Tejada students' experiences in order to question the suitability of CSP to address the poverty and wealth inequality that undermine CSP's social justice commitments. I'll then suggest ways in which some CSP principles might be re-imagined to support political projects that ameliorate inequality and poverty. Fifty years after Dartmouth, a defining characteristic of our time is that vast numbers of people – a disproportionate percentage of them people of color – live in a state of financial distress. In response to these conditions, the central point of this essay is that CSP needs to address economic injustice more directly than it currently does because among the best ways to sustain a culture is to ensure that those who identify with it have enough money.

The limits of cultural pluralism and the myth of equal educational opportunity

Tejada High serves a neighborhood that's known in Chicago as a 'port-of-entry' community for Mexican immigrants, who first arrived in large numbers in response to WWII labor shortages. Currently, over 81% of the community's residents are 'Hispanic', and their influence is evident in everything from the Spanish-language signage of virtually all area businesses to the enormous Mexican flag hanging from the Tejada High cafeteria ceiling. The Tejada principal, who was born in Central Mexico and came to Chicago on a bus when he was 6 years old, has posted a message on the school website that begins, 'En nombre de toda nuestra comunidad, facultad, estudiantes y padres les quiero dar la bienvenida a la familia de la Tejada'. ['On behalf of all our community, faculty, students, and parents, I'd like to welcome you to the Tejada family'.] The message goes on for several paragraphs and is not translated into English. Moreover, among the things I learned during my time at Tejada High is that its teachers consistently include in their lessons topics and materials directly related to the students' experiences as Mexicans and Mexican-Americans.

Still, despite these and many other affirmations of the students' Spanish language ability and national heritage – despite, in other words, having their culture faithfully sustained – Tejada High is imbued with an undercurrent of disquiet due to the financial struggles endured by nearly all its families – a topic that, as I noted earlier, the students talked about continually. Tragically, the Tejada students are emblematic of broader socio-economic trends. According to a Federal Reserve report (2017), the richest 1% of households control nearly 40% of the wealth in the US, while the bottom 90% of families control less than 23% of the nation's wealth, and the poorest half of the families control only 1% of that wealth. These extremes in wealth inequality at once reflect and exacerbate widespread poverty and its long list of deleterious consequences. According the American Academy of Pediatrics (2016), poor children are at heightened risk not only of social effects such as unemployment and incarceration but also of a host of adverse health and developmental outcomes, including chronic cardiovascular, immune, and psychiatric disorders. Moreover, scholars at Columbia University (2017) have concluded that 'research is clear that poverty is the single greatest threat to children's well-being'. According to US Census data, over 21% of US children younger than 18 years lived in households designated as 'poor'. In public health terms, then, poverty is a plague ravaging the lives of over 15 million our nation's young people.

Still, despite what these statistics imply regarding what should be among the highest priorities of a justice-oriented pedagogy, CSP has emphasized not economic equity, but cultural pluralism. In a landmark article, for instance, Django Paris and H. Samy Alim (2014) underscore that CSP represents a shifting of the stance of asset pedagogies 'toward more explicitly pluralist outcomes' (p.87). Moreover, in a previous article that introduced CSP to the nation's educators, Paris (2012) explains that CSP rejects so-called 'deficit' approaches to teaching and instead 'embrace[s] cultural pluralism and cultural equality' (pp.95–96). To be sure, Paris is right to juxtapose cultural pluralism and cultural equality because cultural pluralism without equality sets up a hierarchy that can only result in oppression based on cultural identity – or, in a word, discrimination. And discrimination is, of course, ethically indefensible.

However, as scholars such as Walter Benn Michaels have argued, this CSP ideal of cultural pluralism coupled with cultural equality does not address the problem of poverty that so preoccupied the students at Tejada High.[2] According to the most recent data available (US Census Bureau, 2016), the overall US poverty rate is 12.7%. And a breakdown of poverty statistics by race and ethnicity reveals that, while greater in raw numbers, the poverty rate for Whites is 8.8%, but that rate is 22% for Blacks and 19.4% for Hispanics. These discrepancies are unjust – clearly discriminatory. If, in our efforts to address this injustice, we were able to achieve cultural equality in our culturally pluralistic society, these differences in poverty rates would disappear; which is to say, they would all reflect the overall US poverty rate of 12.7%. This would be progress for the obvious reason that there's no justification for someone's being less likely to be poor just because he's White.

Still, what remains a challenge for CSP advocates is that even if poverty rates were the same across racial categories – in other words, even if we define the problem as discrimination and then were able to solve that problem – achieving such cultural pluralism and equality would not address the fact that 12.7% of Americans (nearly 40 million people) are poor. What would be accomplished, then, is what the historian Barbara Jeanne Fields (1990) has described as the *reallocation* of poverty but not its *abolition* (p.118, italics added). In this way, CSP risks the implication that it's not a priority that people are poor as long as they aren't poor because of their cultural identity. Or, to look at it from the other side of the wealth spectrum, CSP's emphasis on cultural pluralism and cultural equality is compatible with plutocracy, provided that the plutocrats are culturally diverse.

Moreover, Michaels and others have explained why an emphasis on cultural pluralism and cultural equality not only doesn't address economic inequality but also provides a rationalization for it. Cedric Johnson (2007) takes up this idea in his provocative book *Revolutionaries to Race Leaders: Black Power and the Making of African-American Politics*, in which Johnson argues that in the 1960s 'the evolution of black power as a form of ethnic politics' was a conservative development in the sense that more radical social agendas were sacrificed in favor of permitting the rise of an elite African-American political and economic class. This sacrifice, Johnson contends, was a form of ideological consent to liberalism's acceptance of inequality as long as talented and industrious individuals remained free to climb the social ladder. This conceptual coherence between cultural pluralism and liberalism leads Johnson to conclude that while ethnic or identity politics 'may still retain a certain emotive power for its proponents, . . . it is inadequate as an antidote to hierarchy and exploitation' (p.xi).

According to Johnson's thinking, then, CSP runs the risk of being compatible with liberalism (or neoliberalism) because, in seeking eliminate discrimination by foregrounding cultural pluralism and cultural equality, CSP does not trouble the notion that people like the Tejada High students might be poor just because they lack intelligence or ambition. From this point of view, CSP or any other social justice initiative based on cultural identity actually functions as a form of class politics – but, unfortunately, it's a form that favors the rich. Why? Because it provides what Michaels calls a 'meritocratic justification for inequality': namely, that 'if everyone has an equal opportunity to succeed, there's no injustice when some people fail' (2016).

Additionally, CSP's emphasis on equality of opportunity feeds a familiar narrative that over-emphasizes education as a solution to our nation's economic problems (Kinloch, 2017; Irizarry, 2017). In the case of CSP this narrative is that by valuing and sustaining students' cultures, schools will become more universally hospitable places, which will allow more students to succeed in school, thus providing them with greater access to higher education and well-paying jobs. But the problem with the CSP version of this narrative is the same as it is with any other version that relies on schools to solve economic problems, which is that while more and better education may enable a relatively small number of individuals to succeed, on a large scale, more (and more culturally diverse) college graduates won't solve wealth inequality if there aren't more well-paying jobs for those graduates to move into.

Following John Marsh (2011), Michaels (2012) has illustrated this conundrum by citing the job creation outlook for the next several years. According to data from the US Bureau of Labor Statistics (2016), through 2026 about 80% of new jobs will neither require nor reward a college degree. These data also reveal that two of the three top growing occupations are 'personal care aid' and 'home health aid'. Neither of these jobs requires a college degree, and they both pay about $22K a year. These are, of course, important and honorable jobs. But although it's delicate to say so, these are also undesirable jobs in that they pay so little. If our response to this is to adopt CSP's cultural pluralism approach, and if we thus focus on the fact that these jobs are performed by a disproportionate number of women of color, then the solution is to end such discrimination by mandating that the percentage of personal care and home health workers is proportional to their presence in the overall population (which means that about 61% would be White and about half would be men, which isn't remotely the case). That demographic revision would be progress in the sense that it would end cultural (and in this case, gender) discrimination. However, it would *not* be progress in the sense that the people who take these jobs will still make only about $22K a year.

To clarify how the employment forecast relates to the notion of equal educational opportunity, Michaels (2012) engages in a thought experiment in which we imagine that everyone had free access to a good university. This would be desirable for all the same humanistic reasons that it's desirable for people to get a high-quality liberal arts education. However, despite this equal access to education, the job forecast indicates that a great many of these graduates would still enter occupations that pay only about $22K a year. Thus, this imagined solution would do little to ameliorate poverty or inequality. However, what it would do is provide an explanation (and justification) for the likelihood that many people will earn $22K as personal care and home health aides, and that explanation would be that since these workers don't lack a good education, they must lack ability or ambition. The blame, in other words, would land squarely on the victim, and the well-educated victim would have little choice but to accept that blame. In this way, as Michaels (2012) puts it, 'The point of equality of opportunity. . . is not to produce equality but to legitimate inequality, to make sure that even if the (very many) losers feel sad, they won't feel cheated' (p.1008). Because the problem of poverty persists even in this imagined world of equal educational opportunity, an alternative (and more effective) way to address this problem would be to create circumstances toward which CSP does not aspire. Such circumstances would be those in which *all* personal care and home health aides make at least twice what they currently do.

Echoing Paris and Alim's (2014) assertion that CSP fosters cultural pluralism 'as part of the democratic project of schooling' (p.88), Bucholtz, Casillas, and Lee (2017) insist that CSP is important because it not only sustains cultural practices but also 'leverages these as resources both for achieving institutional access and for challenging structural inequality' (p.45). Indeed, this faith that sustaining students' diverse cultures can be a factor in mitigating inequality is the foundational assumption that underwrites CSP's designation as a 'social justice' pedagogy. However, as I have been explaining, among the limits of cultural pluralism – even if all cultures are recognized as equal – is that it leaves undisturbed the economic structures and liberal ideologies that create and justify widespread wealth inequality and poverty. To be clear: this is not an argument against cultural pluralism and cultural equality as such. It is, however, to suggest that in their focused commitment to sustaining students' cultures, CSP advocates may also be unintentionally (and regrettably) playing a role in sustaining the very structures that have rendered so many of the Tejada students poor. In what follows, I'll suggest an alternative to this role by describing the work of two Tejada English teachers who sought to sustain their students' cultures by foregrounding the economic issues that threatened them.

Responding to students' experiences and priorities

Among the benefits of conducting ethnographic research in schools is being able to witness over time the work of exceptional teachers such as Sandy and Peter. Sandy, the Tejada English Department Chair, and Peter, a special education teacher, were co-instructors of the AP Comp class on which I focused during the final year of my study. During the previous school year, the first year in which AP Comp had been mandated for all Tejada seniors, Sandy and Peter had sought to prepare their students for the AP Comp exam mostly by using previous versions of the exam they had found online and other materials they had obtained at College Board workshops. Early in this second year of the AP Comp initiative, however, Sandy and Peter began adapting these College Board materials to cover issues relevant to their students' lives, such as US immigration policy and the tense relationships between the Chicago Police Department and the city's various Latino communities.[3] However, by early November I began to notice yet another shift in Sandy and Peter's materials, for by now they had abandoned College Board materials entirely and had begun using unit plans they had developed themselves. Significantly, these original units focused not on the students' ethnicity or cultural heritage, but on poverty and wealth inequality. When I mentioned this to Peter, he confirmed the shift as deliberate, saying, 'It was like over time, we became more and more irreverent to that College Board system. And we started replacing it with ideas that we were getting from the kids. Things that we heard them talking about and that they would be more interested in'.

This turn toward a focus on economic issues began intermittently in the context of individual lessons. For instance, when the class was brainstorming topics for argumentative essays, Sandy and Peter recommended that the students choose topics that connected their educational experiences with broader developments in the political economy of Chicago – issues such as an impending teachers' strike and the recent closure of scores of schools in poor, racial and ethnic-minority neighborhoods. During discussions of these issues, Peter gave an extended lesson on collective bargaining, while Sandy explained in detail how the school closures were part of an overall strategy by the city to increase future property taxes and improve its bond rating. Subsequently, after the class had read an article and viewed a video on 'Redshirting' – the practice of waiting until a child is six years old to send her to kindergarten in the hope that the child's additional year of physical and cognitive development will give her advantages – Sandy guided the students in exploring why this option is more available to some families than others. During this discussion, Sandy asked, 'Who is most likely to get the advantage?'

'The rich ones,' a student named Carla replied.

'Why does being rich help?' Sandy asked.

'They can afford to keep their kid home for an extra year.'

'Yeah,' Sandy affirmed. 'You can afford to stay home with your kid for an extra year. You don't need your kid to go to school so that you can go back to work, or you don't have to worry about paying for child care.'

'Not me,' said Carla.

It was during an extended unit on satire, however, that Sandy and Peter's emphasis on economic issues became even more explicit, and they underscored this emphasis by guiding the class to identify the 'target' of the satirical pieces they analyzed. To cite just two of many possible examples, when the class viewed a *Saturday night live* sketch mimicking a Taco Bell advertisement for a giant, multi-layered taco, the target was found to be not Mexicans or food associated with Mexican culture, but a corporation that creates outlandish products in a quest for profits. Similarly, the class viewed a video of the comic rap artist Jon Lajoie's performing his song 'Regular Everyday Normal Guy', in which Lajoie declares, 'I'm just a regular everyday normal guy. . ./ I got 600 dollars in the bank. . ./ I make 12 bucks an hour but that's all I need/ I can't afford a car I use public transportation'. During the ensuing discussion, consensus emerged that the target of Lajoie's satire was not rap artists, but a socio-economic system in which a 'regular everyday normal guy' can work full time but still have only $600 in savings and be unable to afford a car.

The students took these lessons to heart, for when they created their own satires, nearly all of their 'targets' were systems or policies that perpetuate various forms of economic injustice. To again cite just two of many possible examples, a group of students made a video about gang members who shocked the local media by conducting 'drive-by's' during which they jumped out of cars and handed strangers cash. Likewise, a Tejada baseball player drew an elaborate eight-panel graphic sequence depicting his arrest by school security guards for selling candy bars in the hallway to raise funds for the athletic program. His 'target' he explained, was not the security guards, but a school system that requires student-athletes, as he put it, 'to sell things to make money for stuff we do'.

Sandy and Peter's focus on economic issues extended beyond the satire unit to the final two weeks of the school year. After the students had taken the AP Comp exam and awaited graduation, they analyzed and wrote personal reflections in response to the documentary film *American movie*, which tells the story of a feckless yet sympathetic amateur filmmaker named Mark Borchardt, whose life's goal of making his *magnum opus* is thwarted by his lack of money. In their conversations about and written responses to the film, the Tejada students made clear that they admired Mark's tenacity and empathized with him as his dream was deferred by poverty.

In end-of-year interviews, I again asked Sandy and Peter why they had so conspicuously abandoned topics rooted in their students' ethnic and national culture and instead focused on issues of political economy. Peter affirmed what he had said several months earlier, saying:

> What we're trying to do is bring up relevant issues that we knew [the students] would respond to. And it's something that we teachers care about because we work with this community, and we love these kids. We realize how wonderful a community it is. So we have this kind of insider's approach, and insider input, when it comes to designing the curriculum.

For her part, Sandy explained that her pedagogical decisions had evolved out of her concerns that her students might be, in her words, 'unprepared for their future because they don't have a lot of money to do anything'. Sandy paused for a moment, then continued. 'My fears are that they won't have the resources to have what they want in their lives, and they are going to get stuck doing jobs that they're going to hate and end up being old before their time'.

At the time of these interviews, Sandy and Peter had been teaching at Tejada High for 17 and 12 years, respectively, and I am convinced that their deep knowledge of and respect for the students and their community was the impetus for their decisions regarding what and how they would teach. As we have seen, among those decisions was to attempt to sustain their students by helping them develop a critical awareness of the relationship between their own experiences with poverty and the economic structures in which those experiences are embedded.

Transforming cultural pluralism into a political project

Although Sandy and Peter never said so directly, their decision to focus their teaching on poverty and wealth inequality reflected theoretical commitments that run counter to at least two of CSP's foundational assumptions. The first of these assumptions is that the 'intersectionality' between race and class is the result of racial and ethnic-minority people's being economically exploited precisely because of their race or ethnicity (or, alternatively, because of the cultural identity that is derived from and that functions as a proxy for race or ethnicity). In contrast, Sandy and Peter's teaching revisions reflected the thought of scholars who insist that race-based oppression – and even the biologically untenable concept of 'race' itself – emerges as a consequence and means of facilitating economic exploitation. In her study of Enlightenment-era colonization, for instance, Lisa Lowe (2015) has noted that race and ethnicity are 'shifting, flexible classifications of difference devised for governing different peoples for labor extraction' (p.31–32). Similarly, Antonia Darder and Rodolfo D. Torres (2004) insist that 'if 'race' is real, it is so only because it has been rendered meaningful by the actions and beliefs of the powerful, to retain the myth in order to protect their own political-economic interests' (p.12). According to Barbara Jeanne Fields, the intersectionality of race and class can be explained by understanding race as an 'ideology'. To Fields, ideology is best understood as 'the descriptive vocabulary of day-to-day existence', a way that people make 'sense of what they do and see' (p.110). Significantly, Fields contends that 'ideology' functions not just to explain, but to justify the way things are and to resolve contradictions between what 'is' and what 'ought' to be. In the context of US history, Fields points out that the most glaring contradiction was the moral and conceptual dissonance created by having millions of people enslaved in a country nominally founded on liberty and equality, and she maintains that the 'Negro' race arose as an ideology to resolve and justify that contradiction. In other words, against the conventional view that White people are racist and so they economically exploit people of color, Fields reverses the cause and effect, insisting that history reveals that (mostly rich) White people have exploited people of color for economic gain and then have justified that exploitation by creating races compromised of people with alleged intellectual and moral deficiencies. Sandy and Peter's decision to teach their students about poverty and wealth inequality reflects this latter view – that while the intersectionality of poverty and race is undeniable, the root of these intersecting injustices is economic (specifically, capitalist) exploitation.

The second assumption of CSP advocates that was challenged by Sandy and Peter's pedagogical choices is that the way people feel about their own or another person's culture is important in advancing social justice. This emphasis on the ways that people think and feel about cultures is evident throughout the CSP literature. For instance, Michael Domínguez (2017), in his call for humanizing teacher education pedagogies that produce teachers capable of resisting 'unjust policies and discriminatory practices' (p.227), argues that teachers must be prepared in a way that produces an '*affective* change. . . in how teachers see and value the diversity of experiences, ways of being, and realities that exist in the world' (p.228, original italics). Thus, to Domínquez and other CSP advocates (Kinloch, 2017; San Pedro, 2017), insofar as the project of sustaining cultures is essentially an affective one, it's a project of fostering in teachers and students an attitude or deeply-felt sense that one's own or another person's culture is valuable and worthy of being sustained and/or revitalized.

I have no doubt that Sandy and Peter were deeply committed to affirming their students' Mexican and Mexican-American cultures. And I am sure, too, that these teachers knew well the importance of their students feeling positive about and secure in their cultural identity. At the same time, however, Sandy and Peter's teaching departed from CSP's emphasis on affect and instead aligns more closely with Wendy Brown's (2004) view that people's feelings or attitudes regarding cultural pluralism are politically irrelevant. According to Brown, to prioritize one's feelings or perceptions regarding diversity is to internalize and psychologize issues that properly belong in the domain of the political. In other words, in Brown's view, the current primacy of individual feelings/perceptions about cultural pluralism represents a retreat from more substantive visions of justice and is part of general trend toward the de-politicization of public life.

If Brown is right about the political limits of affective approaches to cultural pluralism, and if writers such as Fields, Darder, and Torres are right to locate the source of race/class intersectionality in economic exploitation, and if Sandy and Peter were also right to focus their teaching on poverty and wealth inequality, then it seems to me that the central question that educators must address is this: How might we transform a commitment to cultural pluralism and cultural equality into a viable political project that ameliorates economic injustice? In what follows, I'll suggest how certain aspects of CSP itself might facilitate such a transformation.

Political subjectivity and common interests in community practices

Among the downsides of raising concerns like ones I've brought up is that they tend to perpetuate the 'race vs. class' dualism that, in closing (and, perhaps, surprisingly, considering what I've written so far), I'd like to resist. I say so because to acknowledge that a person's race or ethnicity-affiliated identity is a fundamental aspect of her lived experience is also to recognize that cultural identity can potentially play a role in directing activism against poverty and wealth inequality. One of the concepts that has emerged within CSP scholarship suggests a way to move educators in this more overtly political direction. I'm talking, now about the work of Mary Bucholtz, Dolores Inés Casillas, and Jin Sook Lee (2017), who contend that what gets sustained in CSP is multi-faceted. More specifically, these authors point out that CSP is directed not only toward sustaining cultures but also toward securing culture as a medium to sustain in individuals a 'deeply held sense of identity and social belonging' that is necessary for those who seek social justice (p.45). Put another way, Bucholtz, Casillas, and Lee highlight the notion that CSP sustains both cultures and people, and the implied potential of this notion is that these sufficiently-sustained people might deploy their 'community-based resources' (p.44) to combat economic injustice. As George Sánchez has documented, this potential was demonstrated in the ways in which the ethnic identity of Mexican Americans 'engendered political radicalism' that helped fuel the progressive labor movements of the 1930s and 40s (p.12–13). This role of cultural identity in fostering economic activism can also be seen in César Chavez's leadership of the United farmworkers of America, as well as in efforts by the 'Justice for Janitors' organization to win fair wages and working conditions for the mostly Latino maintenance workers in Los Angeles. Historical antecedents such as these affirm Robin Kelly's (1997) observation that 'social movements rooted in race. . . are often the ground upon which class conflicts are enacted' (p.202).

Still, despite their potential to alleviate economic injustice, the obvious problem with such culturally-based efforts is that the resulting benefits are often limited to a particular racial or ethnic group, as well as the likelihood that reliance on this strategy alone would pit different culturally-affiliated groups in competition with each other. Thus, the remaining challenge is to somehow deploy cultural pluralism in support of a broad-based working-class coalition. In my view, this more expansive activist project requires a revision of the notion of 'identity', one that goes beyond CSP's emphasis on locating people's identity in their ethnic or racial culture. Perhaps paradoxically, I believe that such a revision could grow out of the distinction that Paris and Alim (2014) make between cultural 'heritage practices' (things such as traditional values and ways of knowing, rituals, languages) and 'community practices', which evolve fluidly in the shifting contexts of everyday life (pp.90–91).

To apply this distinction to the Tejada High students, these students' daily 'community practices' included not only the struggles of being poor but also their efforts *not* to be poor – their attempts to eliminate poverty from their cultural community. In other words, as an aspect of their community practices, these young people were revising their identity to include specific actions that they hoped would help them escape from poverty. This idea of identity as emerging from justice-seeking actions is precisely what Eddie Glaude (2008) advocates in *In a Shade of Blue: Pragmatism and the Politics of Black America*. Glaude cautions against what he calls an 'archeological approach' to identity, the kind that 'is concerned with uncovering our *true* selves and inferring from that discovery what we must do' (p.53). Glaude's alternative is not to de-racialize notions of identity or construct a fantasy of a post-racial society, but to see re-conceptualize identities as subjectivities that emerge (and continually re-emerge) as the *consequences* of human – specifically, problem-solving – activity. In this view, the 'subject' is a mutable and contingent collection of habits and potentials that have evolved from a person's (that is, a subject's) experiences – like the Tejada students' experiences with poverty. In sum, then, Glaude sees subjectivities not as antecedent identities derived from culture, but as 'the *products* of our efforts to overcome problems' (p.56, original italics). Similarly, as Felix Padilla (1985) explained in his landmark ethnographic study of Latinos in Chicago, in contrast to 'Latin American identities', which are derived from the cultural practices of various regions in Mexico, Central or South America, or the Caribbean, 'Latino' is a multi-ethnic identity that emerges in the context of 'circumstantial conditions of structural or institutional inequality' to achieve a col-lective goal (p.7). In other words, to Padilla, to identify as 'Latino' is to take on a particular role as a political subject committed to ameliorating specific injustices. Considered together, then, Padilla and Glaude depart from familiar understand-ings of culture-based identity in favor of a political subjectivity that is created by engaging in intentional actions. In my view, this shift from an emphasis on cultural identity to political subjectivity provides an ideologically capacious yet materially-grounded method for re-imagining political subjects as emerging from and acting in response to the ever-changing socio-cultural and economic conditions they encounter as part of their community practices.

If the Tejada students were to undergo this shift in their individual and col-lective self-perceptions, I submit that they would do well to choose as their primary identity a political affiliation comprised of people with whom they share a common interest. And who would that be? Is it Arturo Moreno, the Mexican-American billionaire media mogul, famous for his right-wing politics? Or might it be the African-American daughter of a Gary, Indiana, steel worker who was laid off 5 years ago, or the White son of an unemployed West Virginia coal miner? I think that it's the latter two, which leads me also to think that among the ways CSP can fulfill its potential as a social justice pedagogy is to redirect its focus to how cultural identity can be useful in organizing and mobilizing multi-cultural, working-class coalitions. In this sense, failing to sustain or otherwise marginalizing a culture is both a moral offense and – for the poor, anyway – a strategic mistake because it hinders the formation of a cross-cultural solidarity that could challenge the ruling class.

On a balmy June evening, the Tejada High graduation ceremony was held in the Grand Ballroom at Navy Pier on the shore of Lake Michigan in downtown Chicago. It was a festive and fully bilingual event, with everything from the printed program to the valedictorian's and principal's speeches offered in both English and Spanish. Despite the celebratory atmosphere, as I watched the students cross the stage and receive their diplomas, I couldn't help but recall things I had heard them say just a few weeks before. Juana, for instance, her eyes misty with tears, had told me that she turned down an acceptance offer from a well-regarded culinary school because she couldn't afford, as she put it, '4 years of college money'. During a class presentation in which students explained their hopes and concerns for the future, Sarah had confessed that what she worried about most was 'being in debt and being homeless.' Sarah elaborated: 'That just, like, scares the crap out of me. My family is always in debt, and I hate owing people money. And if I go broke, it'll be like I've screwed up my entire life'.

Paris and Alim (2017) have argued that 'CSP demands a critical, emancipatory vision of schooling that reframes the object of critique from our children to oppressive systems' (p.3). I couldn't agree more. Still, by now I hope it's clear that, in my view, the 'oppressive systems' subjected to CSP's 'critique' must more frequently and explicitly be those that result in widespread economic injustice. Such a re-direction of CSP's critical energies would be consistent with the Dartmouth Conference's emphasis on the experiences and priorities of students like those I encountered at Tejada High. In this way, CSP advocates could add to all of the good reasons they rightly provide for sustaining a culture that of sustaining political subjects who are dedicated to and capable of actions that ameliorate the problem of poverty.

Notes

1 All students' and teachers' names, as well as 'Tejada High' are pseudonyms.
2 Much of my critique in this 'Limits of cultural pluralism' section of this chapter draws heavily on the writings of my UIC colleague, Walter Benn Michaels. I am especially, too, indebted to Michaels for insights he provided in a presentation delivered at the University of Chicago on April 5, 2017.
3 Although I'm aware of the rationale for and popularity of the gender-neutral term 'Latinx', I never heard this term used by Tejada High students, teachers, or administrators. Rather, their emic self-identifying term was 'Latino' or 'Mexican'.

References

Bucholtz, M., Casillas, I. C., & and Lee, J. S. (2017). 'Language and culture as sustenance', in Paris, D., & Alim, H. S. eds. (2017), 43–60.
Columbia University, Mailman School of Public Health, National Center for Children in Poverty (2017). *Child Poverty*. www.nccp.org/topics/childpoverty.html (retrieved 18 November, 2017).
Darder, A. & Torres, R. D. (2004). *After race: racism after multiculturalism*. New York: NYU Press.
Domínguez, M. (2017). 'Se hace puentes al andar: decolonial teacher education as a needed bridge to culturally sustaining and revitalizing pedagogies', in Paris, D., & Alim, H. S. eds. (2017), 226–246.
Fields, B. J. (1990). 'Slavery, race, and ideology in the United States of America', *New Left Review*, I/181, May-June, 95–118.
Glaude, E. (2007). *In a shade of blue: pragmatism and the politics of Black America*. Chicago: University of Chicago Press.

Irizarry, J. G. (2017). 'For us by us: a vision for culturally sustaining pedagogies forwarded by Latinx youth', in Paris, D., & Alim, H. S. eds. (2017), 83–98.

Johnson, C. (2007). *Revolutionaries to race leaders: black power and the making of African-American politics*. Minnesota: University of Minnesota Press.

Kelly, Robin D. G. (1997). *Yo' mama's disfunktional!: fighting the culture wars in urban America*. Boston: Beacon Press.

Kinloch. V. (2017). 'You ain't making me write: culturally sustaining pedagogies and Black youths' performances of resistance', in Paris, D., & Alim, H. S. eds. (2017), 25–42.

Lowe, L. (2015). *The intimacies of four continents*. Durham, NC: Duke University Press.

Marsh, J. (2011). *Class dismissed: why we can't teach or learn our way out of inequality*. New York: Monthly Review Press.

Michaels, W. B. (2012). Dude, where's my job? *PMLA*, 127(4), 1006–1009.

Michaels, W. B. (2016). 'What is the Left without identity politics?' *The Nation*, 16 December 2016. www.thenation.com/article/what-is-the-left-without-identity-politics/ (accessed 16 May, 2017).

Padilla, F. (1985). *Latino ethnic consciousness: the case of Mexican-Americans and Puerto Ricans in Chicago*. Chicago: University of Notre Dame Press.

Paris, D., & Alim, H. S. eds. (2017). *Culturally sustaining pedagogy: teaching and learning for justice in a changing world*. New York: Teachers College Press.

Sanchez, G. (1993). *Becoming Mexican American: ethnicity, culture, and identity in Chicano Los Angeles, 1900–1945*. New York: Oxford University press.

San Pedro, T. J. (2017). "This stuff interests me': Re-centering indigenous paradigms in colonizing schooling spaces', in Paris, D., & Alim, H. S. eds. (2017), 99–116.

Smagorinsky, P. (2002). '*Growth through English* revisited', *English journal*, 91(6), July, 23–29.

US Bureau of Labor Statistics (2016). *Employment by major occupational group*. www.bls.gov/emp/ep_table_101.htm (accessed 17 October, 2017).

US Census Bureau (2017). *Income and poverty in the United States, 2016*. www.census.gov/library/publications/2017/demo/p60-259.html (accessed 15 October, 2017).

US Federal Reserve Board of Governors (2017). *Changes in US family finances from 2013 to 2016*. www.federalreserve.gov/publications/files/scf17.pdf (accessed 10 October, 2017).

18

THE DARTMOUTH CONFERENCE REVISITED

Changing views of grammar – or not?

Annabel Watson and Debra Myhill

Introduction

There is little doubt that the Dartmouth Conference in 1966 represents a seminal period in thinking about English teaching, and a turning-point in relation to the teaching of grammar. The conference is properly titled the 'Anglo-American Conference on the Teaching and Learning of English' and it was funded by the Carnegie Endowment in response to growing concerns about the teaching of English in classrooms on both sides of the Atlantic. It was jointly organised by the National Conference of Teachers of English and the Modern Language Association and took the form of a three-week seminar, held at Dartmouth College, New Hampshire. More than 50 scholars, including leading educationalists such as James Squire, Arthur Jensen, Frank Whitehead, James Britton and John Dixon, came together to discuss 'what is English?', but the discussion rapidly moved to focus on the teaching of writing, and with that, the place of grammar. In both England and America, the teaching of writing was typically very product-driven, with an emphasis on accuracy, and including grammar at its core. Grammar teaching was characterised by exercises, drills, labelling and identification. There was an emerging consensus, distilled into a new way of thinking at the Dartmouth Conference, that this product-driven, grammar-heavy approach was not developing confident writers. Instead a process approach, informed by a view of English as personal growth, and energised by the thinking of James Britton and John Dixon, became the dominant theoretical orientation to the teaching of writing. This represented: 'a shift in attention from learning product to learning process, and other changes based on the British "growth model" for viewing the discipline of English' (Smagorinsky, 2002, p.23). With this shift came a new orthodoxy, that grammar teaching was 'a waste of time' (Muller, 1967, p.68) and across the Anglophone world, many countries moved to reform their English curricula and to remove formal grammar teaching. The effect of this has been powerful and sustained. Indeed, in 2003, Haussamen argued that:

> At the start of this new millennium, throughout much of the K-12 English curriculum, grammar is a broken subject. . . Grammar is often ignored, broken off altogether from the teaching of literature, rhetoric, drama, composition, and creative writing. Grammar is the skunk at the garden party of the language arts.
>
> *(Haussamen, 2003, p.x)*

This chapter takes the Dartmouth Conference's rejection of grammar as the starting-point for reflecting on how grammar has developed, or not, since 1966, and whether there has been any change in thinking about the role of grammar in the curriculum. The chapter draws on the perspectives of three writing researchers and educationalists from three different jurisdictions: Judy Parr from New Zealand; Beverley Derewianka from Australia; and Marie-Claude Boivin from Canada. We have included a Canadian perspective, because it is bilingual, and because Quebec, the context of Boivin's research, is dominantly French-speaking, which offers an interesting alternative lens on grammar in a language curriculum. We also draw on our own understanding of the English curriculum context, and documented perspectives from America.

Grammar in the writing curriculum

As noted above, the Anglophone countries all followed the impetus of the Dartmouth Conference and largely abandoned explicit grammar teaching, seen as 'irrelevant and poorly taught' (Derewianka, 2017), in favour of a personal growth model characterised by 'a view of writing as a means of creating, and of expressing ideas' (Parr, 2017). For the bilingual Canadian community in Quebec, Dartmouth had an impact in generating a new emphasis on the process of writing, rather than the final product, but 'grammar instruction, which has a long-standing tradition in the francophone world, was never really abandoned in Quebec' (Boivin, 2017). Yet debates about the place of grammar continued. In New Zealand, the study by Elley et al (1975) demonstrated no significant differences in writing outcomes between students taught no grammar, transformational grammar and traditional grammar, and it also noted that 'large numbers of NZ teachers had deliberately abandoned the teaching of grammar in favour of more 'naturalistic' approaches' (Parr, 2017). In England, the development of the first National Curriculum was preceded by two reports, the Kingman Report (DES, 1988) and the Cox Report (DES, 1989), both of which were intended to halt the freedom of progressive English teaching and reintroduce a traditional curriculum, including a greater emphasis on grammar. In the United States, where the personal growth model was a powerful movement, there were nonetheless efforts to reintroduce grammar, such as the Oregon Curriculum drawing on transformational grammar (see O'Neill, 2010 for an overview) and the rhetorical grammar espoused by linguists such as Martha Kolln and Loretta Gray (2016). The situation in Australia was somewhat different, as the academic field of linguistics was energised by Michael Halliday and Ruqaiya Hasan, whose view of grammar 'not simply as a set of rules but as a dynamic system of choices that varies according to the context resonated with teachers' (Derewianka, 2017). The arrival of Jim Martin from Canada created further impetus for changed views of grammar in the curriculum, particularly as Martin worked with 'educators concerned with equity and social justice, supporting students from disadvantaged backgrounds to meet the language demands of schooling' (Derewianka, 2017). For a fuller analysis of the history of grammar teaching in Australia see Bernard (1999) and Christie (1993).

So how do things stand now in 2018–9? Arguably, although there is still no consensus about the role of grammar in the curriculum, there is a greater emphasis on grammar now than in the period immediately following the Dartmouth Conference. The position in England is probably the most striking. The National Curriculum introduced in 2014 not only makes grammar part of the curriculum but specifies precisely which grammatical terms children should learn in each year of their primary education (see the Grammar Annex DfE, 2014a) on the basis that learning 'the correct grammatical terms in English' is important to give children 'the vocabulary they need to discuss their reading, writing and spoken language' (DfE, 2014a, p.5). For older students (aged 12–14), knowledge of grammar is presented positively as a resource for exploring how texts 'make meaning' (DfE, 2014b, p.4), whilst at the same time there is an emphasis on grammatical accuracy and the use of Standard English. And because there is a national test of grammar at age 11, which tests only labelling and identification of grammatical terms, there is an unclear rationale for grammar's presence in the curriculum. In Quebec, explicit knowledge of grammar is clearly outlined. *Progression of learning* documents 'provide a distribution from the first to the 11th grade of the various grammatical objects to be taught and learned' (Boivin, 2017). The Quebec curriculum positions grammar as having a clear purpose: 'its first and foremost role is accuracy in writing' (Boivin, 2017), but it is seen as valuable in developing knowledge about language, akin to the position in England. Uniquely, in Quebec, the systematic knowledge of grammar is seen as beneficial because it develops both reasoning skills and the use of analytical tools. Nonetheless, the purpose of grammar is multiply defined: concerned with accuracy; with knowledge about language, and with developing abstract reasoning.

The development of the Common Core Standards (CCSSI, 2012) in the United States, which has no national curriculum, is the principal mechanism for shaping curriculum expectations, and is in essence a standards-driven process. Language is a discrete standard in the Common Core and there is both a strong emphasis on grammatical accuracy, and on the integration of attention to language in the context of speaking, listening, reading and writing to support learners in being 'able to make informed, skillful choices among the many ways to express themselves through language' (CCSSI, 2012). The emphasis in the Common Core Standards implies a focus on writing as product, rather than on the process of writing and being a writer, with the associated implication that the teaching of writing will be product-driven. There is ambivalence, nonetheless, about whether this grammatical accuracy and making of effective language choices is founded on expectations of explicit or naturalistic ways of learning about language.

The most recent New Zealand curriculum continues to give primacy to meaning-making: 'making meaning of ideas or information received [listening, reading and viewing] and creating meaning for self or others [speaking, writing and presenting]' (Parr, 2017) and references to explicit grammar are limited to a single statement about language features at the end of primary – 'uses a range of text conventions, including grammatical conventions, appropriately, effectively, and with increasing accuracy' (MoE, 2016, p.13). However, 'the influence of what is known as the Sydney School of functional linguistics and of the Australian genre theorists' is evident in the curriculum emphasis on 'the use of language resources is to achieve the communicative purpose of the writing' (Parr, 2017), although New Zealand has not pursued the genre approach favoured in Australia, focusing instead on the communicative purpose of texts. However, the New Zealand curriculum, despite its apparent liberalism, has been criticised for its lack of emphasis on 'powerful knowledge' (McPhail and Rata, 2016): grammar, as will be discussed later in this chapter, is potentially a tool for genuine empowerment through choice, which perhaps the New Zealand curriculum underplays. In Australia, the impact of Halliday's work on the development of their first National Curriculum was strong:

> the Language strand drew on Halliday's model of language. . . its main principles included seeing language as a resource for meaning-making (rather than simply a set of rules) and understanding language as a system of choices that vary depending on factors in the context.
>
> *(Derewianka, 2017)*

It was underpinned by a principled theoretical framework, exploring how linguistic resources are meaning-making resources, and helping students to earn explicitly how 'to recognise and use grammatical items at the point of need and in the context of actual tasks and authentic texts' (Derewianka, 2017). But despite this strong framing of a role for grammar as a meaning-making resource, the final version of the Australian National Curriculum was somewhat different and 'traditional terms were foregrounded in the pursuit of rigour' (Derewianka, 2017); moreover, subsequent recontextualisation of the National Curriculum by the various states has led to further adaptation, such that in some states 'the original is barely recognisable' (Derewianka, 2017). Here too, despite the influence of Halliday, the role of grammar in the curriculum is unclear.

Assessment

It is evident from the analysis in the preceding section that the role of grammar in the curriculum remains poorly defined and variously interpreted in different educational jurisdictions. Of course, a powerful determinant of what happens in actual classroom practice, regardless of what the curriculum expectations are, is the assessment framework used to evaluate learning in the curriculum. Once again, there is considerable variation across the jurisdictions considered here, both in terms of the nature of the assessment and what view of grammar the assessment implies.

In New Zealand, national mandated assessment is relatively light touch until the final 3 years of schooling. The assessment framework used is enabled through the use of asTTLe (Assessment Tools for Teaching and Learning, which has a specific Writing diagnostic Assessment tool. The asTTLe was developed in a collaboration between teachers and educational researchers, rather than a top-down measure. It was revised in 2012, and one of the changes was to replace the 'notion of language resources with a much narrower vocabulary dimension' (Parr, 2017) and to give more emphasis to aspects of spelling, punctuation and grammar, including, for example 'verb tense, subject-verb agreement, articles and pronouns' (Parr, 2017)

The National Assessment Program (NAPLAN) in Australia is a high-stakes external assessment framework, linked to schools' accountability. The writing assessment criteria which form the major part of the assessment align with curriculum expectations and focus on ideas development, reader engagement, cohesion and sentence structure. However, one component tests understanding of Language Conventions through multiple choice questions which test usage. Derewianka (2017) provides this example:

Our grandfather is ill so we will visit . . . . tomorrow.

( ) us ( ) her ( ) he ( ) him

and observes that:

> the items often don't appear to probe any recognisable usage problem and the distractors are generally not really plausible choices. Given the arbitrariness of items, it is hard for teachers to predict what might be assessed and what could be taught to prepare students.

There are some similarities here with the position in England. Writing is subject to national assessment at age 11 and 16. At age 16, the national qualification GCSE (General Certificate of Secondary Education), the testing of writing is concerned with effective command of writing for a specified audience and purpose, and although the assessment criteria include attention to both accuracy in spelling, punctuation and grammar, and to effective grammatical choices, there is no undue emphasis on grammar. At age 11, there is a teacher assessment of a portfolio of writing pieces representing different genres and purposes, but there is also a national test of grammar, spelling and punctuation, which tests children's proficiency in identifying grammatical errors and in labelling grammatical structures, such as noun phrases or subordinate clauses. The effect of this test has been to increase significantly attention to teaching grammar in the primary school, with almost all schools giving grammar considerably more explicit teaching time than previously. Often, however, because of the test, this is through decontextualized exercises.

Assessment practices in Canadian Quebec appear to present the most sustained and systematic assessment of grammar of all the jurisdictions considered. The assessment of grammar is embedded from primary school to university, and is linked to expectations of what children should know at a particular age or grade level. Assessment is supported by 'a variety of coding instruments or "grids" used to classify the grammatical errors made by pupils and provide a grading' (Boivin, 2017) and takes into account, for example, syntax, punctuation and grammatical spelling. Arguably, it is the Quebec system, drawing on its French linguistic heritage, where assessment is most consistently attentive to grammar, albeit principally in terms of accuracy.

Pedagogical approaches to grammar

What emerges from this brief analysis of the role of grammar in four different jurisdictions is that at the level of curriculum, there remains both evidence that grammar is, to varying degrees, visible in the curriculum, and that there is still no strong articulation of a theoretical rationale for grammar in the curriculum. Beverley Derewianka's account of the development of the Australian curriculum, with an initial strong theoretical rationale and its subsequent dilution by policy-makers, is a salient reminder that grammar is still a contested topic. As a consequence, far less attention has been directed towards *how* grammar is taught, as one effect of Dartmouth has been a perennial deflection of the debate towards *whether* it should be taught.

Any exploration of pedagogy is inevitably more complex than an analysis of curriculum documentation and policy perspectives, as every teacher potentially interprets and recontextualises the curriculum or the testing requirements in their own classroom. Each of the jurisdictions informing this chapter are developing pedagogies of grammar in different ways, though some are complementary of each other. In Quebec, where the influence of Dartmouth on classroom practices in teaching grammar seems to have been least strong, research by Chartrand and Lord (2013) found that explicit grammar was addressed more frequently in French language classes than any other aspect of the language curriculum. This emphasis may, in part, be due to linguistic differences between English and French as languages, with French being much more heavily inflected than English and many of those inflections being silent, causing particular challenges in writing. Towards the end of the twentieth century, dissatisfaction with the effectiveness of traditional grammar in supporting French children in learning to write led to the emergence of *grammaire nouvelle* (new grammar), based on modern linguistics and adapted for use in the classroom. Pedagogically, this focusses learners' attention on active exploration of, and reflection on, language. There are some similarities between this approach and the approach advocated by Haussamen et al (2003) which argues there are three pedagogical goals for teaching grammar: firstly, to achieve effective spoken and written communication; secondly, to have the ability to analyse sentences using grammatical terminology; and thirdly, to recognise language variety and diversity (Haussamen et al, 2003, p.4). In all three countries, the teaching of grammar involves explicit attention to language, including grammatical terminology where relevant, and there is a focus on knowledge and analysis.

There are some resonances between this and the pedagogical practices at play in England. The specification of grammatical terminology to be learned at particular ages and the existence of a national test for all children in their final year of primary school, which requires children to correct grammatically incorrect sentences, and to label grammatical constructions in sentences, means that the explicit teaching of grammatical terminology is widespread. It is often decontextualized from other learning about language, and exercises and practice tests are common. As a consequence, in some classrooms this has led to knowledge divorced from understanding, and to young writers acquiring misunderstandings that good writing requires the deployment, or the 'putting in', of particular grammatical constructions (such as fronted adverbials or complex sentences) regardless of their effectiveness. Myhill and Newman's analysis of metalinguistic talk in English primary classrooms found that where teachers were focused on deploying grammatical constructions in writing, there was less dialogic space for metalinguistic discussion and the classroom talk 'did not enable learners to develop understanding of the linguistic choices they could make in writing, and tended to close down responses, strongly geared towards right answers, and to a norms-driven, formulaic view of writing choices' (Myhill and Newman 2016, p.186). At the same time, however, there is a substantial number of classrooms who are adopting a more integrated approach to the teaching of grammar, particularly informed by Hallidayan meaning-making approaches, and a conceptualisation of grammar as choice (Jones et al, 2013a; 2013b). The notion of grammar as choice stands in contradistinction to the notion of grammar as an arbiter of compliance to rules and customary usages. Instead, it highlights that writing is fundamentally an act of decision-making at multiple levels (What content? What type of text? What layout?. . .) one element of which is linguistic. When Dickens portrays Magwitch in *Great Expectations* as 'A man who had been soaked in water, and smothered in mud, and lamed by stones, and cut by flints, and stung by nettles, and torn by briars' (Dickens, nd) the use of the passive is an authorial choice which subtly positions Magwitch, the aggressor at this point in the story, as simultaneously a victim, one to whom things have 'been done'. Seemingly minor grammatical choices alter how the message is communicated to a reader, and underline the significance of grammatical choice as part of the repertoire of choice central to every act of writing. In these classrooms, high-quality rich texts and authentic communicative contexts are the springboard for considering how language choices shape meaning, with metalinguistic modelling and dialogic talk acting as key pedagogical tools.

The use of modelling is also characteristic of pedagogical practices in New Zealand both 'through making explicit connections between reading and writing, looking at models of how other writers and authors help readers make sense of their stories' and 'through explicit modelling during text construction or co-construction' (Parr, 2017). This reflects a view of grammar needing to be addressed in authentic and purposeful contexts, and being responsive to learners' needs. The same attention to 'meaning in context' is present in some Australian classrooms: Derewianka (2017) describes one school, informed by Halliday's ideas and the tools of Systemic Functional Linguistics as an exemplar of this way of working:

> Over time, the school developed a scope and sequence outlining the key understandings about language to be developed cumulatively across the years. To ensure sustainability, they established guidelines on the school's approach to language teaching, they created repositories of teaching materials for each grade, and they videotaped classroom activities as models. Grammar permeated the curriculum, the teachers felt confident and empowered, and the children actually enjoyed learning about how language works. While the starting point was always 'meaning in context', the students were learning how such meanings are realised through grammatical resources such as clauses and their combinations in sentences, clause components such as noun groups, verb groups, adjective groups and adverbials, cohesive devices such as pronouns, demonstratives and articles, along with interpersonal tools such as speech functions and modality.

At the same time, she notes that as a consequence of the 'theoretical indeterminacy' of the Language strand in the Australian National Curriculum, there are also teachers who 'simply identify the traditional grammar terms and teach them out of context as a list of items from a workbook' (Derewianka, 2017).

Teachers' subject knowledge of grammar

One common factor across jurisdictions is a concern that teachers' grammatical knowledge is not sufficient to cope with the demands of classroom pedagogies of grammar. A legacy of the Dartmouth Conference was to produce a generation or more of teachers who were not taught grammar explicitly themselves, and who consequently lack confidence in their knowledge. In New Zealand, 'few recall ever having received explicit instruction about it' (Parr, 2017), and a similar situation is reported in the USA by Kolln and Hancock (2005). Attempts to address this issue have tended to be piecemeal and often reliant on teachers or schools identifying a need and pursuing professional development opportunities. In New Zealand, for example, teachers report that much of their understanding of grammar developed after their initial teacher education through the process of applying detailed criteria from the asTTLe while 'scoring and moderating writing' (Parr, 2017; Parr, Glasswell and Aikman, 2007).

Often, this gap between teachers' knowledge and the current curricular expectations around grammar results in strong affective responses. Many teachers in Australia are 'anxious about having to teach it' (Derewianka, 2017), and teachers we have worked with in the UK report similar feelings of anxiety and even inadequacy (Watson, 2015). Tackling grammar in the writing classroom places multi-layered demands on teachers: declarative knowledge of grammatical features must be accompanied by an ability to make meaningful connections between features and their effect within particular written contexts, as well as by an ability to judge when and how these features are relevant to the development of students' writing. Pedagogical skills are required to foster students' discussion about language, to model the analysis and creation of texts, and to find ways of making abstract concepts comprehensible to children. It is useful, then, to use Shulman's (1987) categories to draw a distinction between teachers' subject content knowledge of grammar and the subject-specific pedagogical content knowledge required to teach it effectively. The first might be demonstrated in, for example, a teacher's ability to identify and articulate the function of a noun phrase, or their ability to identify the effect of an author's use of adverbials. The second might be demonstrated in their skill in selecting texts which model appropriate language choices for their pupils, or using questions which scaffold a pupil's ability to explain the impact of the linguistic choices they've made in their own writing. It is also valuable to recognise how subject and pedagogical content knowledge are both entwined with teachers' conceptions of grammar and its value.

Despite the fact that grammar 'was never really abandoned' in Quebec, the jurisdiction has not entirely escaped this problem of teacher knowledge. Recent research reveals that 'teachers' grammatical knowledge is still very much influenced by traditional grammar, that the teaching practices observed in the classrooms do not reveal a strong presence of new grammar and that they are rather traditional' (Boivin, 2017). Derewianka (2017) reports a similar trend amongst some older meaning-oriented pedagogies. There is a growing body of evidence that professional development programmes which emphasise pedagogical content knowledge can have a positive influence on teachers' confidence and ability to implement effective pedagogies. Parr (2017) reports that teachers working on a current research project in New Zealand view grammar as 'an important part of learning to communicate effectively', and believe that it should be taught in a contextualised manner which makes use of 'authentic and purposeful writing experiences'. These teachers are able to teach grammar 'in context, in response to needs'. Similarly, in Australia, some states have seen strong support from functional grammar experts, enabling schools to develop coherent, embedded approaches to grammar (Derewianka, 2017). In Quebec, Boivin counterpoints the prevalence of traditional grammar teaching with the presence of 'innovative approaches, involving an active role for the pupils in the discovery and understanding of grammatical phenomena', noting that these approaches foster metalinguistic talk amongst pupils. Such examples illustrate the importance of focusing teacher professional development on pedagogical content knowledge of grammar as much as on grammatical subject knowledge.

Conclusion

Fifty years after the Dartmouth conference overturned the status quo, the place of grammar in the English curriculum is still contested. The past three decades have seen the reintroduction of grammar in jurisdictions where formal teaching had been largely abandoned, but this has often been driven by political and ideological reasons (Clark, 2010; Kolln and Hancock, 2005), rather than by empirical evidence or a coherent theoretical rationale. The debate seems to have been relentlessly characterised by polarised, often evangelical, assertions either for or against grammar and its value, with little evidence of the debate becoming more empirically or theoretically informed.

There also remains a tension between policy makers, who tend to frame grammar within a relatively prescriptive framework with a focus on traditional terminology, accuracy and standard English, and educationalists who emphasise the value of grammar for enhancing creative expression. This can be seen in the watering-down of the strongly Hallidayan Language strand of the original Australian curriculum, as well as the requirement to teach specific grammatical elements in each year of primary school in England. Even where curriculum documents espouse a meaning-oriented view of grammar, methods of assessment can thwart this by encouraging reductive pedagogies focused on identification and naming of features rather than exploration of effect in context (Safford, 2016), or pedagogies which encourage formulaic approaches to writing. Across the jurisdictions explored here, assessment rubrics which detail and rank grammatical constructions (or errors) have acted as an impetus for teachers to address grammar explicitly in their teaching; however, these can also prompt artificial approaches to writing in which teachers and students are encouraged to prioritise or value certain constructions as innately 'good' or 'sophisticated' without appreciating the need to view all language use in context. And yet, an emphasis on the grammar as a resource for considering language choices offers the potential to be a powerful alternative to formulaic, product-driven approaches to writing, focussing instead to the process of writing and the agency of the writer in shaping the text.

Despite this mixed picture, there is a small but growing international consensus that explicit teaching of grammar is best located within a contextualised, functional pedagogy which views declarative knowledge of grammar as a resource for making meaning. In this, we can see the significance of the work of Halliday – most prominently in the Australian curriculum, but also across the jurisdictions discussed here. While terminologies vary, all the regions show the impact of Halliday in the prevailing assumption that students should study language in use: using explicit knowledge of grammar to deconstruct how meaning is encoded within a text, and to make conscious choices in order to shape meaning in their own writing.

This view of grammar underpins a growing body of research which provides evidence that explicit teaching of grammar can have a significant impact on students' writing development. In our own studies, we have demonstrated that a functional approach which uses traditional terminology in the context of creative exploration of writing can benefit young writers. Here, the goal of grammar teaching is to 'open up for young writers a repertoire of infinite possibilities for deliberate structuring and authorial decision-making' (Myhill et al, 2013a, p.104). This is manifest in the focus on selecting grammar points which are relevant to the type of writing being studied, exploring authentic texts, using discussion to unpick the impact of grammatical features, and creating opportunities for playful experimentation in students' own writing. These pedagogical features are echoed in projects outlined by Parr (2017) and Derewianka (2017), but also in the work of Macken-Horarik, Love, Sandiford and Unsworth (Macken-Horarik and Sandiford, 2016; Love, Macken-Horarik and Horarik, 2015; Macken-Horarik, Sandifor, Love and Unsworth, 2015) and Schleppegrell (2011; 2012) in the US. These approaches sit well within a broader rhetorical understanding of language and communication. Internationally we are perhaps now working towards a coherent understanding of how a grammar-rich approach to teaching reading and writing can enhance student outcomes. At the same time, the Quebecois focus on exploration and reflection on language in context with a focus on accuracy is a salient reminder of how the tools of grammar can be used to support grammatical reasoning and problem-solving, particularly where the language, like French, has so many grammatical inflections.

And yet, the time is ripe for further research which sets out not to prove or disprove the value of grammar, but to explore and investigate classroom pedagogies and children's learning. The relationship between explicit knowledge of grammar and the implicit acquisition of grammar through language use is not yet fully understood or theorised, nor is there yet a fully rounded, robust body of evidence of how the explicit teaching of grammar can support procedural facility with language, particularly with attention to different learner groups. There is little research which has addressed how learners' conceptual knowledge of grammar develops and what might be natural steps in cumulative learning. But at the same time, what is emerging from research which has focused on the inter-relationship of grammar and meaning (Macken-Horarik et al, 2015; 2016; Myhill et al, 2012; 2016) is a sense that grammar, reconceptualised as a way of opening up explicit understanding of the way in which grammatical choices shape meaning offers a new way of thinking about the role of grammar in the curriculum. The notion of grammar as choice stands in stark contrast to normative hegemonic discourses about grammar and accuracy, and instead positions grammatical knowledge as a resource for empowerment. Explicit grammatical understanding, which combines a focus on the analysis of authentic texts and on writers' own choices, makes visible implicit choices which exercise both power and control. In line with Martin's argument (1989), we maintain that explicit consideration of the manifold ways in which language choices sculpt meanings in texts challenges the mere reproduction of existing social hierarchies in writing (Myhill et al, forthcoming) and instead gives young writers empowerment, agency and control. Perhaps now is the time for the grammar skunk to come out of the shadows and join the party!

References

Bernard, N. (1999). 'The Fall and rise of grammar in the Australian English curriculum: Factors in continuum of change', *Bundoora: La Trobe papers in linguistics*. Vol 10, 119–157.

Boivin, M.-C. (in press). 'A Review of the current empirical research on grammar instruction in the francophones regions'. *L1 Educational studies in language and literature*.

Boivin, M-C. (2017). Personal correspondence.

CCSSI (2012). *Common Core State Standards for Language Arts*, CCSSI www.corestandards. org/ELA-Literacy Accessed 24 August 2012.

Chartrand, S.-G. & Lord, M.-C. (2013). 'L'enseignement de la grammaire et de l'écriture au secondaire québécois: principaux résultats d'une recherche descriptive'. [Grammar and writing instruction in Quebec secondary schools: main results of a descriptive research]. *Revue suisse des sciences de l'éducation*, 33, 515–539.

Christie, F. (1993). 'The "received tradition" of English: the decline of rhetoric and the corruption of grammar', in B. Green (ed.); *The insistence of the letter: literacy studies and curriculum theorizing*, London: Falmer Press: 75–106.

Clark, U. I. L. (2010). 'Grammar in the curriculum for English: what next?' *Changing English*, 17(2), 189–200.

Derewianka, B. (2017). Personal correspondence.

DES (1988). *The Report of the Committee of Enquiry into the teaching of the English language* (The Kingman Report), London: Her Majesty's Stationery Office.

DES (1989). *English for ages 5–16* (The Cox Report), London: Her Majesty's Stationery Office.

DfE (2014a). *The National Curriculum in England: framework document – grammar annex*. www. gov.uk/government/uploads/system/uploads/attachment_data/file/210969/NC_frame-work_document_-_FINAL.pdf (Accessed 17 August 2013).

DfE (2014b). *The National Curriculum in England: English programmes of study: key stage 3* www.gov.uk/government/uploads/system/uploads/attachment_data/file/244215/ SECONDARY_national_curriculum_-_English2.pdf (Accessed 16 December 2017).

Dickens, C. (nd). *Great expectations*: chapter one. www.johndclare.net/English/Dickens_ Ch1.htm (Accessed 16 December 2017).

Elley, W. B., Barham, I. H., Lamb, H., & Wylie, M. (1975). *The Role of grammar in a second-ary school curriculum: educational research series No 60*. Wellington: New Zealand Council for Educational Research.

Haussamen, B., Benjamin, A., Kolln, M. & Wheeler, R. S. (2003). 'Grammar alive! A guide for teachers'. Available at https://wac.colostate.edu/books/grammar/alive.pdf.

Jones, S., Myhill, D. A. Watson, A & Lines, H. E. (2013a). 'Playful explicitness with grammar: a pedagogy for writing', *Literacy* 47(2), 103–111.

Jones, S. M., Myhill, D. A. & Bailey, T. C. (2013b). 'Grammar for writing? An investiga-tion into the effect of contextualised grammar teaching on student writing'. *Reading and Writing*, 26(8), 1241–1263.

Kolln, M. & Gray, L. (2016). *Rhetorical grammar: grammatical choices, rhetorical effects*. Pearson

Kolln, M., & Hancock, C. (2005). 'The Story of English grammar in US schools'. *English Teaching: Practice and Critique*, 4(3), 11–31.

Love, K., Macken-Horarik, M. & Horarik, S. (2015). 'Grammatical knowledge and its application: a snapshot of Australian teachers' views', *Australian Journal of Language and Literacy*, 38(3), 171–182.

Macken-Horarik M. & Sandiford, C. (2016). 'Diagnosing development: a grammatics for tracking student progress in narrative composition'. *International Journal of Language Studies*, 10(3), 61–94.

Macken-Horarik, M., Sandiford, C. Love, K. & Unsworth, L. (2015). 'New ways of working "with grammar in mind" in school English: insights from systemic functional grammatics', *Linguistics and Education*, 31, 145–158.

Martin, J. R. (1989). *Factual writing: exploring and challenging social reality* (2nd ed.). Oxford: Oxford University Press.

McPhail, G. J., & Rata, E. (2016). 'Comparing curriculum types: "Powerful Knowledge" and "21st Century Learning"'. *New Zealand Journal of Educational Studies*, 51(1), 53–68.

Ministry of Education [MoE] (2016). *The New Zealand Curriculum: achievement objectives by learning area*. http://nzcurriculum.tki.org.nz/The-New-Zealand-Curriculum.

Muller, H. J. (1967). *The Uses of English: guidelines for the teaching of English from the Anglo-American Conference at Dartmouth College*. New York: Holt, Rinehart and Winston.

Myhill, D. A., Jones, S.M., Lines, H. & Watson A. (2012). 'Re-thinking grammar: the impact of embedded grammar teaching on students' writing and students' metalinguistic understanding', *Research Papers in Education* 27(2), 139–166.

Myhill, D.A & Newman, R. (2016). 'Metatalk: enabling metalinguistic discussion about writing', *International Journal of Education Research*, 80, 177–187.

O'Neill, W. (2010). 'Bringing linguistics into the school curriculum: not one less', in Denham, K and Lobeck, A (eds.) *Linguistics at School*. Cambridge: Cambridge University Press: 24–34.

Parr, J. (2017). Personal correspondence.

Parr, J. M., Glasswell, K., & Aikman, M. (2007). 'Supporting teacher learning and informed practice in writing through assessment tools for teaching and learning'. *Asia-Pacific Journal of Teacher Education*, 35(1), 69–87.

Safford, K. (2016). 'Teaching grammar and testing grammar in the English primary school: the impact on teachers and their teaching of the grammar element of the statutory test in spelling, punctuation and grammar (SPaG)'. *Changing English*, 23(1), 3–21.

Schleppegrell, M. J. (2011). 'Supporting disciplinary learning through language analysis: developing historical literacy', in F. Christie and K. Maton (eds.), *Disciplinarity: functional linguistic and sociological perspectives*. London: Continuum: 197–216.

Schleppegrell, M. J. (2012). 'Systemic functional linguistics: exploring meaning in language', in Gee, J. P. and Handford, M. (eds.), *The Routledge handbook of discourse analysis*. New York: Routledge: 21–34.

Shulman, L. S. (1987). 'Knowledge and teaching: foundations of the new reform'. *Harvard Educational Review*, 57(1), 1–22.

Smagorinsky, P. (2002). '*Growth through English* revisited' *English Journal*, 91(6), 23–29.

Watson, A. M. (2015). 'Conceptualisations of "grammar teaching": L1 English teachers' beliefs about teaching grammar for writing'. *Language Awareness*, 24(1).

19

"WHAT IS ENGLISH?"

New directions for the discipline in a transnational world

Allison Skerrett and Saba Vlach

Albert Kitzhaber's keynote speech at the 1966 Dartmouth Seminar was titled "What is English?" His paper, which regarded English as monolithic and unchangeable, represented American thinking about the teaching of English (Sublett, 1973; Trimbur, 2008). However, the British scholars in attendance were interested in a new process-oriented conception of English that was less concerned with the perfection of a final linguistic product. Each group felt that their nation's curriculum was outdated and needed modernizing, but the Americans' goal was to develop a rigorous curriculum in the style of the New Mathematics and New Science (e.g. Project English) founded on scientific principles (Trimbur, 2008), whereas the British wanted to deemphasize the technical and academic aspects of English and build on their students' authentic usage of English (Harris, 1991; Dixon, 2009). Contemporary accounts of the debates and reminiscences of the participants suggest that the Americans wanted to continue to legitimize their nation's ownership of the English language, whereas British educators, who were secure in their literary history, felt no need to flaunt their linguistic heritage (Dixon, 2009; Donahue & Blewett, 2015; Harris, 1991; Trimbur, 2008). The British, particularly, seized this moment of dialogue about English to argue for a more creative, expressive, and student-centered form of English instruction.

Irrespective of the perceived differences at the 1966 seminar, scholars today (Harris, 1991; Smagorinsky, 2002) assert that the Americans and the British agreed upon a growth model for students in English instruction, and that the Dartmouth Conference marked a turning point for both nations, and in turn, for all English-speaking countries, towards a more progressive and student-centered ideology in English education (Sublette, 1973; Smagorinsky, 2002; Dixon, 2009). Scholarly ideas presented at Dartmouth – such as colonization versus decolonization, cultural homogeneity versus cultural diversity, and multilingualism and translingualism – continue to be explored in contemporary work in English education. Likewise, the tensions and debates at Dartmouth surrounding "What is English?" and conversations about approaches and goals for teaching and learning in this discipline remain active in the field today (Donahue & Blewett, 2015; Dixon, 2009; Smagorinsky, 2002; Trimbur, 2008).

The work we present in this chapter represents the conversations at Dartmouth about new approaches to English education in response to sweeping changes in social life within and across world nations. The expanding social phenomenon with which this chapter is concerned is transnationalism. Transnationalism refers to the circumstance wherein people, through a mix of necessity and choice, live their lives across two or more countries. This lifestyle generates familial, social, cultural, economic, sociopolitical and other networks and commitments, and feelings of belongingness, spanning two or more nations (Levitt, 2001). Transnationalism manifests in schools today. Schools, worldwide, are now populated by more transnational youths than ever before (Coe, Reynolds, Boehm, Hess, & Rae-Espinoza, 2011; Zúñiga & Hamman, 2009). Given this situation, it is critical that English education today, in the spirit of the responsiveness, intellectual curiosity, creativity, and social justice stances of Dartmouth, reconsider how the discipline's practices can promote learning for this demographic and all students who sit alongside them in classrooms.

This chapter describes a conceptual approach with related instructional practices for English education called a transnationally-inclusive approach to literacy education (Skerrett, 2015). We discuss how this approach represents a new and productive direction for English teaching and learning. We then report on our researcher-teacher effort to draw upon the principles and practices of a transnationally-inclusive approach to literacy education for teaching and learning with a diverse group of secondary-aged students in the highly transnational and post-colonial Caribbean nation of Dutch St. Maarten. The island's 40,000 plus population represents over 120 nationalities and 54% migrants and immigrants from other Caribbean countries (Cepal.org, 2002; Government of Sint Maarten, 2014). Our goal with this classroom-based research was to further learn about what English could be and accomplish for students and teachers in an increasingly transnational world. In this sense our research represents a microcosm of the dichotomy at Dartmouth and the problems and possibilities we continue to grapple with 50 years later.

Defining transnational students

Transnational students are a diverse group. For example, they vary in terms of the duration of their residence across countries, the regularity of border crossing, and the extent to which formal education across different nations is part of their transnational experience. It is also important to distinguish between immigrant and transnational students. Schools and teachers often mis-categorize transnational students as immigrant students whose primary challenge is to learn how to learn within the language and educational approaches of their new nation's schools (Skerrett, 2015; Zúñiga & Hamann, 2009). Yet transnational students face a distinctively different challenge than immigrant students because transnational students must become increasingly skilled in the languages, cultures, and curriculum and instructional approaches of two or more nations. Teachers are often unaware of which of their students are transnational. Furthermore, when teachers do discover transnational students in their classrooms, they are unsure of how to provide them with appropriate educational supports (Skerrett, 2015; Zúñiga & Hamann, 2009).

Much of what is known about transnational youths' engagements with language and literacy has been produced from research in contexts outside of school (Lam & Warriner, 2012). We understand, for example, that transnational youths develop and employ multilingual and digital literacy practices, as well as trans-cultural identities and global perspectives, through leading transnational lives. In Allison's longitudinal work on transnationalism and literacy education, she has focused on transnational students from the United States, Canada, the Caribbean, Mexico, and Asia, as well as their teachers' experiences in the context of school, through in-depth interviews and curriculum analyses. Allison worked closely for a year and a half with a reading teacher in the US as she implemented a reading curriculum and made it increasingly responsive to the multicultural, multilingual, and multiliterate students she taught, some of whom led transnational lives. The sum of these research experiences and the insights Allison gleaned from these students and educators have allowed her to theorize a transnationally-inclusive approach to literacy education (Skerrett, 2015).

A transnationally-inclusive approach to literacy education

In theorizing a transnationally-inclusive approach to literacy education, Allison drew upon existing theories of teacher learning and practice with increasingly diverse and resource-rich student populations – such as Ball's (2009) theory of teachers' generativity in culturally and linguistically complex classrooms, and theories of literacy as social practice such as the New London Group's [NLG] (1996) theory of multiliteracies pedagogy. Although these theories account for the diversity of students' linguistic, cultural, and literacy practices, and in so doing, reflect the priorities of English education discussed at Dartmouth, these frameworks do not explicitly engage the repertoires and educational circumstances of transnational students. Transnational students expand our understandings of student diversity to include not only students' cultural, linguistic, and multiliteracies diversity, but also their multiple national backgrounds and affiliations, and world knowledge. Transnationally-inclusive literacy education (Skerrett, 2015) extends existing conceptual models for promoting teaching and learning in diverse classrooms to make them intentionally inclusive of transnational students.

Transnationally-inclusive literacy education (Skerrett, 2015) includes three dimensions that broaden in their scope from student to classroom to global networks.

1. Teachers actively inquire with their students into students' social, cultural, and educational experiences in one or more countries, and students' language and literacy practices in outside-school contexts spanning local and transnational contexts.

2. Teachers use the knowledge acquired about students to guide their design of curriculum and instructional methods that uniquely respond to students' educational and social histories, academic strengths, and learning needs. Additionally, teachers' curriculum and pedagogical practices consistently emphasize reading, writing, and critical thinking skills to enable *all* students, notwithstanding their transnational status, to strengthen competencies that are useful in global educational and social contexts.
3. Teachers and students document and share students' academic development and ongoing educational needs with other educational partners. This allows teachers in different countries to gain deeper understandings of their transnational students' academic strengths and needs.

Allison (Skerrett, 2015) has further theorized the unique learning gains that teachers and all students stand to acquire from engaging with a transnationally-inclusive approach to literacy education. These include:

*   Understandings and appreciation of how transnational students and their repertoires comprise part of the diverse and valuable resources for teaching and learning available in classrooms;
*   Greater knowledge and capabilities pertaining to using and strengthening languages, literacies, and sociocultural knowledge to participate productively in and across transnational literacy contexts, including schools;
*   A more comprehensive knowledge base related to the educational, cultural, political, and other aspects of different nations, or particular regions within them, to which transnational students have ties;
*   Identities of global citizenship that include expertise and capacities to identify, care about, critically analyze, and develop potential solutions to social justice concerns of all people and all nations.

Theoretical framing of our classroom-based research

In designing and implementing a transnationally-inclusive approach to literacy education with a group of Caribbean youths, we acknowledged that we would be transporting a literacy pedagogy into a national context that would be distinctive from the pedagogies these students regularly experienced. This knowledge was based in our review of research on English education across the Caribbean, including Allison's own previous research in St. Maarten and at the school in which this work occurred. Yet we believed that such instruction would be generative for students' literacy learning. Ideologically and practically, we framed our work around the principles and practices of a transnationally-inclusive approach to literacy education detailed above, notions of emancipatory pedagogy (Macaluso, 2015) and Canagarajah's (2011) conceptualization of English as a creolized discipline, all of which align with the student-centered focus of Dartmouth scholars and their interest in the grand repertoires of languages, literacies, and cultures that students possess.

Macaluso (2015) offers a pedagogical framework for literature instruction that builds on the principles of Rancièrean emancipatory ethics (Rancière, 1991, in Macaluso, 2015). For Macaluso (2015), readers are emancipated when we insist upon intellectual and social equality among teacher, student, text, and author from the beginning. In line with this thinking, our work with literature was designed to have the students respond to their texts, first with our support and then ultimately on their own. Our instructional questioning aligned with the three questions that Macaluso (2015) provides to support the reader's emancipation: *What do you see? What do you think? What do you say?*

Canagarajah (2011) insists that English education in a globalized world should reflect the practices of a creolized scholarship, meaning, inclusive of multiple languages and language varieties, multimodality, and diverse world perspectives and traditions. Creolization should thus manifest in the processes and content of composition, reading, dialogue, and other domains of the language arts. We hoped that our work with the students, framed by these ideas, would invite students into a generative and participatory literacy pedagogy rather than a literacy pedagogy of colonization (Canagarajah, 2011; Macaluso, 2015). In line with these scholars' thinking, a literacy pedagogy of colonization imposes onto students predetermined texts, textual practices, and meanings, and devalues or delegitimizes students' locally and transnationally developed multicultural, multiliterate, and multilingual identities, competencies, knowledge, and interests.

Research on English education in the Caribbean

Language arts instruction in K-12 Caribbean schools remains primarily teacher-directed and centered on acquisition of knowledge and skills of a "correct" form of grammar, vocabulary, mechanics, and sentence structure, what Canagarajah's (2011) work suggests is a literacy pedagogy of colonization, with limited in-depth engagement with literature or digital literacy experiences for students (e.g., James, 2003, 2004; Seunarinesingh, 2015a, 2015b). This phenomenon persists despite some policy movements that support more culturally responsive, learner-centered instruction that pursues broader academic and social competencies and prepares students to participate successfully in a globalized world (Seunarinesingh, 2015a; Skerrett, 2016). Importantly, these new policy formulations, reflective of the goals of Dartmouth, have been critiqued for their limited attention to professional development and implementation support for English teachers (James, 2003; Skerrett, 2016). The ideological stronghold of the traditions of English has also been faulted for teachers' resistance to change (James, 2004).

Within the literature on English education in the Caribbean examples do exist of pedagogies that are responsive to students' lives, outside-school literacies, and interests, and thus align with the spirit of Dartmouth (Conrad, Forteau-Jaikaransingh, & Popova, 2015; Seunarinesingh, 2010, 2015b). Seunarinesingh (2010) completed a case study of four elementary school teachers in Trinidad and Tobago who used authentic texts from students' everyday lives (for example digital media and newspapers, field trips, and guest speakers) to teach language arts and social studies. The four teachers' desire to secure students' engagement in core literacy learning motivated them to experiment with literacy tools and social literacy practices they had not previously employed in literacy instruction. Conrad et al (2015) employed autoethnography to look back on their own instruction as poetry teachers. The teachers/researchers focused on Rapso, a poetry genre that remains significant in the popular culture of Trinidad and Tobago. Conrad et al (2015) described Rapso as including qualities of articulation, joy, confidence building, enhanced communication, collaboration, and friendship; thus they implemented it in their classrooms to increase students' passion for learning. The authors further described their use of Rapso as a way to push back on the use of traditional English literature and sonnets, and create a space where students could design poetry that bridges the classical and cultural, including all their language varieties. We value these culturally responsive pedagogies that integrate students' local geographies and social lives into the curriculum. However, although Caribbean students, like all people, are members of a globalized world, English education practices in the Caribbean that account for the local *and* global nature of students' literate lives are hard to find.

Implementing a transnationally-inclusive approach to literacy education

The classroom-based project we undertook occurred during spring 2016 and is part of Allison's longitudinal qualitative study on transnational youths' literate lives. In this classroom-based component of the study, we, Allison and Saba, served as teacher-researchers across a four-month period at a school on St. Maarten we call Triumph Multiage School (TMS), where Allison has been conducting research since 2014. The goal of the classroom-based research was to draw upon principles and practices of a transnationally-inclusive approach to literacy education to design and teach a variety of literacy units that could promote students' literacy engagement and development. Allison also hoped that conducting this work would provide conceptual and instructional insights that would strengthen the conceptual principles and practices of the framework she had developed in her recent book, *Teaching Transnational Youth* (2015). We thus drew on qualitative research methods (Miles, Huberman, & Saldana, 2013), elements of design-based research (Reinking & Bradley, 2008) and grounded theory (Glaser & Strauss, 2006).

Instructional design

Allison led the design and implementation of three curriculum units, overviews of which we provide below. We taught a 90-minute block of language arts to six adolescents who, with their parents, consented/assented to participate in the research. We took on dual roles of English teachers to these students, while also maintaining researcher roles of collecting and analyzing data (e.g., student interviews, video-recorded classroom sessions, and collection and analysis of instructional and learning artifacts) to inform our continuous adaptation of curriculum and instruction, and develop increasingly robust scholarly understandings about the processes, challenges, and gains associated with a transnationally-inclusive approach to literacy education.

Allison designed and taught the first two-week long unit, an Inquiry into Literate Lives unit (Bomer, 2011) in which she led students through an investigation into their literacy practices. The goals of this unit were to learn about students' literate lives, facilitate their awareness of the literacy competencies involved in their school and self-sponsored activities (NLG, 1996), and promote students' confidence that they were already highly literate people. Allison encouraged students to notice and name reading and writing in school and other spaces, and facilitated their notice and analysis of other meaning-making activities, such as video-gaming and playing music, they engaged in across different social contexts of their lives. The transnationally-inclusive dimension of Allison's instructional framework was integrated into this unit by explicitly encouraging students to consider both local and global contexts of their literate lives.

For the second unit, we jointly designed and taught a three-week independent reading unit. Based in the knowledge acquired about students' literate lives and interests from the Literate Lives unit, and in students' specific recommendations of books, genres, and topics of interest, Saba led the creation of a classroom library that included at least five books that we knew would be of particular interest to each student. Books were selected from websites devoted to young adult literature such as YALSA (www.ala.org) and more widely oriented websites such as www.amazon.com. We drew on Bomer's (2011) instructional ideas for organizing and teaching independent reading. However, the transnationally-inclusive dimension was addressed through including texts students requested that reflected their participation in a globally-connected world of readers and other literacy practices. The instructional elements of the reading unit (Bomer, 2011) included:

- Students choosing their own books to read, either independently or in a small partnership;
- Sustained time for students to read and discuss texts with peers during class time and encouragement to take their books home to continue reading;
- Regular, brief, teacher-student conferences to understand how students' reading experiences were unfolding and to ascertain and respond to their in-the-moment learning needs;
- Daily mini-lessons taught to the whole class that sometimes emerged from academic needs that were noticed during conferring with students or in whole class sessions. These mini lessons often involved teaching and modeling for students specific socio-cognitive strategies to support their reading comprehension and related tools to externalize and support their cognition. Students were led through guided practice of a selected strategy and then reflected and reported on their experience with using the strategy of focus. Examples of strategies taught included envisioning, predicting, and monitoring understanding, supported by tools such as talk, readers' notebooks, sticky notes, sketching, charts, webs, and diagrams.

Allison designed and taught the third curriculum unit, a week-long unit named Intentionality in Growing our Literate Lives. With this unit coming one month after the reading unit, one goal was to learn from students whether and in what ways they were drawing upon their learning from the Literate Lives and Independent Reading units to purposively build their literate lives, including their reading practices, across different academic contexts of school and social worlds outside school. Allison worked with students on building metacognition of the interrelationships among the socio-cognitive processes we had engaged in the reading unit and reading in other areas of their literate lives. Further, each student developed a Plan for Literate Engagement, in which they articulated in discussion and writing some concrete activities and strategies they would employ to maintain a rich literate life, including reading, over the summer months.

What we learned

We learned much from this project about the role of transnationalism in English education. We focus here on our learning from the Independent Reading unit. All students reported experiencing the traditional forms of reading instruction documented by our literature review and observed by Allison in her previous research at this school. Students were highly motivated to read the texts we brought them. Each student participated in two interviews beyond the reading unit (May 2016, May 2017). All reported that their favorite component of the reading unit was simply reading and enjoying their books in the company of their peers in the language arts classroom. Students deemed instruction around socio-cognitive tools and strategies for improving their reading experiences and meaning-making with their texts as important but also distracting from the pleasure of uninterrupted reading. Students engaged in different ways and to varied degrees – ranging across intellectual curiosity, compliance, and resistance – with the reading tools and practice tasks we presented during class sessions. Yet all students demonstrated some measure of growth in their reading identities and/or practices as evidenced by our data – interviews of students before and after the project, video-recordings of class instruction, and analysis of student talk and student work across time.

Our most compelling point of learning, however, was that the books students requested and self-selected to read were of US and British origin. We were struck by this observation given that the conceptual and instructional design of the classroom-based research was intentionally inclusive of students' transnational lives, which included Caribbean geographies, and that we aligned our work with other emancipatory and de-colonizing literacy pedagogies (Canagarajah, 2011; Macaluso, 2015). We theorized this phenomenon as evidence of the historical and ongoing literary colonization of less dominant world nations, including postcolonial Caribbean contexts (Canagarajah, 2011; Willinsky, 2000), manifesting in the expressed reading preferences of our students. One point of evidence was the nature of the texts that lined the school library shelves. The books were of primarily British and US origin and were often outdated Eurocentric texts. Figure 19.1 represents the shelf containing the most diverse literature in the school library.

FIGURE 19.1 One library shelf at TMS representing some diverse and contemporary texts

Yet we also came to understand the transnational/globalized nature of literate life today was also responsible for the agentive choices and desires of students for particular Euro-Western texts, and that students' choices were not simply reflective of internalization of and acquiescence to literary colonization. Just as with the examples of their transnational literacy practices, such as video-gaming in virtual global spaces and physical border crossing and sojourning for music education across different nations, students' reading choices displayed their belongingness to a transnational world. In this world, global media and technologies, uneven flows of cultures, and ideologies about the nations and cultures that hold more worth (Appadurai, 1996), surely influenced students' reading choices. By this we mean, for example, when, nearing the end of the Literate Lives unit, Allison provided students with laptops or allowed them to use their phones to search for texts they wanted to read, the returns of their searches were usually books based in US and British contexts, with few returns on Caribbean texts. Thus, online spaces provided students with little opportunity to explore the wide vista of available world literatures, including those based in Caribbean geographies, in which they might have found interest.

As an example, Table 19.1 below displays the texts and genres one student, Sabrina (pseudonym), expressed preference for or explicitly requested, those purchased with her in mind based on what she shared with us, and other texts that

TABLE 19.1 Sabrina and the Independent Reading Unit

Sabrina's Expressed Reading Interests	Texts Sabrina Read: Titles, Genres, and Overviews
• Nancy Drew series • Books based on Disney television shows • Fantasy • Mythology • Strong female characters	1. *Nancy Drew the new case files #1: Nancy Drew vampire slayer* by Stefan Petrucha, Sarah Kinney, and Sho Murase, 2010. This is a new version of the classic Nancy Drew series as a graphic novel. 2. *Sabriel (Old Kingdom)* by Garth Nix, 1997. This is the first installment in the trilogy, *Abhorsen*. It is a fantasy novel with a strong female lead, who must take charge, enter a new world, to save her father. 3. *The lightning thief, Percy Jackson and the Olympians, Book 1* by Rick Riordan, 2005. This text was selected for Sabrina because she expressed an interest in Greek mythology, and it is a favorite among many readers with strong male and female characters that live across the worlds of humans and gods. 4. *Pax* by Sara Pennypacker, 2016. This is an award-winning adventure story of the extraordinary friendship between a boy and his fox, and their epic journey to be reunited. 5. *There you'll find me* by Jenny B. Jones, 2011. This is a YA novel that deals with loss, love, and a search for God. 6. *When you reach me* by Rebecca Stead, 2009. An award-winning novel for middle-school readers that bridges themes of family, friendship, and time travel.

Sabrina engaged with that were available in the classroom library we created based on the interests of all student-participants.

A significant and ongoing area of reflection for us is our reasoning and decision-making as scholar-teachers in relation to the text selection process. We intentionally refrained from imposing texts set in Caribbean geographies onto students based on an assumption that they should or would want to read such texts because of their Caribbean identities and locations. Rather, we chose a position from which we could view students as literate agents in a transnational world with rights to desire and choose texts, regardless of these texts' origins, that *students* felt represented their interests, identities, and lived experiences. Thus, the textual choices students made provided us with evidence of how students understood, or wished to situate, themselves in a globalized world of literacy practices. At the same time, students' textual selections prompted our scholarly critique of the globalized ideologies that continued to privilege Euro-Western culture, and buried within world media other available texts that reflected these and other youths' cultural lives and geographies, that we believed our student participants would also enjoy (Appadurai, 1996; Canagarajah, 2011; Willinsky, 2000). We further recognized that as US-based teacher-researchers our very affiliations with that global power may have influenced students' requests for Euro-American texts. Finally, critically reflecting on our own practices, we realized that although we encouraged students to visit their local libraries to feed their reading lives, we did not organize any field trips to local libraries as part of our instruction; neither did we research into local availability of Caribbean literature.

Discussion and implications

The project we undertook, framed by a transnationally-inclusive approach to literacy education (Skerrett, 2015), enabled us to underscore the intersections of the local and the global in students' literacy practices, and the influence of ideologies, now more pervasive through advanced technologies and global media, in shaping youths' reading choices. Taking on dual roles as researchers and teachers in a transnational nation that bear remnants of colonization, and in which many youths claim and pursue globalized identities and literacy practices, heightened our notice of this phenomenon. Our dual teacher-researcher roles further allowed us to study these influences and theorize their meanings while we carried on with the work of supporting students' literacy development. We avoided a contemporary project of colonization (Canagarajah, 2011; Willinsky, 2000) by designing a curriculum based in what students informed us about their literate lives. However, doing so required our responsiveness to students' simultaneous positionings in local and global worlds and the different weights they placed on particular identities and literary desires at the particular period of their lives in which we worked with them.

Certainly, the human experience and students' interests are represented in texts situated both within and beyond their immediate local and cultural worlds. However, given the power of global media and ideologies that continue to privilege Euro-Western culture, we propose that teachers augment students' reading choices by making *available* to them (not *imposing* onto them) texts that reflect their local *and* global affiliations. To do so, teachers would take a stance of inquiry into learning from students about the multiple geographies, cultures, and literacy practices that comprise students' lives, and make efforts to include texts that reflect those landscapes in classroom offerings. Such a pedagogy would further involve examining with students their reading preferences and the ways in which global ideologies, as spread through global media and technology (Appadurai, 1996), may be shaping their reading identities and preferences. Such critical questioning aligns with the critical inquiry dimension of a transnationally-inclusive approach to literacy education. Questioning textual choices in these ways can enhance students' noticing, exploration, and appreciation of their own and other geographies that contribute to the world of reading opportunities.

We thus propose that greater emphasis on the critical inquiry dimension of a transnationally-inclusive approach to literacy education (Skerrett, 2015) is one way to advance emancipatory pedagogies and further resist colonizing pedagogies (Canagarajah, 2011; Macaluso, 2015; Willinsky, 2000) in the teaching of English. Our teacher-researcher effort, and the learning we acquired, thus stands as a current example of the spirit and future of Dartmouth. We forged deeper conceptual understandings and practices of why and how English education should and could be more centered on students' diversity and learning processes (Dixon, 1991; Donahue & Blewett, 2015; Harris, 1991). We re-examined and further debunked the mythical idea of a monolithic (and in our case, mono-national) student and academic discipline, and the monocultural content s/he may consume or produce within the boundaries of "English" (Sublett, 1973; Trimbur, 2008).

References

Appadurai, A. (1996). *Modernity at large: cultural dimensions of globalization*. Minneapolis, MN: University of Minnesota Press.

Ball, A. F. (2009). 'Toward a theory of generative change in culturally and linguistically complex classrooms'. *American Educational Research Journal*, 46(1), 45–72.

Bomer, R. (2011). *Building adolescent literacy in today's English classrooms*. Portsmouth, NH: Heinemann.

Canagarajah, S. (2011). 'English studies as Creole scholarship: reconfiguring the discipline for postcolonial conditions'. *Changing English: Studies in Culture and Education*, 18, 251–263.

Cepal.org. (2002). 'The Impact of immigration on Caribbean microstates: Bahamas, British Virgin Islands, Saint Maarten, United States Virgin Islands'. Accessed May, 2015 at 1 www.cepal.org/publicaciones/xml/0/10340/carg0540.pdf.

Coe, E., Reynolds, R. R., Boehm, D. A., Hess, J. M., & Rae-Espinoza, H. (2011). (eds.). *Everyday ruptures: children, youth, and migration in global perspective*. Nashville, TN: Vanderbilt University Press.

Conrad, D. A., Forteau-Jaikaransingh, B., & Popova, D. (2015). 'Poetry to rapso: localized narrative in the classroom'. *Caribbean Curriculum*, 20, 1–29.

Dixon, J. (2009). 'English renewed: visions of English among teachers of 1966'. *English in Education*, 43(3), 241–250.

Donahue, C., & Blewett, K. (eds.). (2015). *The Power of writing: Dartmouth '66 in the twenty-first century*. Hanover, NH: Dartmouth College Press.

Glaser, B. G., & Strauss, A. L. (2006). *The Discovery of grounded theory: strategies for qualitative research*. Chicago, IL: Aldine Publishing Co.

Government of Sint Maarten. (2014). *SintMaartenGov.org. The official website of the government of Sint Maarten*. Accessed 23 November, 2014 at www.sintmaartengov.org/Pages/default.aspx.

James, C. (2003). 'The Status of literature in six types of Trinidad secondary schools: issues, implications, and recommendations'. *Caribbean Curriculum*, 10, 1–36.

James, C. (2004). 'Breaking the silence: using journals to stimulate self-evaluation toward change in the Trinidad primary school system'. *Caribbean Curriculum*, 11, 85–113.

Harris, J. (1991). 'After Dartmouth: growth and conflict in English'. *College English*, 53(6), 631–646.

Lam, W. S. E., & Warriner, D. S. (2012). 'Transnationalism and literacy: investigating the mobility of people, languages, texts, and practices in contexts of migration'. *Reading Research Quarterly*, 47(2), 191–215.

Levitt, P. (2001). *The Transnational villagers*. Berkeley, CA: University of California Press.

Macaluso, K. (2015). 'Literary interpretation as poetic translation: envisioning a Rancièrean emancipatory framework for literature instruction'. *Reading Research Quarterly*, 50(2), 205–218.

Miles, M. B., Huberman, M., & Saldana, J. (2013). *Qualitative data analysis: a methods sourcebook*. Thousand Oaks, CA.: Sage.

New London Group. (1996). 'A Pedagogy of multiliteracies: designing social futures'. *Harvard Educational Review*, 66(1), 60–92.

Reinking, D., & Bradley, B. A. (2008). *Formative and design experiments: approaches to language and literacy research*. New York: Teachers College Press.

Seunarinesingh, K. (2010). 'Primary teachers' explorations of authentic texts in Trinidad and Tobago'. *Journal of Language and Literacy Education*, 6(1), 40–57.

Seunarinesingh, K. (2015a). 'Managing a paradigm shift in language arts pedagogy: a case study of effective literacy practice'. *Caribbean Curriculum*, 9, 47–64.

Seunarinesingh, K. (2015b). 'Revisiting "Writing in spite of teachers: issues in teaching writing (Trinidad and Tobago)" 20 years later'. *Caribbean Curriculum*, 22, 35–66.

Skerrett, A. (2015). *Teaching transnational youth: literacy and education in a changing world*. New York: Teachers College Press.

Skerrett, A. (2016). 'Refiguring a Caribbean school within and across local and global communities'. *Journal of Professional and Community Capital*, 1(4), 254–269.

Smagorinsky, P. (2002). '*Growth through English* revisited'. *The English Journal*, 91(6), 23–29.

Sublette, J. R. (1973). 'The Dartmouth conference: its reports and results'. *College English*, 35(3), 348–357.

Trimbur, J. (2008). 'The Dartmouth conference and the geohistory of the native speaker'. *College English*, 71(2), 142–169.

Willinsky, J. (2000). *Learning to divide the world: education at empire's end*. Minneapolis, MN: University of Minnesota Press.

Zúñiga, V., & Hamann, E. T. (2009). 'Sojourners in Mexico with US school experience: a new taxonomy for transnational students'. *Comparative Education Review*, 53(3), 329–353.

INDEX

Page numbers in *italics* refer to figures. Page numbers in **bold** refer to tables.

Aboriginal texts 153–154
abstraction 103–104
abstract objectivism 167
Accelerated Reader 222–223
accountability 49–50
Achievement Certificate 71–73
Adult Needs 114, 117, 136, 138, **139–140**
agency 118–120
Aims of English Teaching, The (LATE)
    18–20, 21, 22, 23
Aldrin, B. 206
Alim, H.S. 228, 230, 232, 237, 239
Allen, D. 34
American Academy of Pediatrics 229
American movie 234
Analysis of Literature in Australian Schools
    (ALIAS) database 152
And When You Are Young (LATE) 24
Anita and me (Syal) 195
Applebee, R. 31, 37, 46–48, 126
Archer, M. 118–119
Arendt 82
Armstrong, N. 203–204, 206
Arnold, M. 53, 55, 60, 61
Assessing English (Johnston) 162
assessment frameworks 244–246, 250
asTTLe (Assessment Tools for Teaching
    and Learning) 245, 248
Atherton, C. 30–31
Atwell, N. 85
Atwood, M. 218
Auden, W.H. 82, 83

Australia 65–77, 133–143, 146–156, 177,
    178, 242–243, 245, 248
Australian Association for the Teaching of
    English 147
Australian Curriculum: English, The (AC: E)
    152–154, 156
Australian National Curriculum 244, 248
authoritarian approach 125–126
autobiography 167
autoethnography 259

Backchat 72
Baker, K. 184
Ball, A.F. 256
Ball, S. 37
Barclay School 207
Barker, P. 206
Barnes, D. 16, 18, 22, 24, 76, 81, 99
Barnsley, G. 219
'Bear Grylls' (Rosen) 212
Beavis, C. 68
Beazley Report 71, 74, 75
Benjamin, W. 168
Bennett, B. 71
Benyon, E. 210
Berchini, C. 130
Berliner, D.C. 195
Bernard, N. 243
Bernstein, B. 81
'Better-Never' position 89
Blue Books 52–62
Board of Education (BoE) 53

Board of Secondary Education (BSE) 71–72, 73
Boas, F.C. 52
Boivin, M.-C. 242, 249
Bomer, R. 260
books, access to 220–221
Boomer, G. 148
Booth, W. 81
Borchardt, M. 234
'bottom-up' approach 17–18
Bradley, A.C. 52
Brand, S. 87
Brexit 110–111, 125, 192
British Council Study Boxes 18
'British Model' 47
Britton, J. 16–20, 22–24, 29–30, 34, 62, 71, 76–77, 81–84, 86–88, 90, 99, 102–103, 128, 140, 163–164, 167, 241
Brock, P. 65–66, 133, 134, 140
Brown, W. 236
Bruner 62, 82
Buber 82
Bucholtz, M. 232, 237
Buckingham, D. 179, 182, 184, 188
Bullock, A. 76
Bullock Report 115
bullying 128
Burgess, T. 18, 23
Butt, B. 166

Cabrera, N.L. 194
Calkins, L. 85
Campbell, N. 212
Campbell's law 195
Canagarajah, S. 257, 258
canon, restoration of 191–200
'Cargoes' (Masefield) 208
Caribbean 258–259
Carlin, N. 71
Carnegie Foundation 44–45, 241
Carr, N. 87
Carter, D. 215–216
Casillas, D.I. 232, 237
Cassirer 82
Cavarero, A. 167
Centre for Cultural Studies, Birmingham University 116
Certificate of Secondary Education (CSE) 62
Chartrand, S.-G. 246
Chavez, C. 237
child-centredness 34, 59, 60, 61, 62; see also student-centred teaching
Children and their primary schools (Plowden Report) 58–59

Children's Choice project 221
Chorny, M. 81–82
Christenson, B. 100
Christie, F. 159, 165, 166–167, 243
Churchlands Teachers' Training College 71
civic online reasoning 89, 90
Claremont Training College 70
class: culture and 193; race and 235–237
Clayfield, R. 205
Clements, S. 21–22, 95–96, 97
close reading 31
cognitive psychologists 45, 46, 49
Cold War 44, 49, 110
Coleridge 82
colonization 235, 254, 258, 260–261, 264
Common Core State Standards 124, 128, 187, 243
Commonwealth Literary Fund 151
community practices 237
'compelling comprehensible input' 224, 225
conative forms for speech 83
Conrad, D.A. 259
copyright 90
Copyright Agency Cultural Fund 154–155
Corbin, R. 47
Cormack, P. 43, 148
Cox, B. 54, 112, 113, 181, 184, 186
Cox Report 109, 112–118, 136–137, 181, 183, 184, 242
Creative Commons 90
creative writing 56, 102–103, 141–142
creativity 55, 56, 58, 60–61, 101–102
creolized discipline, English as 257, 258
Critical Literacy 116, 136, 138–139, **139–140**
Critical Realist theories of identity 109–110, 118–120
Critical Whiteness Studies 130
Cross-Curricular model 115, 136
Cult of the Amateur, The (Keen) 87
Cultural Analysis model 109, 114, 115–118, 136, 138–139, **139**
cultural diversity 112
Cultural Heritage model 28–29, 33, 96, 112, 115, 117, 126, 136, 138, **139**, 149–150, 152–156, 160
cultural literacy 48, 196
Culturally Sustaining Pedagogy 227–239
Culturally Sustaining/Revitalizing Pedagogy (CSRP) 228
cultural modelling approach 199–200
cultural pluralism 48, 228, 229–232, 235–237
culture 191, 192–194

Culture and Environment (Thompson and Leavis) 116
culture of reading, developing 221–222
Curriculum and Assessment in English 3 to 19: a Better Plan 187

Dahl, R. 181
Daiches, D. 97
Darder, A. 235, 236
'Dartmouth II' 48
Dartmouth Seminar (1966): LATE and 22–24; London English and 15–24; re-reading 42–50; revisited 241–251; *see also Growth through English* (Dixon); *Uses of English, The* (Muller)
'data-driven' management 49
Davis, R. 205
Dearing, R. 185
de la Mare, W. 205–206
Derewianka, B. 242, 245, 246, 248, 249, 251
Dettman Report 71, 75
Development of Writing Abilities, The (Britton et al.) 162, 164
Dewey, J. 111, 112, 119
dialect 19–20, 55, 76, 96, 102
Dickens, C. 82, 247
dictionaries 85–86
digital era 87–90, 110, 223–224
discourse analysis 176–177
Discrimination and Popular Culture (Thompson) 116
Dixon, J.: on abstraction 103–104; Australian context and 65, 67, 69–70, 76, 77, 133, 147–148; on authoritarian approach 125–126; 'British Model' and 47, 49; as context 191–192; continuity with 114–115, 118, 120; creativity and 102; on cultural heritage vision 28–30; 'cultural heritage' vision and 156; at Dartmouth 15–16, 24, 27, 32, 42–44, 45–46, 50, 81; as documentary evidence 176; on experience 33–37; experience and 103, 159–163, 168; on imagination 62; on Infant Schools 204–205; influence of 146; on keeping language alive 212; language-in-use-in-context and 140; LATE and 20, 21–23, 59; Learmonth and 183; on literature 148–150; Muller and 93; on panicked reactions 188; Personal Growth model and 109, 110, 112, 124, 126–127; process approach and 241; on societies during rapid change 125; on

sociopolitical contexts 86; on teaching approach 58, 60; Whitehead and 100; *see also Growth through English* (Dixon)
documentary research 176
Doecke, B. 196
Dolin, T. 152, 156
Domínguez, M. 228, 236
Doughty, P. 18
Douglas, W. 101
Dowsett, P. 70
Drummond, P. 182, 184
Dunmore, H. 212
Dunn, S. 206
Dyson, A.H. 210

Eagleson, R.D. 75–76
Eagleton, T. 191
Early, M. 43–44
Eddo-Lodge, R. 193
educated imagined 86
Education Act (1944) 16–17
8-year study 46
11-plus examinations 61
Elley, W.B. 242
emancipatory pedagogy 257–258
Empire of Words, The (Willinsky) 85–86
English and Media Centre (EMC) 179–180
English Association, The (EA) 52, 53
English Coalition Conference 48
English for maturity (Holbrook) 60
English for the rejected (Holbrook) 60, 205
English in Australia 65, 75–77, 147
English in harmonious practice 117
English in Secondary Schools (NSW English Teachers' Association) 34
English Journal 129
English Teachers' Association of Western Australia (ETAWA) 71
English Teachers in a Postwar Democracy (Medway, Hardcastle, Brewis and Crook) 21
English Working Group (EWG) 181–184
Enright, D.J. 83
equal educational opportunity 229, 231–232
ERIC 176
'evidence-based' education 49
experience: creative writing and 102–103; Dixon on 97; language and 19–20, 22, 23, 28, 30, 55, 56, 66–67, 159–169; literature and 30–32, 33–37; Personal Growth model and 126, 128–129; responding to 232–235
'expressiveness' 20
expressive speech 83

Fairclough, N. 176–177
'Fake News' 111
Far From the Madding Crowd (Hardy)
    207–208
'fidelity to experience' 20
Fields, B.J. 230, 235, 236
Finding a Language (Medway) 162
Findlay, K. 137, 139
Fishman, J. 81
Fletcher, R. 84–85
Foer, F. 87
Forster, E.M. 207
Fort Street Model School 70
foundational elements of subject 37–38
found poetry 211
Foyle Young Poets of the Year 212
Framework for English, The 117–118
Freire, P. 82, 95
Froebel 70
Frye, N. 86
'functional' approach to language 20

Gaffield, N. 212
Gallagher, K. 218
Gay, G. 196
GCSE examinations 118, 195, 196,
    197–198, 245
Gee, J. 208
Gelder, K. 151–152
genre-based writing pedagogy 34
'genre' pedagogy 165–167
genre theorists 244
Gill, M. 219
Glaude, E. 237–238
globalisation 110
Golden Treasury of Poetry (Untermeyer) 208
Goodman, P. 82
Goodwyn, A. 134, 137, 139, 192
Gopnik, A. 89
Gove, M. 179, 192, 195, 196
grammar study 20, 57, 68–69, 76, 241–251
Graves, D. 77, 84–85
Gray, B. 165–166
Gray, L. 242
Great expectations (Dickens) 151, 247
Green, B. 35, 43, 73–74, 148
Greer, G. 217
growth model *see* personal growth model
Growth through English (Dixon): on
    abstraction 103–104; Australian context
    and 65, 67, 69–70, 72, 76, 133;
    consensus in 15–16; as context 191–192;
    context for 94–97; creativity and 102;
    on experience 103, 111, 159–160,

166–167, 168–169; experience and
    33–37; on Infant Schools 204–205;
    influence of 146; LATE and 20, 21,
    23–24; National Curriculum for English
    (NCE) and 114; nation and 27–30;
    nuance of 38; partiality of 93; Personal
    Growth model and 110; progressivism
    of 42–44; re-reading 159–169;
    on sociopolitical contexts 86;
    sociopolitical contexts and 48; on
    teaching approach 58
Gurrey, P. 17
Gutierrez, K.D. 194

Habermas, J. 177
Hales, B. 208, *209*
Half our future 62
Halliday, M.A.K. 18, 83, 242–243, 244,
    247, 248, 250
Hancock, C. 248
Harding, D.W. 23, 149–150
Hardy, T. 207–208
Harris, J. 42–43, 96
Harry Potter series 193
Hasan, R. 242–243
Haussamen, B. 241–242, 246
Heaney, S. 209
Hemingway 82
Herbart 70
'Hermit Crab' (Porter) 212
Hesse, D. 87, 88
Higher School Certificate 141, 150, 152
High School Instruction Today (Squire and
    Applebee) 31
Hirsch, E.D. 48, 125, 196, 205
Hoggart, R. 116
Holborow, M. 193
Holbrook, D. 59–60, 62, 94, 101, 205
home language 19–20, 21, 23, 48, 55, 124
Homer, D. 34, 65, 133
Hook, J.N. 47–48
Hourd, M. 162
Howards End (Forster) 207
Humanist Manifesto II 97

identity: Critical Realism and 118–120;
    re-conceptualization of 237–238
Illich, I. 82
immigrant students 255
imperialism 86
Importance of Teaching, The (DFE) 179–180
In a Shade of Blue (Glaude) 237–238
Indigenous literature 153–154
Infant School 204–206

information literacy 88–90
informative forms of speech 83
Inglis, F. 34
initial teacher education, poetry in 210
'In memory of W. B. Yeats' (Auden) 83
innoculation theory 111
Inside a Dog (website) 223
International Federation of the Teaching of English 147
internet 86–89, 110, 119
Ishiguro, K. 195

Jackson, C. 70
Jaquette, O. 194
Jasper Jones (Silvey) 155
Jenkins, H. 88
job creation outlook 231
John Dixon in Australia 147
Johnson, C. 230–231
Johnson, Dr 55
Johnston, B. 162
'Justice for Janitors' 237

Keen, A. 87
Kelly, G. 82, 83
Kelly, R. 237
Kent, V. 221
Kingman Report 116, 175, 181, 183, 242
Kitzhaber, A. 28, 99, 254
knowledge, literature and 30–32, 38
Knowledge about Language 116
Koch, K. 85
Kohn, A. 128
Kolln, M. 242, 248
Krashen, S. 216, 224

Lady Chatterly's Lover (Lawrence) 82
Lajoie, J. 234
Lamborn, G. 52–53
Langer 82
Language, the learner and the school (Barnes et al.) 60
Language and Learning (Britton) 19, 81, 82–83, 85, 90
Language for Life, A (DES) 115
Language in Use materials 35
Lawrence, D. H. 82
Learmonth, J. 182–183
Learning to Divide the World (Willinsky) 86
Leavis, F.R. 31, 111, 116, 192
Lee, C.D. 194, 199–200
Lee, J.S. 232, 237
linguistics 102

listening: Blue Books on 55; Personal Growth model and 126–127
literacy/literacy education 74–75, 76, 114, 260; *see also* reading
literature: Australian 151–155; in Australian context 147–151; experience and 27–38
Literature as Exploration (Rosenblatt) 46
Literature Board 151–152
Little, G. 68, 70, 76
Loban, W. 47
London Association for the Teaching of English (LATE) 16–24, 59, 95
'London English' 15–24
London Institute for Education 17, 70, 71–72, 104
London Plan 17
Lord, M.-C. 246
Lorde, A. 212
Love, K. 251
Lowe, L. 235
Luria 82

Macaluso, K. 258
Macken-Horarik, M. 251
Mackey, M. 221
Manuel, J. 215–216, 218–219
Marckhardt, A. 102
Marsh, J. 231
Martin, J. 165
Martin, J.R. 243, 251
Martin, N. 17, 71, 76
Martinez, D.C. 194
Martin Report 71, 72–74
Marx, R.W. 194
Masefield, J. 208
Masterman, L. 182, 183
McCulloch, G. 176
McDougall, J. 186
McGaw Report 71
McGough, R. 207
Mead, P. 196
meaning-making 244, 247
Media Education 112, 116, 117
media in English curricula 175–188
Medway, P. 104, 162
Meek, M. 82
Merchant, G. 216
'meritocratic justification for poverty' 231
Mexican-American Studies 194–195
Michaels, W.B. 230, 231–232
Milem, J.F. 194
Miyazawa, K. 212
Modern Language Association (MLA) 44, 241

Moffett, J. 31, 35, 45, 67–68, 70, 76, 81, 100, 103–104, 138, 140
Moll, L.C. 194
Monterey Pop Festival 81
Montessori 70
Moreno, A. 238
Mossenson, D. 73
Muller, H. 15, 27–32, 37, 43, 93, 97–99, 101–102, 104, 148, 176
Muller, J. 196
multiculturalism 111–112, 191–200
Murray, D. 76–77
Murray, J. 85
'My Bus Conductor' (McGough) 207
Myhill, D.A. 247

nation, literature and 27–30
National Assessment Program (NAPLAN) 245
National Association for the Teaching of English (NATE) 59, 179, 203
National Conference of Teachers of English 241
National Council of Teachers of English (NCTE) 44–46, 47, 49
National Curriculum for England and Wales 54
National Curriculum in English (NCE) 109, 112–113, 116–118, 175–176, 178–187, 242, 243, 244
National Defense in Education Act (NDEA) 44–45
National interest and the teaching of English, The (NCTE) 44
nationalism 110–111
National Literacy Strategy 117
National Union of Teachers 116
National Writing Project 46, 47, 124
natural grammar 60
Nelson-Addy 197–199
neoliberalism 111, 120
'Never-Better' stance 89
Never let me go (Ishiguro) 195
Newbolt 54, 55, 59, 61
Newbolt Report 160
New Critics 31, 71, 124, 126, 130
'New English' movement 2, 6, 16, 17, 18, 20, 42–43, 71, 74, 133
New London Group (NLG) 256
Newman, R. 247
Newsom Report 62, 94
New South Wales 65–70, 75–77, 133–143
New Zealand 177–178, 242, 244, 245, 247–248, 249
Nichols, S.L. 195

Nixon, R. 49
NSW English syllabus for forms I–IV 65–70
NSW English Teachers' Association 34

OECD PISA tests 217
'O' level language examination 18
Olive, S. 195
omniculture 110, 111–112, 113
O'Neill, M. 70, 71–72
Ong, W. 81
online information 87–90
Opie, I. 211
Opie, P. 211
Oregon Curriculum 242
Oswald, A. 212
'otherness' 154, 156, 192
Oxford English Dictionary 85–86

Padilla, F. 238
Paris, D. 228, 230, 232, 237, 239
Parker, R.B. 76
Parr, J. 242, 249, 251
participant role 23, 34, 83–84, 88
participatory culture 88
patents 90
pedagogical approaches to grammar 246–248
'pedagogy of permission' 210
Penguin Education series 82
Perkins, R. 155
Personal Growth and Social/Cultural Agency 110–120
personal growth model: agreement on 254; in Australia 65–77; Australian context and **139**; class and 159; Dartmouth and 24, 42–49; influence of 60; social perspective on 123–131; updating of 109–120; *see also Growth through English* (Dixon)
Personal Growth model and, Australian context and 133–143, 146–156
Pestalozzi 70
Petch Report 71
Piaget 82
Plowden Report 58–59, 61, 101
poetic forms of speech 83
poetry 52–53, 56, 58, 83, 195, 198, 203–212, 259
political subjectivity 236
Porter, P. 212
portfolio approach 210
postmodernism 118
poverty 227–239
Prendergast, M. 211
Prentice Hall literature series 130

'process writing' approaches 76–77
professional agency and autonomy 140–141
Progression of learning documents 243
progressivism, post-Dartmouth 46–48
Project English 15, 44–45, 47
publishing 84–85
Purves, A. 81
Putin, V. 110

Quebec: assessment frameworks in 246; curriculum of 243; grammar teaching in 249
Quin, R. 72

race: class and 235–237; poverty and 230
radical optimism 111
Rain Won't (Miyazawa) 212
rappers 130–131
Rapso 259
Rata 178
'readicide' 218–219
reading: Blue Books on 55; for meaning 186–187; for pleasure 215–224; Plowden Report on 59; *see also* literacy/ literacy education
Reflections (Dixon, Clements and Stratta) 21–22, 23, 33, 95, 97
'Regular Everyday Normal Guy' (Lajoie) 234
Reid, I. 146, 147, 156
Reid, J.-A. 74
reification 164–167, 168
Response to Literature (NCTE) 31–32
Response to literature (Sawyer et al.) 149
'results-based' educational systems 104
Revolutionaries to Race Leaders (Johnson) 230–231
rhetoric, move towards 67
Rhym, D. 130–131
Rogers, A. 192
Rogers, G. 20, 95
Romantic poets 168
Rosen, C. 82, 95
Rosen, H. 16, 18–25, 62, 71, 82, 95, 101–102, 167, 208
Rosen, M. 212
Rosenblatt, L. 46, 83, 124
Rosen. C. 81
Rose Where Did You Get That Red? (Koch) 85
Rothery, J. 165
Rowling, J.K. 193

Said, E. 193
Salzman, P. 151–152
Sampson, G. 53
Sánchez, G. 237

Sandiford, C. 251
satire 233–234
Sawyer, W. 74, 133, 134, 140, 148
Schleppegrell, M.J. 251
Schools Council Writing 76
Scientific Reading Association (SRA) 218
Scott, D. 60
Scribener 62
Scrutiny 23
Secondary School 207–208
Secondary Teachers' College (STC) 71
self-cultivation 138
self-expression 56–57, 96, 128
'Self Unseeing, The' (Hardy) 208
Seunarinesingh, K. 258–259
Shallows, The (Carr) 87
Shayer, D. 21, 61
Shulman, L.S. 249
'Silver' (de la Mare) 205–206
Silvey, C. 155
Skerrett, A. 256–257, 259
'skills' model 15, 49, 96, 112, 114–115, 126, 138, **139–140**, 160
Smagorinsky, P. 156, 228
Smith, F. 223
social dimensions of language and experience 19–20
social nature of learning 192
Some suggestions for the teaching of English in secondary schools in England (BoE) 53
speaking: Blue Books on 55; Personal Growth model and 126; Plowden Report on 59, 61
spectator role 23, 29, 34, 36, 83–84, 88
Spoken Word 209–210
Squire, J. 31
Squire, R. 149–150
Squires, J. 81, 128, 163
standardized assessments 48, 141, 218
state-controlled education systems, federal interventions into 49
State Library of Victoria (SLV) 223
Stevenson, R.L. 56
St. Maarten 255, 257, 259
Stratta, L. 21, 95, 162, 169
streaming and segregation 94, 101
student-centred teaching 46, 124, 127, 128, 138, 139, 254; *see also* child-centredness
student choice for reading 220–222, 261–264, **263**
'subject paradigm' 136
Suggestions for the consideration of teachers and others concerned in the work of Public Elementary schools (Blue Books; BoE) 52–62

Summerfield, G. 52, 55, 60–61, 62
Swenson, M. 208
Syal, M. 195
Sydney School of functional linguistics 244
Systemic Functional Linguistics 164–165, 248

Task Force on Teaching English to the
  Disadvantaged (NCTE) 47
teachers: education for 210; grammatical
  knowledge of 248–249; poetry and 204
Teachers' book (Dixon, Clements and
  Stratta) 21–22, 95
Teaching the Universe of Discourse (Moffett)
  67–68, 103, 138
Teaching Transnational Youth (Skerrett) 259
Tejada High 228, 229, 230, 231, 232–235,
  237, 238–239
Thatcher, M. 49
Theory of Communicative Action, The
  (Habermas) 177
Things Being Various 95
third spaces 194
Thompson, D. 81, 101, 116
Thompson, I. 193
thought, language and 19
Topping, K. 222–223
Torres, R.D. 235, 236
Torres Strait Islander texts 153–154
tracking reading 222–223
transactional speech 83
transnationalism 254–265
transnationally-inclusive approach
  255–257, 259–261, 264–265
transnational world 254–265
Triumph Multiage School (TMS) 259
Trump, D.J. 87–88, 110–111, 125, 192
Tucker, E. 222

Unsworth, L. 251
Untermeyer, L. 208
US Bureau of Labor Statistics 231
Uses of English, The (Muller) 15, 27–29, 38,
  43, 93, 97–99, 101, 104

Voices 60
Vološinov 167
Vološinov, V.N. 160
Vygotsky, L. 19, 62, 82, 160

Wagner, J. 212
Wallace, R. 207–208
Walshe, R.D. 76–77
Walworth School 20–22, 33,
  59, 95
'Was Worm' (Svenson) 208
wealth inequality 229, 231, 235–236
Western Australia 65, 70–77
'What is English?' (Kitzhaber) 28
Whitehead, F. 23, 30, 34, 99–100
Whole Earth Catalog 87
'wide reading' programmes
  219–220, 222
Wilkinson 76
Williams, R. 33, 163–164, 196
Willis, K. 70
Wilson, H. 62
Wilt, M. 101, 102
Wineburg, S. 88–89
Winnicott 82
Wordsworth 82
Workers' Educational Association 59
World Without Mind (Foer) 87
'Writer's Shed' (Hales) *209*
writing: Blue Books on 55, 56–57; creative
  56–57, 102–103, 141–142; grammar
  study and 242–244; Personal Growth
  model and 126
Writing Narrative – and Beyond (Dixon and
  Stratta) 162
Writing Research Unit 35

Yandell, J. 149, 196–197
Yates, C. 212
Yiannakis, J. 152
Young, M. 196

Zitlali Morales, P. 194